T0319536

HARVARD HISTORICAL STUDIES ◆ 193

Published under the auspices
of the Department of History

from the income of the
Paul Revere Frothingham Bequest
Robert Louis Stroock Fund
Henry Warren Torrey Fund

COCONUT COLONIALISM

Workers and the Globalization of Samoa

HOLGER DROESSLER

HARVARD UNIVERSITY PRESS

Cambridge, Massachusetts

London, England

2022

Library of Congress Cataloging-in-Publication Data
Names: Droessler, Holger, 1982– author.
Title: Coconut colonialism : workers and the globalization of Samoa / Holger Droessler.
Other titles: Harvard historical studies.
Description: Cambridge, Massachusetts : Harvard University Press, 2022. | Series:
Harvard historical studies | Includes bibliographical references and index.
Identifiers: LCCN 2021017940 | ISBN 9780674263338 (cloth)
Subjects: LCSH: Globalization—Samoan Islands—History. | Cultural fusion—
Samoan Islands—History. | Coconut industry—Samoan Islands—History. |
Samoan Islands—Colonization—History. | Samoan Islands—Relations—History.
Classification: LCC DU817 .D76 2022 | DDC 996.1 / 3—dc23
LC record available at https://lccn.loc.gov/2021017940

To my parents

E suamalie a niu ʻaʻati.

The coconut is sweet, but it was husked with the teeth.

SAMOAN PROVERB

CONTENTS

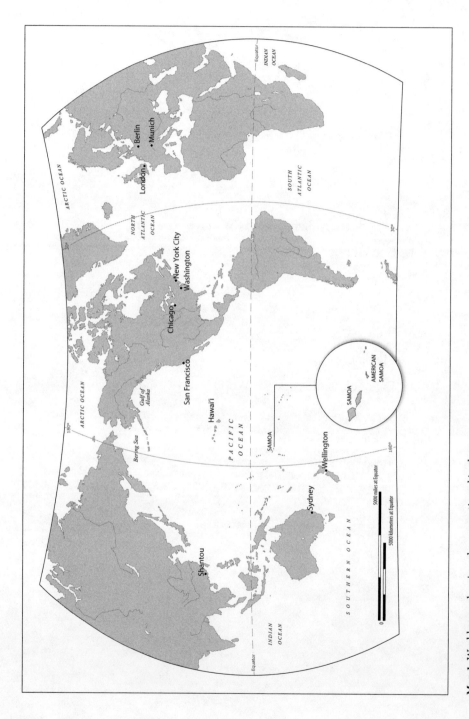

Map 1. World map, showing places mentioned in the text.

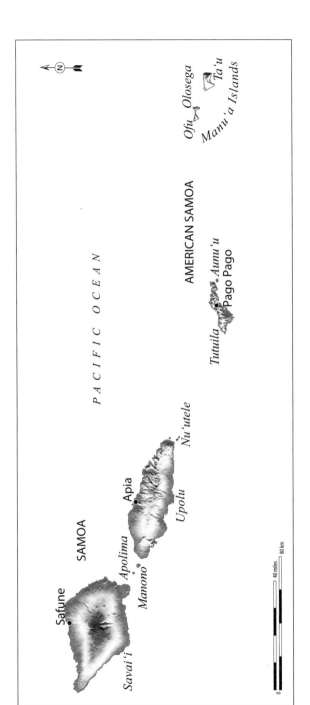

Map 2. Map of the Samoan Islands, showing places mentioned in the text.

INTRODUCTION
Samoans on the Move

On a humid morning in late November 1901, Charles Thomas Taylor left his Samoan home to see the world. With little luggage but plenty of excitement, the thirty-year-old Samoan boarded the steamer *Manapouri,* which would take him to Sydney by way of Suva, Fiji. From Australia, it would take eight long weeks and a dramatic passage through the Suez Canal before he would finally reach the northern German port city of Bremerhaven. Months earlier, Wilhelm Solf, the governor of German Samoa, had decided to send Taylor on a ten-thousand-mile journey to improve his German language skills and learn about German culture. Since Solf spoke only basic Samoan, he and his fellow German officials depended on Samoans—many of mixed-race heritage—to do the translating and interpreting crucial for running the colony.

Taylor was born in 1871 in Moto'otua near Apia, the biggest town on Samoa's most populous island of Upolu, to an English father and a Samoan mother. After his father moved to New Zealand, Taylor was adopted by German-speaking parents. Because Taylor was fluent in Samoan and English and also spoke good German, he was hired in 1900 as an interpreter for the new German administration. With his gift for languages and winning personality, Taylor became a powerful broker in Samoa. Over the course of a decade of colonial service, Taylor would build a close personal relationship with Solf that transcended matters of work and even the colonial rule of difference. It was partly because Taylor was on good terms with the governor that he was allowed to travel to Germany.

During his six months in Germany, Taylor spent most of his time at the German Colonial School in Witzenhausen, but he also visited other German cities. In a tailor's shop in nearby Hannover, he bought three tailored shirts,

Figure 1. Charles Thomas Taylor (1871–1911), 1905, Wellington, New Zealand. FamilySearch.

three tailored slacks, three suits, a blanket, and an umbrella.[1] In May 1902, Taylor paid a visit to the nearby Wartburg, where a famous predecessor had done important translation work nearly four centuries earlier. And later that summer, Taylor reunited with Solf in the spa town of Bad Kissingen, where Solf was spending his home leave. However, beyond this meeting and sending Taylor some pocket money, Solf wanted little to do with his trusted interpreter during their overlapping stay in Germany. After their meeting, Taylor asked Solf if he could visit him in Berlin, the empire's capital and largest city. To Taylor's disappointment, Solf rejected Taylor's wish because, as he explained to him in a letter, such a big city as Berlin would, without proper guidance, pose a great danger for Taylor.[2] Solf further justified his decision by reassuring Taylor that he had only his best interests for his "colonial career" in mind.[3]

Undeterred, Taylor hoped for more opportunities to travel. He not only wanted to see Berlin but wanted to explore other parts of the world as well. As Taylor would soon find out, Solf's affection for him had further limits. Months before his scheduled departure to Samoa, Taylor had asked Solf to change his original ticket, which had Taylor returning on the same itinerary, from Bremen to Apia via Sydney. Solf had plans to return to Samoa across the Atlantic, making diplomatic visits in the United States. Anxious to accompany his boss to visit the other colonial power in Samoa, Taylor asked in a letter written in German: "Couldn't I go with you, Mr. Governor, via America? That way, I could see more of the world."[4] With an insistent and personal tone, Taylor appealed to the governor of German Samoa to take him along in his circumnavigation of the world. Unfortunately for Taylor, Solf again politely declined his request. But the Samoan interpreter continued his travels. In the years following his return to Samoa, Taylor took his two young daughters to vacation in Wellington and visited Tonga twice. Then, in summer 1909, he petitioned for a second extended stay in Germany—which Solf rejected.

Taylor's travels and Solf's denials capture the global aspirations of Samoa's workers at the turn of the twentieth century and, at the same time, their limitations. Colonialism created new opportunities for Samoans—such as traveling around the world—but also circumscribed the extent and purpose of their movements. Samoans in the age of empire had to navigate their way through strong crosscurrents. Multilingual mediators like Taylor became adept at managing and, at times, even manipulating the expectations of Euro-American colonial officials like Solf. In a strategic appropriation of Solf's paternalist self-description as the "father" of all Samoans, Taylor repeatedly fashioned himself as the German governor's son to further his personal interests. Yet as governor and employer, Solf did have the final word with regard to Taylor's travel plans, his work conditions, and even his finances.

Charles T. Taylor was among the first Samoans to visit Germany, but he was not the only Pacific Islander who traveled the world at the turn of the twentieth century. From the 1880s on, thousands of contract workers from New Guinea, Kiribati, and China endured thousands of miles at sea to work on coconut plantations in Samoa. In the decades before World War I, several groups of Samoan and fellow Polynesian performers visited Europe and North America to provide ethnographic edutainment to metropolitan audiences. And the first Samoan women, who worked for the U.S. Navy in American Samoa, journeyed across the Pacific to receive medical training in San Francisco. As this book will show, these wide-ranging movements were both old and new. Samoans had been "travel-happy" ever since their ancestors had settled in the South Pacific roughly three millennia earlier.[5] Yet as Samoa became a target of European and U.S. colonialism in the late nineteenth century, long-grown paths of spatial and social mobility were curtailed even as new ones opened up.

• • •

Long before the European age of empire, Samoa had been at the crossroads of people on the move. Located halfway between Hawai'i and Australia, Samoa emerged as one of the cultural centers of Oceanian life. Genealogy, trade, and occasional war linked Samoans with fellow islanders, particularly in Fiji to the southwest and Tonga to the south, and as far away as the Marquesas Islands in the eastern Pacific. Austronesian voyagers from the western Pacific had first settled on this group of volcanic islands as they expanded a shared oceanic culture, known as the Lapita. Likely the direct ancestors of most Polynesians, the Lapita people were highly mobile seaborne explorers, who, starting around 1,500 BCE, spread from northern New Guinea across eastern Melanesia into central Polynesia, including Tonga and Samoa. Archaeologists, who found shards of Lapita pottery in the Mulifanua lagoon in northern Upolu in the late 1960s, date the earliest human presence in Samoa to around 800 BCE.[6] Over three millennia, Samoans had come to share a collective identity (*Samoa 'uma*), which would shape their encounter with foreign newcomers (*papālagi*) in the nineteenth century.[7]

Like other islanders, Samoans sustained their Oceanian culture through travel and movement. According to *fa'a Samoa* (the Samoan way of life), Samoans demonstrate kinship by traveling to see relatives for important life events and conduct diplomacy by consulting with allies in times of crisis.[8] Samoans call these traveling parties *malaga,* which also refers to travel, movement, and mobility more generally. More than simple travel, *malaga* are crucial to maintaining *vā*—the "links, pathways, and networks that people reestablish as they move."[9] As a central principle of the Samoan moral economy, *vā* denotes spaces in between people, places, and environments that need to be in balance and reciprocal. By moving back and forth between relational spaces, Samoans nurture social harmony and ensure the integrity of their culture. According to Damon Salesa, the popularity of *malaga* increased throughout the nineteenth century as new people, places, and objects were incorporated into the practice. After 1899, colonial and Samoan governments alike were "concerned with restricting and regulating *malaga* for, as much as any Samoan practice, *malaga* troubled colonial intentions of controlling and disciplining Samoans and Samoan politics."[10] Yet Samoans would not be easily contained.

By the close of the nineteenth century, colonial boundaries around space, race, and political sovereignty threatened Samoan traditions of mobility and cultural exchange. As colonial boundary-makers introduced new spaces that

separated people, Samoans continued to spin their own webs of social, economic, and environmental relationships. Wherever they went, Samoans
sought to reconstitute existential relational spaces threatened by the forces
of colonialism. To understand the "rewiring of Samoa" in the context of
unprecedented global interest in the islands at the end of the nineteenth
century, it is essential to follow the workers who were busy updating old wires
and laying new ones.[11] Building on their long-grown practices of mobility,
Samoans extended *malaga* from their villages and islands to the wider Pacific world and beyond. In doing so, Samoans enlarged their lifeworlds even
as colonial officials sought to narrow their paths and visions.

The nineteenth century brought fundamental changes to the culture of mobility that Samoans had created over generations. As Europeans and Americans scrambled for the Pacific as one of the last colonial frontiers, scores of
outlanders visited and settled on Pacific islands such as Samoa, beginning
with the beachcombers. In the early nineteenth century, Euro-American
sailors who had escaped the hard work of whaling ships settled in Samoa,
where they were joined by criminal escapees from New South Wales and
Tasmania. Beachcombers became crucial mediators between islanders and
outlanders, introducing new tools, such as metal goods and rifles.[12] Hard on
their heels followed the missionaries. Even before the first European missionaries sailed for the South Pacific, the Samoan sailor Sio Vili brought
Christian beliefs home in the late 1820s from visits to Tahiti and other Pacific
islands.[13] Not long after, in 1830, Rev. John C. Williams, the first emissary of
the London Missionary Society, landed in Sapapali'i (Savai'i) together with
a group of Tahitian and Rarotongan teachers. Apart from bringing the gospel to Samoa, Williams also built himself a trading vessel, established a general store in Apia, and began exporting coconut oil in 1842.[14] Within years
of the missionaries' arrival, many Samoans had converted to Christianity
and ventured to other parts of the Pacific to spread the gospel. Samoan
missionaries who followed in the footsteps of Vili initiated new forms of
movements brought about by Euro-American colonialism. By mid-century,
Euro-American trading houses and shipping companies joined Christian
missions in reshaping the ways in which Samoans moved about their home
islands and beyond.

By the 1850s, Samoa had become the target of coconut colonialism: the extension of initially informal and subsequently formal Euro-American control over tropical islands to extract their resources, such as coconuts.[15] In 1857,

the Hamburg-based trading house J. C. Godeffroy & Sohn established its Pacific headquarters in Apia on Upolu's northern coast. Within years, Godeffroy & Sohn expanded its trade in tropical fruit, especially coconuts, copra, and cocoa, from Samoa to New Guinea and the Marshall Islands. Shipped to San Francisco and Hamburg, copra—the dried endosperm or meat of the coconut—was processed into vegetable oil, margarine, and soap. At the same time, British and American merchants opened the first trading stores, turning Apia into a bustling commercial center for trans-Pacific trade. In the 1860s, Godeffroy & Sohn and its successor company, Deutsche Handels- und Plantagen-Gesellschaft der Südsee-Inseln zu Hamburg (DHPG), began to purchase land from Samoans around Apia and along the northwestern coast of Upolu. In return, Samoan chiefs (*matai*) received foreign goods, such as metal wares and rifles, which they used to expand their political influence over rivals.

Throughout the 1870s, a vicious cycle of selling land for arms destabilized the economic and political systems of Samoa. In a series of violent clashes, German, British, and American officials and settlers allied with different Samoan parties competing for royal titles and political power. Recurrent fights between Malietoa Talavou and his nephew Malietoa Laupepa over the rightful successor to the Malietoa title had subsided with Talavou's death in November 1880. However, civil war broke out again soon after, as holders of other paramount chiefly titles—Mata'afa Iosefo and Tamasese Titimaea—and the two houses of the Samoan legislature (Ta'imua and Faipule) openly challenged Malietoa Laupepa's title. With the political and military support of the German Empire, Tamasese Titimaea crowned himself "king" of Samoa in November 1884, only to be attacked by Mata'afa Iosefo, who enjoyed the support of a majority of Samoans.

In June 1887, delegates from Great Britain, Germany, and the United States convened in Washington, DC, to negotiate a new colonial arrangement in Samoa. But the predominance of German interests—especially in trade—combined with Anglo-American disagreements prevented a more lasting solution. Samoans themselves were never asked to join the debate about the future of their islands. More than anything, outlanders consistently misunderstood Samoan politics, which was based on local and genealogical sources of authority—what Malama Meleisea has described as Samoa's "unitary system of dispersed power."[16]

Shortly after the inconclusive Washington conference, Tamasese Titimaea was again crowned "king" over all Samoa with German backing. Most Samoans, however, disputed Titimaea's ascension to power because he failed to unite all four paramount chiefly titles (*pāpā*) to claim the paramountcy (*tafa'ifā*). Undisturbed by Samoan objections, German naval officials declared war on Malietoa Laupepa, Titimaea's most formidable challenger to the paramountcy. With substantial support from the Imperial German Navy, Titimaea prevailed over Laupepa and his supporters in September 1887. German officials then deported Laupepa and his chief advisors to Jaluit Atoll in the German Marshall Islands, eighteen hundred miles from Samoa. In December 1888, German troops attacked the supporters of Mata'afa Iosefo, who had continued his challenge to Titimaea's claim to power. Underestimating the battle-hardened skills of Iosefo's troops and the challenging terrain, the Germans suffered a devastating defeat, with 56 out of 140 troops killed, and had to retreat. German soldiers eventually prevailed and exiled Iosefo, but not without serious damage to their reputation and considerable public outcry throughout the German Empire.[17]

In January 1889, U.S. consul William Blacklock called for warships to defend U.S. interests against escalating shelling by German ships. On March 11, 1889, three U.S. battleships under the command of Rear Admiral L. A. Kimberly arrived in Apia. Events began to spin out of control as the decades-long proxy conflict threatened to turn into all-out war between Germany, Great Britain, and the United States, with Samoans caught in the line of fire. Then, on March 15, a tropical cyclone sank three German and three American warships, which had been dangerously eyeing each other in the harbor of Apia. Hundreds of Samoans died in the cataclysmic storm, along with ninety-two Germans and sixty-three Americans.[18] Still in shock, the colonial powers agreed to a system of tripartite rule over the islands at a conference held in Berlin in the early summer of 1889.

Under this so-called tridominium, sovereignty over the Samoan islands and their forty thousand residents was not split along territorial lines but shared equally among the three "great powers." In reality, most Samoans outside the municipal district of Apia continued to live under their traditional laws, while the three consuls were busy determining which national laws applied to which non-native colonists. Throughout the ten-year life span of the Samoan tridominium, the treaty powers were constantly trying to change the status quo to their advantage but managed to avoid direct military confrontation. As I have argued elsewhere, the tridominium was a deliberate strategy of deferral, designed to regulate the transition of colonial rule over Samoa from three to eventually two powers.[19]

In early 1899, Mataʻafa Iosefo, who had returned from his exile, defeated his opponents and reinstalled himself as paramount titleholder of Samoa. In December 1899, the unprecedented experiment in tripartite rule came to an end. A trilateral convention divided Samoa between Germany and the United States, while Great Britain gained exclusive rights over nearby Tonga and further German concessions in the Solomon Islands. In 1900, the two biggest western islands, Upolu and Savaiʻi, officially became part of German Samoa. Under Governor Wilhelm Solf's administration, Samoan cultural practices were tolerated, while German officials stepped up their control over political matters through a flurry of regulations. Meanwhile, the U.S. Navy took control over the major island to the east, Tutuila, in 1900, along with the smaller Manuʻa islands in 1904.[20] As a coaling station run by a small group of naval governors, American Samoa entered a historical trajectory connected to, yet distinct from, neighboring Upolu and Savaiʻi. Outlanders had succeeded in dividing Samoans' long-grown unitary system of decentralized power into two separate colonies. Most importantly for political self-determination, Samoans had suddenly lost their ability to play off one colonial power against the others. After decades of proxy wars, international treaties, and hundreds of casualties, a new era had begun for Samoans as they struggled to keep millennia-old kinship networks and travel routes alive.

When world war reached the shores of Samoa in August 1914, German authorities did not put up a fight against the overwhelming show of force by marines from Great Britain and New Zealand. New Zealand occupied German Samoa during the war and took over the islands under a League of Nations mandate into the 1920s and beyond. In the fall of 1918, the flu pandemic that trailed the millions of casualties of the world war hit Samoa especially hard, killing one out of five Samoans in New Zealand–controlled Western Samoa within months. By contrast, nobody died in the neighboring U.S. territory. Many in Western Samoa blamed the staggering human toll on the botched response by New Zealand administrators and called for greater self-determination. By the mid-1920s, the Mau movement began to challenge colonial administrations head-on through international lobbying, public demonstrations, and economic boycotts.[21] Western Samoa would gain its formal independence in 1962, the first colonized Pacific island to do so. American Samoa, by contrast, remains an unincorporated territory of the United States to this day.

• • •

This book tells the story of Samoa's relations with the rest of the world from the closing decade of the nineteenth century until the end of World War I through the eyes of working people like Charles T. Taylor. Thousands of workers—locals and newcomers—laid the foundation for Samoa's integration into the world. Independent Samoan producers who sold surplus copra to traders were essential to the prosperity of German and American Samoa. So were the thousands of Melanesian, Micronesian, and Chinese contract laborers who picked and processed coconuts and cocoa, tapped rubber trees, and weeded plantation grounds. Workers also built the colonial infrastructure necessary to connect Samoa internally and with the rest of the world: trails, roads, docks, and even a radio station. Cash crops found their way to market on these very roads and docks.

Samoans and migrants from around the Pacific forged new connections with one another and the wider world because and in spite of colonial regimes of difference. As Samoa was drawn into the orbit of Euro-American empires at the turn of the twentieth century, the islands' working people extended their networks and interests outward, into the wider Pacific and beyond. Even as they were coerced co-makers of colonial globality, workers in Samoa created their own way of relating to the world, which—inspired by Oceanian intellectual Epeli Hauʻofa—I call *Oceanian globality*.[22] Confronted with coconut colonialism, Samoans and other islanders counterposed their own definition against the limiting form of globality that colonial officials and capitalists sought to force on them. In doing so, they filled the foreign and abstract notion of global space with their own culturally specific and relational meaning. Over the course of the nineteenth century, the makers of Oceanian globality struggled to extend their shared values of social reciprocity into the wider world. Crucially, the global connections that bound Samoa to Euro-American traders, planters, and politicians depended on the very local connections that Samoan, Melanesian, Micronesian, and Chinese workers made with one another.

Indeed, most Samoans did not distinguish between the "global" and the "local" in any meaningful way because their far-reaching *malaga* were designed to attend to interpersonal relationships all along. But even though Oceanian cosmopolitanism had deep roots, Samoan travels at the turn of the twentieth century—from Sydney to Munich to San Francisco—were unprecedented.[23] Through traveling and meeting fellow Pacific Islanders around the world, these globe-trotting Samoans grew increasingly aware of shared struggles against colonial exploitation. Samoans realized their version of Oceanian globality in different ways, from projecting their *malaga* into the world to entering into a Polynesian Confederacy with their Hawaiian and Tongan kin in 1887.[24] Ultimately, as Samoans became more conscious of the global dimensions of colonialism, they began to challenge outlander rule over their islands more directly in the wake of World War I.

The decades before and after 1900 formed an important transition period for Samoans and many other Pacific Islanders. As new means of communication and travel sought to annihilate space and time, the turn of the twentieth century brought profound economic, political, and social change to the Pacific. Samoa in 1889 and Samoa in 1919 were very different places. First, the islands had lost their formal political independence as Great Britain, Germany, and the United States struggled over control. After 1900, the forty miles of ocean separating the islands of Upolu in German Samoa and Tutuila in American Samoa became an international boundary. Initially, the border was weakly policed and easily crossed; over time, however, it hardened into a substantial barrier that slowed down exchange between Samoans in the western islands and those in the eastern islands. As Samoans adjusted to formal colonial rule after 1900, the economic and political trajectories of German and American Samoa began to diverge, with far-reaching consequences for their political status and migration patterns.

Second, the patchy array of foreign-owned copra plantations in the 1880s experienced explosive growth in the following decades. As a result of an expanding plantation agriculture, Samoa became home to a diverse group of people from around the Pacific world. Besides the forty thousand Samoans who lived on the islands, several thousand migrant workers came to work on Samoan plantations from other parts of the Pacific, particularly the Gilbert Islands (now part of Kiribati), the Solomon Islands, and New Guinea. Beginning in the early twentieth century, they were joined by several thousand more from China. As a result, Samoan farming practices came under increasing pressure from a growing plantation economy dominated by foreign traders and worked by migrants from China and other Pacific islands.

Third, Samoa became increasingly entangled in shipping, communication, and entertainment networks that encircled the globe at the end of the nineteenth century. The expansion of copra plantations and regular shipping lines tied Samoa ever tighter to global trade networks. Workers erected new hospitals, administration buildings, and a coaling station for the U.S. Navy in Tutuila. Radio stations in American and German Samoa connected the islands to imperial metropoles and warships, and offered easier access to news. For their part, Samoan performers in ethnographic shows used the new infrastructure to travel to distant places, becoming cultural ambassadors in the process. And the new languages of the colonizers created new forms of employment for Samoans, who became interpreters and clerks. Uncovering the aspirations of workers on plantations, on show stages, and in governor's offices reveals a social world beyond the control of colonial officials and, too often, beyond the purview of historians.

Coconut Colonialism is a history from way below and far away, but it is also a history from close up. It traces the struggles of workers in Samoa from the plantation grounds up and across thousands of miles of land and sea, while staying firmly anchored in the South Pacific. For both islanders and outlanders at the turn of the twentieth century, Samoa was not at the margins of world history but, to the contrary, at the very center of events. For U.S. naval strategists in the 1890s, Pago Pago on Tutuila was a harbor "so central, and otherwise so suitable in case of operations in that quarter, that it is recommended to be retained."[25] Samoa's global importance in the age of empire deserves renewed attention from historians of globalization, colonialism, and capitalism. Histories of modern capitalism and globalization are typically set in Europe or its settler colonies, and more recently in China.[26] But Pacific islands, in general, and Samoa, in particular, are ideal places to rethink the history of colonialism and the colonial roots of globalization.[27] During the European age of empire, the Samoan islands emerged as objects of imperial competition over access to tropical cash crops, shipping lines, and coaling stations in the South Pacific. Given these Euro-American claims on Samoa, the general terms of its integration into global circuits of trade, migration, and information were often beyond the direct control of workers on the islands. What set colonial Samoa apart from other plantation colonies at the time, however, was the fact that Samoans were able to protect a communal land base on which they continued sustainable farming. With their own food supply secured, Samoan farmers sold their surplus production of coconuts and copra to foreign merchants in German Samoa and the U.S. Navy in American Samoa. As a result, Samoans exercised considerable power in shaping their relationship with the rest of the world.

The globalization of Samoa at the turn of the twentieth century also adds a new chapter to the history of modern capitalism.[28] Recent works by historians of capitalism have focused on commodities, railroads, and slavery in North America and around the world.[29] To date, there are very few histories of capitalism that engage with the Pacific and its extensive networks of trade, agricultural production, and labor.[30] Most significantly, the story of labor in Samoa offers a new take on the transformation of the global countryside at the turn of twentieth century. This process took place in many parts of the world, at different times and under different circumstances, but was generally linked to colonization projects by powerful states and companies.[31] The expansion of commercial plantation agriculture in Samoa and the recruitment of contract laborers from all over the Pacific to work on these plantations was part of this global transformation. By the close of the nineteenth century, Samoa had joined other Pacific islands, such as Fiji and Hawai'i, to become part of a tropical plantation complex built in the long shadow of legal slavery.[32] As the Samoan case shows, Pacific islands deserve more scholarly attention as one of the major postemancipation commodity frontier zones, marked by globally traded cash crops and unfree labor regimes.[33]

Despite several global commonalities, local particularities made the Samoan case different from others. To be sure, rural cultivators around the world preferred local trade and farming over long-distance markets.[34] But few farmers, especially in Euro-American colonies, were able to resist growing outside demands and thrive at the same time. Facing mounting pressures to sell their land and their labor power, Samoan farmers were able to hold on to their sustainable farming practices for a number of reasons. First, Samoa remained at best partially integrated into global commodity chains at the turn of the twentieth century. Steamship and communication lines improved access to the South Pacific, but other tropical cash crop zones—in the Caribbean and in Africa—were geographically closer to major consumer markets in North America and Europe. Second, Samoans had a long history of violent resistance against colonial intervention, which made colonial officials hesitant to enact more aggressive methods of extraction. Last but not least, colonial officials pursued paternalistic policies that protected Samoan ways of life from wholesale commodification by more aggressive planters. Although this policy of paternalism undermined long-standing political structures, it did help Samoans adapt to global trade largely on their own terms. As Samoans held their own in this precarious balance between external pressure and internal change, they developed new bonds of solidarity with one another and with non-Samoans.

Workers were prominent actors in the dramatic expansion of capitalism to Samoa and to the Pacific more broadly. In the eyes of plantation owners and colonial officials, the "labor question" was central to colonialism, its political economy, and the integration of Samoa into capitalist trade networks. In Samoa and elsewhere in the Pacific, unfreedom and coercion survived the legal abolition of Atlantic slavery as different postemancipation labor regimes came to coexist. Euro-American capitalists introduced wage labor on large copra and cocoa plantations, putting pressure on independent Samoan farmers to sell their surplus crops for export, often under coercive conditions. At the same time, foreign-owned plantations attracted migrant workers from neighboring Pacific islands and as far away as New Guinea and the Gilbert Islands. Faced with widespread Samoan resistance to land enclosure and wage labor, plantation owners resorted to recruiting more and more contract laborers, including thousands from China. Samoan islanders and this diverse group of newcomers engaged in various forms of manual and intellectual labor. In their own ways, all of them were involved in shaping Samoa's relationship with the wider world. Asking big questions in a small place, the case of Samoa shows that historians need to focus on workers' struggles and do so from a global perspective.[35]

Workers in colonial Samoa faced physical and emotional challenges in their different work environments. Melanesian, Micronesian, and Chinese workers on copra plantations, for example, confronted a form of labor that strained not only their bodies, through heavy lifting and long work hours, but also their minds, through the monotony of the work rhythm. Some plantation workers developed what colonial doctors called "coolie legs," painful ulcers on their lower legs, resulting from constant standing, walking, and carrying crops on plantation grounds. Meanwhile, workers who helped build the coaling station in Tutuila developed their own, no less exacting relationship to the natural environment. As they cut into the hillside to gain soil for the land fill stretching into the bay, workers used shovels, carts, and often their bare hands to handle the dirt. Although the workers with leg ulcers and dirty hands were not present when international treaties about the future of Samoa were signed, they were the ones who turned the islands into contested terrain in the first place.[36]

Samoan government employees who helped translate and interpret documents and speeches experienced very different demands. While they did not face the same physical challenges, their personal proximity to the center of colonial power taxed them in emotional ways. Some developed such intimate relationships with their employers that lines of authority became blurred. And for those Samoan women and men who joined ethnographic show troupes to travel to the United States and Europe, working acquired yet another meaning. Theirs was a movable workplace that took them from their home islands to unfamiliar places to be exhibited in front of unfamiliar audiences. Over time, their particular kind of performative labor enabled forms of sociality with fellow colonized peoples unimaginable at home.

Like their counterparts in other parts of the Pacific, working people in Samoa sought social interactions with their colleagues.[37] Whether on the plantation grounds or in the government hospital, labor was rarely a solitary endeavor. Chinese plantation workers had dens where they smoked opium and gambled. Samoan soldiers shared the same barracks. And Samoan performers in ethnographic shows spent almost every moment of their worldwide travels together. Inspired by Thomas Andrews, I will refer to the contested terrain of social and material interactions in which working people in Samoa participated as a *workscape*.[38] Different workscapes enabled different forms of interaction, giving rise to different forms of sociality. Samoans in Savai'i who were farming to feed their family members followed time-tested ways of labor organization according to gender, age, and status. Meanwhile, construction workers who transported soil from cut to fill for the U.S. Navy coaling station in Tutuila followed the commands of their white bosses—at least most of the time.

Occasionally, states of sociality turned into more robust bonds of solidarity in a contested workscape. Through shared experiences, workers came to acquire a sense of common interests that became the basis for collective action. In most cases, the kinds of political acts workers engaged in were far from revolutionary. For instance, plantation workers intentionally worked more slowly than their employers required, ethnographic performers demanded opportunities to earn additional cash through the sale of craftwork, and construction workers struck for better wages. In rare moments, however, concerted political action took the form of economic boycotts that threatened the very foundations of colonial rule, such as when a charismatic *matai* from Savai'i organized a powerful movement in the early twentieth century. It was not until the early 1920s when the social bonds forged in the crucible of labor congealed into a more sustained solidarity movement among Samoans, who directed their demands for cultural autonomy and respect against both the U.S. Navy and the New Zealand civil administration. By analyzing the bonds of solidarity that emerged in different workscapes in Samoa in the preceding decades, *Coconut Colonialism* maps out the understudied labor roots of the anti-colonial Mau movement.[39]

Due to the multiracial and transitory nature of labor in Samoa, solidarity among workers did not emerge primarily from an awareness of common goals. Instead, workers shared a sense of vulnerability to cultural, economic, political, and environmental change. To varying degrees, workers were drawn into a colonial world beyond their control. Samoan families, for instance, had to deal with the commodification of their natural resources, from food crops such as coconuts to the very lands they lived on. The thousands of migrant workers who came to Samoa from all over the Pacific world were exposed to different kinds of vulnerabilities. Bound by contract to their employer, they had to obey orders, work hard, and endure regular physical and financial punishment. Because most contract laborers came alone, they could not rely on the social networks that sustained Samoan communities. Even though workers experienced different degrees of vulnerability in the face of coconut colonialism, they came to share a common understanding of themselves as structurally exposed to forces beyond their control. While it would be too much to speak of a class consciousness shared by all workers in Samoa, this sense of solidarity in the face of shared vulnerability emerged clearly on several occasions at the turn of the twentieth century.

Solidarity materialized, for instance, when Samoans protested against the continuing commodification of their food supplies by German plantation owners seeking quick profits. In protecting their own agricultural economy, Samoans slowed down the advance of commercial plantations on their islands and, indirectly, mitigated the further exploitation of plantation workers from elsewhere. Likewise, Samoans who participated in ethnographic shows in Europe and North America were vulnerable to exploitative managers, aggressive audiences, and local authorities. By socializing with fellow people on display, such as hula dancers from Hawai'i, Samoans recognized their own vulnerabilities as participants in the politics of colonial representation. Yet when they laughed and danced with fellow Polynesians in faraway Chicago, Samoan performers also transcended official protocols and shaped their own form of Oceanian globality.

• • •

Samoan history at the turn of the twentieth century has usually been told from the perspective of the European and American diplomats whose voluminous records are readily accessible. In an influential study, Paul Kennedy characterized the negotiations, conferences, and treaties involving the islands as "the Samoan Tangle."[40] Rather than approaching Samoan history at the turn of the twentieth century as a diplomatic tangle, *Coconut Colonialism* puts Samoa's entanglements in the global webs of capitalism and labor migration front and center.[41] In doing so, the book relies on the foundational work of Samoan, New Zealand, and Australian historians writing in the late 1960s and 1970s. James W. Davidson wrote the first political history of the newly independent Western Samoa, but only his opening chapters focus on the period before World War II, with scarce attention to the experience of working people.[42] Richard P. Gilson, while broadening his view to include culture and religion, ends his account of multicultural Samoa with partition in 1899.[43] Malama Meleisea does highlight the role of workers in colonial Samoa, but aside from his important oral history of Melanesian workers, he did not produce a major monograph or analyze forms of labor beyond plantations.[44] Other studies of labor in Samoa tend to focus on specific groups of migrant workers—for example, those from Micronesia, Melanesia, and China.[45] In contrast, *Coconut Colonialism* connects the experiences of all workers in colonial Samoa together in a Pacific and global context. More recently, Patricia O'Brien has put Samoa back on the world stage with her biography of Ta'isi O. F. Nelson.[46] However, O'Brien's study of an influential businessman, plantation owner, and charismatic politician has little to say about the everyday experiences of working people and their own global travels. One of this book's main arguments is that the thousands of lesser-known workers on plantations and show stages at the turn of the twentieth century were the trailblazers for Nelson's anti-colonial lobbying and the success of the Mau movement.

Earlier than many of their counterparts, historians of the Pacific islands have worked to overcome the national, racial, and cultural boundaries erected by outlanders since James Cook.[47] Two major fault lines dating back to Euro-American colonization of the late nineteenth century continue to run right through the Samoan archipelago today: the international date line and the border between (Western) Samoa and American Samoa. The international date line, created in 1884 at a conference in Washington, DC, represented the counterpart to the zero meridian at the Royal Observatory at Greenwich, Great Britain. With the Atlantic world foremost on their minds, conference delegates solved the geometric "problem" by drawing the line right through the middle of the Pacific Ocean. As far as Euro-American delegates were concerned, there were too few islanders living in the region to matter. In fact, representatives from the Kingdom of Hawai'i were the lone voices from the Pacific in Washington. Since 1884, Samoa jumped across the date line not once but twice. Only eight years later, Samoa celebrated two consecutive Fourths of July to join the eastern side of the line. American merchants had lobbied for the time alignment since the creation of the date line, hoping to facilitate business with their main shipping destination in San Francisco. And over a century later, on December 30, 2011, Western Samoa jumped back west across the date line. That Friday was simply skipped on Upolu and Savai'i, forcing hundreds of surprised residents to move their birthday parties.[48] Samoan prime minister Tuilaepa Aiono Sailele Malielegaoi had argued that the date switch would improve business relations with major trading partners in Australia, New Zealand, and China. Since hundreds of thousands of Samoans lived in Australia and New Zealand, crossing the date line would also make it easier to communicate with family and friends in the diaspora. Considerations of political economy had influenced Samoa's first jump across the date line in 1892, and they did so again in 2011. In both cases, workers seeking opportunities for a better life bound Samoa closer to other parts of the Pacific.

   Likewise, the international border between the independent nation-state
of (Western) Samoa and American Samoa, an unincorporated territory of
the United States, was the product of colonial boundary-makers. Since the
Tripartite Convention of 1899, which created German and American Samoa,
an international border has separated the western islands of Savai'i and
Upolu from their eastern neighbors, Tutuila and Manu'a. With the stroke of a
pen in distant Washington, long-standing political, economic, and genealogical links among the islands of Samoa were put under strain. Through this
rewiring of Samoa from the outside, Apia gained in economic significance
while the paramount titleholders of Tutuila and Manu'a lost political influence vis-à-vis their counterparts in Upolu and Savai'i.[49] During the influenza pandemic of 1918–19, the international border allowed the U.S.
naval administration to more effectively quarantine Tutuila and Manu'a
from Western Samoa, likely saving hundreds of lives. Since Western Samoa
gained its independence in 1962, the border has served to separate an independent Pacific country from a colony of the U.S. empire. While American
Samoan nationals are free to move to fully incorporated parts of the United
States for work or family visits, Samoans in (Western) Samoa traveling to
American Samoa face the comprehensive and changing border regime of the
U.S. empire.
   To understand the differential distribution of rights and resources across
the border between Upolu and Tutuila today, Coconut Colonialism analyzes
the intertwined colonial trajectories of Western and American Samoa together. To date, there is no book-length study that brings together the histories of Western and American Samoa during the crucial time when the
islands redefined their relationship to the world at the turn of the twentieth
century. Both the international date line and the international border are
products of Euro-American colonialism that continue to affect migration,
trade, and family networks in postcolonial Samoa and still-colonial American Samoa. Given renewed attention to the Pacific Ocean and its peoples, historians of the region need to build more bridges to national and international
conversations without losing sight of the very local traditions of genealogy,
identity, and connection.[50]
   Beyond Samoan and Pacific history, Coconut Colonialism pushes historians of the United States and Germany to broaden their horizons toward the
Pacific. Despite rising interest in the history of German and U.S. colonialism in recent decades, there has been no book on Samoa that situates the

islands within the region and within the histories of the two colonial empires.[51] This book offers a detailed analysis of Samoa's role in both German and U.S. colonial projects, highlighting the central role played by working people. For a long time, scholars of U.S. and German labor history have ignored the experiences of workers beyond the imperial center and without citizenship. This study of German and American Samoa is part of a growing wave of scholarship that tries to break that silence.[52] Workers in Samoa played important roles in the expansion of global trade and shipping networks, which fueled capitalist production and consumption in metropolitan markets. And some Samoan workers even traveled to Berlin and New York to entertain German and American spectators anxious to see exotic islanders from the Pacific. These cultural workers collapsed distinctions not only between center and periphery but also between colonizer and colonized. In sum, historians of German and American history have a lot to learn by turning their eyes toward the South Pacific.[53]

• • •

Samoa at the turn of the twentieth century was riven by tensions over trade, labor, and mobility. To flesh out the intimate dynamics of working in Samoa, *Coconut Colonialism* is structured topologically, linking particular *themes* to particular kinds of *places*. Theme and place come together in five different workscapes. Each chapter captures a global process within the local context of Samoa: the commodification of the Samoan economy (Chapter 1), unfree labor migration (Chapter 2), the performative labor involved in ethnographic shows (Chapter 3), the construction of transportation and communication lines (Chapter 4), and the careers in the colonial service (Chapter 5).

Chapter 1 opens with the tropical fruit that sparked outside interest in the Samoan islands in the nineteenth century: the coconut. Samoans resisted Euro-American coconut colonialism by holding on to their vibrant farming practices, which acted as a safeguard against their exploitation as wage laborers on plantations. In insisting on the limits of commodification of natural resources, especially food crops such as coconuts, Samoans succeeded in protecting long-standing ways of life. At the same time, Samoans also adapted selectively to the new colonial world by performing occasional wage labor on plantations and, especially, by founding copra cooperatives. In both German and American Samoa, this form of worker mutualism was aimed at greater economic self-determination on the part of the powerful Samoan producers.

While the cooperative movement eventually gave in under political coercion, it helped form the nucleus of a more sustained challenge to colonial rule in the 1920s.

Chapter 2 sketches out the colonial world made by copra, the dried meat of the coconut. As the main cash crop of the islands, copra structured the lives of thousands of Melanesian and Chinese plantation workers and independent Samoan producers. Plantation workers struggled to turn shared sociality into the more concrete bonds of solidarity that would enable them to resist their exploitation in more lasting ways. Moving across lines—spatial, racial, and even spiritual—was one of the main strategies of resistance pursued by workers. Chinese workers defied the coercive conditions on large copra plantations by running away, appealing to their home government, and sometimes resorting to physical violence. Workers from Micronesia and Melanesia created communities of cultural kinship with one another in a related but distinct islander society. Those migrant workers who made Samoa their home after their contracts had expired often intermarried with Samoans to form multicultural families still visible today.

Chapter 3 follows the travels and travails of Samoan performers who participated in ethnographic shows in the United States and Europe at the turn of the twentieth century. No less than the workers cutting copra on the islands, the men and women who left their homes to enact Samoan culture abroad played a crucial role in the making of empire in Samoa. Easily the most mobile of all workers, troupe members charted out their own pathways on unfamiliar terrain and, in the process, complicated lines of authority and cultural authenticity. Balancing the exploitation of the colonial gaze against opportunities for travel and self-representation, Samoan performers became powerful diplomats of their own. Over time, they learned to circumnavigate the demands of their Euro-American managers by reinterpreting their participation in ethnographic shows as diplomatic missions and making friends with fellow colonized peoples, finding new forms of solidarity out of earshot of colonial officials.

The building of the material infrastructure of empire in Samoa is the focus of Chapter 4. Shipping and telegraph lines presaged Samoa's entry into an age of deepening global connections, a process bookended by the two date line crossings in 1892 and 2011. Despite their aura of annihilating time and space, new technologies such as the telegraph and radio still required manual labor. Communication and shipping lines helped link Samoa to Euro-American audiences and markets while giving islanders little control over the terms of interaction. But construction workers who built the roads, telegraph lines, and U.S. naval station in Tutuila were far from mere auxiliaries of Euro-American colonialism. By contrast, these construction workers not only regularly fought for better working conditions but also succeeded in making the new material environment their own. In the end, the building of infrastructure went hand in hand with the building of structures of solidarity among those who did the work.

In the fifth and final chapter, the white-collar counterparts to the blue-collar plantation workers take center stage: soldiers, interpreters, and nurses. Colonization brought new forms of employment to the islands. Many of the workers in the colonial service were of mixed-race heritage and used their intermediary positions to become powerful brokers between colonizers and the colonized. Interpreters like Charles T. Taylor gained political clout in German Samoa because of their proximity to colonial power. Female nurses like Grace Pepe received training from the U.S. Navy in Tutuila and California, turning them into essential brokers between Samoan traditional healing and Euro-American medicine. Above all, soldiers, interpreters, and nurses in the colonial service used their acquired skills not only for individual advancement but for political activism as well. With their intercultural education and personal networks, service workers emerged as leaders of the anti-colonial resistance movement that shook Samoan society after World War I.

Coconut Colonialism is a book about those who shaped Samoa and its place in the world. It covers the span of three decades, from 1889 to 1919, to tell the story of Samoa's fraught integration into global capitalism and its lasting effects into the present. Workers, merchants, and colonial officials play major roles in this story, as do plantations, ships, and show stages. Tracing the experiences of workers in Samoa moves the narrative far beyond the Samoan islands of Upolu, Savaiʻi, and Tutuila, to cities like San Francisco, Berlin, and Shantou. As it turns out, interpreter Charles T. Taylor, whose global travels opened this introduction, was only one of many Samoans who moved thousands of miles and remade their home islands in the process. The journey into this contested past begins in the South Pacific with the tropical fruit at the center of Samoan culture and, eventually, global commerce: the coconut.

1

COCONUTS

As nourishment for body and mind, the coconut has fed Samoans for millennia. Coconut trees are among the most widespread plants in the South Pacific, providing Samoans and other Pacific Islanders with both calories and canoes. A medium-sized coconut yields more than fourteen hundred calories and is rich in iron, potassium, and saturated fat. Coconut trees are highly versatile plants whose entire organism—from the palm leaves to the roots—can be used for different purposes. Because growing coconut trees (*niu*) required little attention, Samoans were fond of saying: "Give a coconut a day and it will give you a lifetime."[1]

A well-known story from Samoa and other parts of Polynesia explains the origins of the coconut tree. According to oral tradition, a beautiful girl named Sina had a pet eel (*tuna*) who fell in love with her. Afraid, Sina ran away, but the eel followed her to a pool in a neighboring village. Before village chiefs could kill the eel, Sina granted him his last wish: cut his head off and plant it in the ground. From her planting grew the first coconut tree. The face of the eel—two eyes and a mouth—can be seen in the three round marks of the husked coconut.[2] The round form of the coconut with its three indentations also resembles a human head, an association that influenced even Samoan plantation pidgin: "White man coconut belong him no grass he stop [The white man's head is bald]."[3] And when Portuguese explorers brought back the first coconuts to Europe in the mid-sixteenth century, they called the fruit *coco*, or grinning face.

The coconut's anthropomorphic appearance was matched by its great practical use for humans. Shells served as drinking cups and to carry water, the palm and midrib were used to make baskets, and fiber from the husk (coir) was plaited into sennit to build houses and canoes.[4] The husking and splitting of nuts, followed by the grating and squeezing of the meat inside, were arduous and time-consuming labor processes. As a consequence, the time invested in the preparation of a coconut tended to correlate with the special occasion or the status of the guests to be served.[5]

An average family coconut grove was less than one acre in size but could yield up to sixty nuts per tree per year.[6] Coconut trees took between five and eight years to mature, but some trees bore fruit for up to seventy years, longer than the average life expectancy of Samoans at the time. Samoans did not plant coconut trees in a particular order or distance from one another, but they made sure to plant them close to taro and yam fields to have quick refreshment available for workers.[7] That way, Samoans knew that no spot on their islands was further than half an hour from the nearest coconut, which could provide food and drink in times of need.[8] While coconut trees were owned by the families on whose ground they stood, passersby had the right to pluck a few nuts to refresh themselves.[9] Fallen nuts were usually left to themselves and were free to be picked up by anyone who found them.[10]

To harvest the fruits while they were still green, Samoan men climbed up coconut trees that grew as tall as a hundred feet. Using only a sling wrapped around their feet as support, they hugged the tree trunk with their arms and scaled the tree like a caterpillar. Once at the top of the tree, the climber plucked the green fruits from their stems and dropped them onto the ground.[11] Mature coconuts could be more conveniently picked up from the ground and collected in baskets, usually made out of coconut leaf midribs.[12] Ripe coconuts also made better copra. Traditionally, young women carried the harvested fruits in two baskets, one in back and one in front of their bodies, connected with a stick across their shoulders.[13] Filled to the top, two baskets of coconuts could weigh up to 150 pounds. Young men then processed the coconuts, to make use of their individual components. First, the husk of the coconut was split off and removed by pounding the nut against a sharpened wooden stick (*mele'i*) rammed into the ground. Next, the young Samoans straddled a wooden stool (*'ausa'alo*) to scrape the open coconut against the seashell-like part of a coconut shell fastened to the stool's point. The scraped-off pieces of the coconut kernel were then collected in a vessel or on a leaf placed below the stool. Finally, the scrapings were poured into a strainer and the juice squeezed into a bowl for further mixing with other foodstuffs.[14]

Figure 2. Samoan man under coconut tree near Pago Pago, Tutuila, 1884.

[Pango Pango (sic). Cocoa Nuts], 1884, by Alfred Burton, Burton Brothers studio, Dunedin. Purchased 1943.
Te Papa (C.018079).

Because coconuts and other food crops required little sustained attention, Samoan labor was sporadic in nature. Experienced in this noncapitalist mode of agricultural production, Samoans gradually seized the new opportunities that presented themselves with the increasing presence of Euro-American missionaries and traders beginning in the 1830s. After the introduction of commercial agriculture by German traders in the 1860s, Samoans fought to maintain their economic and cultural autonomy and to shape the copra economy according to their own values and interests.

Copra World

The origins of foreign copra plantations in Upolu and Savai'i in the mid-nineteenth century were bound up with the sale of Samoan land. Soon after the first outlanders decided to stay on the islands, Samoans began leasing and selling them land, likely unaware that the buyers expected exclusive and indefinite access.[15] According to one Samoan historian, the possibility that Samoans "could lose in perpetuity, in return for one payment in cash or kind, control over the land, authority over the conduct of its occupants and jurisdiction over the future transfer or inheritance of land they bestowed, was outside their experience or comprehension."[16] A trading company from distant Germany played a major role in the alienation of Samoan land.

In the mid-nineteenth century, the German trading house J. C. Godeffroy & Sohn began its business activities in the South Pacific, establishing its headquarters in Apia in 1857.[17] From Apia, Godeffroy & Sohn expanded its trade in tropical fruit throughout Polynesia and into Melanesia and Micronesia. In its early years, the trading house relied on local Samoan producers to supply the increasingly valuable cash crops. In the mid-1860s, the young and energetic Godeffroy manager Theodor Weber took advantage of a series of environmental disasters to purchase twelve acres of land from starving Samoans and set up the first cotton plantation.[18] During the global cotton famine caused by the U.S. Civil War in the mid-1860s, a few Samoans worked for wages on these cotton plantations.[19] By 1868, when the cotton boom began to subside, the firm owned twenty-five hundred acres, almost 1 percent of the total land area of Upolu.[20] After its reorganization into the Deutsche Handels- und Plantagen-Gesellschaft der Südsee-Inseln (DHPG) in 1878, the German firm continued to prosper.[21]

By the 1870s, copra had become Samoa's main export to Europe and North America, where it was processed into a variety of products, including high-quality soap, margarine, and even dynamite.[22] Driven by growing demand for copra, the DHPG dramatically expanded its plantation holdings by purchasing land from Samoans at war. Trading land for firearms and other supplies, Weber managed to purchase around twenty-five thousand acres of prime plantation lands during the Malietoa succession war between Talavou and Laupepa (1869–1872).[23] At the same time, the Central Polynesian Land and Commercial Company—a group of land speculators based in San Francisco—acquired claims to an area of more than 300,000 acres, or nearly half the land area of all the Samoan islands.[24] Samoan land became so scarce after this rush in the 1870s that at the beginning of the twentieth century, an acre of land was selling for up to £500 ($100).[25] Samoans were divided over these escalating land sales to outlanders. Many feared that foreign ownership would undermine long-standing ways of life based on sustainable agriculture, while some welcomed the considerable profits they reaped from the sales. These profits usually came in the form of imported rifles, which *matai* used to gain an advantage over their rivals. The result was what outside observers innocently called "civil war," which belied the active support Euro-American traders and plantation owners provided to different sides of competing Samoan parties. Fueled by demand for copra in the United States and Europe, the vicious cycle of selling Samoan land for arms accelerated.

Land sales had far-reaching consequences for Samoans and their relationships with outlanders. Euro-American planters were so desperate for Samoan land (and regulations so minimal) that newly "land-conscious" Samoans were able to sell the same parcels of land to several buyers.[26] As a result of widespread fraud, the area claimed by Euro-American speculators amounted to a grand total of 1.7 million acres, or more than twice the overall area of Samoa.[27] In 1893, a land commission installed by the colonial powers recognized only about 8 percent of these outlander claims to Samoan lands, but these included 35 percent of overall cultivable land and 60 percent of cultivable land in the plantation belt between Apia and Mulifanua.[28] Decades after the Great Māhele in Hawai'i, Samoans fought their own struggle against colonial enclosure.[29]

Selling land also increased the power of Samoan men over women and of *matai* over those without title. Since ownership of property conferred social

prestige, the increasing commodification of plantation land intensified conflicts between and within Samoan families.[30] With the arrival of Euro-
American capitalists and their ideas about private property, claims to land
ownership in colonial Samoa moved from genealogical title to usufruct
occupation. In American Samoa, Euro-American settlers and the U.S. Navy
used the common law doctrine of adverse land possession, based on individual land titles derived from at least ten years of cultivation, to undermine
customary Samoan land tenure, based on family (*'aiga*) and village (*nui*)
rights.[31]

Besides the German company and a handful of Euro-American merchants,
another group rose in size and power in colonial Samoa: Samoans of mixed-
race descent (*afakasi*). As the interracial offspring of Samoans and Euro-
American newcomers, the first generation of mixed-race Samoans was born
in the early nineteenth century. As outlanders arrived in greater numbers and
decided to stay, the mixed-race population of Samoa expanded. Interracial
liaisons and marriages were often motivated by economic interests. Euro-
American men sought out marriages with high-ranking Samoan women to
gain access to coveted land. After establishing a foothold in Samoan family
and village networks, these newcomers were able to expand their landholdings or establish trading stations. Their interracial offspring were usually
classified as "European" by Euro-American law, which allowed them to
hold land, enter into individual contracts, and participate in political self-
representation. Generally accepted by other Samoans, mixed-race Samoans
used their language and intercultural skills to seize new opportunities presented by coconut colonialism. For colonial officials, mixed-race Samoans became "troublesome half-castes" because they muddled the colonial rule of
difference by crisscrossing well-defined boundaries of race, class, and culture.
Furthermore, many Samoans of mixed-race descent traveled widely within
Samoa and beyond, which challenged restrictions on mobility passed by
colonial administrators.[32]

Among the mixed-race Samoans was a young man by the name of Ta'isi
Olaf Fredrik Nelson. Born in Safune (Savai'i) in 1883, Nelson was the fourth
child of a Swedish merchant and a Samoan mother. Twelve years younger
than interpreter Charles T. Taylor, Nelson likewise grew up between European and Samoan cultures and languages. When he was a young teenager,
Nelson quit the Marist Brothers' Commercial School and began working for

the DHPG as an office clerk. While there, he learned basic accounting skills and gleaned insights into the political nature of business in Samoa, both of which would be crucial for his future career in business and politics. Tellingly, Nelson refused to speak German, even though his superiors at the firm had ordered him to do so.[33] In February 1900, four years into Nelson's job at the DHPG, the German flag was raised over Upolu and Savai'i. Nelson's DHPG manager had been suspicious of his loyalty to the German kaiser for years, and a recent kerfuffle between Nelson and a group of German marines at the Lindenau restaurant in Apia had made matters worse. When the German judge ordered Nelson and his friends to pay fines as punishment for the public confrontation, Nelson was fired from his job. As O'Brien wryly notes, Nelson's dismissal from the DHPG a mere week after formal annexation "did not help endear the new German regime to him."[34]

In retrospect, Nelson's firing from the DHPG set him up for a successful business career. After he returned to his birthplace of Safune on Savai'i, the seventeen-year-old joined his father's prospering trading company and was made junior partner in 1905. In 1908, Nelson returned to Apia and worked hard to extend the network of trade stores his father had started in the 1870s. With an expanding trade empire of his own, Nelson would once again run afoul of German political and economic interests in the context of Lauaki's Mau a Pule. Mixed-race Samoans, like Nelson, were innovators in the commodification and cultural transformation of Samoa—contested processes that colonial administrators preferred to control.[35] As in other colonies at the time, it was ambitious Samoans of mixed-race descent that would later emerge as leaders of decolonization.

• • •

After partition in 1899, the Samoan labor system was subjected to severe strains by the increasing demands of colonial administrators and foreign plantation owners. Samoa's communal social and economic system increasingly clashed with the new plantation system introduced by Euro-American traders, who pursued their own economic interests and desperately needed workers. The famed Scottish writer Robert Louis Stevenson, who had moved to Samoa in 1889, understood this gradual transformation of the Samoan political economy as well as anyone. In his plantation estate in Vailima, Stevenson exploited the social hierarchies among the Samoan workers he employed by presenting himself as a caring father and welfare capitalist.[36]

German colonial officials, who had formally taken over the main islands of Upolu and Savai'i in 1900, were acutely aware of the long-grown and complex nature of the Samoan labor system. Widespread Euro-American stereotypes about the alleged laziness of colonized people, in general, and Samoan "communism," in particular, did not stand the test of social reality. In a letter to a German geographer from the fall of 1906, Governor Solf defended his policy of protecting Samoan ways of life from overly aggressive planters:

> The assumption that the Samoan does not work is wrong. . . . Every young Samoan, who is working for planters, is, of course, missing with his labor power inside his community. The Samoan idea is that everybody who is working outside of his community owes his pay to the community because his labor power is withdrawn from the community. Hence, the little interest of Samoans to work for foreigners. For they have to, according to the communistic outlook of their community, give back to the community part or all of what they earn. In addition, working as a servant for pay is seen as despicable.[37]

Forcefully changing this deeply ingrained labor system, Solf reasoned, would lead to nothing but economic disaster for the white settlers. Samoans would stop buying imported goods and rely on family farming to satisfy their basic needs. Most importantly, Solf warned, Samoans would refrain from cutting copra for the white traders. In light of the recent Herero rebellion in German Southwest Africa, Solf reassuringly added, Samoans would threaten the lives of the white settlers only in cases of "utmost outrage." They would, however, more readily destroy foreign plantations, Solf concluded.

While social rank, age, and gender determined the kinds of labor Samoans were engaged in before the colonial era, German and American colonial officials and plantation owners tried to impose their own boundaries on Samoa's social landscape. Samoans were increasingly reduced to laborers who were expected to produce cash crops in ever greater quantities. To be sure, Samoans had always produced a small surplus of food crops to have a reserve in case of environmental disasters and to host *malaga*.[38] But before 1830,

Samoan agricultural production was geared toward securing livelihood, not making a profit. As in most Oceanian societies, social prestige in Samoa came from "the generous distribution, not the accumulation of wealth."[39] Most Samoans continued to practice their sustainable farming regardless of the increasing presence of outlanders and sold their surplus crops to Euro-American traders. And occasionally, Samoans worked on larger Euro-American plantations to earn cash.

Coconut colonialism changed Samoan economic, social, and cultural practices in profound ways. Beginning in the 1830s, Euro-American traders and missionaries introduced new goods into the Samoan economy, some of which, like firearms and ammunition, quickly became indispensable to Samoan warfare and politics. Other new manufactured goods (*mea palagi,* or "foreign goods") included such diverse objects as umbrellas, watches, and sewing machines. Many of these manufactured goods were sold by Euro-American traders in their own stores or in stores owned by large plantation companies. A German trade report from May 1900 documented some of the imported goods that changed everyday life among Samoans: "Every evening, one can see a lamp burning in every Samoan hut, nearly every Samoan family owns as part of their inventory a sewing machine, which is expertly handled by the women and girls. Extraordinarily high is the demand for umbrellas, which serve as protection against rain and sunshine, at the same time, however, are also seen as a symbol of certain refinement and therefore are very popular with both sexes."[40]

Samoans needed cash to pay for these desirable goods as well as for government taxes and church services. Additionally, missionaries raised substantial amounts of cash through donations and sports competitions, which were used to finance the construction of new church facilities and schools. A critical observer quipped in the 1890s that missionaries rang a big bell three times a day: "the first bell: a summons for the natives to bring to the priest all the taros which they have gathered, the second: all the coconuts and bananas, the third: fresh fish."[41] In a trade report from April 1898, German consul Rose worried about the large sums of money Samoans were donating to the Christian missions, such as the London Missionary Society (LMS).[42] For instance, losers of cricket matches, hosted by the mission on two or three afternoons a week, had to pay 1 shilling ($0.25) to the church's construction fund.[43] Some missionaries—like the LMS in Malua and the Catholic mission in Vaia—operated their own plantations, albeit on a much smaller scale than the DHPG.[44] As colonial officials and traders were quick to notice, British, French, and American missionaries were formidable capitalists in their own right.

Missionaries also introduced Samoans to new crops, agricultural techniques, and accounting practices. Mission school plantations proved to be important training grounds for Samoan farmers, who learned more efficient cultivation practices and gained work experience. Since accounting skills were indispensable to the management of construction projects, such as the large churches built by missionaries around Apia, Samoans were trained in basic commercial practices.[45] Christian missionaries had a lasting impact on Samoans' rhythm of work. By the end of the nineteenth century, most Samoans began their labor-free Sundays by attending church service before they enjoyed their elaborate meals and found time to relax.[46]

Apart from the missionaries, the colonial administrations also demanded cash from Samoans for school and marriage fees, dog and gun licenses, head taxes, and fines. New means of transportation, such as boat launches and buses, and new forms of entertainment, such as dances and restaurants, cost money as well. Samoans also began saving cash as insurance against environmental disasters, such as droughts, pests, or volcanic eruptions. The gradual emergence of a cash nexus by the close of the nineteenth century made new commodities and services available to Samoans but also confronted them with new challenges.

Over time, Euro-American money became part of the Samoan system of reciprocal exchange.[47] Since the Samoan political economy was based on the mutual exchange of food and fine mats for ceremonial reasons and to enhance one's social prestige, cash money was merely a new kind of currency. If fine mats remained qualitatively different from cash, many Samoans by the late nineteenth century had adopted the Euro-American approach in measuring the value of fine mats in exclusively monetary terms for their own exchange transactions.[48] Traders were mostly interested in copra, so Samoans increased their production whenever they needed cash or wanted to purchase goods in the trading stores. This new need for cash made copra production more important to the Samoan economy and contributed to a more regular and regimented work rhythm on copra plantations. And as more and more ships came to call at the islands, Samoan women earned cash by selling craft products, such as baskets, ornaments, and clothing, to visitors.[49] By the turn of the twentieth century, Samoans had incorporated the rules of the cash crop economy into their own system of economic exchange, so much so that a New Zealand soldier in 1914 complained of Samoans selling fruit "at exorbitant prices."[50]

Before the arrival of outlanders, labor in Samoa was associated with status, age, and gender. In general, the labor of Samoan men tended to be heavier and dirtier, while Samoan women performed lighter and cleaner types of labor. If masculine labor was largely utilitarian, aimed at the production of food and tools, feminine labor was predominantly ceremonial, producing *kava* and fine mats (*'ie tōga*).[51] Fine mats played a crucial part in a range of social and political events, such as marriages, funerals, visiting parties (*malaga*), and formal apologies (*ifoga*). The labor of producing fine mats thus provided women with a degree of influence in political and economic matters, which were usually dominated by men. Most importantly, Samoan women performed most of the reproductive labor necessary to sustain family life and Samoan society as a whole. They not only regulated biological reproduction but also cared for the social reproduction of their *'aiga*.

Outside their families, Samoan men and women rarely worked alone but formed labor groups according to their gender. Untitled men belonged to the *'aumāga*, a voluntary society and cooperative work group that represented the main labor force in Samoan villages.[52] Its main function was to provide manual labor and particularly military service to the village. The *'aumāga* was usually headed by the *manaia*, the son of the village's paramount *matai* and his most likely heir, who had a vested interest in proving his dedication to service. The male work group was engaged in a wide range of community activities, such as cutting copra to raise money for the church, maintaining village roads, building houses, ferrying passengers and cargo, planting and harvesting taro, fishing, cooking, and serving *kava* at village council meetings (*fono*). Besides work, the *'aumāga* offered an arena for socializing for young men who played cricket and drank together. The female counterpart of the *'aumāga* was the *aualuma*. It originally consisted of the female servants of the *taupou*, the daughter of the leading *matai* in a village. Headed by the *taupou*, the *aualuma* brought the sisters and daughters of the *fono* members as well as the *'aumāga* together. In contrast to the practical labor performed by the *'aumāga*, its function was largely ceremonial, such as entertaining guests on *malaga*.

Occasionally, members of the *aualuma* assisted in the construction of houses by carrying cane leaves and baskets of pebbles or weaving thatching sections and blinds. As a result of the increasing presence of missionaries in Samoa after the 1830s, the *aualuma* assumed responsibility for the public health of the village, especially its infants, and helped raise money for the church.[53]

Overall, reproductive labor was a decidedly communal affair in Samoa. Since the household was the basic unit of production and the center of Samoan life, individual households in a village cooperated in food production and cash cropping. Households also pooled resources to contribute to the village church and family ceremonies. Family members maintained the surrounding household area, prepared food, took care of livestock, produced household items, gathered fruit and seafood, and hunted for pigeons.[54] Daily social reproduction, carried on by Samoan women, was thus inextricably linked to the production of copra, carried on by Samoan men. As the guardians of family life, women guaranteed the continuity of cultural practices as well as the material foundations of Samoan society.

Gendered forms of Samoan labor underwent a major transformation under coconut colonialism. The increasing presence of missionaries and traders had different effects on Samoan men and women. On the one hand, Christian concepts of specifically masculine and feminine duties and responsibilities denigrated forms of labor outside the household that Samoan women traditionally performed, such as lagoon fishing. On the other hand, the need for cash to pay for new goods gave a boost to traditionally masculine forms of labor, such as heavy plantation labor and military service. After 1900, Samoan men by and large stopped fighting one another in large and drawn-out wars; quit the manufacture of handcrafted tools, including fishhooks and weapons; and went fishing far less frequently. Instead, they increasingly focused on producing cash crops and went to secondary school to train for the new white-collar occupations on which colonial administrations depended.[55]

By contrast, mission schools for girls, such as the boarding school run by the LMS in Papauta, taught Samoan girls basic literacy and numeracy, childcare, and housekeeping. Domestic work and nursing, two of the new paths to social mobility open to Samoan girls, were primarily seen as interim occupations that would bridge the time between the end of school and marriage. Heavily influenced by the doctrine of separate spheres, missionaries (and, to a lesser extent, colonial officials) regarded Samoan higher education

as the exclusive domain of boys. As wealth and education along the colonizers' model became the new avenues for prestige and status, they remained
barred to most Samoan women. Until the 1920s, only a select few Samoan
women had careers of their own as domestic workers or nurses.[56]

As missionaries imposed their doctrine of separate spheres and plantation
owners expanded their cash crop economy, Samoan women saw their traditional forms of labor both marginalized and domesticated. Because many
Samoan children attended mission schools, Samoan mothers did not have
to spend as much time supervising their children in the mornings. Instead,
new household tasks emerged: sewing, washing, ironing, cooking, baking,
and cleaning the new appliances and furniture that decorated many Samoan homes by the early twentieth century.[57] Cooking in the earth oven
(umu) remained the duty of Samoan men, both on the islands and in ethnographic shows abroad. In addition, women were often called to help men in
food production, as well as copra cutting and drying at peak times. At the
same time, Samoan men handled the marketing of the cut copra and received the payments. Hence, Samoan men retained their dominant position
in the social hierarchy and gained additional power in the economic realm
through cash cropping and preparing for white-collar jobs that required
higher education. In sum, Samoan men's work was oriented toward the
capitalist future—owning and managing land, earning cash, receiving higher
education—while the work of most women remained entrenched in the
pre-capitalist past—gardening and domestic work.[58]

Despite these diverging gender trajectories, Samoan women seized the new
opportunities that the colonial world presented. For example, Samoan girls
were highly sought after as domestic workers in the households of wealthy
Euro-American plantation owners, colonial officials, and missionaries. Some
Samoan women also washed clothes and cooked for the young, male, and predominantly single plantation workers from Melanesia and China. A group
of Samoan women in Leone, Tutuila, even produced tapa cloth (siapo) for
local sale and export.[59] Led by master artist Kolone Fai'ivae Leoso, the Samoan artists produced thousands of siapo in multiple colors. In the late 1920s,
they sold their siapo to Mary J. Pritchard, the daughter of a Samoan mother
and white American father, who exported Samoan products to traders in Honolulu.[60] Finally, Samoan women's committees continued the long tradition
of female-only work groups and church women's auxiliaries. Founded in 1919

by Dr. Mabel Christie, the women's committees were initially set up to improve public hygiene in American Samoan villages. The committees also spread to Western Samoa and broadened their mandates to include fundraising, making them leading actors in the Mau movement against American and New Zealand colonial rule in the mid-1920s.[61]

Making Samoans Work

As in most Pacific colonies at the time, Samoans under German and American rule were not directly forced to work for the export economy.[62] It was the very strength of the Samoan agricultural economy and the military muscle it supported that forced colonial officials in both German and American Samoa to pursue a strategy of accommodation. This paternalistic policy of *salvage colonialism* was most visible in the German-controlled part of the islands. Governor Solf fashioned himself into the "father" of his Samoan "children," protecting them from the corrupting influence of Euro-American capitalist modernity—especially in the form of wage labor and consumer commodities.[63] In Solf's eyes, his duty in Samoa was "merely to guard it as what it is—a little paradise—and to do my best to keep the passing serpent out of our Garden of Eden."[64] Using the colony as a living experiment in social engineering, German colonial officials deemed Samoans worthy of protection from the brutal forces of coconut colonialism they themselves had helped unleash.[65] Not incidentally, Solf's policy left Samoans firmly tied to small-scale agriculture and at a safe distance from some of the new opportunities that colonization opened up. And while Solf's salvage colonialism aimed to maintain order among the colonized, the paternalism practiced by plantation owners sought to extract as much of their labor power as possible. After a violent revolt by the Herero and Nama in German Southwest Africa broke out in the spring of 1904, Solf's less overtly confrontational "native policy" gained even more legitimacy in the eyes of Euro-American settlers and the colonial press.[66]

Since Samoans were not forced to work and continued to rely on sustainable farming, it is little wonder they found the cash incentives of plantation labor insufficient. Most Samoans remained landholding producers, and only a small number performed casual day labor on foreign-owned copra plantations. If subaltern workers are, by definition, forced to sell their labor power,

then Samoans did not belong in this category.[67] Accustomed as they were to
the sporadic nature of communal labor in service of their families, most Samoan men found it hard to adjust to the radically different time and labor
discipline prevailing on large-scale Euro-American plantations. Perhaps the
most significant difference lay in the ability of Samoan workers engaged in
farming to choose the timing and intensity of their labor tasks. Plantation
labor, by contrast, demanded continuous physical exertion to produce crops
that would not directly benefit one's community but instead be shipped to
distant markets in San Francisco and Hamburg. Samoans quickly came to
realize the fundamental difference between their traditional agricultural
labor as service to one's community (*tautua*) and the alienating labor required
on foreign-owned plantations (*gālue*). Workers attached different meanings
to their labor, which influenced their willingness to perform it. In doing so,
Samoans reshaped the forces of colonial globality, which pressured them to
become plantation workers, into Oceanian globality, centered around the core
values of their moral economy.

Under the official policy of salvage colonialism, German colonial officials
were constantly preoccupied with boosting copra production. Their concerns
were understandable because throughout the nineteenth century and into the
colonial era, Samoans were, by far, the largest producers of copra. In 1896,
Samoans produced as much as 80 percent of the overall copra exports that
year on their family plantations.[68] The remaining 20 percent were produced
by the DHPG, the largest foreign trading company operating in Samoa at the
time. Given Samoans' preponderant role in copra production and their general unwillingness to work on foreign plantations, Euro-American plantation
owners, traders, and colonial officials sought to devise different means for
increasing agricultural output.

Throughout the nineteenth century, violent conflicts among competing
Samoan parties, fueled by Euro-American colonialists themselves, had put
severe limits on the time and resources Samoans could devote to food production, sometimes resulting in famines.[69] During the turbulent years of
the tridominium between 1889 and 1899, German diplomats in Apia regularly reported on the relationship between war and economic stagnation.
German consul Biermann noted in April 1894 that during times of Samoan
war, agricultural production was interrupted, forcing many Samoans to con-
sume their coconuts instead of selling them as dried copra. Even worse, the

consul observed, Samoans had to be supplied with provisions from German plantations, which offered the only sources of food in times of war. As a result, Biermann concluded, the copra trade came to a halt, plantation output decreased, Samoan purchasing power declined, and imports and exports dropped.[70] Because continued warfare among Samoans—fueled in no small part by the competing interests of the colonial powers—had a negative impact on agricultural exports, the pressure to ensure political stability on the islands increased.

Political tension subsided in 1899, when Samoa was divided into a German part in the west and an American part in the east. Driven by the economic interests of German traders and plantations owners (especially the DHPG), the German colonial administration lost little time in exerting pressure on Samoan farmers. On August 31, 1900, only a few months into formal annexation, Governor Solf passed a regulation requiring every Samoan head of family to plant fifty coconut trees a year. On average, it took around six thousand mature Samoan coconuts to produce a single ton of copra. Samoan officials were appointed to inspect plantations on a regular basis and punish individuals who failed their quota.[71] This stricter policy was hard to enforce, but it did lead to a considerable increase in the number of coconut trees in German Samoa. By 1908, there were 455,280 coconut trees on German plantations, of which more than 90 percent belonged to the DHPG.[72] Between 1900 and 1913, more than one million new coconut trees were planted in Savai'i and Upolu.

Over the same period, however, overall copra output did not increase significantly.[73] This was mainly due to the fact that most Samoans, while following the official mandate to plant new trees, did not substantially increase their workload and produced and sold only as many coconuts as they needed to survive and earn cash. Even so, Samoan stands of coconut trees covered three times the area of European copra plantations.[74] In line with Solf's salvage colonialism, Samoan landholdings, on which sustainable farming depended, had come to be legally protected. To secure the "natural fruit lands of Samoans," the Berlin Act of 1899 had prohibited the sale of all lands outside the municipal district of Apia.[75] In November 1907, a regulation passed by the German colonial administration confirmed this ban in principle but enlarged the area in which the sale of Samoan lands was allowed.[76] From then on, no Samoan lands were to be sold outside the "plantation district"—an

Figure 3. Map of DHPG plantations in German Samoa, 1900. Table no. 1 in *Ländereien und Pflanzungen der Deutschen Handels- und Plantagen-Gesellschaft der Südsee-Inseln zu Hamburg in Samoa: Uebersichtskarten und Ansichten.* Hamburg Chamber of Commerce/Library of Commerce, 1964/546 Anhang.

area of roughly seven square miles around Apia, where most of the foreign-owned, large-scale plantations were located. In addition, every Samoan was guaranteed at least 3.2 acres of land to cultivate. Its good intentions notwithstanding, the regulation clearly benefited the largest landholder outside the plantation district: the DHPG.[77] The German company now enjoyed a "virtual monopoly of land which other Europeans could buy."[78] A DHPG business report from 1907 duly noted that the company could proceed to sell the majority of its uncultivated lands at a profit.[79]

Other strategies the colonial administrations pursued to increase agricultural production among Samoans included restrictions on Samoan travel, the introduction of copra kilns, and head taxes. Samoans had a long tradition of visiting relatives in other villages and islands to strengthen the bonds of family and forge political alliances. Visiting parties (*malaga*) were treated to huge displays of generosity punctuated by political conversation and the ceremonial exchange of goods. Because some *malaga* could last for weeks, the economic burden on both hosts and guests could be great. At the same time, *malaga* allowed families suffering from food shortages to temporarily relieve their plantations and helped them address local economic crises.[80] In any case, Samoans rarely approached cultural traditions such as *malaga* in purely economic terms. A Samoan *matai* interviewed in the early 1930s defended this comprehensive outlook on life, shared by many Samoans: "The white people condemn many Samoan customs as being wasteful. Their idea is that customs that interfere with working and making money are bad. But such customs give pleasure to the Samoans and are almost their only form of amusement. To travel and to entertain those who travel makes life interesting. A life filled with nothing but work would not be worth living."[81]

Euro-American colonial officials had different views. Intent on putting the new colony into value, they saw Samoan *malaga* as a quaint nuisance at best and an inexcusable waste of time and resources at worst. As a result, in 1903 Solf reached an agreement with the U.S. naval administration in American Samoa that prohibited Samoans from going on *malaga* between Upolu and Tutuila. In line with his policy of paternalistic preservationism, Solf refused to ban all Samoan *malaga* outright.[82] Samoans experienced the partition of their islands in 1899 most directly when they went on *malaga* to visit relatives across the new interimperial boundary between Upolu and Tutuila. These trips, while not impossible, became increasingly troublesome

as German and American authorities stepped up control of population movements.[83] At the same time, Solf and other high-ranking colonial officials
adopted the practice of visiting different parts of the colony, often to great
effect. The ban on visiting parties caused considerable opposition among Samoan *matai,* who saw one of their traditional privileges threatened. The first
Mau movement led by Lauaki Namulauʻulu Mamoe in 1908 emerged partly
in response to this ban on *malaga,* as did the second Mau movement against
New Zealand rule in the mid-1920s.

The introduction of copra kilns by colonial officials was another attempt
to increase Samoan copra production. While the larger trading companies
like the DHPG had been using copra dryers and kilns since the early 1890s,
Samoans continued to rely on the traditional method of drying coconut meat
in the sun.[84] On average, green copra yielded up to 68 percent dried meat.[85]
Compared to sun drying, kilns made the drying of coconuts more reliable
and efficient. Up to five days of drying coconuts in the sun could be reduced
to one day in the kiln, using the shells as fuel.[86] Colonial officials followed
the DHPG in giving preference to the "plantation copra" over the "trader
copra," primarily because of its higher quality and storage life.[87] In the fall
of 1907, a member of the German Colonial Economic Committee recommended to the German Colonial Office that it purchase copra kilns and rent
them out to Samoans during the rainy season.[88] Shortly thereafter, a DHPG
manager wrote to Governor Solf about the need to increase the use of
copra kilns among Samoans. The DHPG, the manager noted, had "already
repeatedly tried to induce the natives to sell their copra either green or in
nuts in order to be dried in the kilns on the trading stations of the whites.
These attempts unfortunately had failed due to the resistance of the natives."[89]

While colonial officials pushed for copra dryers, Samoans continued to
prefer their traditional method of drying coconuts in the sun. During the several days of drying, Samoans kept constant watch of the copra to protect it
from sudden rain or wandering dogs and pigs. Overnight, the copra was
brought indoors and stored in containers.[90] Although sun drying ran the risk
of diminishing the copra's quality (especially during the rainy season) and
took longer, this mattered little in an agricultural economy with abundant
crops. Far from resisting technological innovation, Samoans held on to established ways of agricultural labor and refused to give up autonomy over
this crucial part of the production process. Besides, by keeping control over

Figure 4. Copra dryer, DHPG plantation in Mulifanua, c. 1910–1915, Alfred J. Tattersall.
Alexander Turnbull Library, Wellington, New Zealand (PAColl-3062-2-06).

copra drying, Samoans maintained the option of short-weighting Euro-American traders by soaking copra or adding small stones and sand to their deliveries.[91] In this way, Samoan producers fought back against Euro-American traders who often shortchanged them for their copra deliveries.

Apart from travel restrictions and copra kilns, the German colonial administration also introduced a head tax in 1901. The main aim of the head tax was to raise revenue for the colonial administration to pay Samoan government officials, but it was also meant to create an incentive for Samoans to enter into wage labor. It was the robust nature of Samoan agriculture that made the introduction of a head tax feasible in the first place.[92] A head tax had already been introduced during the days of the tridominium, but collecting the taxes proved to be difficult. Consul Rose reported in April 1897 that apart from a stronger demand by Samoans for imported goods, better enforcement of the head tax would help increase planting activity among

Samoans. Rose suggested collecting the head tax more regularly and com-
prehensively, which would motivate Samoans to work.[93] When the German colonial administration reintroduced the head tax in 1901, it had more
success.

Initially set at 4 German marks ($1) for every Samoan in 1901, the head
tax was limited to adult males only after 1903. *Matai* had to pay 12 marks
($3), while untitled men continued to pay only 4 marks ($1). By 1914, the head
tax had risen to 24 marks ($6) for *matai* and 20 marks ($5) for untitled men.[94]
While Chinese contract workers were exempt from the head tax, Samoans
and other Pacific Islanders living in German Samoa had to pay or face serious penalties. To be sure, part of the local taxes and import duties were
used to build a rudimentary infrastructure, including roads, docks, and
later telegraph lines. Yet contrary to what Euro-American planters claimed,
Samoans—let alone Melanesian or Chinese workers confined to plantations—
were unable to enjoy much of this newly built infrastructure. Responding to
the demands of the growing export economy, these internal improvements
primarily served the interests of the plantation owner class. Taxes and duties also ensured the workings of the colonial administration, especially its
courts and police force, accessible only to Samoans.[95] If the head tax gave testament to the resilience of Samoan farming, it was a form of punishment for
the Melanesian workers who saw little of its benefits. Through the head tax,
Samoan and Melanesian workers, who had created the wealth of the colony
and had made German Samoa independent of subsidies from Berlin by 1909,
helped support a colonial system aimed at their further exploitation. Out
of a fear of organized resistance, colonial officials introduced a head tax
with uneven reach partly to undermine interracial solidarity among working
people in Samoa.

Despite these efforts by colonial administrations to force Samoans into
wage labor on foreign plantations, the overwhelming majority of Samoans
continued sustainable farming practices on family and village plots, which
offered greater control over their lives. Since Samoans held on to most of the
land on which coconut trees grew, their surplus production dominated the
copra export market throughout the colonial era. Agricultural resilience provided Samoans not only with insurance against environmental disasters
but, more importantly, with a strong foundation to protect their political and
social self-determination against colonial demands. Samoans were thus able

to shape the introduction of a plantation economy geared to global trade largely on their own terms.

Earning Cash and Taking Fruit:
Samoans on Euro-American Plantations

On rare occasions, Samoans chose to enter into wage contracts on Euro-American plantations. Because most Samoans preferred working independently and selling their surplus to traders, wage labor on foreign-owned plantations remained the exception throughout the colonial era. As early as the 1850s, Samoans had worked on foreign plantations on a casual basis. They demanded equal wages to those paid to Europeans, which proved to be unprofitable for Euro-American planters, who preferred recruiting workers from other Pacific islands. But even after 1900, Samoans continued to work for Euro-American plantation owners as temporary laborers and overseers. During acute labor shortages, Samoans could earn as much as 3 marks ($0.75) a day plus food working on Euro-American plantations. In 1901, Samoans earned an average of one U.S. dollar for a day's plantation work, which was considerably more than what the DHPG paid its Melanesian workers ($21–$23 a month).[96] In neighboring U.S.-controlled Tutuila, Samoans also earned one dollar a day, including board.[97]

Business reports from German and British trading companies operating in Samoa at the turn of the twentieth century provide documentation for the Samoan presence on foreign plantations. Reports from the Safata-Samoa-Gesellschaft (SSG) from 1905 and 1906 list the number of Chinese and Samoan workers employed on its copra and cocoa plantations. In 1905, the SSG employed between thirty and forty Samoan workers to cultivate its newest plantations. Roughly the same number of Chinese workers, whom companies like the SSG had eagerly recruited to Samoa, were supervised by Samoan, and later also white, overseers.[98] In the following year, over one hundred new Chinese workers joined the SSG workforce, while an unidentified number of Samoans continued to work for the company. As the business report from 1907 noted, for heavy labor, such as clearing bush, Samoans could only be hired on temporary contracts.[99] By the end of 1911, the SSG employed 187 Chinese workers, but managers still complained about the lack of manpower to cultivate existing plantations, let alone expand them. According to the business report from 1911, this perceived lack of workers had to be compensated by hiring "expensive" Samoans.[100] In addition to these temporary plantation laborers, two mixed-race Samoans worked as overseers on the SSG plantations.

One of the SSG's competitors in cocoa production, the British-owned Upolu Rubber and Cacao Estates Ltd. (URCE), also employed mainly Chinese workers on its rubber plantation in Alisa and on its cacao plantation in Tagamapua. Samoan workers performed contract labor for the URCE for higher rates than their Chinese counterparts. As an URCE business report from 1910 noted, many Samoan workers reengaged for one or two months after the end of their original contracts.[101] Samoan workers also worked for other foreign companies, such as the German Samoa-Plantagen-Gesellschaft (SPG) and the British Upolu Cacao Company (UCC), particularly cutting wild bush for new plantations.[102] The Samoan workers hired by the UCC in early 1902, however, had all left the plantation within a few months.[103]

Working on Euro-American plantations, if only for limited amounts of time, posed considerable challenges to Samoan men. Timing, techniques, and general labor discipline differed greatly between small Samoan family plantations and the larger commercial enterprises. Due to the tropical climate, Samoans tried to complete most of the heavy agricultural labor in the early mornings, before the sun became too intense. By contrast, Euro-American plantations were larger in size, organized toward producing large amounts of cash crops, and generally more rigidly organized. Contract workers from Melanesia and China were specifically recruited to perform this kind of exhausting and monotonous plantation labor and tried to resist these coercive measures as much as they could. Samoans, who engaged in casual wage labor on Euro-American plantations, were unaccustomed to such a profit-oriented labor regime and usually arrived at the plantations exhausted from their family labor in the mornings.[104] Agricultural techniques, too, were different. While Samoans cut as much copra as they needed to buy clothes or food, coconuts on DHPG and other plantations were usually not cut before they had fully matured and fallen to the ground.[105]

In the summer of 1903, the issue of Samoan labor contracts with Euro-American traders and plantation owners erupted into a heated debate between Samoan leaders and the German colonial administration. In June 1903,

Samoan paramount chief Mataʻafa Iosefo wrote a letter of complaint to Solf. Disturbed by recent reports, Iosefo voiced the contentious issue of labor contracts for Samoans who worked on copra plantations owned by German settlers. Such contracts should be limited to one month, Iosefo argued, "because it is our custom that no one on these islands be engaged in menial labor."[106] Iosefo recounted rumors that Solf had planned to force Samoans into slave-like labor, allegations probably fueled by several "uncomfortable incidents" involving Samoan workers and Euro-American employers. In his letter, Iosefo painted an idealized picture of the Samoan labor system: "Since childhood, we have grown up in perfect freedom and everybody is allowed to work and sleep as he pleases because our Mother Earth provides all goods through her great fertility."[107] He concluded his complaint by criticizing the colonizers for their blasphemous greed: "The foreigners only want to gain money through the lives of others . . . , because they do not at all know the love of God in heavens."[108] In his defense of Samoan workers, Iosefo clearly adopted some of the stereotypes about Samoan indolence and carefree living propagated by the colonizers, not to mention their Christian rhetoric. But since most *matai* supported the petition, Iosefo's concerns about broken contracts and labor exploitation at the hands of Euro-American settlers were undeniable. For the time being, Solf managed to dissipate these complaints in a heated *fono* meeting, but Samoans remained sensitive to the dignity of the labor they performed.

As these examples show, Samoans did make use of the new opportunities of wage labor on Euro-American plantations, if only temporarily and selectively. Their choices depended on a range of factors, such as the wages they received, the current copra prices, and their need for cash to buy imported goods and pay for taxes or fines. Thus, when the end of World War I brought higher copra prices and higher wages, a greater number of Samoans engaged in wage labor on Euro-American plantations.[109] The cash earned from wage labor frequently flowed back into practices central to Samoan culture, such as organizing *malaga*. Some enterprising Samoans even used their cash income to expand their own plantations. For most Samoans, however, working on plantations was not a sign of assimilation to Euro-American capitalist values but rather a way to maintain social cohesion in the face of rapid change.

Beyond wage labor, Samoans engaged with Euro-American plantation owners in a more direct manner: they took their crops. What Samoans saw as their right to make use of the natural bounty growing on their islands, settlers, who had come to Samoa to make a living by selling cash crops, interpreted as outright theft and a challenge to colonial authority. Samoans had been "taking" from foreign plantations ever since German traders "took" their lands in the 1860s. The taking of crops continued throughout the second half of the nineteenth century into the colonial era, spiking in times of war and when food was scarce. In 1886, German consul Knappe reported that gangs of up to ninety Samoan men were forcefully entering German plantations to steal crops. Plantation managers had complained that they could no longer protect their Melanesian workers, who, in turn, were hired to protect the plantations against the Samoan intruders. An investigation had been started, Knappe noted, and the entire village of Matafaga was fined 300 marks ($75), or the current price for one ton of copra.[110] Because individual thieves were difficult to identify or arrest, punishment in the form of fines was usually leveled at the entire village neighboring the plantation.[111] According to one DHPG manager, Samoans gained access to foreign plantations under the pretext of intending to shoot pigeons but then proceeded to steal crops.[112]

Three years later, reports on Samoan thefts from German plantations resurfaced. An acute food shortage had led to an increase in Samoans stealing fruit, then consul Stübel reported. These thefts resulted in friction and, at times, violent encounters between the Samoan thieves and the Melanesian plantation workers. The DHPG manager in Vailele, Kurt Hufnagel, had been punched to the ground and seriously injured by Samoans looking for breadfruit, Stübel noted. Trying to defend their plantation, a group of Melanesian DHPG workers had retaliated in August 1889 by beating a Samoan man named Liku to death.[113] In the following months, Stübel continued to express concerns about the "persistent anarchy," especially on the two largest German plantations in Vaitele and Vailele. According to the consul, Samoan men had been "brutalized" by the ongoing civil war between Malietoa Laupepa, who had returned from exile in Jaluit in September 1889, and the reigning but disputed Mata'afa Iosefo. The DHPG estimated the damage done to its plantations by Samoan "looting" to be as high as 80,000 marks ($20,000), or a good quarter of its profits for 1889.[114]

By October 1889, things had calmed down. Thefts had become rarer, as the food shortage subsided.[115] In 1894, however, reports on Samoan crop thefts and clashes with Melanesian workers reappeared. As Consul Biermann noted, the sentences dealt out by the Imperial Court against thieves in the preceding years did not have the desired effect.[116] In the summer of 1895, the DHPG management complained to the consulate in Apia about a series of new crop thefts on its plantations. The letter noted that Samoans had stopped stealing as publicly as they had done before and now used the early morning hours to do so. The DHPG also explicitly accused mixed-race Samoan and U.S. citizen Alfred Schuster and his family as major instigators of the thefts.[117] In May 1896, Schuster was arrested by German DHPG employees and locked up in the plantation jail for one night.[118] By 1898, Consul Rose happily reported that thefts had declined again. He mentioned several reasons for this decrease: first, the Imperial Court had finally finished determining property boundaries; second, large parts of plantations had been secured with barbed wire to keep out roaming cattle; third, a more effective enforcement of prison sentences was in place to punish thieves; and last, an extraordinarily rich harvest of food crops, including bananas and breadfruit, had diminished incentives to steal crops elsewhere.[119]

Yet Samoans continued taking crops from Euro-American plantations even after formal annexation in 1899. Different conceptions of space and property among Samoans and their colonizers shaped this restive practice.[120] Samoans defined agricultural property on the basis of practical use rather than formal ownership. German and American traders and plantation owners, by contrast, had little tolerance for such a definition of property rights. After all, most settlers had come to Samoa to prosper by exporting tropical fruit. As a result, they showed little patience for the persistent Samoan incursions into their plantations. The colonial administration in German Samoa asserted its power by protecting German property against what they considered theft and punished violators severely. The fact that Samoans continued taking what they needed from the foreign plantations reflected the changing nature of Samoan agriculture at large. As Euro-American capitalists bought up more and more land to grow cash crops, Samoans had less and less flexibility in food supplies. This limitation became particularly pressing in times of war or environmental disaster. Samoans understood these threats

to their economic self-determination and fought back, following the logic of
their own moral ecology.[121]

Cutting Out the Colonizers: Samoan Copra Cooperatives

While Samoans produced the vast majority of copra, Euro-American traders had come to dominate the copra trade by the mid-nineteenth century. Together with British and French missionaries, German traders were the first
to open trading stations in Upolu between 1830 and 1870. Methodically, they
moved to monopolize the import and export of goods essential to the Samoan
economy. In the eyes of Samoans, traders seemed to adjust prices for the copra
they bought and the goods they sold at leisure. Thus, Samoans had long been
resentful of the domineering influence of Euro-American traders.[122] Samoans realized that Euro-American traders deceived them by thirty to fifty
pounds in every one hundred pounds of copra they delivered at the trading
stations.[123] Over time, Samoans devised various strategies to resist the power
of the traders. For instance, they took out large amounts of credit from traders and deferred their payments. Lack of effective legal enforcement of debt
defaults protected Samoans from punishment. Samoans also resorted to manipulating the quantity and quality of the copra they delivered to traders by
soaking the copra in water before weighing it or mixing greener nuts of poorer
quality with better nuts.[124]

   A few years into formal colonial rule, Samoan producers launched a more
fundamental attack on the monopoly of Euro-American traders on the lucrative copra trade. In 1904, a movement to found cooperative companies
swept through German and American Samoa, taking different trajectories.
Led by Lauaki and the German Samoan Carl Pullack from Savai'i, the so-
called 'Oloa movement—'oloa meaning "goods" or "business"—sought to
wrest economic control over the copra trade from dominant Euro-American
traders such as the DHPG. Copra cooperatives built on a tradition of cooperative work groups—the male 'aumāga and the female aualuma—had been
part of Samoan society long before the arrival of Europeans. The chief aim
of this Samoan-run copra cooperative movement—also known as the
kumpani—was to cut out the Euro-American intermediaries, who profited
from the labor of Samoans. Since Samoan producers followed copra prices
in London and San Francisco, they were aware of the fact that Euro-American

traders were underpaying them for their copra while overcharging them for imported goods.[125] A slump in the global market price for copra from 9 pfennigs ($2.25) to 5 pfennigs ($1.25) a pound provided the final spark for the economic independence movement.[126]

In response to depressed copra prices, Pullack promised Samoan copra producers no less than 16 pfennigs a pound—an appealing, if unrealistic, figure.[127] Samoan leaders supported the 'Oloa movement as a way to regain political power through economic power, and they campaigned for participation in the company as a patriotic venture.[128] At the same time, conflicts among white German settlers—especially between Governor Solf and the newly arrived plantation owner Richard Deeken—further encouraged Samoans in their attempts at economic cooperation.[129] Samoan cooperatives were part of a wider move toward cash crop cooperatives, which swept across the world at the turn of the twentieth century.[130] Similar to cooperative movements in other parts of the world, the Samoan 'Oloa movement was based on democratic decision-making, profit sharing, and mutual solidarity. Confronted with coconut colonialism, Samoans adapted to new circumstances and became savvy actors in the global copra trade themselves.

The Samoan cooperative movement not only posed an economic challenge to the most vocal part of the Euro-American population but also threatened the political legitimacy and racial superiority of the colonial state itself. As O'Brien aptly summarizes the conundrum at the heart of race-based colonial claims: "If Samoans could be enterprising, economically independent, and politically empowered, where could European colonial power reside and what would become of the notion of European superiority?"[131] Given this profound economic and political threat, Governor Solf moved to suppress the 'Oloa. Colonial officials criticized the self-government of the cooperatives as mere window dressing and directly threatened their leaders with punitive measures.[132] The colonial administration was also concerned about potential alliances between the Samoan 'Oloa movement and some of the newly arrived small-holding settlers who challenged the colonial administration on its handling of labor relations. In a letter to Solf from February 1905, acting governor Schultz wrote that his fears that the "machinations of the Deeken clique would be an evil example for the natives" had unfortunately materialized.[133] Deeken, the leader of these small settlers, was even said to be the potential successor to Pullack as the manager of the 'Oloa. Schultz added that there were rumors that Deeken was busy collecting signatures among Samoans for a petition against Solf.[134] It is not clear whether these rumors turned out to be true, nor did Deeken ever become formally involved in the predominantly Samoan-led 'Oloa movement. Seen from the governor's mansion, however, the 'Oloa cooperatives were closely associated with challenges to colonial authority from white settlers.

In December 1904, the 'Oloa company introduced a tax (*lafoga oloa*) ranging from 4 to 8 marks ($1–$2) on all Samoans to finance its business activities.[135] The German colonial administration moved quickly to suppress this direct challenge to its control over taxation and the copra trade. At the end of December, Solf prohibited the payment of any copra tax to the cooperatives, sowing seeds of disunity among the supporters of the 'Oloa. When Solf left for a trip to New Zealand at the end of the year, the threat seemed on the wane. Solf's departure, however, sparked a revival in the cooperative movement. Rumors began circulating that Solf was conspiring with Euro-American traders against Samoan producers and had been recalled by the kaiser.[136] One of the Samoan village mayors, Malaeulu, even encouraged his fellow Samoans to "scrape his [Solf's] body with *pipi* shells" if he continued to oppose the 'Oloa.[137] Under heavy pressure, acting governor Schultz decided to arrest Malaeulu and another movement leader in late January 1905 for disturbing the peace and spreading false rumors about the governor. On January 31, several *matai* broke into the prison in Vaimea and freed the two prisoners as a sign of Samoan independence and solidarity.[138]

Meanwhile, internal conflicts within the movement were rising to the surface. Members of the Mata'afa party returned the freed prisoners to jail and pleaded with Schultz for a full pardon, which he refused. When Solf returned in mid-March 1905, the 'Oloa movement was nearly defunct.[139] With a series of powerful speeches and a calculated show of strength, Solf exploited the divisions within the Samoan leadership and ordered the Samoan government in Mulinu'u to be dissolved. Apart from dismissing government officials, Solf also fined all *matai* of the offending districts, confiscated prime land partly owned by Lauaki's *'aiga* in Safotulafai (Savai'i), and ordered the offending *'aumāga* to help construct a new administration headquarters.[140] By aggressively suppressing the copra cooperatives, Solf succeeded in curtailing Samoan self-government more broadly.

If the German colonial administration managed to quell the spread of
the 'Oloa movement for the time being, ideas for greater Samoan self-
determination survived and resurfaced after a few relatively quiet years. As
one of the most gifted *matai* from Savai'i, Lauaki had been at the forefront
of the original 'Oloa movement before abruptly retreating from it when the
administration's strong opposition became evident. Indeed, Solf and Schultz
had been warned back then to send Lauaki into exile while they could, but
Solf had decided to pardon him.[141] When Governor Solf left Samoa for another leave of absence in mid-1908, Lauaki revived the idea of copra cooperatives as part of a more general challenge to colonial rule. A short visit by
the U.S. Navy's so-called Great White Fleet to Pago Pago in August 1908 further encouraged Lauaki in his challenge to German colonial rule.[142]

Initially supported by Mata'afa Iosefo, Lauaki made plans to reorganize
cooperatives in Upolu and Savai'i. In later testimony, Lauaki recalled that
Iosefo explained the plan to found an independent copra trading company
at a meeting at his residence in Mulinu'u: "A large wooden shed would be
erected in Mulinu'u here, for the receiving of all the goods and then disperse
them to all the districts of Samoa. A large ship would be obtained for the purposes of bringing the goods from America."[143] Two Samoan clerks were to
organize production and trading in each district. Samoan producers would
receive 4 cents per pound for their copra. Moreover, the copra cooperatives
would set up an insurance policy against the risk of bad weather at the time
when government taxes were due. Lauaki's Mau a Pule aligned with the economic interests of a burgeoning class of mixed-race Samoans, like Nelson,
who sought to undermine the quasi-monopoly of the DHPG. After silent
support for the first 'Oloa movement four years before, Nelson now more
forcefully supported his fellow Savai'i native in his campaign for restoring
Samoan self-determination. In a private meeting, Nelson told Deputy Governor Schultz that he "thought Lauaki a great man who was sincere in his intentions for the good of Samoans."[144]

Lauaki's rebellion lasted longer than the first 'Oloa movement and posed
the most serious challenge to German colonial rule in Samoa. On the one
hand, Lauaki's Mau a Pule fought to restore the privileges and political
influence of talking chiefs from Savai'i like himself.[145] On the other hand,
Lauaki's rebellion was part of broader Samoan efforts to shape coconut colonialism in the image of shared Oceanian values, such as reciprocity and social

harmony. Copra cooperatives, as envisioned by Lauaki and supported by Nelson, promised to reconcile Samoan labor mutualism with the new realities of long-distance trade and the overbearing power of the DHPG. Ultimately, however, Lauaki's second challenge to German colonial rule failed as well. Internal divisions between Lauaki and Iosefo, along with Solf's return, combined to end the rebellion. Schultz politely listened to Nelson but refused to hear him. In March 1909, Lauaki and eight other *matai* were arrested and sent into exile in Saipan in the German-controlled Mariana Islands. Although unsuccessful in the face of an entrenched colonial administration, copra cooperatives illustrated the ways in which Samoans creatively adapted the world of copra to their own needs and shaped their own version of Oceanian globality.[146]

Lauaki's severe punishment by the German administration left his supporters angry and willing to continue the fight. In protest against Lauaki's exile, Nelson and a group of European citizens in Apia signed a petition to the German Reichstag in February 1910. In their petition, the five self-described "certain residents of Western Samoa" complained bitterly about unfair business competition by the DHPG, taxation without representation, and general mismanagement by German officials. The petitioners concluded their list of grievances with a prescient plea for greater political and economic self-determination: "Our chief complaint has been against the overgovernment, and the retrospective taxes levied; but self-control at this end is really our main desire, and, we honestly think, the best and easiest of all cures for our present disordered state."[147]

When New Zealand took over German Samoa in August 1914, Nelson's economic fortunes brightened. During World War I, trade in tropical fruit, such as coconuts and cocoa, boomed, which benefited Samoan producers and traders of mixed-race descent. In 1916, acting administrator Robert W. Tate liquidated the vast plantation holdings and other assets of the DHPG. With the removal of the largest German plantation and trading company in Western Samoa, Nelson and other traders were able to expand their own economic influence. At the same time, Samoan producers used their increased economic clout vis-à-vis traders. *Matai* committees imposed boycotts (*sa*) on outlying trading stations that refused to buy village copra or sell consumer goods at Apia prices. Guards, appointed by *matai,* policed stores to prevent villagers from purchasing goods until traders agreed to the prices demanded.[148]

Emboldened Samoan growers tried to revive copra cooperatives during World War I. Founded by leading *matai* in 1914, the Toeaina Club was a social club and political association created to promote Samoan unity and settle land title disputes.[149] The club also relaunched the prewar 'Oloa movement with a copra cooperative and trading company, managed by Afamasaga Toleafoa Lagolago.[150] Funded by capital from Samoan villages, the cooperative sought to gain better returns on Samoan copra by running its own motorboat to Apia. In the tradition of the 'Oloa, the Toeaina Club was part self-help organization, part anti-colonial protest. As the New Zealand administration began liquidating DHPG assets in early 1916, club members competed with Nelson for control over German resources. When economic losses and misconduct by Toleafoa put the club in dire straits, Tate referred to the cooperative as "the greatest political danger" and, in April 1916, dissolved the trading company.[151] The Toeaina Club, meanwhile, would continue into the 1920s.

Across the channel in American Samoa, the cooperative movement assumed a different form. The U.S. naval administration, in control of the main port of Pago on Tutuila, pursued a paternalistic policy similar to that of its German counterpart to the west. Because the U.S. Navy was mainly interested in securing a deep-sea port and coaling station in the South Pacific, the naval administration had little mandate and resources to meddle in Samoan affairs. In addition, regular job rotation made consistent policy making difficult, as most naval governors did not stay longer than eighteen months in American Samoa. In line with the Berlin Treaty of 1899, Governor Benjamin F. Tilley passed the Native Lands Ordinance in 1900, which prohibited the alienation of Samoan land. Thus, in both American and German Samoa, foreigners were not allowed to purchase Samoan land. To raise revenue and increase copra production, the U.S. administration introduced a tax in 1901 to be paid in copra deliveries. Samoans were slow to pay this new tax and were supported by Euro-American traders who even tried to keep the Samoans from cutting copra to pay taxes rather than sell it for export. In the eyes of the naval administration, the fact that taxes needed to be paid in copra protected "child-like" Samoans from exploitation by scrupulous traders. By

1902, Samoans sold copra below market price, while the naval government took great care to use the collected taxes for their benefit. "In some villages," Tilley's successor as governor, Uriel Sebree, noted, "the natives have already resolved to sell wholesale rather than individually, and thus get a higher price."[152] Even without the aid of colonial paternalism, copra producers in American Samoa, too, came to appreciate the advantages of collective bargaining in a cash crop economy.

In 1903, the naval administration cut out the Euro-American traders and formally took over the sale of Samoan copra. In doing so, the U.S. Navy acquired the monopoly on the copra trade in Tutuila, a position similar to the DHPG's in German Samoa. Samoan producers delivered their copra to stations run by the government, where they received a standard price per pound, somewhat lower than the projected annual bid. This margin allowed the government to pay additional expenses, such as transportation and wages for Samoan weighing clerks. After the annual output was awarded to the highest bidder from an American or Australian firm, the remaining surplus was returned to the *matai* in proportion to the copra cut by their family members. Instead of cash, copra receipts were issued to Samoans payable by the government, which could be used to purchase goods in trading stores with official licenses.[153]

The year before U.S. naval administrators took over the copra trade, Samoans in Manu'a had founded their own copra cooperative. The Manu'a Cooperative Company took over the copra trade between the main island Tutuila and the smaller Manu'a islands seventy-five miles to the east. The company operated stores in several villages across the islands and owned three motorboats to ship copra to Pago Pago for export to San Francisco. For a few years, the cooperative worked well, but since Samoan members could buy goods on credit, company debt continued to rise. By 1907, rumors of embezzled funds and accumulating debt led Governor Moore to act as a trustee for the company, a role his successors continued.[154] Since this involvement in the Samoan copra business put the highest political representative of the United States in competition with local merchants and antagonized them, Governor Stearns decided to withdraw his personal liability in September 1913. In January 1914, the people of Manu'a gave their consent to selling out their company, but they could not reach an agreement satisfactory to the government and creditors. To avoid the comingling of political authority and economic interest, the supervision of the company was turned over from the governor to the secretary of Native affairs, Alexander Stronach, in May 1914.[155] Stronach and Stearns agreed that the cooperative had failed economically and recommended shutting it down as soon as all the remaining debt was collected. As Stearns put it, "The natives are absolutely incapable of managing their own affairs in financial matters and it is believed that permitting them to establish co-operative stores and co-operative schooners has been a mistake."[156] What looked like failure to paternalistic U.S. officials in Pago provided Samoans in Manuʻa with a much-needed way to pool resources and mitigate risk, albeit only for a few years.

In stark contrast to the ʻOloa cooperatives in German Samoa, the Manuʻa cooperative came under indirect navy control, run by white American managers.[157] When a tropical cyclone devastated Manuʻa in January 1915, the cooperative was practically put out of business. Half of the fifteen hundred inhabitants of the Manuʻa islands had to be relocated to Tutuila because most of the food crops had been destroyed, including the larger part of the cooperative's copra stock.[158] It took several years for agricultural production in Manuʻa to recover, but the cooperative venture never did. By 1919, the former store of the cooperative was used as a naval dispensary and wireless radio office.[159] The following year, the Manuʻa Cooperative Company officially shut down.[160]

Despite these difficulties, the system of selling copra through the naval government in American Samoa proved so successful that Samoan producers in neighboring German Samoa began demanding higher prices for their copra.[161] As a form of economic paternalism, the copra system in American Samoa had clear parallels to Solf's salvage colonialism in German Samoa. In both colonies, the Euro-American administrations feared Samoan naivete vis-à-vis scrupulous traders and proceeded to regulate copra production and sales. In German Samoa, regulations were passed to increase production and protect Samoans, who produced two-thirds of all copra, from Euro-American traders out to make a profit. In American Samoa, the U.S. Navy assumed a similarly paternalistic attitude toward Samoan copra producers and even became their agent in securing higher prices. Since virtually no foreign-owned plantations existed in American Samoa and the copra market remained relatively small, the naval government could become the go-between for the Samoan producers who cut almost all copra themselves. Given the powerful interests of the DHPG and competing smaller plantation owners, the colonial administration in German Samoa could not aspire to such a powerful role. The American Samoa government-run copra economy worked quite smoothly until 1921, when difficulties in paying out the surplus money to communities led the government to introduce individual payments.[162]

In their own ways, Samoans in both Western and American Samoa grew more adept at navigating the capitalist marketplace and, in doing so, became powerful actors in the global copra trade. Determined to defend their economic and cultural autonomy, Samoan copra growers transformed the colonial globality imposed on them into their own Oceanian version.

• • •

Samoans shaped coconut colonialism in two major ways. First, their sustainable farming practices allowed Samoans to retain much of their self-determination in the face of Euro-American traders and officials. More than just supplying a vital source of food, Samoan agriculture provided a kind of insurance in times of crisis and, over time, the basis for anti-colonial resistance. Particularly in comparison to other colonized people at the turn of the twentieth century, Samoans by and large managed the introduction of export-oriented plantation agriculture on their own terms. As large tracts of Samoan land were sold to Euro-Americans over the course of the nineteenth century, long-grown social and economic structures, such as the *matai* system and household-centered farming, came under pressure but survived through the colonial era. In Samoa, the traditional owners of the means of subsistence prevailed over the new owners of the means of cash crop production. Confronted with coconut colonialism, Samoans remained powerful protagonists in the dramatic commodification of the global countryside at the turn of the twentieth century.

Second, Samoans remade coconut colonialism by creatively exploiting new opportunities for trade and economic gain. Emboldened by independent food production, Samoans only occasionally engaged in wage labor on Euro-American plantations, primarily to earn the cash needed for imported commodities, government taxes, and church donations. More importantly, Samoans founded copra cooperatives to undermine what they perceived as the monopolistic practices of Euro-American plantation owners and traders. Samoan copra cooperatives were an attempt to beat the coconut colonizers at their own game. Taken aback, German and American colonial officials understood this fundamental challenge to their policy of extracting resources from the islands and sought to suppress cooperative movements as soon as they emerged. While the copra cooperatives eventually gave in under coercion, they helped form the nucleus of a more sustained challenge to colonial rule in the 1920s.

2

PLANTERS

In April 1904, Ko Tuk Shung was confronted by a group of angry plantation workers from China. As personal servant of the governor of German Samoa and interpreter at the Imperial Court, Shung was one of the most influential Chinese living in the colony. The workers wanted Shung's advice in a delicate matter. Their boss, the German plantation owner Richard Deeken, had complained that cash money and vegetables had been stolen on his two-thousand-acre cacao plantation in Tapatapao, a few miles south of Apia. When the thefts remained unresolved, Deeken had decided to punish his Chinese workers by cutting their wages. The outraged workers demanded to know from Shung if Deeken had the right to do so. Unsure himself, Shung in turn asked Governor Solf, who replied that the laborers could make a complaint in the German Imperial Court. But before Shung could pass on Solf's suggestion, the workers decided to take matters into their own hands and composed a letter of complaint against Deeken, accusing him not only of withholding their wages but also of repeatedly humiliating and beating them. In a gesture of social deference, they then asked their Chinese overseer, Ah Tsung, to forward their letter to the court.

In the letter, the workers defended themselves against Deeken's accusations by pointing out that "after a good hard day's work we feel more inclined to lay down and have a good rest instead of roaming about at night to steal things from our own master's house."[1] When Deeken found out that his overseer had assisted the workers' protest, he set out to punish Tsung, probably because he could not imagine his own workers to be savvy and courageous enough to file a complaint on their own. Past midnight on April 28, four Chinese laborers carried Tsung on a stretcher to the colonial administration building in Apia. There, imperial doctor Julius Schwesinger confirmed that Tsung had been severely whipped and had suffered heavy injuries on his face and arms. As court investigations revealed, Deeken had hit Tsung with a "dangerous tool"—a leather whip—and "in blind anger" had tried to hit him "wherever he could." Tsung eventually recovered from his life-threatening wounds. In June 1904, the Imperial Court sentenced Deeken to four months in jail for physically abusing his overseer.[2]

Deeken's trial revealed the realities of plantation life in Samoa—a world of broken contracts, physical violence, and organized resistance by Chinese workers. Relying on their close personal links, Chinese workers in German Samoa used an underground communication line that stretched from Deeken's plantation all the way to the governor's kitchen. Chinese workers shared information and organized collective action across workscapes. By making public what should have remained secret, Tsung and his fellow Chinese workers had challenged the colonial order of things. And in the end, the workers succeeded in bringing Deeken's abuses to light, paving the way for future resistance against violent plantation owners.

As plantations remade the lives of thousands of Samoans, Melanesians, and Chinese, this diverse group of workers carved out precarious livelihoods in the new world of copra. Since work discipline on plantations was strict, workers resisted the heavy demands on their bodies through a broad arsenal of behaviors, from keeping crops for themselves to making appeals to the state to waging violent attacks on overseers. Resistance against colonial subjection turned workers in Samoa into subjects of their own lives and allowed them to forge bonds of solidarity beyond the spatial, social, and racial boundaries maintained by colonial administrations. In doing so, Samoa's workers shaped their own version of Oceanian globality.

The People Trade to Samoa

Throughout the nineteenth century, Samoans continued their sustainable farming practices in the face of increasing outlander pressure on their land and labor. Under its paternalistic veneer, Governor Solf's salvage colonialism was an acknowledgment that the economic, political, and military strength of Samoans made forced labor impossible. As a consequence, plantation owners had to turn elsewhere for their labor supply. In the 1860s, J. C. Godeffroy & Sohn had built its trading empire in the South Pacific by recruiting

laborers mostly from the Gilbert Islands (now part of Kiribati). Beginning
in the late 1870s, contract workers also came from Bougainville and the
Bismarck Archipelago in New Guinea, from Malaita in the Solomon Islands,
and from the New Hebrides (Vanuatu).[3] Located between Samoa and the
Godeffroy trading stations in the Marshall Islands, the Gilbert Islands offered an ideal recruiting pool for company ships on their way back to Apia.
More importantly, severe droughts on these low-lying coral atolls forced
their inhabitants to seek alternative means for survival, including contract
labor in Samoa, Fiji, and Tahiti.[4] Unlike other Pacific Islander contract laborers at the time, most Gilbertese Islanders went to Samoa in family groups,
which made them even more attractive to Godeffroy because women and
children were better at picking and weeding and could be paid less.[5] By
1885, a total of nearly five thousand Pacific Islanders—almost half from the
Gilbert Islands—had been recruited to Samoa, most of them by the DHPG.[6]

In the early 1880s, the DHPG sought to diversify its labor pool by recruiting laborers in Melanesia, especially in New Guinea, the New Hebrides, and
the Solomon Islands. Living in a similar tropical environment, Melanesian
men had the skills and experience necessary for plantation labor in Samoa.
On Melanesian islands, however, the DHPG faced serious competition from
recruiting vessels bound for Queensland and Fiji. Seen from Apia, Melanesian workers were creatures of the DHPG, but in reality, Samoa was only one
of many destinations for Pacific Islanders looking for work at the time. Besides, recruiting Melanesian workers involved additional costs. Not only were
so-called beach payments needed to convince local chiefs and relatives to
allow recruits to leave their islands, but nearly all were single men—as opposed to the Gilbertese Islanders, whose women and children provided
cheaper labor.[7] After 1889—the year when the tridominium introduced a
greater degree of political stability on the islands—imports of laborers from
Melanesia increased further.[8] Between 1885 and 1913, the DHPG recruited
a total of 5,746 laborers from German New Guinea to Samoa.[9] As copra
prices continued to soar in the years after German annexation in 1900, more
and more Melanesian workers arrived in Samoa.[10] Since these recruiting trips
from New Guinea to Samoa were long (nearly three thousand miles) and
arduous, one out of every seven recruits passed away en route.[11]

The DHPG maintained exclusive access to laborers from Melanesia into
the years of formal German rule—a crucial basis for its business success.[12]

Other plantation owners, especially newcomers with little seed capital, took offense at this competitive advantage for the biggest economic player in German Samoa. To circumvent the labor monopoly of the DHPG, smallholders, led by Deeken, pushed the colonial government to recruit contract laborers from China.[13] Earlier regulations passed by Samoan leaders and Euro-American diplomats in the 1880s had explicitly prohibited the recruitment of Chinese workers. With its labor monopoly in Melanesia, the dominant DHPG opposed the import of Chinese workers by its smaller competitors. In the end, the new settlers prevailed. After months of difficult negotiations between a German agent and local authorities in Shantou, the first transport of three hundred Chinese contract workers arrived in Apia in April 1903. Since Chinese laws prohibited the emigration of contract laborers, the Chinese recruits signed their labor contracts only after they had boarded the steamer in Hong Kong.[14]

In German Samoa, the Chinese workers took up a number of jobs. Most worked on plantations cutting copra, overseeing fellow workers, and cooking. Others chose domestic work or helped the colonial administration build roads and docks. A handful of the new arrivals from China worked as traders, bakers, tailors, and box makers. From the beginning, Euro-American traders feared competition by their Chinese counterparts and called on the administration to withdraw their licenses—with limited success.[15] Between 1905 and 1913, six additional transports brought a total of almost four thousand Chinese workers to Samoa.[16] Contract workers had to spend most of the three-week journey from mainland China to Samoa on bunk beds in the hot and stuffy holds of the ships.[17]

Chinese labor migrants, most of them young men, had a long and complex history of movement and settlement throughout the Pacific world, dating back to at least the sixteenth century.[18] Tens of thousands of Chinese men worked on plantations in the Dutch East Indies, Malaya, Queensland, Hawai'i, and as far as the Caribbean, enduring the hardships of exhausting work for little pay and even less legal protection.[19] With their meager earnings, workers helped support their families back home in China.[20] The Chinese workers who had filed a complaint against Deeken in 1904 had stressed family remittances as one of their main motivations for coming to Samoa: "We are very poor and have come all the way from China to earn a little money for the maintenance of our aged parents and relatives in China who are exceedingly poor."[21] Beginning in the early twentieth century, Chinese labor migration to Samoa constituted a small yet consequential episode in this global story.[22] Resilient and enterprising, the first generation of Chinese workers who stayed on the islands laid the foundations of a dynamic Chinese Samoan community still present today.[23]

The recruitment and treatment of workers on Samoan plantations were shaped by racial hierarchies of labor. While Melanesians did most of the unskilled physical labor, some Chinese recruits also performed skilled labor tasks, such as tapping rubber trees.[24] In contrast to Samoans and other Pacific Islanders, Chinese workers were generally portrayed as obedient, experienced, and hardworking plantation workers. Some German planters even had plans to produce a more efficient workforce by racial mixing, preferably between Samoans and Javanese.[25] Plantation owners and colonial officials used racial stereotypes to divide workers and make them more productive, but the workers' identities remained in flux. As the migrants on Samoan plantations came to hold tighter to their distinctiveness as New Guineans, Solomon Islanders, and Chinese, they also developed affective ties with their fellow workers.

As the labor demands of plantation owners brought workers from around the Pacific to Samoa, a diverse and global community emerged on the islands. At the close of the nineteenth century, German Samoa's capital, Apia, was a small settlement of a few hundred souls. John La Farge, an American painter who visited Samoa in the fall of 1890 together with Henry Adams, described Apia as "an orderly little place strung along what might be called a street or two, the main of which is on the beach, and goes by that name. There are stores, a few hotels and drinking places, warehouses and residences of the consuls. . . . Further back and right and left all is Samoan and native."[26] Less than two decades later, *The Cyclopedia of Samoa* captured the global origins of the people living in the Samoan capital in only slightly hyperbolic fashion: "And surely there never was a spot on the face of the globe which in proportion to its population had so many nationalities represented in it as Apia, the capital of Samoa. Germans, Britishers, Americans, Frenchmen, Danes, Norwegians, Swedes, Chinese are all represented."[27] At the dawn of the twentieth century, Apia had become a truly global place.

And yet this listing of mostly Euro-American residents of Apia ignored the even larger number of Pacific Islanders who had come to Samoa in the preceding decades. By 1907, German Samoa was home to almost 1,500 non-

Figure 5. Apia harbor, 1904. View of Apia, 1904, Samoa, by Thomas Andrew. Te Papa (C.001486).

Samoan Pacific Islanders, of whom 886 were Melanesian contract laborers for the DHPG and 583 free settlers, including 185 Tongans, 167 Niueans, and 65 Solomon Islanders.[28] The roughly 1,000 workers from China alone out-numbered the Euro-American settlers in Samoa by far.[29] On the eve of World War I, no fewer than 12,500 Pacific Islanders and 3,800 Chinese had, at one point, worked as contract laborers in Samoa.[30] Global in their origins and outlook, the forty thousand people living in Samoa at the turn of the twentieth century found themselves in radically different circumstances. If coconut colonialism limited the ways in which places like Samoa related to the wider world, the islands' diverse inhabitants found creative ways to transcend these constraints.

Copra Plantations

Since the mid-nineteenth century, coconut colonialism had transformed the natural environment of Samoa in profound ways. Coconut trees, which had been growing in uncontrolled fashion in Samoa for centuries, were replanted

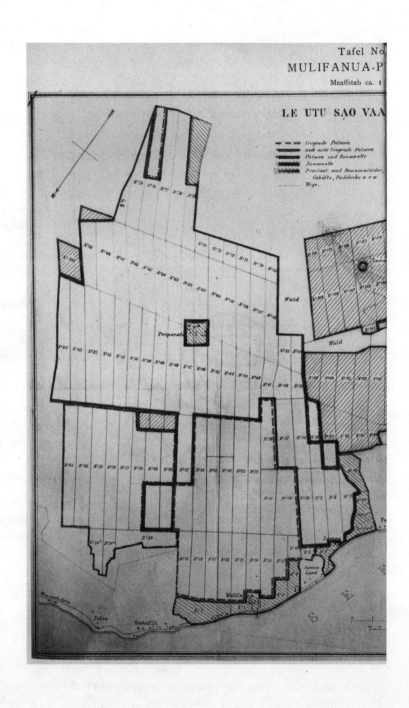

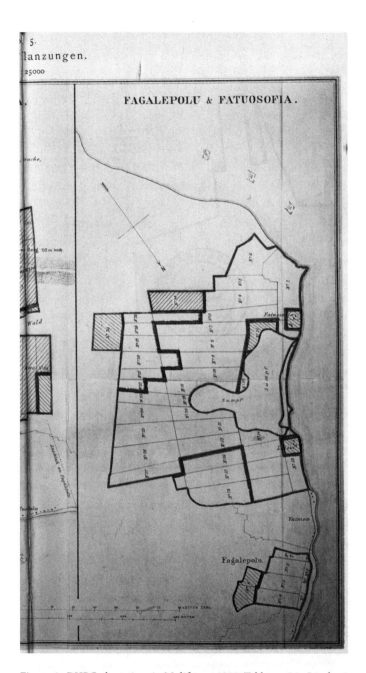

Figure 6. DHPG plantations in Mulifanua, 1900. Table no. 5 in *Ländereien und Pflanzungen der Deutschen Handels- und Plantagen-Gesellschaft der Südsee-Inseln zu Hamburg in Samoa: Uebersichtskarten und Ansichten.* Hamburg Chamber of Commerce /
Library of Commerce, 1964 / 546 Anhang.

in straight lines to discipline workers and measure their work progress. Samoans usually planted coconut trees twenty to twenty-six feet from one another, while on foreign-owned plantations the average distance between trees
was increased to thirty-three feet.[31] Plantation owners also introduced clear
divisions both between different plantation lands and within them according to the different uses to which they were put. A map of the largest DHPG
plantation in Mulifanua twenty-five miles west of Apia, for instance, listed
five distinct categories of plantation lands: first, ripe palm trees; second, not-
yet-ripe palm trees; third, palm trees and cotton; fourth, cotton; and fifth, a
mixed category, including provisions, bananas, and sheds.[32] Every parcel of
land was carefully classified into one of these categories and numbered from
1 to 115. A system of pathways bounded and linked these different categories of land in straight and parallel lines. The resulting geometrical system
of lands with different degrees of exploitation provided a grid of intelligibil-
ity for plantation managers and allowed for better control of the workers
who were tasked with making the land useful.

Despite such maps, the ability of overseers to exert visual control over their
workers was not evenly distributed across plantation lands. Various factors
determined the limits of their visual regime of power: the thickness of the
vegetation, the steepness of the hills, the accessibility on roads and paths, and
the proximity to villages and other plantations. Workers used their superior
knowledge of these environments to escape the hardships of plantation
discipline.

Since coconut trees took more than six years to mature, only a small percentage of the substantial plantation lands, which the DHPG had amassed
over the decades, were under cultivation at any time. In 1893, the DHPG
owned a total of 6,900 acres of coconut trees, of which 4,450 acres (65 percent)
were in full cultivation, yielding about 2,100 tons of copra ready for export.[33]
One acre of good plantation land could yield more than half a ton of copra
per year, with one worker able to cultivate around five acres.[34] Managers were
ever hopeful of expanding the areas under cultivation. For workers, plantation areas that appeared empty on maps meant full days of planting, nour-
ishing, and weeding. As the DHPG plantations expanded at the turn of the
twentieth century, a larger labor force was needed to turn wild strips of coconut trees into marketable tons of dried copra.

Figure 7. Workers cutting copra, Samoa, n.d. Copra making, Samoa, New Zealand, by Muir & Moodie studio. Purchased 1943. Te Papa (C.017590).

Life on Samoan plantations alternated between backbreaking work and soul-crushing boredom. A usual day on a copra plantation began before sunrise around 6 a.m. Workers were woken either by overseers or by a signal that had to be answered from the workers' barracks.[35] After putting on their clothes, workers lined up on a parade ground in front of their barracks to be physically examined by the plantation doctor (looking especially for wounds on legs and feet) and were then assigned their daily labor tasks by the plantation manager.[36] Workers toiled under a searing sun from early morning until the hour-long lunch break at noon. In the hottest summer months from December to February, temperatures could reach more than 100°F, with humidity levels of up to 95 percent. After lunch, workers went back to cutting copra from 1 p.m., when the South Pacific sun was most intense, until around 5:30 p.m. Half an hour later, dinner was served, looking much the same as lunch.[37]

According to oral testimonies, Melanesian workers on DHPG plantations received sufficient food rations, including fresh and tinned beef; rice; and local produce such as taro, yams, and bananas, along with tea, sugar, and tobacco.[38] One worker even recalled the amount of food wasted after dinner: "Generally the boys were not great eaters and when we sat down for an evening meal we drank a lot of tea but ate only a small amount of food. Leftovers were given to the pigs."[39] According to government regulations, Chinese workers received rice together with five ounces of fish and another five ounces of vegetables.[40] Although Melanesian and Chinese plantation workers had enough food to eat, they—in stark contrast to Samoan workers—still depended on their employers to ensure their survival. Food rations and monopolistic trading stores gave plantation owners additional leverage over migrant workers.

Workers cleared underbrush, cut copra, and carried loads of harvested coconuts every day of the week except Sunday. Some particularly motivated workers used their time off-contract to work for other employers, often illegally, receiving one mark for half a day.[41] To curtail this practice, the DHPG ran a series of newspaper ads that warned other employers not to hire the company's Melanesian workers without explicit permission.[42] According to government regulations for Chinese workers, Sundays ought to be free from plantation work and reserved solely for the maintenance of buildings (and other time-sensitive tasks) as well as for the cultivation of the workers' own vegetable plots. In addition to Sundays, four traditional Chinese holidays, such as Chinese New Year's Day, were also declared work-free.[43] The original Chinese labor contract limited daily working hours to a maximum of ten hours, with a pay of 10 marks ($6) per month. At the end of their contracts, workers were guaranteed free passage back to China. A wage book was required to list the wages of each worker, potential reductions as a result of penalties, and other relevant information concerning payment. In the early 1900s, Chinese workers on DHPG plantations earned roughly 1.90 marks (47 cents) a day.[44] Workers received their pay in two monthly installments, one on the second Sunday and the other on the last Sunday of each month.[45]

Many migrant workers took time to get used to plantation life. Like in other parts of the global plantation belt, control over the timing of work emerged as a central bone of contention on Samoan plantations. Melanesian workers recalled that plantation work was divided into several work gangs headed by a "boss boy." This boss boy was in charge of keeping a steady eye on the workers to prevent unnecessary loafing during work hours. A white overseer or Samoan police officer would check on the workers' progress in regular intervals, usually every hour.[46] Among Chinese workers, several overseers were selected to ensure that production continued smoothly. These so-called *tandyls* were often fluent in Cantonese and used Samoan plantation pidgin—a simplified form of pidgin English sprinkled with words from New Guinean languages, Samoan, and German—to communicate with their white superiors. While most of the Melanesian and Chinese overseers were selected on the basis of their language and leadership skills, some vied for these positions to escape the physically more demanding stoop labor. Time discipline on plantations even affected the realm of language. Melanesian workers conversant in Samoan plantation pidgin coined a new word—*belo*—to describe the bell that announced the noontime break on plantations.[47] This aural sign introduced a new *zeitgeber* (time-giver) into workers' lives, which provided a stimulus to set their biological clocks according to the plantation schedule.[48]

Plantation workers in Samoa experienced the global commodification of agricultural labor firsthand. Under constant supervision by overseers and managers, workers were gradually socialized into a time discipline geared toward the incessant movement of their bodies—by physical force, if necessary. Since plantation owners owned land and hired the labor power of their workers, they tried to get as much out of them as possible. In the eyes of a plantation owner, every minute lost in idleness or unfocused work was money wasted. In response, workers crafted intimate and idiosyncratic ways of engaging with their natural surroundings.

Ti'a Likou, a labor recruit from New Britain who had arrived in Samoa around 1910, was one of the many plantation workers tasked with collecting fallen coconuts and weeding young trees.[49] On average, one coconut tree carried around sixty coconuts.[50] Mature coconuts—known to Samoans as *popo*—at some point become too heavy for the branches to carry them and dropped down from the crowns. Workers like Likou were sent to roam through the plantation to look for these fallen coconuts and collect them. When they found a coconut on the ground, workers bent down, picked the fallen fruit up with a swift and coordinated movement of arm and hand, and repeated this movement over and over again. Experienced workers tried to avoid the physical pain of sustained stoop labor by using their bush knives to pierce the nuts, pick them up from the ground, and toss them into baskets. Some workers carried their own baskets on their back, while others preferred the help of mules, which transported two sheet iron baskets on either side of their bodies.[51] Full baskets were initially unloaded on the sides of the rectangular paths crisscrossing the plantations.[52]

For the next step, so-called ox boys picked the harvested nuts up in light carts drawn by oxen and brought them to the station and copra kilns for further processing. At the kilns, the young male workers split up the nuts with axes, before female and older male workers cut out the meat from the husk. Finally, workers moved the coconut meat into a kiln, where it was dried for twenty-four to thirty-six hours. Coconut husks were used to fire the kilns.[53] Through extended exposure to hot air, the copra shrank, sometimes up to 40 percent. Before being loaded onto ships for export, the copra was usually cooled down in a storage shed and then collected in bags, which could weigh up to sixty-five pounds.[54] The ashes left over from the kilns were later reused as fertilizer on the plantations.[55] In addition to the physical burden, the drying process also taxed the workers' noses, since the odor of dried copra was "extremely disagreeable and penetrating."[56]

If collecting fallen coconuts exerted a heavy toll on workers, weeding young coconut trees did so even more. As the DHPG map indicated, copra plantations in Samoa did include other crops (such as cotton, cocoa, or rubber), but they grew increasingly monocultural as global demand for copra began to soar around 1900. And with monoculture came the imperative to protect the most valuable crop—the coconut—from natural competition by other plants and insects. As plantation managers turned coconut trees into cash crops, other plants transformed into weeds, and insects, which fed off coconut trees, into pests. A sturdy and fast-growing plant with a telltale name posed a particular threat to the efficient management of copra plantations: the touch-me-not. Touch-me-not plants concealed fallen coconuts and also stung human and animal feet. Concerned about the plant's spread, plantation owners introduced buffalo grass from North America, which successfully pushed the touch-me-nots aside.[57] Since cattle grazed only on young touch-me-nots, plantation managers decided to cut older plants and allow cattle to take care of the rest. Soon, however, the buffalo grass threatened to replace the touch-me-nots it was meant to contain by depriving the soil of humidity. At that point, the buffalo grass had to be checked by fires.[58] Alongside the controlled

Figure 8. Solomon Islanders cutting copra, c. 1900. Soloman [sic] Island workers making copra. From the album Samoa, c. 1918, by Alfred James Tattersall. Te Papa (O.041889).

fires and the cattle, which plantation owners allowed to graze freely, workers had to help protect coconut trees from this new threat.[59] Hence, Likou, like many other plantation workers, again bent low to cut smaller bushes and ferns around coconut trees and ensure their efficient growth into cash crops. As the hands who picked up fallen coconuts and cut weeds around trees, workers suffered the physical toll of export-oriented plantation agriculture in Samoa. Susceptible to new species like buffalo grass, plantation monoculture changed the Samoan environment in lasting ways.[60]

Islands of Labor

While producing copra for export was the primary goal of Samoan plantations, their impact on the people working on them went far beyond. Since workdays were long and only Sundays were off, workers spent most of their waking hours at work on plantations, with little distraction for their bodies and souls. Migrant workers from Melanesia and China also lived on the plantations where they worked. Samoans, by contrast, retained the comfort and familiarity of their homes and followed a more flexible work schedule.

Workers were confined physically within the limits of the plantation, both day and night. They were not allowed to move around or leave the plantation at will. During field work, workers were under constant surveillance by overseers, their fellow workers (who sometimes reported other workers), and plantation owners themselves. In the eyes of the largest employer of plantation laborers, Chinese workers adapted to this coercive work environment well. In a business report from 1907, the DHPG managers in Samoa reported their "general satisfaction" with the newly arrived workers from China, "after overseers have now gotten sufficiently used to their treatment."[61] Remarkably, the DHPG managers maintained that plantation overseers, rather than the workers themselves, had to go through a process of "seasoning" to get adjusted to their new workplace and its harsh discipline. The concern with overseers foregrounded the challenges in the "proper" management of the Chinese labor force, rather than the serious challenges faced by those being managed. Chinese workers, the statement revealed, had to be "educated" into accepting the new constraints on their bodies, sometimes even by violence. In their attempt to displace this seasoning process from worker to overseer, the DHPG managers highlighted the conflict-ridden nature of solving the "labor problem" in Samoa.[62]

Surveillance and work discipline were harsh, particularly on the bigger plantations. In his first report to Berlin after the arrival of the Chinese in April 1903, Governor Solf was already complaining of "unfortunate misdemeanors in the treatment and provisioning of the Chinese" on the part of planters.[63] Chinese workers were also severely limited in their physical mobility outside the plantation. Chinese laborers had to carry a badge with an identification number and a legitimation card everywhere they went.[64] They were not allowed to leave the plantation without the explicit consent of the plantation owner. If they wanted to go to Apia, they needed a special pass from the plantation boss. The legal contract, which most Chinese workers had agreed to in Shantou without knowing its full details, revealed its true face on the plantations in Samoa.[65] Colonial law reduced human beings with more than physical needs into mere hands satisfying the burgeoning demands of a cash crop economy. Squeezing as much labor power out of workers while maintaining order was the principal aim of labor contracts. Hence, workers who refused to work were severely punished for breaching the contract. After lobbying from European and American merchants in German Samoa, Chinese workers who wanted to stay on the islands beyond their contracts were prohibited from purchasing land or engaging in trade. Some still decided to stay.[66]

Most of the larger plantations in Samoa were located far away from bigger settlements. In many ways, these plantations formed islands within islands, where workers experienced the isolation of plantation life both physically and socially. In the rare instances when workers were allowed to leave the plantation, they felt the sheer geographical distance that separated them from the outside world. The three main plantations of the DHPG on Upolu were Vailele (four miles east of Apia), Vaitele (four miles west of Apia), and Mulifanua (25 miles west of Apia). Given the lack of well-maintained paths or roads, Mulifanua and Vaitele were located at considerable distances from the commercial capital Apia. To reach the plantation in Mulifanua, for example, it took three to four hours by horse and, depending on weather conditions, up to six hours by boat.[67] The physical isolation of the plantations also heightened the sense of social isolation among workers. Beyond the plantation boss, his family, and his overseers, workers were on their own. As one Melanesian worker remembered, plantation life was exceedingly boring. For most, a normal day consisted of little else than working, eating, talking, and sleeping.[68]

Colonial officials were acutely aware of the dangers of social isolation on plantations. When the first three hundred Chinese contract laborers arrived in April 1903, Governor Solf and recruiting agent Friedrich Wandres advised planters outside Apia to take at least three laborers to prevent their running away to join their fellow countrymen.[69] Since some of the smaller plantation owners could afford only a few of the expensive new Chinese laborers, the governor's advice was not always heeded. Although German colonial officials had organized the recruitment of additional workers from China, they had little influence over exactly which plantation owner took how many laborers. Some of the "surplus" laborers were contracted to the colonial government itself, mainly for domestic work, office work, and construction (see

Chapters 4 and 5). As a consequence, a few Chinese workers ended up alone or virtually alone on smaller plantations. They combatted their social isolation by holding on to institutions and practices from back home: forming mutual benefit societies, smoking opium, and gambling.

Melanesian workers, who had been settling in Samoa for decades, initially shared a sense of social isolation with Chinese workers. Over the years, however, labor recruits from the same islands developed lasting bonds during their time in Samoa. Similar language and customs helped newly arrived workers, known as *nubois,* to rebuild social ties severed by migration and hardship. Labor migration of able-bodied men had direct consequences for the Melanesian agricultural economy, as women and children were forced to increase their own labor contribution. Not all of the Melanesian men who came to Samoa were alone, however. According to Ti'a Likou, the worker from New Britain, "quite a few Melanesian women" were working on Samoan plantations in 1910.[70] Exact numbers were not collected, but roughly one in four Melanesian recruits was female.[71] As wives of the Melanesian labor recruits, they joined their husbands in cutting and especially in preparing copra.[72] They soon earned a reputation for their skills and speed—and their lower wages.[73] To prevent conflict, plantation owners erected separate tin-roofed barracks with concrete floors and timber walls for couples and simpler barracks for the overwhelming majority of single men.[74]

At the same time, the fact that most workers from Melanesia had signed three-year contracts posed considerable challenges to the formation of more permanent community life. Most Melanesians returned to their home islands after their contracts ended, but some decided to stay in Samoa. After World War I, around 120 *olbois* and a smaller number of so-called *Teine uli* (Black girls) remained in Mulifanua and later Vaitele. As they intermarried with Samoans, they put down the roots of Samoa's mixed-race Melanesian Polynesian community.[75] The overwhelming majority of Melanesians, however, returned home after one or two contracts and offered useful advice for the next generation of labor recruits.[76]

Some of the Melanesian workers who went home had managed to amass a considerable fortune (mostly in the form of Western goods, such as clothes, jewelry, knives, and watches), which they leveraged to climb the social ladder of their home societies. Their years as plantation workers in Samoa, especially their acquisition of Samoan plantation pidgin, conferred both useful skills and social prestige on the Melanesians who returned to their homes in New Ireland and elsewhere.[77] Many returning workers used their experiences in Samoa to rejoin the agricultural economies of their native islands. As early as the mid-1880s, the German consul in Apia had defended the recruitment of workers for Samoa by suggesting that returning workers become the originators of plantation agriculture in their home islands.[78]

For some migrant workers, isolation from their fellow islanders was the price to be paid for lighter work. Workers employed by plantation owners or colonial officials generally had less demanding physical work but, at the same time, were often excluded from the social life of their peers on plantations. Tapusini Peni Maluana from Nissan Island, for instance, came to Samoa around 1909 and was hired as a domestic worker in the home of the German manager of the DHPG plantation in Vailele. Recalling his early days in the new workplace, Maluana noted that he missed the company of fellow Melanesians and local Samoans, which field workers, especially on large plantations, enjoyed.[79] Other Melanesians who came to Samoa and worked as servants on plantations had different experiences. Tui Sakila, for example, described his job as a messenger boy on a large plantation as "very tiring."[80] As a messenger boy, he had to run from plantation house to the fields and back several times a day to deliver messages for his boss. Like Tapusini, Tui appreciated any opportunity to chat with friends and fellow workers on his way. But because speedy delivery of certain messages (for example, concerning changes in the work schedule) mattered a great deal on copra plantations, Tui and other messengers had little time to waste. Their world, too, was driven by the employer's clock.

As these cases of Chinese and Melanesian workers illustrate, the experience of social isolation depended on the size and location of the plantation as well as the type of work. To a certain degree, white settlers, plantation owners, and officials shared a sense of social isolation with the workers they employed. Both Euro-American and non-Samoan laborers were minorities in Samoa and had traveled a long way from their families and homes in Europe, the United States, and the Pacific. But this is where the similarities ended. White Europeans and Americans in Samoa had, by and large, come to the South Pacific voluntarily, while the contract laborers arrived under much more coercive circumstances. As workers, most Chinese and Melanesians shared a more pronounced sense of alienation, not only as a consequence of being uprooted from their home societies but also due to the difficult new work environments they found themselves in. For them, Upolu, Savai'i, and Tutuila were indeed islands of labor.[81]

In this respect, Chinese and Melanesian workers also had different experiences than most Samoans, who were generally not geographically displaced and continued to maintain their long-standing community ties in the face of colonization. Since Samoans were not forced to work on foreign-owned plantations, they also remained relatively shielded from the worst excesses of work discipline directed at contract workers from elsewhere. Throughout the colonial period, Samoans continued to rely on their sustainable farming practices, which guaranteed the continuity of the larger contours of Samoan community life. By resisting the wholesale commodification of their labor power, Samoans managed to escape the most violent forms of discipline and punishment exacted on plantation workers from Melanesia and China.

When efforts to manage the labor force through spatial and temporal discipline failed, plantation owners resorted to more aggressive methods. Workers who broke one of the many formal and informal regulations that governed life on the plantation could face serious consequences. Depending on the severity of the transgression, the spectrum of punishment stretched from monetary fines and imprisonment to flogging and the death penalty. Physical violence against workers on Samoan plantations was not uncommon, though it was less common than in other German colonies or in the Pacific colonies of other colonial powers.[82] As in other German colonies at the time, corporal punishment in Samoa helped colonial authorities to routinize their precarious claim to power.[83] Yet in German Samoa, it was rarely the colonial authorities that resorted to corporal punishment but rather plantation owners and their overseers themselves. As the largest employer in German Samoa, the DHPG even ran its own jail in Vaitele, where workers were interned and, in some cases, punished with forced labor.[84]

Flogging was the most widespread form of physical punishment for workers who violated plantation regulations. Plantation owners generally cited running away, laziness, disobedience, insulting behavior, and not bowing low to masters as reasons for the flogging of their Chinese workers.[85] Employers were all too aware of the symbolic power of flogging, as the terror of physical pain and public humiliation of one worker disciplined many others.[86] Physical violence on Samoan plantations even entered the linguistic realm.

In Samoan plantation pidgin, the verb "to kill" meant "to hit," as in "white man he kill a plenty" ("the white man gave me a good beating").[87] From the receiving end of plantation workers, the act of hitting was comparable to the ultimate punishment of death. Other workers were subjected to solitary confinement. Many Chinese workers feared imprisonment most of all because of the well-known cruelty of Samoan police wardens.[88] A Melanesian worker recounted this dreadful experience in an interview over a half-century later, describing solitary confinement as a common practice on plantations.[89] Workers were typically confined in a small hut without light overnight to numb their senses. As a form of punishment, solitary confinement amplified the stifling atmosphere of physical and social isolation that dominated plantation life more generally.

Monetary punishment in the form of fines represented the softer but no less coercive end of the spectrum of work discipline on Samoan plantations. Workers were fined for the smallest violations of their work contracts, including coming late to work or working too slowly. Plantation owners used fines to counter the weapons of the weak wielded by workers who struggled to hold on to their humanity in an adverse environment. Since contract workers had only agreed to the coercive work environment in Samoa in return for wages and free passage, fines imposed by employers hit workers particularly hard. Some plantation owners punished workers who did not fulfill their quotas by adding labor tasks on Sundays.[90]

Plantation owners and colonial administrators were acutely aware of the disciplinary power of handing out fines to workers. In an article about the death sentence for the Chinese worker Jso Hoo, the *Samoanische Zeitung* in 1909 reminded its readers that the Chinese workers feared fines more than corporal punishment or a jail sentence.[91] Consequently, the article argued that only the death penalty could have a deterrent effect on the Chinese workers. Perceptions among the workers themselves were certainly different. If some workers might have worried more about being fined than being whipped, this preference was surely not a general rule, as the article claimed. In the eyes of employers, fines had the advantage of effectively withholding wages for already performed labor, which was precisely why workers thought them unfair.

Violence, and the threat of violence, permeated plantation life. If plantation work can be understood as a form of physical torture through repetition, then plantation workers in Samoa experienced their share, day after day

and year after year. The torture of everyday plantation routines represented
one part in a series of violent experiences that workers endured. These experiences ranged from physical punishment in the form of whippings, beatings,
and confinement, to the ultimate punishment: death. Whether through tuberculosis, accidents, or as the consequence of physical punishment, death
came to plantation workers in many forms. Workers were also disciplined
by being made to witness spectacles of violence, as most plantation owners
understood the power of such displays in deterring future resistance. But at
the end of the day, plantation managers had to strike a fine balance between
the imperatives of profit maximization and social peace to ensure the smooth
workings of their plantations. And it was this need for balancing exploitation with social order that opened up opportunities for workers to resist.

Resisting Plantation Discipline

While plantation owners had a vested interest in getting as much labor out
of their workers as possible, workers carved out moments of freedom under
this oppressive system. Some workers tried to resist the new and demanding
work rhythm head-on, only to find out that their bosses did not shirk from
using violence to get their money's worth. Many others succumbed to the re-
strictive plantation rules on the surface, while resorting to other means of
subversion under the radar of official control. Labor regulations on Samoan
plantations proved easier to compose than enforce.

Resistance among plantation workers took many shapes and changed over
time. Plantation workers relied on a wide array of practices to defy the demands of their employers and improve their living conditions. Among the
most lasting forms of resistance was the workers' refusal to give up their cultural traditions in the face of unfamiliar environments. On plantations,
workers fashioned new forms of living and communicating, such as pidgin
languages. Language was a central arena in the conflict between plantation
owners and workers. Hence, the names given to these practices differed widely
between workers and their bosses. What plantation owners called "theft," for
instance, many workers simply understood as "taking" a fair share of their
fruits of labor. Not only in name, Euro-American notions of private property clashed with the moral economy shared among the workers of the
Pacific. As in other parts of the colonial world, a pragmatic sense of mutual

solidarity emerged on copra plantations in Samoa. Examples of this growing sense of solidarity abound, both within racial groups and increasingly
without. Over time, plantations became important crucibles out of which
interracial solidarity among workers emerged.

In early 1906, four hundred Chinese workers banded together and sent a
letter to the Chinese embassy in Berlin, by way of Honolulu and Washington, to complain about their working conditions. In their petition, the workers wrote about the cruel treatment they faced on German plantations and
asked for an official to be sent to Samoa to protect them.[92] Later that year, more
than sixty Chinese workers on Deeken's plantation in Tapatapao struck in
protest against a cruel overseer, while some Chinese workers even committed
suicide.[93] Apparently, conditions for Chinese workers on Samoan plantations
had not improved since Deeken's conviction in summer 1904.

Outraged at these and other abuses, the Chinese government sent a special commissioner to German Samoa to represent the Chinese workers. In
March 1908, commissioner Lin Shu Fen arrived in Apia to investigate the
work conditions on the islands.[94] Touring the plantations, Lin Shu Fen caused
quite a stir among German plantation owners and colonial officials. At the
end of his monthlong visit, Lin Shu Fen confirmed the allegations made by
the workers about their cruel treatment and sent a damning report back to
China.[95] The following year, a second commissioner, Lin Jun Chao, visited
the plantations and reached a similar conclusion. Lin Jun Chao recommended
a series of reforms, including the abolition of flogging and identification
badges, and called for better food for the workers.[96]

In contrast to their fellow workers from Melanesia and Micronesia, Chinese workers came to enjoy legal protection and political support from their
home government. In May 1911, Chinese in German Samoa achieved legal
status equal to Euro-American settlers.[97] And by 1913, the German colonial
administration had met most of the Chinese calls for legal equality and better
working conditions.[98] Beginning in the 1890s, Chinese officials had imple-
mented policies to protect overseas Chinese communities and attract migrants back to their homeland. These efforts by officials of the Qing Empire
intensified after the Chinese Revolution in 1911. In fact, German Samoa
emerged as one of the test cases for Chinese nationalist agitation.[99] On
May 28, 1912, Lin Jun Chao, who had been promoted to Chinese consul,
informed his U.S. colleague in Apia that China had become a republic and

that the new national flag would be flown from the consulate starting June 1.[100] Political change at home, however, went beyond mere symbolism for the Chinese workers in German Samoa.

While the majority of Chinese workers at the time were formally "free" migrants who signed labor contracts upon arrival in Southeast Asia and other parts of the Pacific world, German plantation owners recruiting Chinese workers to Samoa could simply not afford this legal nicety. Together with the lack of a Sino-German treaty regulating the emigration and employment of Chinese workers in German territories, this impression of "coolie labor" fueled opposition by the Chinese government.[101] Combined with a desperate need for workers among new plantation owners, legal and political protection by their home government gave Chinese workers a powerful avenue for redress. As a result, Chinese workers were less vulnerable to excessive punishment than their counterparts from Pacific islands. As Melanesian workers later recalled, better legal protection also translated into better living conditions for Chinese workers.[102]

In August 1914, New Zealand occupied German Samoa. For Chinese workers, the transfer of power from one empire to another did little to change their living conditions. Conflicts over withheld and reduced wages continued throughout World War I. As in other areas, the new rulers from New Zealand maintained the German labor regulations.[103] Recruitment of new workers from China and Melanesia came to a halt during the war as German plantations were expropriated. In fact, New Zealand military governor Robert Logan's main motive to repatriate Chinese plantation workers was to reduce the productivity and value of the former German plantations.

Since the outbreak of the war, Euro-American plantation owners had put their Chinese workers on short rations for fear of a large-scale rebellion. Logan did nothing to change that.[104] In late August 1914, hundreds of Chinese workers left their plantations and came to Apia to protest against the reduced rice rations.[105] Following Logan's orders, Samoan police officers set out to quell the rebellion and started clubbing the Chinese workers. According to a New Zealand soldier who witnessed the brutal suppression of the Chinese rebellion, the Samoan officers "used their batons freely and blood flowed."[106] Several Chinese were beaten up so severely that they had to be treated in the hospital. One of them later died of his injuries.[107] The following May, Logan issued an ordinance that punished the exclusively Chinese crime of "loafing" with a fine of up to 30 shillings ($7.50).[108] Influenced by widespread fears of the "yellow peril," Logan soon thereafter began sending Chinese workers back home. Between 1914 and 1920, over twelve hundred Chinese workers returned to China without being replaced.[109]

The repatriation of Chinese and then Melanesian workers created a large-scale labor shortage on Samoan plantations. Copra production peaked in 1917 but then nose-dived as workers left the islands.[110] At war's end, a copra boom intensified the labor shortage. The flu pandemic of 1918–19 that had killed over a fifth of the Samoan population had also destroyed plans to force Samoans onto plantations. Beginning in August 1920, the New Zealand administration reversed its policy of repatriation and started recruiting new Chinese workers. Between 1920 and 1934, eight new transports brought a total of over three thousand Chinese workers to Samoa.[111]

Gradually, the most severe labor regulations were dismantled, culminating in the abolition of contract labor itself in 1923.[112] Labor protests, however, continued. In August 1929, three hundred Chinese workers went on strike over the failure to resolve a dispute over their foremen. A dozen Chinese strikers received gunshot and baton wounds when the New Zealand police attacked them.[113] Only a few months later, the police used similar methods to suppress a demonstration by the Samoan Mau movement, which challenged colonial rule. In many ways, the "weapons of the weak" used by plantation workers since the 1880s had helped prepare this fundamental challenge to colonial rule.[114] Apart from appeals to the state and large-scale protests, working people in Samoa found other ways to resist plantation discipline and, in doing so, forged new bonds of community with one another.

At the beginning of the twentieth century, colonial officials introduced a policy of racial segregation to prevent contact among Samoans, Melanesians, and Chinese. Most fundamentally, Melanesian and Chinese workers on copra plantations were not allowed to mingle with Samoans who lived in neighboring villages. Officials and plantation owners alike were afraid of interracial mixing for moral and security reasons but had fewer qualms about taking Samoan wives themselves. Samoan leaders, too, were arguing against the importation of Chinese workers mainly because they feared that sexual liaisons with Samoan women would put the purity of the Samoan race in danger. Despite efforts to curtail interracial relationships, social realities in German Samoa turned out differently. Many of the Chinese workers who wished to stay became gardeners, fishermen, and tailors. One of the men, Tsung Sui, was employed as a plantation overseer and in 1911 applied to settle permanently as a tailor. Others, like Wong Kau and Lai Man, who were working as police officers for the colonial administration, changed their careers and became gardeners and fishermen.[115] Freed from plantation life, it was primarily these Chinese workers and others like them who started families with Samoan women.[116]

Melanesian workers, too, crossed the colonial color line. Many Melanesian workers stayed in Samoa after their contracts ended (some voluntarily and many not), and a good number of them also started families with Samoan women. Over time, a full-fledged Melanesian enclave emerged around the London Missionary Society in Tufutafoe on the western tip of Savai'i. Apparently, the Melanesian workers who remained in Samoa wanted to be as far away as possible from the plantation belt around Apia. Despite feelings of racial superiority on the part of many Samoans (reinforced by Christian missionaries and colonial officials), Melanesians tried to escape the boredom of everyday plantation life by seeking out Samoans for friendship and romantic encounters. Their desire to leave behind the stifling air on the plantations was great. Ignoring the official ban on interracial mixing, some Melanesian workers stole themselves away from the plantation and attended Samoan church services in nearby villages. To make communication easier, church services for plantation workers were held in Samoan plantation pidgin until the 1960s.[117]

Tui Sakila, a labor recruit born in the Bismarck Archipelago who had arrived in Samoa around 1912, remembered that "some New Britain boys (probably Tolai) had had mission contact before being recruited. They would get up early on Sunday morning, wash and get dressed up and sneak off to church in a village adjoining the [DHPG] plantation [in Mulifanua]. They would come straight back after services, put on their old clothes and sit around as though nothing had happened."[118] Sakila quickly added that he never joined these clandestine church visits because he was too scared. According to Sakila, Samoan village leaders and pastors "had been warned to report such incidents to the [German] authorities."[119] Nevertheless, Sakila recounted that

Samoan villagers "had friendly feelings to the church-going laborers partly because the laborers generously gave them sticks of tobacco."[120] It was not until the end of World War I that the New Zealand authorities, which had taken over German Samoa, relaxed the ban on interracial mixing and recruited Samoans to work on plantations to relieve the acute labor shortage.[121] Governor Logan forced those Melanesian workers whose contracts had expired to stay in Samoa because he needed them to do the dirty work for the New Zealand soldiers.[122] In December 1914, the disgruntled Melanesian workers went on strike for better wages, but tensions soon subsided.[123]

Melanesian workers who secretly joined Samoan church services on Sunday mornings were innovators in forging ties of interracial solidarity. By joining the spiritual and communal space that Christian churches provided for Samoans, these Melanesian workers risked serious punishment from their employers. Given widespread Samoan racial prejudice toward Melanesians, the initial personal encounters between Melanesians and Samoans in these small churches perched on the edge of plantations must have been charged. Melanesians left their plantations to join Samoans to worship and socialize with them and one another out of the purview of Euro-Americans. In doing so, they crossed not only spatial but also racial and spiritual boundaries.

Workers also resisted the hardships of cutting copra through social and physical escape from the plantation. Many workers absconded from their workplace, sometimes for days, sometimes for years, sometimes never to return. Their superior knowledge of the inaccessible terrain surrounding many plantations aided workers in their escapes. Likewise, lack of comprehensive supervision made leaving plantations easier. When La Farge and Adams visited a village close to the DHPG plantation in Mulifanua, La Farge noted "two blacks, or Solomon islanders, dressed in lava-lavas in the Samoan way, who have taken refuge here, having escaped from the German plantation further on." The local Samoan *matai* told La Farge that the two runaways "are quiet and well-behaved, and that they go to school like the others about them."[124] As reports from plantation companies attest, desertions like the one recorded by La Farge were quite common. In March 1893, for instance, Krüger, a DHPG manager in Mulifanua, reported that Ragaub, "a good, docile boy and competent worker," had deserted from the plantation a month earlier.[125] Apparently, a worker by the name of Ratonga, who had already run away three times, had visited the workers' barracks on the plantation and tried to

persuade the DHPG workers to run away as well. According to the DHPG
manager, Ratonga had told the workers that "living with the Samoans is
much nicer than living on the plantations—you do not need to work, you
can do what you like, etc."[126] Ragaub seemed to have been converted by Ratonga, and he decided to follow him. The DHPG manager suspected that
"old deserters" like Ratonga were sent by Samoans to convince more workers to quit their contracts. Outraged at the "despicable" refusal by Samoans to
surrender these runaways, Krüger called on police officers to be sent all the
way from Apia to catch them, but to no avail. As this example shows, plantation managers were acutely aware of the lived solidarities among Samoans
and other Pacific Islanders.

Chinese workers ran away from their plantations as well. A Chinese workers' register kept by the German colonial administration offers a unique
window into the constant movements across the plantation landscape. Begun
by the German Chinese commissioner around 1913, the register consisted of
a standard ledger book with categories in German and entries kept in English.[127] The New Zealand military administration that took over German
Samoa at the beginning of World War I deemed the register useful enough
to maintain it through the early 1930s. To keep track of Chinese workers, the
register recorded a running number of the Chinese workers who lived in
German Samoa and when they had arrived. All in all, the register, which
spanned the years 1913 to 1932, consisted of 847 entries. A second column
recorded the "control number," which since May 1904 was given to every
newly arrived Chinese worker to be carried on an identification badge at all
times. Chinese workers had to wear the control number on their left upper
arm for everybody to see and could be arrested and punished for failing to
do so.[128] Individual names of workers were not listed until after this control
number, in a third column. Next to the name, the number of the transport
on which the worker had arrived from China was included. The proximate
columns were titled "monthly pay" and divided into the three years of a standard contract, but actual entries in the register frequently withheld this
information and instead listed the date when a new note had been entered.
Another column was reserved for the name of the employer, and the final
column included miscellaneous "notes" on the worker. It is this final column
that opens up an entirely different perspective on Chinese workers in permanent defiance of plantation discipline.

The German Chinese commissioner (and New Zealand officials after 1914) used this last column in the workers' register to record the current whereabouts of workers, in addition to other occurrences deemed noteworthy. Among the most common pieces of information listed were "returned to plantation," "fishing in the seaside," "arrested by policeman," "arrested by natives in the bush in Malua," "came to Chinese Commissioner's Office," and "sentenced for disobedience." The comments also included several false alarms of desertions ("returned himself to plantation") and information about the successful repatriation of a worker or notes like "deserted to avoid repatriation." The fact that a majority of the workers included in the 1913 register had such comments attached to their names belied the official rhetoric of tightly regulated plantation life found in so many of the regulations passed by colonial administrations.

Judging from the register, Chinese workers were almost constantly on the move. Most workers left their plantations only briefly to visit friends on other plantations or simply to go fishing. Others ventured away for much longer, and some never returned. Wong Sang, for example, who had arrived in Samoa on June 24, 1913, was listed as a "runaway about four years ago from Saninoga." Where Sang had run away to, much less why, was unknown. Intriguingly, Chan Mow Quan was listed on the same day as Sang with a similar comment: "Runaway to Sydney about four years ago. Seen by Policeman No. 3455 in Sydney about three years ago." To be sure, Sang and Quan had arrived in Samoa on different transports and had worked for different employers. And yet the fact that they were both believed to have run away from their plantations sometime in 1909 and were listed next to each other in the register was striking. Did they run away together? Was Sydney, where Quan was last seen by policeman No. 3455, a fellow Chinese, also Sang's new home? And how did they get to Australia in the first place? Unfortunately, the available historical sources do not provide answers to these and related questions. Still, the stories of Wong Sang and Chan Mow Quan—as incomplete as they are—point to a community of Chinese workers in defiance of the constraints of plantation life.[129]

If only a small minority managed to escape Samoan plantations, many other Chinese workers resisted exploitation in other ways. The register is replete with cases of Chinese workers actively seeking redress for the wrongs inflicted on them. On March 1, 1915, for instance, Fong Kin "came to office with complaint re wages," the register recorded. Kin worked for Upolu Rubber and Cocoa Estates Ltd., a London-based company that had survived the colony's takeover. Apparently, conflicts over wages also survived into the new colonial regime. The brief comment did not specify what Kin's complaint was exactly about, but judging from earlier instances of wage conflict, the likely cause for Kin's complaint was either withheld or reduced wages. For Chinese workers like Kin, then, the transfer of power from one empire to another in August 1914 did little to change their labor exploitation.

A few particularly courageous workers chose to leave the oppressive atmosphere on plantations completely behind, seeking a new life beyond the plantation belt. As in plantation colonies in other parts of the world, these runaways evaded the control of plantation owners and colonial officials alike and established a precarious form of living alongside the plantations they had fled. In the spectrum of resistance, this act lay somewhere between the everyday forms of resistance many workers practiced and Chan Mow Quan's decision to leave the islands and find a new start in Australia. Runaways chose permanent escape from plantation life, even if they stopped short of leaving Samoa.

In January 1901, a young male Solomon Islander found refuge aboard the USS *Abarenda* under the command of Benjamin F. Tilley. According to Tilley's report, the unnamed man was found "in the woods of Tutuila where he had been a fugitive for more than twelve years." Through an interpreter in Apia, the anonymous man related his incredible life story in an idiosyncratic mixture of Solomon pidgin, English, and German. Originally, he had been recruited to work on a DHPG plantation in Upolu when he was a young teenager. Apparently, he was treated badly on the German plantation and decided to run away. In 1884, he, a friend named Malua, and two other comrades escaped their plantation and crossed the forty-mile-wide channel to Tutuila on a self-made raft. "There they fled to the woods and remained as outcasts," Tilley noted.[130]

By the time Tilley took the young islander on board in 1901, two of his fellow runaways had already passed away, but his friend Malua was still alive. The unnamed man confessed that he was terrified of the Samoans, but when Tilley offered him passage home to the Solomon Islands, he refused.[131] Although a "perfect savage" in Tilley's eyes, the forty-five-year-old Solomon Islander was "very industrious and useful on-board ship, doing willingly all kinds of menial work." Perhaps because of his work ethic, the ship crew took a liking to the courageous man and gave him clothes. Tilley concluded his report to Washington with a request to continue the ration he had issued his unnamed guest and to retain him on board.[132]

Remarkably, Tilley was not the first person to tell the story of a group of workers who had fled from Upolu to Tutuila. In his famous *A Footnote to History* (1892), Robert Louis Stevenson rendered the great escape in gothic detail: "There are still three runaways in the woods of Tutuila, whither they escaped upon a raft. And the Samoans regard these dark-skinned rangers with extreme alarm: the fourth refugee in Tutuila was shot down (as I was told in that island) while carrying off the virgin of a village; and tales of cannibalism run round the country, and the natives shudder about the evening fire."[133] Little else is known about this man from the Solomon Islands who, together with three friends, had successfully escaped the plantation discipline on Upolu for a different kind of life in the backcountry of Tutuila. After a dozen years of relative freedom, he returned from the margins of the colonial world and joined the crew of a U.S. Navy ship. As it turned out, he was not the only runaway worker who had survived in the mountains of Tutuila.

More than twenty years later, Governor Edwin T. Pollock included the story of a "wild man" captured by a young Samoan in a letter to the Department of the Navy from June 1923.[134] Pollock recounted the unexpected turn of events from May 8, 1923:

A Samoan, among the hills north of Pago Pago Bay, saw this fourth "wild man," clad only in nature's vestments, descending a coconut tree. The young Samoan overcame the "wild man," bound his hands and brought him into the Naval Station, where he was the sensation of the day among the Samoans, and the whites as well. The Samoan who made the capture was an escaped prisoner. After the return to the Naval Station where the prisoner gave him up, the "wild man" would not separate himself from his captor for any length of time. Up to the present time no one has been able to converse with this man; although one other black boy, who has lived in the island of Tutuila for some years, tried to talk to him. However, they apparently spoke a different language. The "wild man" is naturally well along in years (his hair is almost white), and he is not strong physically. He appears quite contented and satisfied to remain here peacefully where he is well treated.[135]

Figure 9. Samoan Ielu (left) and
Melanesian Malua (right), Tutuila,
1923.
National Archives and Records Administration, Washington, DC, RG 80, file 3931, box 37.

As Joseph Kennedy has reconstructed, the young Samoan was a famous
climber by the name of Ielu, who had run into the "wild man" by sheer accident.[136] Ielu himself had been sentenced to prison for theft and made to join
a prisoner road crew. When he decided to escape, he fled into the nearby
mountains, where he encountered and captured the unnamed "wild man."
But as soon as Ielu had brought his naked captive to the courthouse in Pago,
Samoan locals recognized the so-called wild man as Malua, the fourth and
last surviving runaway from the Solomons. According to rumors, Malua had
been roaming the mountains surrounding Pago ever since his companion
had fled to Governor Tilley in 1901. In his sixties and with graying hair, Malua
was well-received by Pago residents. According to a local newspaper report
on which Kennedy based his account, Malua "was groomed, fed, given sweets
(which he is said to have loved), and made to feel like a long-lost member of

the family."[137] After their consequential encounter, Malua and Ielu became inseparable friends. In their own ways, both Ielu and Malua—the young Samoan and the old man from the Solomons—were captives of the colonial world that enveloped them. Ielu had escaped a prison sentence for theft, while Malua had left the world of copra behind, much earlier and with similar courage. As it turned out, Malua had only three months to enjoy his new friendship with Ielu before he fell ill with pneumonia and passed away on September 5, 1923, at the Naval Hospital in Pago. More than anything, this odd Samoan-Melanesian couple shows that Pacific Islanders succeeded in forging affective ties with one another beyond the control of their colonizers. By escaping the confines of colonial globality, runaway workers like Malua lived out their own form of Oceanian globality.

• • •

Plantation agriculture reshaped Samoa in fundamental ways. As Euro-American settlers turned the natural environment of Samoa into natural resources to be sold on a world market, they also transformed the social landscape on the islands. The new global and unequal community of workers in Samoa struggled to retain a sense of humanity in the hostile world of copra. In a strategy of divide and rule, Euro-American authorities segregated the colonial workforce along racial lines and sought to prevent contact among Samoans, Chinese, and Melanesians. Maximizing profits from the sale of copra, plantation owners argued, necessitated this racial segregation and strict work discipline. A range of factors determined how vulnerable workers were to violence and death: the kind of labor tasks they performed, their gender and race, the distance of their plantation from Apia, and whether or not they enjoyed support from state institutions—those within the colony or back home.

Resistance to the demands of plantation agriculture came in many guises and, over time, transcended racial boundaries. Chinese workers successfully improved their working conditions through appeals to their home government. Many Melanesian workers defied the coercive conditions on large copra plantations through physical escape, whether temporary or long term. Samoans, who could not be forced to work on Euro-American plantations, managed to maintain much control over their daily lives through sustainable farming and selling surplus copra to traders. With a vibrant social life based on substantial economic self-determination, Samoans succeeded in protecting their ways of life from outlander demands while refashioning the new world of copra around them. Forging interracial solidarity with newcomers was one of the ways in which Samoans shaped Oceanian globality—a practice that would prove critical for the more substantial challenge to colonial rule that would shake Samoan society in the 1920s.

3

PERFORMERS

On a sunny day in May 1893, a group of Samoans were busy chatting with a group of Hawaiians. Their meeting did not take place in Honolulu or on one of the many ships crisscrossing the Pacific at the time but on a busy street in downtown Chicago. As the entertainment area of the World's Columbian Exposition, the Midway Plaisance hosted an international crowd of performers in front of an equally international crowd of spectators. Amid this mixture of languages from around the world, Samoan and Hawaiian words could be heard. Lola, Siva, Fetoai, and Mele—the four female members of the Samoan troupe performing in Chicago—found a way to communicate with the six hula dancers from Hawai'i, turning the Midway into a Polynesian middle ground. By the time the fair shut its gates in October, two of the Hawaiians had become so close to their fellow Polynesians that they decided to make a stop in Samoa before returning to Hawai'i. Far from being mere conscripts of colonial interests, Samoans on American and European stages made new friends in unfamiliar places.[1]

As one of the most popular forms of urban entertainment at the turn of the twentieth century, ethnographic shows offered Euro-American visitors a glimpse into foreign cultures without the cost of long-distance travel. The shows presented the everyday lives of "primitive" peoples, emphasizing and eroticizing their physical attributes in picturesque "natural" settings, ranging from zoos and theaters to world's fairs and colonial exhibitions. Combining popular entertainment with didactic elements, the ethnographic shows also functioned as advertisements for the white civilizing mission and colonial trade.[2] As "ethnological show business," the performances were marked by a tension between claims for cultural authenticity and commercial success.[3] Samoans who participated in ethnographic shows offered indispensable labor power for this form of metropolitan edutainment. Like many other colonized people on show stages at the time, Samoans were powerful participants in increasingly global entertainment networks, lining the pockets of ruthless impresarios and savvy show managers across Europe and North America.[4] In spite of fierce competition, Samoans were among the most popular and hence most profitable performers at the turn of the twentieth century. Over the course of a quarter century, Samoans participated in seven ethnographic tours to Europe and the United States. The first tour, from 1889 to 1891, brought the Samoan performers to the United States and Europe, while the tours that followed included three exclusive visits each to the United States (1893, 1904, 1915) and Europe (1895–1897, 1900–1901, 1910–1911). Since the tours featured several stops, sometimes even two stops in the same city, Samoans were among the most widely seen ethnographic troupes at the time.[5]

Samoan performances on American and European stages served contradictory purposes. On the one hand, colonial authorities generally encouraged Samoans to participate in ethnographic shows and even assumed direct control over the logistics of travel. By exhibiting Samoan ways of life, American and German colonial officials hoped to convince metropolitan audiences of the success of their respective colonial projects in the South Pacific. More than other ethnographic shows at the time, the Samoan shows blended the natural beauty of the islands and the physical beauty of island inhabitants into a harmonious whole, offering Euro-American spectators a seductive alternative to industrial modernity.[6] At the same time, the organizers of the ethnographic troupes sought to impress on the minds of the Samoan visitors the economic, military, and cultural superiority of the colonizers.

Samoans themselves, on the other hand, pursued their own interests with their participation in ethnographic shows. Over time, Samoan performers used their trips to Europe and the United States more and more consciously as a way to represent their own culture, including the pivotal role of social rank within their community. High-ranking *matai,* such as Te'o Tuvale and Tupua Tamasese Lealofi I, came to understand their travels as diplomatic missions in the spirit of Samoan *malaga,* or traveling parties. They brought gifts and prepared speeches for their German and American hosts and insisted on meeting with top political leaders in person. In addition, going on a trip abroad promised a strategic advantage to Samoan leaders in their power struggles with competitors at home.

The contradictions of performative labor—representing the fruits of colonization as well as the interests of the colonized—distinguished the ethnographic show from other workscapes. Since Samoans were asked to perform specific labor tasks onstage—such as collecting coconuts or preparing *kava*—they reenacted forms of material labor through the labor of performance. While climbing a tree to fetch a coconut in a zoo certainly involved physical exertion, it remained an isolated action, to be performed at specific times and in front of an audience as entertainment. Collecting coconuts in Samoa rarely featured these explicitly performative elements. The preparation of *kava* and the performance of dances and songs, however, blurred the lines between cultural practice and performative labor because Samoans participated in these activities both at home and abroad. Samoan singers tried to reproduce an authentic version of their cultural repertoire when they performed in ethnographic shows, not only because they were expected to do so by the organizers and visitors (who included high-nosed ethnologists) but also because they wanted to do a good job in front of their Samoan and Polynesian peers. When performing Samoan cultural practices, then, Samoans operated under the constraints of a double audience with related but not coextensive cultural references and quality standards.

Samoans who traveled the world to perform *fa'a Samoa* were hard workers, just like their colleagues on plantations and in consular offices. They faced similar constraints in their own workscape—from broken contracts to abusive managers to restrictions on their mobility—and resorted to similar means of resistance, from pushing for better work conditions to escaping from tours altogether. Most importantly, Samoan performers created their own version of Oceanian globality by redefining their tours as cultural and diplomatic missions. As ambassadors of Samoan culture, Samoans on *malaga* performed the crucial labor of representing their home islands on the world stage. The first tour in 1889 set the scene for many of the challenges and opportunities that Samoan performers would face in the future.

Bad Omen: The First Samoan Troupe in the United States and Europe, 1889–1891

In June 1889, Robert A. Cunningham arrived in Apia in search of a Samoan troupe to tour the United States and Europe. Born in Quebec, Cunningham had moved to California in 1856 to mine for gold, but then turned to other

sources of wealth in San Francisco's entertainment industry. He first worked
for the famous Barnum & Bailey Circus and then as an independent impresario of popular shows featuring "freaks" and exotic peoples. In 1883, Cunningham tricked a group of Aboriginals from Queensland into taking part
in an ethnographic show in San Francisco.[7] Six years later in Samoa, Cunningham sought to recruit another troupe of "exotic" peoples to be showcased
in front of American and European audiences. Against strong opposition
from leading *matai,* including Tamasese Titimaea and Mataʻafa Iosefo, and
lacking official permission from the tripartite government, Cunningham had
to move on to Tutuila to find Samoans who were willing to go with him.

The nine Samoans recruited in Tutuila included five men (Atofau, Manogi,
Leasusu, Lealofi, and Letuugaifo) and four women (Mua, Foi, Tasita, and Tu).
Cunningham offered the first Samoan troupe a three-year contract that
included expenses, free clothing, and free passage to and from the United
States. The monthly wage for the Samoan performers was $12.50, half of what
Samoans could earn working on Euro-American plantations at the time but,
considering the free food and clothing, substantially more than what Melanesian ($8.45 a month) and Chinese ($11.70 a month) plantation workers were
making. Samoans preferred the less physically demanding labor of performance to stoop labor on copra plantations. Besides the financial compensation, participating in an ethnographic show offered other opportunities as
well: "travel-happy" Samoans could steam around the world, see new places,
and meet new people.[8] Visiting the United States and Europe also allowed
Samoan travelers to buy Western commodities, such as jewelry and sewing
machines, which would confer prestige and economic clout upon their return
home.[9] Samoans who went on tour overseas shared similar hopes with contract laborers from Melanesia and later China who returned from Samoan
plantations with trunks of valuable goods.

In August 1889, Cunningham and his hastily assembled Samoan troupe
shipped to San Francisco on the steamer *Alameda.*[10] There, they were joined
by Silaulii, who had been sent by missionaries to a local school years earlier.[11]
According to newspaper reports, the troupe performed *siva* dances to great
acclaim in San Francisco and other parts of California. At the end of August,
the troupe moved on to Chicago, where an American visitor, J. S. Cottrell,
fell in love with "Princess" Silaulii. Cottrell followed her to Minneapolis,
where the troupe was giving performances at the Dime Museum, and eloped

with her on September 19, 1889. The couple was alleged to have begun their return to San Francisco because Silaulii intended to go back to Samoa. According to a newspaper article, Silaulii said that she did not "expect to marry her American lover. He was only to look after her until she reached California."[12] As it happened, Silaulii died on her way back to California, probably of a combination of malnutrition and fever. Contemporary U.S. newspaper reports and Samoan oral memory confirmed that the whole troupe suffered from malnutrition throughout the tour.[13] Unfortunately, Silaulii would not be the last victim on what would turn out to be a disastrous first tour.

In October 1889, the rest of the troupe made their way to the Atlantic coast and performed at Koster and Bial's Music Hall in New York City, among other venues. A New York newspaper referred to Atofau as a "stalwart Samoan" and described the other male members as "warriors" and "exceedingly muscular."[14] To advertise his Samoan show, Cunningham produced a pamphlet featuring photographs and a lurid narrative of their alleged capture.[15] Cunningham's macabre marketing strategy turned out to be closer to reality than expected as the troupe crossed the Atlantic in spring 1890. While giving shows in Belgium in April 1890, troupe leader Atofau passed away, probably as a result of a pulmonary disease.[16] Atofau's body remained an object of anthropological interest even after his death. Belgian scientists removed the skin of the lower body of his corpse to study Samoan tattooing.[17] Neither Cunningham nor Atofau's fellow Samoans had enough influence to prevent his corpse from being used for these "scientific" purposes. Atofau's fellow traveler Tu died shortly afterward in Cologne, Germany, on April 25, 1890.[18] Since both Atofau and Tu succumbed to pulmonary diseases after a European winter that Samoans were not used to, it became clear that Cunningham's bad management was directly responsible for this human tragedy.

In the summer of 1890, the remaining troupe of seven Samoans moved on to the capital of the dominant colonial power in Samoa: Berlin. While there, they performed at popular entertainment venues such as Castan's Panoptikum and the Flora of Charlottenburg, "one of Berlin's more luxurious entertainment establishments that combined a park, palm garden, and stage with an excellent location beside the river Spree."[19] Beyond these commercial venues open to paying customers, the Samoans also gave a "lecture-performance" to the Berlin Society for Anthropology, Ethnology, and Prehistory. Anthropologists at the time relied on impresarios like Cunningham to deliver study objects from far-off places and, in turn, offered to authenticate them in order to both shield the impresarios from police scrutiny and attract visitors.[20]

Introduced by one of the leading German anthropologists, Rudolf Virchow, the Samoan troupe's visit straddled the border between science and entertainment. After the performance, Virchow proceeded to take their body measurements—a common practice among physical anthropologists at the time, who were keen on empirical data on the peoples they studied.[21] A heated debate ensued among the white German anthropologists present about the authenticity of the Samoans, who themselves must have been puzzled by the sight of bearded white men fighting about their "Samoanness." Virchow defended the Samoan troupe by arguing that "beneath the potentially deceptive signs of theatrical performance" lay the core of authentic Samoan culture.[22] The politics of cultural authenticity shifted with the particular settings in which ethnographic troupes, like the Samoans in Berlin, appeared.

The troupe's extended stay in Berlin also involved a story of interracial romance and a mysterious death.[23] In July 1890, the wife of wealthy retired Berlin merchant Max Hauke took a liking to Leasusu and Lealofi and convinced them to desert their troupe. Mrs. Hauke went on to scandalize the bourgeois neighborhood of Charlottenburg by having the two Samoan men accompany her in a carriage, dressed in fashionable European outfits. Only ten days later, her forty-five-year-old husband suddenly passed away under dubious circumstances. Nobody knew if his unexpected death was connected to his wife's Samoan romance, but newspapers—from as far away as the United States—suspected as much. Soon after, the widowed Mrs. Hauke paid the two men's early passage home to Samoa, which prompted Cunningham to sue her for the portly sum of $100,000 for the loss of "his savages."[24] It is unlikely that Cunningham ever received his compensation. In the fall of 1890, he returned to New York with the remaining five Samoans.

In New York, Cunningham transferred the Samoan troupe to an agent named Marshall, allegedly telling him, "I've got all out of them that I could. Now you take them and see what you can do."[25] Such a transfer was nowhere mentioned in the labor contract the Samoans had signed at the beginning of the tour in summer 1889. Apparently, Cunningham had enough of the problems his Samoan troupe had created and decided to sell them to another manager at a discount. Marshall then went on to tour the troupe through the

United States in the fall and winter of 1890–1891. Exhausted from the severe climate and even more severe travel schedule, Letuugaifo died of tuberculosis in Denver, where his body was embalmed by a local undertaker and placed on display in a pine box.[26]

Marshall then abandoned the remaining four members—Manogi, Tasita, Mua, and Foi—in New York. Van Cullen Jones, a reporter for the *New York World,* found them there "in a deplorable condition" and managed to arouse the attention of the federal government with his reports on their plight.[27] Secretary of the Treasury Charles W. Foster eventually appointed Jones to escort the Samoans home, with expenses shared by the federal government, the *New York World,* and a public subscription.[28] Jones took the four Samoans with him on a train to California, but Manogi did not live to see the Pacific: he died in a private Pullman Palace railway car en route through the Rocky Mountains and was interred in Rawlins, Wyoming, with a headstone marking his grave. Only half of the original ten members—Tasita, Mua, Foi, Leasusu, and Lealofi—made it back alive to Samoa.

Not only had five of the original ten troupe members died by the end of the tour, but their ruthless impresario had abandoned the remaining members and had cheated them out of their rightful wages. As the surviving members of the first Samoan troupe to tour the United States and Europe complained after their return to Samoa, Cunningham had withheld parts of the wages guaranteed under their contract. Cunningham had even "borrowed" $41 from each member, which was all they had left on their return to New York in fall 1890.[29] Cunningham's tour was a human tragedy with lasting consequences for all subsequent troupes. If five Samoans—Silaulii, Atofau, Tu, Letuugaifo, and Manogi—had to die in the service of empire, the performers who followed in their wake made sure things would go differently.

Polynesian Encounters: Samoans at the World's Columbian Exposition in Chicago, 1893

After this disastrous start, it took two years until plans to take another troupe of Samoan performers abroad resurfaced. Charles Mason Mitchell, U.S. consul in Apia and an occasional actor himself, came up with the idea of taking a Samoan troupe to the World's Columbian Exposition in Chicago in 1893. Mitchell told his American friend and fellow Apia resident Harry J. Moors about his idea. Born in Detroit, Moors had worked as a labor recruiter in Kiribati before coming to Samoa in 1875. There, he had become a successful trader and planter and married a Samoan woman. In the 1890s, Moors expanded his trading and planting interests into the entertainment sector, which, at the time, was virtually nonexistent in Apia. A gifted amateur showman himself, Moors built the first theater in Apia and became the first to show films and put up a wrestling match.[30]

Moors jumped at Mitchell's suggestion and intended to recruit a dozen Samoans, two dozen Wallis Islanders, five Tongans, and a Fijian.[31] Malietoa Laupepa strongly opposed another recruitment of Samoan performers, given the bad experiences with Cunningham's first tour and Moors's long-standing support of his archrival Mata'afa Iosefo.[32] Resorting to the dubious recruiting skills he had acquired in the blackbirding business, Moors managed to circumvent this powerful opposition and enlisted four mixed-race Samoan women (Lola, Siva, Fetoai, and Mele), two Wallis Islanders / Uveans (Sesefa and Pasilio), two Rotumans (Amosi and Sali), and one Fijian (Simi).[33] According to the contract, performers were to receive $12 a month for their services.[34] Moors's original plan to bring at least a dozen Samoans and even more Wallis Islanders failed, so he had to settle for a much smaller group.[35]

Moors's "Samoan" troupe consisted of a heterogeneous crew from Polynesia and Melanesia. Only four of the nine troupe members were actually from Samoa. The four Samoan women probably knew each other from the islands, while the rest of the group came from neighboring but culturally and linguistically different Pacific islands. Simi, who was described as a former sailor from Fiji, had probably been to Samoa and other major ports in the Pacific before. By the late nineteenth century, Melanesian and Polynesian navigators had already been traveling from one Pacific island to another for millennia. Simi and his fellow travelers in Moors's ethnographic show troupe thus stood in a long line of Pacific Islanders on the move.

Amosi and Sali were born in Rotuma, a tiny group of islands north of the Fijian main islands and part of the British colony of Fiji since 1881. An ethnic minority within Fiji, Rotumans shared more cultural and linguistic similarities with their neighbors in the east and south—those from Samoa, Wallis Island / Uvea, and Tonga—than with Fijians. Sesefa and Pasilio, finally, were from Uvea, a Polynesian kingdom sandwiched between Rotuma and Samoa. Part of the Tongan maritime empire from the thirteenth to the sixteenth centuries, Uvea had become a French protectorate in 1887. Culturally and linguistically, then, the Samoans shared many traits with their fellow travelers from Rotuma and Uvea. And even the Fijian sailor Simi, whose ethnic roots mixed Melanesian and Polynesian elements, was familiar with the cultures and languages of his Polynesian neighbors. Their common experiences on ships and on stage in Chicago brought the group even closer and enabled them to forge deeper bonds of solidarity.

As a Samoan newspaper noted, when in Chicago, the performers were "to give dances, sing songs and in every way treat visitors to a faithful representation of Samoan manners, customs and mode of living."[36] To provide such a "faithful representation" of Samoan culture, the troupe took along a seventy-foot canoe, several smaller boats, three large houses, *tapa* costumes, weapons, fire sticks, fishing devices, *kava* bowls, and ceremonial headdresses.[37] In spring 1893, the troupe embarked for Honolulu, where they had a break-in performance at the Opera House.[38] They reached Chicago via San Francisco just in time for the opening of the World's Columbian Exposition on May 1, 1893. The huge canoe (*taumualua*), used for large *malaga*, needed two thirty-four-foot railway cars to transport it from San Francisco to Chicago. To Moors's chagrin, people autographed the Samoan canoe with their names and addresses at almost every freight stop, after which he ordered the thousands of penciled inscriptions to be sandpapered off. Despite this involuntary mail service and the narrow tunnels of the Sierra Nevada Mountains, the canoe arrived safely at the fairgrounds only a few days after the troupe did.[39]

Celebrating the four hundredth anniversary of Christopher Columbus's first voyage to the Americas, the World's Columbian Exposition was a gigantic feat of engineering—both in concrete and in human beings. Its two main sections—the White City and the Midway Plaisance—mirrored in layout the fair's central message of racial and cultural evolution: the fruits of white civilization in the form of huge machines and beautiful art in the White City and the exotic bustle of titillating but racially inferior nonwhite peoples on the Midway.[40] Frederic Ward Putnam, director and curator of the Peabody Museum at Harvard University, was originally in charge of the historical and cultural exhibits at the fair. When it became clear that Putnam knew more about science than entertainment, the fair organizers replaced him with San Francisco–based entrepreneur (and later New York congressman) Sol Bloom. Inspired by his visit to the Algerian Village at the Exposition Universelle in

Figure 10. The Samoan Village on the Midway Plaisance, World's Columbian Exposition, Chicago, 1893. C. D. Arnold and H. D. Higinbotham, *Official Views of the World's Columbian Exposition* (Chicago: Chicago Photo-Gravure, 1893), plate 96.
Widener Library, Harvard University.

Paris in 1889, Bloom set up more exotic and dramatic showcases on the Midway to appeal to visitors.[41] Other attractions on the Midway included Carl Hagenbeck's animal circus and a number of "native villages," representing Germany, Ireland, Java, and China.[42]

The Samoan troupe set up their village on the corner of Madison Avenue and Sixtieth Street, right between the South Sea Islander exhibition and Hagenbeck's animal show. Many of the troupe's six daily performances in Chicago continued those of Cunningham's first tour: *kava* ceremonies, war dances, sitting *sivas,* and boat races. The official fair concession also granted performers the right to manufacture and sell woven hats and mats, fiber cloths, filigree, and carved work in their village.[43] Produced in public by the female members of the troupe, these items gained in cultural authenticity and, hence, in cash value.[44] Performative labor, regulated in contracts, thus enabled other forms of earning money, but woven mats were not the only elements of Samoan culture on sale in Chicago.

With their physical beauty, the four women in the troupe attracted special attention from male visitors. Judging from surviving photographs, the Samoan women were required to cover their breasts, and their dances were probably less sexualized than earlier ones in the private show rooms of Europe.[45] However, Moors had selected the Samoan women Lola and Fetoai partly because of their attractive looks. Lola, in particular, aroused the interest of both visitors and photographers. In a photographic collection of the fair, Lola was described as a "Polynesian Belle" and "one of the great features of attraction in the South Sea Island Exhibit." The caption emphasized Lola's natural beauty in visual as well as auditory terms: "Her name is Lola. She is a pure Samoan, but her features are European in every lineament. Lola has a magnificent physique which with jet black eyes and stately bearing gives her the appearance of a queen. And yet as she softly lisps the letters which spell her pretty name, her smile and manner are as soft and gentle as it is possible to imagine."[46] By the time of the Chicago fair, Lola's characterization as a royal beauty, with manners as lush as the tropical vegetation of her home islands, had congealed into a recognizable trope in Euro-American perceptions of the South Pacific and its inhabitants. Photographs with poetic captions formed part of a larger colonial discourse, conveying the availability of feminized Pacific islands to predominantly male spectators.[47]

The Samoan performers on the Midway found other ways of confounding expectations and asserting their own wills. As a Chicago newspaper reported, the Samoans had given one another haircuts and begun dressing in American clothes soon after their arrival in Chicago. Moors, the article reassured its readers, had to put a halt to this "civilizing process."[48] In an act of colonial mimicry, the Samoan performers developed their own sense of fashion and succeeded in subverting the clear-cut lines between "civilized" and "uncivilized" peoples. By the 1890s, Euro-American goods, such as dresses and umbrellas, had been introduced in Samoa and had come to be regarded as status symbols. It is no wonder, then, that Samoans and their fellow islanders would grasp the opportunity to wear American clothes and get Western-style haircuts when they were in the United States for an extended period. Their new dresses and haircuts were made possible partly by the monthly wages they received as ethnographic performers.

Dancing and singing were central elements of the performances in the Samoan Village. *Siva* dances were an indispensable part of Samoan hospitality, as many Euro-American visitors to the islands knew.[49] Over time, the Samoan *siva* evolved into a metonymy of Samoan culture, a ritual straddling the line between authentic Samoan custom and commercialized performance for non-Samoans.[50] The eroticism of some of the dances performed by Samoan women certainly added to their appeal among male visitors of ethnographic shows. In Chicago, the Samoan troupe performed club and sitting dances accompanied by call-and-response songs on a regular basis. A handful of these memorable Samoan performances on the Midway were recorded on a phonogram by the American ethnomusicologist Benjamin Ives Gilman.[51] Samoan performative labor became nowhere more palpable than in these dances and songs.

While most of the troupe's time was spent inside their village, the Samoan troupe also ventured outside it. For performers even more so than for visitors, the Midway was a bustling middle ground to meet, mingle, and make new friends. The Samoans in Chicago were no exception. Right next to the Samoan Village, a South Sea Islander exhibition had set up its operations, with daily show performances similar to the ones in the Samoan Village. The South Sea Islander exhibition hosted its own performance troupe, the Polynesian Star Company, which included all of the more than three hundred Pacific Islanders at the fair. While the troupe consisted mostly of Javanese performers, who had their own village as well, there were also Fijians, Tongans, and Samoans among them.[52] Thrown together in the Polynesian Star Company, the performers came from various parts of the Pacific—including Java in the Dutch East Indies—with different cultural and linguistic traditions. In between show breaks, the Polynesian Star Company must have been a polyphony of Pacific languages, stories, and music. Bringing so many different Pacific Islanders together so far away from home, the Polynesian Star Company offered a sense of community for the Samoan travelers in Chicago.

The Samoans preferred mingling with a group of fellow Polynesians who had their own show at the fair: the Hawaiian hula dancers. To fill up their three-hundred-seat theater five times a day, the six hula performers from Hawai'i played with the erotic expectations of the mostly male visitors, but they rejected requests to dance topless and sometimes had to resist the physical advances of particularly aggressive men with punches.[53] Compared to the Samoans' monthly wage of $12, the hula dancers from Hawai'i received $20 a month under a six-month contract.[54] They, like the four Samoan women in Moors's troupe, were exposed to the lurid gaze of the white male visitors—part and parcel of the fair's aim to present their home islands as available targets for virile colonizers.[55]

But the Polynesian women proved adept at deflecting the colonial gaze by fostering a sense of female solidarity beyond the public view. The Samoan women certainly had much to talk about with the Hawaiian women, and because Hawaiian and Samoan share similar grammar and vocabularies, they learned to communicate without interpreters.[56] One of the Hawaiian hula dancers, Kini Kapahukulaokamamalu Wilson, vividly remembered her interactions with the neighboring Samoans: "We used to go over [to see them] from the back entrance. We talk all the time."[57] A group of Hawaiians was also present when the Samoans hosted French American zoologist Paul du Chaillu in their village, preparing a roasted pig for him and over forty fellow performers from the Pacific.[58]

What exactly the Polynesian performers talked about remains unknown. Between tales of shared exploitation as cultural workers in an exoticized entertainment setting, there must have been moments of fun, laughter, and the surprising joy of cultural familiarity far from home. Two of the Hawaiians—Nakai and Kanuku—had become such good friends with the Samoans that they decided to join them and visit Samoa before returning home to Hawai'i.[59] A chance encounter at Lake Michigan thus resulted in lasting friendships among Samoan and Hawaiian performers.[60] In making new friends, they shaped their own version of Oceanian, or even Polynesian, globality. Samoans and Hawaiians in Chicago were not the only Pacific Islanders who appropriated turn-of-the-century exhibitions for cultural exchanges with fellow islanders. At the International Exhibition of Arts and Industries in Christchurch, New Zealand, in 1906–1907, for instance, Maoris exchanged gifts and ceremonial greetings with Cook Islanders and Fijians.[61] On future travels to Europe, Samoan performers would continue to meet fellow performers from Africa, Asia, and the Pacific. These encounters prompted globe-trotting Samoan performers to rethink their own place in the colonial world.

As the fair came to an end in late October 1893, the Samoan Village was dismantled. H. N. Nichols, manager of the South Sea Islands Village, sold more than seventy Samoan objects to Putnam, who passed them on to the newly founded Field Columbian Museum. Among the objects were fans, clubs, bowls, two slit drums, and four canoes. The Samoan craftspeople and owners of these objects, however, did not receive their fair share of the $500 Nichols charged the museum.[62] According to Moors, the museum paid $1,500 for the large *taumualua*, but it was probably Moors himself who kept the money.[63]

Indeed, Moors must have made money with his Samoan troupes in Chicago because he came back to the Louisiana Purchase Exposition in St. Louis in 1904 with a larger troupe. Upon his return to Samoa, he also bought large tracts of land around Apia and in Savai'i, where he planted cocoa and grazed horses and cows.[64] Besides the performers who joined the Barnum & Bailey show, two of the Chicago veterans (Siva and Mele) reenlisted when two German brothers took the next troupe to Europe in 1895. Their experiences in Chicago—despite initial fears of a repeat of Cunningham's first tour—were positive enough to make them feel comfortable signing up again.

The "Belles of Samoa": Marquardt's Troupe in Europe, 1895–1897

In the summer of 1895, less than two years after the Chicago troupe had returned, a third Samoan troupe prepared for their tour, this time bound for Europe. Carl Marquardt, whose brother Friedrich was the Apia police chief at the time and was married to a mixed-race Samoan woman, had probably heard about the success of Moors's trip to Chicago.[65] A German-born writer and amateur ethnologist himself, Carl teamed up with his brother to recruit Samoans for a tour to Germany and other parts of Europe.[66] Despite concerns about the members' health after Cunningham's first tour, during which five Samoans died, Marquardt succeeded in convincing forty-two Samoans to join his troupe—an unprecedented number. Aware of these earlier difficulties, Marquardt negotiated a detailed contract with Malietoa Laupepa, which set out the conditions of employment in English and Samoan. The length of the trip was limited to two years, the performers would receive 64 marks ($16) per month (40 marks to be paid on tour, the rest to be paid upon return), and they had to agree to specific duties, including obeying Marquardt's orders.[67]

Most importantly for the Samoan performers, the organization of their troupe followed the logic of social rank and duty within Samoan society. Of

Marquardt's originally intended forty-two members, thirty-two Samoans actually went on tour, including twenty-five women and seven men. Nearly all the performers were recruited in villages around Apia and were members of influential Samoan families.[68] Amitua, for example, was the son of a district judge under Tamasese Titimaea, while the other six men were sons of *matai*.[69] One of them, Phineas—son of Laiataua, governor of Manono—had been a police sergeant in Apia in 1893.[70] Among the women were Faagalo, who knew Phineas from their common childhood in Apia, and her younger sister Manaima, a gifted weaver.[71] Siva and Mele were the two women who had already been to Chicago with Moors. They jumped at the opportunity to join the next troupe and explore different places.

On June 26, 1895, the group of thirty-two Samoans and their manager, Carl Marquardt, boarded the steamer *Taviuni* to Sydney. During their weeklong stop there, the Samoan women bought warm clothes, veils, and gloves, no doubt remembering the tragic deaths on the first tour.[72] At the end of July, the troupe reached Bremerhaven in northern Germany and began its first set of shows at the Passage-Panoptikum in Berlin in September 1895. At this commercial entertainment theater, the Samoans sang original songs about their long travels, including a sorrowful farewell song that became popular among visitors.[73] Their eight performances a day also featured boxing matches and a staple of the earlier tours: the preparation of *kava*.[74]

Since the local press had described Fai Atanoa as the most beautiful, dubbing her "Princess Fai," panoptikum director Richard Neumann selected her to prepare the *kava* during the shows. This outside intervention into long-standing Samoan custom sparked strong opposition among the other members of the troupe. Some male members threatened outright violence against Fai because other women were of higher social rank and deserved the right to perform the task. Other men tore down pictures depicting Fai as a princess and threatened, upon return to Samoa, to parade her through the villages strung to a stick like a pig to be roasted. Given these explicit threats, Fai wisely refused to go along with the theater director's request. When Malietoa Laupepa was informed of the events in faraway Berlin, he sent an indignant protest letter to Marquardt, which convinced the German press to change Fai's title from "Princess" to a simple "Miss." This episode showed the long reach of high-ranking Samoans, who projected their political power across thousands of miles.[75] Ultimately, the confusion about Fai's proper rank and its resolution according to Samoan custom proved that the Samoan performers, backed by their leaders at home, were able to protect their own interests more forcefully than on earlier tours.

While in Berlin, the troupe gave another special performance at the Berlin Society for Anthropology, Ethnology, and Prehistory, but this time without live body measurements. Again, the Samoan performers had increased their bargaining power. As part of his recruiting permission, Marquardt probably had to vouchsafe the safety of the Samoan women vis-à-vis Tamasese Titimaea and Malietoa Laupepa.[76] This time, their bodies remained out of reach of the German anthropologists, but a photographer shot a series of pictures of the troupe, which the performers went on to sell afterward.[77] Following stops in Copenhagen and Düsseldorf in the spring, the troupe began a four-week stay at the zoo in Frankfurt am Main at the end of June 1896. With five daily shows, the Samoans were quite busy performing their Samoanness for the benefit of record numbers of visitors.[78] When troupe members were beginning to feel exhausted only a few days into their stay, Marquardt extended their lunch break for one hour and reduced their daily workload from ten to nine hours.[79] According to amused newspaper reports, the Samoans swam and dived once a week in the zoo pond, some cleaning their bodies and hair with soap—that "yardstick of civilization"[80]—while others started fishing in the pond.[81] Some Samoan women had picked up the German children's game of klicker, which—similar to marbles—involved throwing small clay balls into holes in the ground.[82]

Most of the other daily routines, like eating, were not within public view. In the mornings, the Samoan performers received tea and 120 fresh rolls, and for lunch and dinner, boiled beef or ox meat with rice, cucumbers or salad, and mixed bread, as much as they desired. A female cook prepared their food in a special kitchen, a newspaper noted.[83] In stark contrast to these daily meals, pigs were roasted in an earth oven (*umu*) on Sundays—an event explicitly advertised in local newspapers. The Samoan men who prepared the meal received the pig ready to be roasted directly from the zoo's butcher and served the dish, first to the women in their troupe and then to hungry visitors, who found the meat "soft and mellow, but too little salted for German tongues."[84] If food functions like a cultural grammar, then the *umu* symbolized to German spectators the Samoan culture of communal labor and sharing.[85]

After stops at the zoos in Leipzig, Dresden, and St. Petersburg, the troupe returned to Berlin for a second stop in March and set up shop again in the Passage-Panoptikum. As during their first stay at the theater, the performers became embroiled in another scandal. In May 1897, the Berlin press reported that Marquardt had encouraged the Samoan men of the troupe to castigate their women with whips. On top of this physical mistreatment, reports also claimed that the Samoan men and women were kept in a small dark room, were fed insufficient and bad food, and received no pay.[86] Marquardt defended himself against these accusations in a thirty-two-page pamphlet in which he provided precise details on the food and payment given to the performers. According to Marquardt, they received one pound of meat per day per person, plus potatoes, rice, bread, milk, and tea at their pleasure.[87] As Marquardt's testimony stood against the newspaper allegations, the Samoans themselves were given no voice at all in the debate. A police investigation, including medical examinations of the Samoan women, failed to confirm the accusations, and it was eventually dropped.

Meanwhile, another conflict arose between the Samoan women and the theater director, Neumann. German men who came to the Samoan shows—some even equipped with Samoan dictionaries—had repeatedly tried to touch the Samoan women on stage and in some cases succeeded.[88] While some of the most aggressive men had to be kicked out of the theater, Neumann surely appreciated the informal advertisement for his erotic performers. In an attempt to avoid another scandal and potential repercussions in Samoa, Marquardt defended the moral integrity of Samoan women against advances from their overly intrusive male admirers. Six Samoan women even fled the panoptikum and sought refuge at a female cashier's home in Rixdorf.[89] Eventually, a compromise was reached: the Samoan women did not have to sit at the customers' tables but still had to make contact with the audience. At some point, Neumann accused Marquardt himself of sexually abusing the women—a claim that was difficult to prove and probably a ploy to create publicity for the show.[90]

As in the allegations concerning mistreatment, lack of food, and withheld wages, the Samoan women did not figure in these debates among the white men. Yet the female troupe members were by no means helpless victims. For example, they used their European travels to spend part of their wages on fashionable hats, red scarves, and fur coats.[91] They also actively resisted the supervision of their white managers by secretly absconding from the panoptikum. Mamele and Pola simply took matters into their own hands and fled the theater with a young German man. They were eventually found in a hotel in Swinemünde on the Baltic Sea island of Usedom, with a guy named Alfred. The twenty-one-year-old technician had been visiting the panoptikum every day for as many as five hours at a time, eventually convincing two of his objects of interest to run away with him.[92] Alfred was only one of several young German men who were so smitten with the Samoan women onstage that they followed them across Europe.[93]

In August 1897, after stops in Vienna, Dresden, and Leipzig, the Samoan troupe returned to the zoo in Frankfurt am Main for a second stint. Apart from the daily performances, which were similar to their first stay, a local photographer began selling postcards to zoo visitors with portraits of the Samoan women.[94] Visitors to ethnographic shows collected signed postcards as souvenirs that provided proof of personal contact with the performers.[95] If similar rules prevailed in the Frankfurt zoo as in Chicago, the Samoan models received a fee for their labor or a percentage of the postcards sold.

In 1893, the Samoan performers in Chicago had mingled with their fellow Pacific Islanders, particularly the Hawaiian hula dancers on the Midway. Four years later, in the zoo in Frankfurt, the Samoan troupe received another visitor: Gumma, the "warrior-queen" from Dahomey. Gumma, who had visited the Frankfurt zoo as part of a troupe of Amazon warriors in August 1891, was then staying in nearby Darmstadt.[96] Whether she had heard about the Samoans performing in Frankfurt or not, Gumma, with a male companion (and interpreter), came to visit them just after they had finished a sumptuous *umu* dinner. She chatted freely with the Samoans, some of whom spoke English, and held the infant Peter, born in St. Petersburg in February, in her arms.[97] Le Pupa, whom the local press had dubbed the leader of the troupe, took a keen interest in Gumma's dark skin color—an interest he evidently shared with German anthropometrists like Virchow. But Le Pupa's physical contact with his fellow performer might have signaled a more intimate connection among peoples whose strangeness became familiar under the unlikely circumstances of the ethnographic show. Gumma herself seemed not to have minded Le Pupa's keen interest in her skin and immediately bought one of his photographs before giving two of her own to the Samoan women. They appreciated the gift and exclaimed in

German *"Fein, fein!"* (Fine, fine!) as they passed them around.[98] Among ethnographic performers like Gumma and Le Pupa, self-portraits functioned both as souvenirs to be sold to white visitors and as business cards that could be exchanged as tokens of respect and shared memory.[99] Gumma responded with a dignified smile to the Samoan women's giggles and proceeded to take a tour of the zoo, which must have stirred up memories from her earlier stay.[100] From the Chicago Midway to the Frankfurt zoo, Samoan performers defied official transcripts in surprising ways. Through their curiosity, they turned ethnographic shows staged for the colonizers into spaces of cross-racial encounter that attested to the shared humanity of the colonized.

In the fall of 1897, after two-and-a-half years abroad, the troupe ended its tour through Europe and returned to Samoa, arriving in December.[101] Many of the performers brought loads of gifts and Western goods back home with them, including three bicycles.[102] Marquardt's first tour not only was the longest (30 months) and best paid ($16 a month) but also included the highest percentage of female performers (78%) of all the ethnographic tours at the turn of the twentieth century. Somewhere along the way, Faagalo and Phineas, the former police sergeant, discovered they shared more than a sense of adventure. They fell in love on tour and got married upon returning to Samoa.[103] Newly wed, they moved to Fiji to work as lay preachers for the Samoans living there. They bought some land and ran a laundry, staying for seven years. In 1905, they returned to what had become German Samoa, and Phineas decided to pick up his old job and entered the German colonial police.[104] Phineas had not only found love on tour but also discovered the benefits of serving the colonial empire he had visited a decade earlier.

"Our New Compatriots from Samoa": Tuvale's *Malaga* in Europe, 1900–1901

In 1900, the German flag was raised in Apia. Following the Berlin Treaty of 1899, Upolu and Savai'i became German colonies, while the U.S. Navy took control over Tutuila. Given this change in political status, German colonial officials thought it would be fitting to send another ethnographic troupe from the new colony to Europe. The Marquardt brothers again offered to recruit a group of Samoans, but this time with the direct involvement of a leading Samoan: Te'o Tuvale. Born into an affluent family of pastors and civil servants,

Tuvale was a powerful *matai,* who had spent time in Fiji in the 1880s and had worked as an assistant clerk to his half brother, Le Mamea, a government interpreter. Marquardt hoped that under Tuvale's leadership, his second tour to Europe would avoid the conflicts about rank and gender that had plagued the 1895 tour. With the respect he commanded among his fellow Samoans, Tuvale managed to recruit a more cohesive and stable group of performers and successfully organized its travels. Even more importantly, Tuvale did not see the tour primarily as an ethnographic show but rather as a *malaga,* with its Samoan members offering song and dance in exchange for European hospitality and respect.[105] As a result, the Samoan group consisted of a diplomatic delegation, led by Tuvale himself, and a cultural group made up of a *taupou* and a number of talented performers.[106] The high status of *matai* like Tuvale freed the group from performative labor abroad. With this division of labor grounded in Samoan traditions, the travelers used the tour to carve out their own version of Oceanian globality.

Marquardt himself, in line with German colonial officials, planned to use the tour to stress the fact that Samoa was now a German colony. Consequently, he highlighted the martial prowess of Samoan men more than the beauty of Samoan women, as opposed to earlier tours.[107] Marquardt's and Tuvale's conceptions of the tour, however, were not mutually exclusive. While Tuvale opened the troupe performances with a speech that conveyed his joy about the fact that Samoa was now German, he also made sure that he would meet up with German dignitaries, including Emperor Wilhelm II himself.[108] The official theme of the meeting of two warrior peoples on equal terms could be made compatible with the Samoans' understanding of a "goodwill" tour.[109] And as businessmen like Marquardt knew, exotic visitors with royal heritage rarely failed to attract visitors.[110]

Marquardt and Tuvale recruited a group of twenty-nine Samoans, including ten men and nineteen women.[111] Among the male members were many direct acquaintances of Tuvale's, which ensured greater discipline. Most prominent among the female members was Naitua, the only daughter of *matai* Atoamalefuaiupolu So'onanofo. A mere seventeen years old at the time, Naitua became the official *taupou* of the troupe, in accordance with her father's rank. Taking a large collection of objects with them, including arms and household items, the troupe departed Apia on January 17, 1900.[112] Their performances in Europe featured many of the same elements from earlier tours: songs, dances, collecting nuts from a coconut tree, preparing *kava,* war scenes, fistfights, and, as a new addition, showcases of Samoan cricket. Probably due to Tuvale's direct involvement in the planning of the tour, the maximum number of shows per day was reduced from eight to six.

After initial stops at a panoptikum in Cologne and the Berlin zoo in the spring, the Samoan troupe moved on to the political highlight of their tour. At a navy parade in Kiel on June 28, 1900, Tuvale achieved one of the major goals of his diplomatic mission and met with the German head of state, Wilhelm II. Both Tuvale and Wilhelm II gave obligatory speeches in their native tongues, while in a reversal of colonial hierarchies, Carl's brother Friedrich helped interpret the speeches.[113] After this formality of both Samoan and German diplomatic culture, Wilhelm II and Tuvale had a friendly conversation before the kaiser turned his attention back to the parade. Three weeks after their encounter in Kiel, Tuvale received a golden wristwatch from Wilhelm II through German consul Rose, while the Samoan women were given rings, bracelets, and scarves. The German officials even sent a collection of toys for young Peter. Upon receiving these gifts, the Samoan troupe reportedly broke out in an improvised show to give thanks to the Kaiser.[114] The Samoan performers were so impressed by these gifts that even a year later when they returned to one of their mainstays, the Frankfurt zoo, they set up a table to exhibit the collection of watches and rings they had received from the kaiser.[115] Lying not far from the cultural objects they had brought with them from Samoa, these royal gifts were easily incorporated into the symbolism of Tuvale's diplomatic mission.[116]

In May 1901, while the troupe was in Germany, the Colonial Department of the German Foreign Office issued a ban on recruiting colonial subjects for public display.[117] Modeled on existing bans on exporting laborers from German colonies, the new ban prohibited the export of ethnographic troupes from German colonies for the purpose of exhibiting them abroad.[118] The German Colonial Society had lobbied for such a ban since the mid-1890s, when a series of widely reported scandals involving ethnographic performers (particularly at the 1896 German Colonial Exposition in Berlin) dominated the German press.[119] Advocates argued that a ban on exhibiting German colonial subjects abroad would protect the physical and moral integrity of the performers and, even more importantly, help contain the escalating voyeurism of their white German spectators.[120] In addition, supporters cited the alleged loss of cultural authenticity among performers, who wore Western clothes, spoke European languages, and were not afraid to mingle with "racially superior" Germans.[121] Against considerable odds, performers had succeeded in transforming ethnographic shows into cultural bridges and a kind of performative labor based on ethnic diversity. As the predominantly white visitors were turned into passive spectators, the threat to white supremacy could only be contained by banning the shows altogether.[122] The following tour with Tamasese Lealofi I in 1910–1911 would need special permission to circumvent this ban.[123]

Meanwhile, the Samoan troupe visited Zurich and Cologne in winter 1900 before moving on to Munich in April 1901. There, the Samoans performed at the Hammers Panoptikum, a commercial entertainment theater known for its exotic as well as erotic shows. While the rest of the troupe gave shows in the theater, Tuvale continued to pursue his diplomatic mission in other parts of town. After some inquiries, he managed to meet up with Prince Regent Luitpold, who presented him with a portrait with a personal dedication. As a follow-up to his meeting with the German head of state in June 1900, Tuvale had succeeded in shaking hands with the leader of the Bavarian royal family, who held a somewhat similar position to the one Tuvale occupied in Samoa.[124]

After stops at zoos in Dresden, Frankfurt am Main, and Leipzig in the summer of 1901, the troupe returned to Samoa in December.[125] According to his own report, Marquardt did not make a profit from the two-year tour. With Cunningham's tour in mind, he also made sure to receive official confirmation that he brought the Samoans back healthy.[126] The actual manager of the Samoan troupe, Tuvale, was in more than good health upon his return. While on tour, he had fallen in love with Naitua, the *taupou*, when he cared for her during a sickness. Like Faagalo and Phineas four years earlier, Naitua and Tuvale got married right after their return, and they would go on to raise nine children together.[127] Even before his return to Samoa, Tuvale, together with Tolo, was hired by Imperial Court judge Schnee as a clerk.[128] Several other young *matai* who were part of the troupe entered the German colonial service as police officers when they returned.[129] One of Tuvale's sons, Atoa Teʻo Tuvale, followed his father's path into the colonial service and became chief interpreter of independent Western Samoa's Legislative Assembly. Tuvale himself did not live to see the day of Samoan independence in 1962; he passed away in 1919, one of the many victims of the Spanish flu.

Meet the Samoans in St. Louis, 1904

Two years after the return of the last troupe, another world's fair was on the horizon in the United States: the Louisiana Purchase Exposition in St. Louis in 1904. Commemorating the centennial of Jefferson's Louisiana Purchase in 1803, the world's fair was designed to showcase the rising global power of the United States. Under the leadership of the president of the American Anthropological Association, W. J. McGee, the fair's anthropological exhibit was the largest to date and included more than two thousand human exhibits from around the world.[130] To represent the largest colony that the United States had recently acquired, an enormous Philippine Reservation was mounted on the fairgrounds in St. Louis, stretching over forty-seven acres and filled with six native villages and a total of seventy-five thousand exhibits. More than one thousand Filipinos participated in the performances, including Igorots, who attracted large numbers of visitors because they publicly consumed dog meat.[131]

Given the unprecedented numbers and diversity of the ethnographic performers, the St. Louis fair was a veritable field research station for the study of nonwhite racial types.[132] Modeled on the Midway Plaisance in Chicago, the Louisiana Purchase Exposition was designed with a mile-long entertainment strip called the Pike, where a number of exotic shows took place.[133] As in Chicago, Hagenbeck's animal show performed in St. Louis and added to the sensationalist character of the Pike. Other visitors from abroad had more difficulties attending: the Chinese delegates to the fair were subjected to excessive restrictions, primarily because the U.S. government and several western states had passed exclusion acts to keep Chinese migrant workers out.[134] A year after desperate German plantation owners had finally succeeded in importing Chinese workers to German Samoa, public debate and policy in the United States aimed in the opposite direction. Avoiding these diplomatic crosscurrents, a team of Chinese and American impresarios organized a Chinese village on the Pike, complete with theater, bazaar, and teahouse.[135]

Unlike the Chinese delegation, the Samoan performers were more than welcome in St. Louis, since the 1901 ban did not prohibit exhibitions outside

Germany. Again, it was the entertainment veteran Moors who ventured to recruit a group of Samoans to bring to the world's fair. Given his success in Chicago a decade earlier, Moors, who had in the meantime become one of the largest taxpayers in German Samoa, was probably eager to go on another tour. The troupe of fifty Pacific Islanders, most of them Samoans, who went with him to St. Louis seemed to be eager as well. Most of them knew about the tragic first tour organized by Cunningham in 1889 but had also heard about the exciting adventures, material gain, and love stories of the subsequent tours. Some Samoan *matai* in Tutuila were so willing to go to St. Louis that in June 1903 they approached Governor Edward B. Underwood, who was sympathetic to the idea. Similar to his German colleagues, Underwood reasoned that a Samoan presence at the fair would showcase U.S. colonial interests and, at the same time, educate Samoans about the superiority of their colonizers. He even suggested to arrange an interview with President Theodore Roosevelt either in St. Louis or in Washington, DC.[136] Unprecedented in number and ethnic diversity, Moors's St. Louis troupe brought a gigantic number of props and objects with them. A whole ship had to be chartered to transport the troupe and its stage materials across the Pacific.[137]

Upon arrival in San Francisco in April 1904, Moors first bought warm clothes for the troupe members who were not used to the chilly spring temperatures of Northern California. In St. Louis, Moors needed to aggressively advertise the Samoan troupe to fairgoers, who had by then acquired some experience in ethnological slumming. Newspapers praised the show for "the best dancing in the Plaisance. It makes no pretense to grossness, but is simply downright savage."[138] One reporter even pointed out that the Samoans were not "cannibals" anymore and were, to the contrary, so Christianized that, alone among the exposition's companies, they refused to perform on Sundays.[139] Among the show's many visitors was a familiar face from back home: Richard Williams, the Irish-born governor of Savai'i, who had spent a few months of his vacation in Europe before traveling back to Samoa through St. Louis.[140]

The Gilbertese Islanders among the troupe members were the most popular dancers among fair visitors. As Moors knew all too well from Gilman's recordings in Chicago in 1893, traditional Samoan music relied mainly on percussions. To produce a more wholesome musical experience for the visitors, Moors simply hired the services of a Mexican orchestra to accompany

Samoan dancing.[141] Polynesian dancers thus received musical support from the eastern fringes of the Pacific. Moors's mixed-race daughter also participated in the performances and later remembered that the Samoan women in the troupe "cautioned her not to encourage cheap skates by stooping to pick up anything smaller than a quarter."[142] By 1904, the Samoan performers had grown wise to the rules of the erotic marketplace at world fairs.

As on earlier tours, the performers made extra money by selling postcards and curiosity objects from their islands that they produced during show breaks. In these side shows of receiving tips and selling curios, performative labor enabled other forms of paid labor and additional opportunities for profit. To be sure, Samoans and other Pacific Islanders had been selling native objects as souvenirs to visitors to their islands since the early nineteenth century. From this historical perspective, their sales at world fairs were a logical extension of this conscious participation in the commodification of Polynesian culture. And yet the fully commercialized setting in which the performers appeared in ethnographic shows lent these interstitial economic transactions a different flavor. If Samoan performers were already offering their cultural authenticity onstage, they continued to make money with it when the spotlights were off. By selling fine mats and other Samoan curios, the female troupe members actually received cash for work that went unpaid at home.

Besides selling curios, the performers used their spare time to explore different parts of the fairgrounds. Provided they remained in "native costume," they enjoyed free entry to all other shows on the Pike.[143] Samoan performers were particularly drawn to fellow Pacific Islanders and people under U.S. colonial rule, such as the Hawaiians, whose products were exhibited at the fair.[144] Since the Philippine Reservation was the largest exhibit at the fair, the Samoans probably ran into one of the thousand Filipino performers from time to time. What they talked about during these encounters (and in what language) remains unknown. Judging from earlier exchanges with the Hawaiian hula dancers in Chicago and Gumma the "warrior-queen" in Frankfurt, the Samoan performers must have been good listeners, equipped with an extraordinary curiosity for foreign cultures and languages. And on one of their strolls through the fair, the Samoans might have even come across a collection of plants from their home islands—part of the German Educational Exhibition in St. Louis.

When the fair drew to a close in December 1904, Moors continued the tour to other cities in the United States. For another year and a half, the troupe barnstormed the country from coast to coast, performing as much as twice a day.[145] As had happened on earlier tours, the Samoan women, in particular, became the objects of intense interest among male spectators, at times aggressively so. Following a series of incidents, Moors decided to set up more stringent rules to prevent Samoan women from socializing with the men in the audience. As a result, the women started dancing with their chins up in the air to prevent eye contact with unwanted suitors.[146] Samoan dancers had few problems incorporating Moors's disciplining measure and adapted their performances accordingly. After seven months in St. Louis and an additional eighteen months on the road, the Samoan troupe finally returned home in mid-1906.

Tamasese's Diplomatic Mission to Europe, 1910–1911

In the following years, both Moors and Marquardt tried to bring more Samoan troupes to Australia and Europe, but the German Colonial Office rejected their requests. It was not until 1910, when Marquardt, with strong support from Governor Solf, succeeded in organizing another Samoan tour to Europe. Starting in July 1909, Marquardt had begun lobbying the German Colonial Office by arguing that the Samoans saw themselves as Germans and should be allowed to visit Germany.[147] According to Marquardt, Samoans themselves were saying, "We are, after all, Germans. Why would anyone want to ban us from seeing Germany?"[148] In addition, another Samoan troupe in Germany would reinforce the benevolent reputation of the colonial administration, now in its tenth year of rule. At the time, Tupua Tamasese Lealofi I, who offered to lead the troupe, and his rival, Malietoa Tanumafili, clashed over the question of who would succeed Mataʻafa Iosefo as *aliʻi sili* (paramount chief). In light of these tensions, Solf reached an agreement with his superiors in Berlin by framing the tour as a diplomatic mission.[149] Marquardt received special permission to recruit another troupe only after Solf had begun to actively support a temporary lifting of the ban in Berlin.

Conflicts with the German Colonial Office did not end with this special permission granted to Marquardt. The terms of the labor contract that Marquardt offered his recruits in January 1910 caused another wave of criticism from Berlin. As with all earlier tours, travel expenses, accommodation, food, and even medical treatment were paid for. For their services, the Samoan performers were to receive 24 marks ($6) per month, with an additional 4 marks ($1) for performances on Sundays. Half of this monthly wage was to be paid every first of the month and the rest upon the troupe's return. This was, by far, the lowest monthly wage of all the Samoan tours. The contract also included wage cuts for breaches of contract if, for example, performers, who were referred to as Marquardt's "servants," refused to follow his orders or protested against the censorship of their correspondence to family and friends back home.[150] Furthermore, the performers were not allowed to wear European clothes, and the women among them could not cut their hair.[151]

The German Colonial Office took exception to several elements of the contract, especially the potential wage cuts and—remembering the premature return of Leasusu and Lealofi in summer 1890—the lack of a deposit in case of an early return home. Solf defended the terms of the contract as modeled on earlier versions and personally vouched for Marquardt's good record. In the end, the Samoan performers signed Marquardt's contract under the original terms and even spread rumors that the colonial administration would pay for Tamasese's travel expenses and probably had something special planned for him.[152] Not unlike the contract laborers from Melanesia and China who had come to Samoa to work on copra plantations, the Samoan performers' desire to travel, earn cash, and make new friends outweighed the strict labor discipline they would face on tour.

On February 10, 1910, a group of twenty-eight Samoans—ten men and eighteen women—left Apia for Hamburg via Sydney and London. Carefully selected by Tupua Tamasese Lealofi I himself, all performers came from high-ranking families whose individual names were, for the first time, listed in Marquardt's official show brochure.[153] Alongside Tamasese's wife Va'aiga and two daughters from earlier marriages, his son Mea'ole, who would become the first cohead of state of independent Samoa in 1962, joined the troupe.[154] Similar to the 1901 tour, the show program included dances, fights, *kava* preparation, rowing in outrigger canoes, and, as a popular addition, water-sliding on a specially constructed rock modeled on the waterfalls of Papas-eea.[155] Tupua Tamasese Lealofi I, like Tuvale before him, did not participate in these performances.

At the first stop, the Hamburg zoo, in May and June 1910, tens of thousands of visitors, including many school classes, came to see the Samoans slide down their replica waterfalls. Even more so than on earlier tours, the

Figure 11. Samoan women in Hagenbeck Zoo, Hamburg, Germany, 1910. Courtesy of Hilke Thode-Arora.

performers sold postcards showing portraits and Samoan scenes and kept the proceeds from these sales to themselves.[156] In late May, the Samoans took off their performer hats and toured the zoo themselves, feeding the giant and unfamiliar elephants. Defying their preconceived roles as exotic performers, the Samoans became interested spectators of another ethnographic show when they visited the premiere of the circus show Farmerleben (A farmer's life), then on tour in Hamburg, which featured scenes and stunts set in the American Wild West.[157]

For his part, Tupua Tamasese Lealofi I used his time to visit an old friend from Samoa who had retired to Hamburg: former DHPG manager Otto Riedel. Married to a Samoan-born wife, Riedel was surprised when Tamasese and his wife suddenly rang their doorbell. In his memoirs, Riedel recounted the scene:

> One day—we were then living on Adolphstraße—my wife and I heard some commotion at the front door. Our Hamburg maid gave a shrill scream, and a dark voice hollered into the house: "Bella! Bella!"—My wife [Bella Decker, born in Samoa] rushed outside. There there stood Tamasese and his second wife Vaainga [sic]. The huge Samoan simply pushed our maid aside when he was sure that the Riedels were living here and then rushed towards my wife and me. Tamasese envisioned his trip to Germany a little different from his managers. He probably looked at it as a kind of visit with new friends. He did not like the fact that he would be shown in zoos, the more so as he was not housed adequately. Marquardt apparently did not want him to come close to me. But Tamasese and his wife simply jumped into a car and told the Hamburg driver: "Otto Riedel!" He could not imagine that there would be anybody in Hamburg who did not know me. The driver, with whom Tamasese naturally could only communicate through gestures, reacted very wisely. He looked into a phone book, found my address there, and brought his exotic guests right there where they wanted to go.[158]

Riedel himself agreed with Tamasese's disgust at being exhibited in zoos, feeling that "good faith was betrayed here."[159] In any case, Riedel was happy to see Tamasese, as was his wife, who immediately started speaking Samoan with the unexpected guests. While they stayed in Hamburg, Tupua Tamasese

Lealofi I and his wife would visit the Riedels' home several times, prompting Riedel to admire "the self-assurance with which these Samoans found their way around [in Germany]."[160] While on earlier trips the Samoan travelers had made new friends with Hawaiian hula dancers in Chicago and Gumma in Frankfurt, Tamasese was keen on seeing old friends again in Hamburg.

After a series of stops at zoos in Frankfurt, Cologne, Breslau, and Dresden, the Samoan troupe set up their exhibition at one of the most famous entertainment fairs in Germany: the Oktoberfest in Munich.[161] For the entire two weeks of the beer festival's centennial, the Samoans had a native village set up on a huge separate exhibition space, north of the Theresienwiese, where they rowed on a small lake, slid down rocks, and roasted pigs. The Samoans competed with other more or less exotic attractions at the Oktoberfest, such as a show featuring dwarfs and giants, an agricultural exhibition (including cows and pigs), an airship, and a so-called Eskimo troupe.[162] Carl Gabriel, the organizer of the Samoa in Munich show, had complained about the presence of this other troupe, which had been arranged by a rival impresario. The Munich city administration, however, would hear none of it.[163] Despite this direct competition, Gabriel's Samoa show turned out to be a huge success. A well-known actor and experienced impresario based in Munich, Gabriel operated Hammers Panoptikum, where Tuvale's troupe had performed in April 1901, and had organized a successful Tunis show together with Carl Marquardt in Munich in 1904.[164] Gabriel had probably relied on his old contact Marquardt to bring the Samoans to Munich.

On September 26, 1910, the Samoan troupe received a guest of honor: Prince Regent Luitpold of Bavaria. For two hours, Luitpold strolled through the Samoan Village and chatted with the performers. Tupua Tamasese Lealofi I even explained the intricacies of Samoan tattooing to Luitpold, who in return bestowed on Tamasese a centennial medal and a golden ring.[165] Later on, Tamasese met with the future Bavarian king Ludwig III, and gave him a fine mat, a *kava* bowl, and a fan.[166] Like Tuvale before him, Tamasese understood his travel to Europe as a diplomatic mission and welcomed every opportunity to exchange gifts and speeches with Germany's political leadership. He succeeded in securing meetings with high-level officials in Munich and, more importantly, with the top brass in Berlin.

After spending the three-month winter quarter in a villa in Joachimsthal outside Berlin, the Samoan troupe returned to Castan's Panoptikum in Berlin for a two-month stint in February 1911. Toward the end of their stay in Berlin, Wilhelm Solf—former governor of German Samoa and current head of the Colonial Office—hosted a lavish dinner in the posh Hotel Adlon, which more than one hundred select guests attended. To represent Solf's credentials as a skilled colonial administrator, the Samoans gave a special performance at the dinner.[167] Afterward, Tupua Tamasese Lealofi I was even more impatient to see the German emperor and reiterated his request to Solf. Tamasese's incessant pressure finally paid off on May 26, 1911, when he and three aides (including the old *matai* Ai'ono) were invited to a spring parade of the German military in Tempelhof. Donning a brand-new tailor-made white suit that had cost 70 marks ($17.50), Tamasese was introduced to Wilhelm II by Solf. Tamasese kissed the emperor's hand and struck up a friendly conversation with him. To make this chat among royals possible, Tamasese's wife Va'aiga interpreted the kaiser's German into Samoan.[168] Central to Samoan diplomatic etiquette, Tupua Tamasese Lealofi I handed two fine mats to Wilhelm II, who later reciprocated by sending Tamasese his portrait and a gold watch. Tamasese also gave a speech in which he stressed the lasting friendship between Samoa and Germany. The Berlin press lauded Tamasese, calling Samoans good carriers of colonial propaganda.[169]

Despite this instrumentalization for colonial purposes, Tamasese never forgot that day and, allegedly, even continued to believe in a German victory until the very end of World War I.[170] In an interview with a Sydney newspaper on his way back to Samoa, Tamasese remembered his encounter with German royalty in exuberant terms: "Everybody was very kind to us. I was given a seat in one of the Royal carriages, and was taken to one of the Kaiser's castles. It was wonderful."[171] He also said that he was very impressed by the size of the German army and the electric trams in Berlin.[172] Critics of the ban on allowing German colonial subjects to travel for exhibition purposes were certainly glad to hear Tamasese's remarks. After all, it was they who had argued as early as the 1890s that visiting ethnographic troupes from the German colonies would be impressed by Germany's technological and cultural superiority and, consequently, think twice about armed resistance. Tamasese, for his part, while duly impressed by the size of the German army, pursued his own diplomatic agenda while on tour. Following Samoan traditions, Tamasese, like Tuvale in 1901, insisted on meeting with his aristocratic counterparts in Germany eye to eye. With a mix of pressure and politeness, he managed to turn the tour of an ethnographic troupe, originally designed to present Samoans as "kindred spirits" to German audiences, into a *malaga* among equals.[173] On their way home, the performers were chatting "pleasantly enough of the long 'malaga' (journey) they had made to the Fatherland."[174]

After almost a year abroad, the Samoan performers returned home on November 22, 1911.[175] According to family memory, Pu'emalo, Tamasese's daughter from his first marriage, enjoyed her travels through Europe immensely and would have liked to stay longer. Her reluctance to go back to Samoa probably had something to do with the fact that she had fallen in love on tour. Pu'emalo and Eteloma had become a couple while traveling through Europe and were expecting a child when they returned to Samoa. Like Naitua and Tuvale before them and Faagalo and Phineas even earlier, Pu'emalo and Eteloma had found love in unexpected places far from home.[176]

The Samoan Village at the Panama-Pacific International Exposition in San Francisco, 1915

Half a year into a world war that brought a new colonial power to Western Samoa, another Samoan troupe left Apia to perform abroad. Celebrating the opening of the Panama Canal under U.S. control, the Panama-Pacific International Exposition began in San Francisco in March 1915.[177] Since German Samoa had come under New Zealand military administration in the first weeks of the war, chances for recruiting performers there were slim. Instead, the American impresario Richard Schneidewind went to American Samoa to put together a group of Samoan performers for San Francisco. Born in Detroit, Schneidewind had been a private in the Medical Corps of the U.S. Army during the War of 1898. He stayed in Manila working as a mail clerk until he was fired for smuggling.[178] After visiting the Igorot Village at the Louisiana Purchase Exposition in St. Louis in 1904, Schneidewind founded the Filipino Exhibition Company, which brought three separate Igorot troupes to the United States between 1905 and 1908. In 1913, he cheated a troupe of fifty-five Igorots, whom he had brought to the Ghent Exposition in Belgium, out of their contractual wages (a meager $5 a month) and simply abandoned the group, eight of whom died there. Responding to a protest letter sent by two Igorots to President Wilson in October 1913, the U.S. consul in Ghent took charge of the troupe and eventually paid for their passage back to Manila.[179] Schneidewind's ruthlessness in Ghent harked back to Cunningham's irresponsible management of the Australian Aboriginals and the first Samoan tour to the United States and Europe in 1889. Partly in response to this scandal, the Philippine Assembly prohibited further exhibitions of Filipinos in 1914.[180]

In early February 1915, the Samoan troupe under Schneidewind's management boarded the steamer *Niagara* in Pago Pago bound for Vancouver via Honolulu. The troupe consisted of twenty-three Samoans: thirteen men and ten women.[181] According to the passenger list, eight of the performers were married and all were listed as U.S. citizens, which they technically were not.[182] In stark contrast to the 1904 tour to St. Louis, when impresario Moors had chartered a whole ship for the performers and their equipment, the troupe traveled to San Francisco third class. It was not without irony that they were on their way to an exposition that celebrated the opening of the Panama Canal as a crucial passageway to U.S. political and economic claims in the Pacific.[183]

When they arrived in San Francisco on February 16, the performers set about constructing a Samoan Village in the fair's "Joy Zone"—a staple of U.S. world fairs since Chicago's highly successful Midway Plaisance.[184] As at earlier fairs, the Samoans performed dances and songs, including "It's a Long, Long Way to Tipperary"—a song that had become popular among British soldiers during the world war that overshadowed the fair from the start.

According to American author Laura Ingalls Wilder, who visited the fair in September 1915, the Samoan performers "all seemed very much pleased with themselves that they could sing it and all smiled when they began."[185] Wilder went on to note that the Samoans "seemed cold, poor things . . . when they left the stage wrapped up in heavy bathrobes."[186] For the freezing Samoans, San Francisco was a long way from their tropical home. As early as April 1915, the Samoan performers had requested permission to surround their exhibition stand with glass. As the assistant director for concessions and admissions noted, the Samoans "cannot stand the cold and several of them have contracted severe illness from exposure."[187] It is not recorded if the permission was granted, but judging from Wilder's comments half a year later, the Samoan performers had to wear heavy bathrobes to shield themselves from the notoriously chilly winds hitting San Francisco from the Pacific.

Figure 12. Samoan dance, Panama-Pacific International Exposition, San Francisco, 1915.
San Francisco History Center, San Francisco Public Library (AAF-0037).

The Samoan troupe was, however, not alone in San Francisco's cold. As in Chicago, fellow Polynesians from Hawai'i were present at the San Francisco fair, this time even with a village of their own. In it, visitors could admire reproductions of Waikiki beach and the Kilauea volcanic crater, while scantily clad Hawaiian women dove into the water.[188] If the organizers of native villages, such as the Samoan and Hawaiian villages in San Francisco, promised visitors a titillating journey through time and space, the Polynesian performers themselves experienced their journeys no less dramatically. The Samoan performers in San Francisco again mingled with their counterparts from Hawai'i, as they had in Chicago more than two decades earlier. Backstage, in the shabby quarters where the performers were living, Polynesian languages, food, and dances merged into an alternative middle ground of colonized people.[189]

Besides the Samoan and Hawaiian villages, fairgoers could walk through a replica of Beijing's Forbidden City. All parts were shipped from China and then reassembled on the other side of the Pacific by Chinese laborers, who, according to a local newspaper, "wore American clothes [and] did their work effectively with ineffective tools—the best test of good workmen."[190] Chinese workers were helping to build the infrastructure of empire not only on copra plantations and dock stations in Samoa but also on the fairground in San Francisco. If skilled labor unions and fair organizers had agreed to what became known as the "Pax Panama-Pacifica" ahead of the fair's opening, the thousands of unskilled fair workers, including the various ethnic performers, had their own battles to fight.[191]

In line with the fair's representation of labor was the miniature model of the Panama Canal itself. Spread over five acres, it allowed visitors to watch miniature ships pass through the model canal as they listened to educational lectures, emphasizing technology's triumph over nature.[192] However, the workers who built the canal in Panama—as well as its miniature model in San Francisco—played no visible part in the exhibition.[193] Similarly, when Samoans were building their own villages on the fairground, their material labor played no part in the performative labor it enabled and that, in turn, represented other forms of material labor, such as picking coconuts from trees. This representation of "traditional" forms of labor also helped transport racial stereotypes, which justified the ongoing exploitation of workers in U.S. colonies such as Samoa.

When the Panama-Pacific Exposition came to an end in December 1915, the Samoan troupe returned home to a world transformed. Global war had disrupted the copra economies of both American Samoa and New Zealand–occupied German Samoa. Copra prices in the city from where the performers had returned were at an all-time low. While the Samoan performers struggled to find their bearings in a newly unstable economic and political environment, their manager Schneidewind went back to his native Detroit to work as a cashier at a street railway company. He, too, had to look for new opportunities.

• • •

On long journeys on ships and railways, from Sydney to Hamburg and San Francisco to Chicago, the experience of communal traveling through unfamiliar territories united Samoans who went on tour abroad. During their travels, they discovered the joys of performing together and the empowering feeling of forming intimate yet fleeting communities with fellow colonized peoples. But the Samoans overseas also discovered that performing for Euro-American audiences was hard work that demanded discipline and sometimes created conflicts within the group as well as without. Euro-American impresarios saw profit as the only measure of success, while fellow troupe members tested established hierarchies of rank and gender far away from the social control of their home islands. On their global *malaga*, Samoan performers transcended the limitations of colonial globality imposed on them and fashioned their own way of navigating the world based on shared Oceanian values and practices. Going abroad to earn money and respect, Samoan performers were the precursors of today's labor diasporas overseas, stretching from Auckland to Honolulu to Los Angeles.

As they crisscrossed the globe, Samoans extended their *malaga* from their home islands and the Pacific world to Europe and North America. The cultural tradition of going on *malaga* differentiated Samoan performers from other ethnographic troupes of the time. Most comparable to the Samoan traveling parties were the Hawaiian hula dancers who toured the world around the same time and encountered their fellow Polynesians in Chicago in 1893 and in San Francisco in 1915. As Adria Imada argues, "Hawaiian performers were not merely passive objects in Euro-American tourist economies, but resisted and negotiated with colonization through their own 'traveling cultures' and consumer practices. They carved out their own homes, political expressions, and diasporic networks in view and out of view of foreign audiences."[194] Like their Samoan counterparts, Hawaiian hula dancers preferred their participation in a commodified spectacle over the alternatives at home: the hard toil of plantation labor or low-level service jobs.[195] And if the commodification of Hawaiian hula performances by the end of the nineteenth century had turned dancers into wage laborers in a capitalist spectacle, the embeddedness of hula in Hawaiian culture set equally firm limits to its commodification.[196] Samoans, too, defended the integrity of the cultural practices they performed in front of Euro-American audiences, even as they seized the new opportunities for travel, money, and prestige.

While the Samoan performers worked far from home, they shared many similarities with their fellow workers back home. Most obviously, their packed show schedules, sometimes with up to eight performances a day, revealed the physical demands of performative labor. At every stop, the performers had to build their own accommodations and stages on which they would reenact the physical labor of collecting coconuts for the entertainment of visitors. The labor contracts the performers signed before going on tour introduced a strict regime of labor discipline and managerial control reminiscent of plantation labor in Samoa. The workscape of the ethnographic show might have been mobile and far away from Deeken's whip in Tapatapao, but it nevertheless limited the movement of the performative laborers beyond the impresario's eyes. Finally, going on tour with an ethnographic troupe was a gateway to and from other jobs in the colonial economy in Samoa. While the performative labor on stage was, in part, colonial service, moving to other positions in the colonial administration back in Samoa was relatively easy and common. Several show veterans—such as Phineas and Tuvale—joined the colonial service upon their return to Samoa. Driven by its own dynamics, performative labor in ethnographic shows remained intimately connected with other forms of labor in the islands.

4

BUILDERS

When Samoa came under formal German and American control in 1900, the world around the islands was growing smaller. Steamships carried people, goods, and information ever farther. Trade interests went hand in hand with military planning of the growing naval forces of Imperial Germany and the United States.[1] After the War of 1898, the U.S. Navy established coaling stations in the Philippines, Guam, and Hawai'i. For its part, the Imperial German Navy set up its Pacific fleet in the treaty port of Kiaochow, southeast of Beijing. One of the leading German naval strategists, Admiral Alfred von Tirpitz, argued in 1899 that the Samoan islands would be of "great strategic value to the German navy, as an important stopping place on the voyage from Kiaochow, via our possessions in the South Seas, to South America."[2] And when plans for building a canal through the isthmus of Panama resurfaced at the beginning of the twentieth century, the strategic importance of coaling stations was increasingly hard to ignore. Euro-American competition for control over Samoa was fueled by and subsequently fueled the expansion of colonial infrastructure, such as steamships, telegraph cables, and wireless radio.

In the South Pacific and elsewhere, technologies of communication and power projection were not simply "tools of empire."[3] By contrast, the expansion of infrastructure in such places as Samoa actively produced colonial spaces dependent on access to markets for cash crops and vulnerable to gunboat diplomacy. As historians of Euro-American imperialism have argued, infrastructure was central to colonial state building more broadly, from the U.S.-occupied Philippines to German Southwest Africa.[4] Both German and U.S. officials saw the building of colonial infrastructure as a way to impose modern ways of life on Samoans and other colonized people. Since Germany and the United States entered the colonial scramble at a time when new technologies were becoming available, integrating colonies like Samoa into global transportation and communication lines reinforced their claim to "enlightened" colonial rule.[5] New transportation and communication links in the colonies also redirected the circulation of people and commodities in the service of Euro-American capital.[6] In the closing decades of the nineteenth century, rising consumer demand for tropical fruit in Europe and North America required improvements in transportation and communications in the global plantation belt. In German Samoa, settlers and traders began lobbying the colonial administration to boost trade by expanding shipping and telegraph lines. Across the channel, U.S. Navy officials in Tutuila were concerned less with the circulation of commodities and more with the projection of naval power. In both places, infrastructure was key to the success of the colonial project as a whole.

Colonial officials welcomed the improved communication lines with their superiors in distant metropoles, even as they worried about the workers who built them. The annual reports by German and American colonial officials were filled with references to the various construction projects underway on the islands, but they frequently relied on the passive voice to distract attention from the actual workers who were building the infrastructure. Whereas the so-called labor question played a prominent role in debates on Samoan plantations, workers figured less explicitly in reports about the building of new infrastructure. In the eyes of colonial officials, the latest technologies, such as steamships and radio stations, operated by an invisible hand. In reality, the economic and military significance of colonial infrastructure turned those who built it into important actors. Not only did construction workers contribute their labor to extract economic and strategic value for foreign traders and military officials, but they also put this new infrastructure to their own uses.[7] The hundreds of Samoans, Melanesians, Micronesians, and Chinese who built the coaling station in American Samoa and the wireless radio station in German Samoa developed a shared sense of exploitation as both colonized and working people. Even prison laborers who were forced to work for the colonial administrations found moments of sociality with fellow workers and relatives, to the anger of white settlers. As workers helped build the material infrastructure of Samoa, they created structures of solidarity that brought them closer to one another, across both racial and colonial boundaries.

Over time, the building of material infrastructure in Samoa exposed the ways in which environmental, political, and economic vulnerabilities intersected. Mudslides became a more frequent occurrence as workers cut into coastal hillsides to fill up areas for new buildings for the U.S. naval station in Tutuila. The extension of shipping facilities in the shallow harbor of Apia likewise increased the risk of damage from seasonal cyclones. And the formal integration of German and American Samoa into wider circuits of colonial naval power, including regular visits from German and American warships, raised the stakes of large-scale Samoan resistance against colonial rule. Steamships and telegraph lines allowed colonial officials in the Pacific not only to communicate better with their colleagues in faraway capitals but also to request military support in the form of gunboats. The sheer vastness of the Pacific Ocean made long-distance technologies such as the telegraph and wireless radio all the more significant for colonial control. In this way, Samoa's integration into global communication networks shifted the balance of power toward colonial administrations.

As environmental, political, and economic vulnerabilities intertwined, workers in Samoa gained new opportunities to delay and disrupt the smooth workings of ports, roads, and telegraph lines. Workers fortifying old roads or building new ones knew the natural environment better than anyone else, including their own employers. This familiarity with the local terrain—the firmness of the soil, the availability of shade, the existence of dense bush— proved to be useful knowledge in the hands of workers seeking to escape hard manual labor. Workers engaged in the monotonous work of maintaining government buildings and roads, for instance, found comfort in regular interactions with familiar parts of the natural environment and with fellow workers.

At the same time, the infrastructure workscape challenged workers in unique ways. In contrast to plantation or service labor, most of the construction labor was short term, often a matter of weeks or months. Contracts on plantations lasted three years or more, while careers in the colonial service sometimes transcended generations. Thrown together for much shorter periods, construction workers had fewer opportunities to get to know one

another and organize collective action. In addition, construction workers relied more heavily on imported machines and techniques than did plantation
workers, whose agricultural skills made them desirable to plantation owners
in the first place. Given the short-term and more mechanized nature of construction labor, bonds of solidarity among workers took longer to form and
only occasionally bridged racial lines. A strike in Tutuila in 1905 against wage
cuts remained one of the rare direct confrontations between a cross-racial
coalition of construction workers and their employers.

Carrying Coal to Pago Pago

In the context of the new navalism of the 1880s, Samoa gained in importance
for the U.S. Navy because of its strategic location between Hawai'i and Australia and its potential as a coaling station for the expanding steamship fleet.[8]
In 1872, U.S. Navy commander Richard Meade had negotiated a treaty with
Samoan *matai* that guaranteed the right to build a coaling station in the port
of Pago Pago on the eastern island of Tutuila. But given the growing influence of other imperial powers in the region—including Great Britain and
France, and later Germany and Japan—the U.S. Navy's claims on one of the
finest harbors in the South Pacific were hotly disputed. In 1887, the U.S. Navy
secured the right to establish a coaling and repair station in Pearl Harbor
from Hawaiian king Kalakaua, but the search for other useful naval bases
continued. In the summer of 1898, the General Board of the U.S. Navy found
the location of Pago Pago "so suitable in case of operations in that quarter,
that . . . political possession of the whole island in which the port is, or at least
of ground sufficient for fortifications, is desirable."[9] Military planners and
politicians became even more alert after 1898, when the United States annexed Pacific islands from the Philippines and Guam to Wake Island and
Hawai'i. During the war against Spain, U.S. admiral George Dewey was
forced to purchase British coal in Hong Kong before attacking Manila because
there was no U.S. coaling station in the area. A year later, Bartlett Tripp, the
U.S. member of a commission sent to Samoa, urged policy makers in Washington to keep Pago Pago as the "Gibraltar of the Pacific."[10]

Later that year, the Berlin Treaty united Savai'i and Upolu into a German colony, while the United States was guaranteed the harbor of Pago
Pago in Tutuila. Pago Pago harbor was one of the best in the entire Pacific.

With an anchorage depth of over forty feet, Pago Pago harbor stretches nearly two miles inland along a rectangular bend to the west. Millions of years ago, the harbor formed the crater of a volcano, whose ridges today rise up to twenty-three hundred feet from sea level. Except for the occasional cyclone or tsunami, Pago Pago harbor offered an ideal anchorage for the steamships of the late nineteenth century. Anchored westward, a surveyor noted, the harbor could accommodate a dozen ships, all "well protected against wind and swell."[11]

By contrast, the new German colony to the west lacked a well-protected harbor. While Apia harbor was equipped with a short wharf and leading lights, it was not as deep as Pago Pago's and its entryway was a mere third of a mile wide. Besides a coral reef that divided the harbor in two, Apia was exposed to the north to cyclones, such as the one that hit in 1889 and sank several German and American warships. Apia harbor usually stored around one thousand tons of coal, but loading sometimes proved difficult due to heavy seas. The German colonial administration estimated that approximately 2 million British pounds ($400,000) would be needed to make the harbor safe and, given the more suitable harbor of Pago Pago nearby, decided not to go ahead with the improvement of Apia port.[12]

Initially, the U.S. Navy refrained from investing in the expansion of infrastructure in Pago Pago. After Meade secured the right to establish a coaling station in Pago Pago in 1872, little construction took place. For over two decades, coal was sent only sporadically to Pago Pago "because it had been deemed more advantageous and economical to purchase coal when required by vessels in those waters."[13] Most coal for Pago Pago and Apia came from the U.S. East Coast, from Cardiff in Wales, or from closer-by Australia and New Zealand. By 1897, the U.S. Navy had purchased "certain lands on the shores of Pago Pago to be used as a Naval station" and had successfully surveyed the harbor.[14] In fall 1898, a civil engineer was sent to Tutuila to purchase additional land for the erection of a coaling station and other facilities.[15] Six months before the Berlin Treaty granted official recognition to U.S. interests in the eastern islands, the expansion of the navy facilities began. In February 1899, Healy, Tibbetts & Co.—a company based in San Francisco—was awarded the contract to oversee the construction and began sending construction material, manufactured in Pittsburgh, to Pago Pago.[16]

Samoan workers did most of the dirty work for the U.S. Navy in Tutuila. To increase anchorage and construction space, they added a huge land fill at

Swimming Point in Pago Pago harbor. Over the years, workers transported hundreds of thousands of cubic feet of soil from a cut in the hills just behind Swimming Point. This "fill dirt" was usually drawn from the subsoil and contained little organic matter to prevent the settling of the soil over time. Fill dirt was a mixture of rocks, stones, and sand, which made it difficult to transport. To alleviate the burden of manual labor, workers laid tracks for a small cable car from the cut to the land fill to help them move the soil.[17] Cable cars soon became the preferred way to lessen the cost of hauling heavy material to construction sites in Tutuila. In contrast to the iconic ninety-five-ton Bucyrus steam shovels used in the Panama Canal Zone around the same time, workers in Pago Pago had to rely on more basic tools.[18]

On the new land fill, a series of new buildings were erected. The largest structures were two sheds that could store up to four thousand tons of coal for navy ships calling at Tutuila.[19] In front of the coal sheds, a broad, steel-reinforced coal wharf was built into the bay to allow for the loading of coal. In addition to these coaling facilities, the land fill provided space for a copra shed, a storehouse, and, by 1904, an icehouse and a carpenter and blacksmith shop. From the start, members of the U.S. Navy stationed in Tutuila or visiting on warships participated in construction and maintenance.

Commandant Benjamin Franklin Tilley, the first naval governor of the U.S. naval station in Tutuila, personally brought additional construction material, such as wooden piles and timber, by ship from Auckland in February 1900. According to Tilley, construction work proceeded slower than expected, partly because of heavy rains and partly because the U.S. contractor had problems with its workforce. "The climate at this season," Tilley reported to Washington, "is rather hard on the workmen and it is difficult to make them do much. Quite a number of the contractor's men have become dissatisfied and have gone home and he now has but twelve of the party of twenty-five workmen who came out from the United States last summer."[20] To fill this labor shortage, the construction company recruited Samoan workers for the comparatively low daily wage of 1 dollar. At the same time, common laborers from the U.S. mainland earned around 2 dollars per day.[21] Tilley noted that the contractor did not "know how to get along with the natives and at times they refuse to work for him although they are always glad to work for the Government at the same price." Despite these delays, Tilley was optimistic that the coal wharf and shed would be completed by September 1901.[22]

As in neighboring German Samoa, the management of workers posed a
threat to the plans of colonial officials. Tilley's comment hinted at competing notions of work between Samoans and Americans. While the U.S. contractor supervising the building of the coaling station expected Samoans to
simply follow instructions, the workers themselves had different ideas about
their work conditions. Given a long tradition of cooperative work in Samoan
villages, construction workers for the U.S. Navy demanded more than just a
living wage; they wanted to be treated in a fair and respectful way as well. A
foreign contractor who did not "know how to get along" with them violated
a crucial principle of Samoan culture. Even though little is known about the
precise details of these conflicts, Samoan workers in neighboring German
Samoa engaged in wage labor only in times of need and under conditions
similar to established ways of cooperative work. The U.S. contractor brought
in from the mainland by Tilley did not take into account these significant
cultural differences. Samoan workers welcomed earning cash, but refused to
work when they felt disrespected. Tilley's final remark that Samoans were "always glad to work" for the naval government revealed more about the navy's
paternalistic self-image than the realities in the colony. In several instances,
Samoans refused to work for the naval administration, especially when they
felt mutual trust had been betrayed.

Contrary to Tilley's plans, the coaling station was not yet finished in September 1901. Commandant Uriel Sebree, who replaced Tilley as naval governor in November 1901, expected the dredging of coal to be completed by
the next steamer in mid-January 1902. Sebree went on to note: "Some grading has been done on the Station by native labor. Forty to fifty natives being
employed at a time, per week. They have been taken from the different villages each week."[23] The Samoan workers faced a daunting task. In March 1901
alone, they moved more than seventy thousand cubic feet of soil from the
coastline at Swimming Point and dumped it in the land fill. At the same time,
forty workers were busy grading the area around Observation Point to the
east. They were blasting out stone and removing material that had been ex-
cavated before but had subsequently rolled down and piled up.[24]

American Samoa's tropical climate continued to defy plans by U.S. Navy
officials to remodel it for their own purposes. Mudslides were a common danger to workers and the maintenance of buildings, roads, and docks. Tutuila's
tropical vegetation posed an ongoing threat to human-made infrastructure.

"A great deal of labor is necessary," a 1908 report noted, "to prevent the quick growing tropical vegetation from over-running everything." To domesticate nature, the report went on, human labor was in constant demand: "A gang of men are almost continually employed removing the debris and rotting vegetable matter carried into the station by the excessive rains from the steep surrounding hills."[25] This uphill battle against American Samoa's natural environment was waged predominantly by Samoan workers. In contrast to short-term construction labor, maintenance labor allowed workers a more regular interaction with the natural environment and with fellow workers.

In addition to their efforts to contain nature, navy officials sought to manage Samoan labor power. As Sebree noted in his report, workers were recruited from different villages each week. By rotating Samoan workers, navy officials ensured that regular maintenance and plantation work continued alongside the navy's own construction projects. Grading work remained a continuous necessity as well as a problem in Tutuila. In 1903, grading had to be discontinued for several months because not enough workers could be found. The arduous nature of the work was certainly part of the reason why not many Samoans or other Pacific Islanders could be recruited.[26] Despite these difficulties, workers hired by the naval government completed a concrete dam that formed a new water reservoir in December 1904.[27] By 1905, when workers finished two additional land fills and a causeway to Goat Island, "all grading was done by dump cars filled and operated by hand."[28] The use of machines like dump and trolley cars distinguished the construction work from plantation work, where mechanization remained limited to copra kilns.

In February 1902, work on the coaling station was finally complete. Along with delays in the shipment of material and the labor shortage, navy engineers and their workers also faced other challenges. The sea bottom around Swimming Point, it turned out, was "peculiarly unstable." As a result, the wharf had to be built twice. Overall, the costs for material and labor for the coal sheds, the wharf, and the storehouse amounted to over $282,000 (roughly $8.6 million in 2021 dollars).[29] But the completion of these major construction projects did not spell an end to the labor shortage.

Securing labor remained a constant problem throughout the first decade of formal U.S. colonial rule over Tutuila. In August 1903, government carpenters were busy working on the foundations of a new courthouse and other office buildings. The new courthouse next to the old government house at Pago Pago harbor occupied an area of eighty by seventy-six feet and, according to a newspaper report, was set to be "quite a handsome structure."[30] Rumor had it that Governor E. B. Underwood would even follow Samoan custom and give the workers a "blow-out," with tea and cake upon move-in. It is not known if Underwood followed through on this promise, but only a few months later he offered a more pessimistic view of the labor situation in Tutuila.

In November 1903, Underwood complained about the "great scarcity of labor" that thwarted construction plans for necessary buildings, including an additional coal shed, an office building, and a quarter for officers. To tackle these pressing construction projects, Underwood reported, only a handful of skilled workers were available: "We have two very good carpenters, who came out from the United States under contract last February, one good white carpenter, and two fair half-castes, carpenters. Other so-called carpenters have been given trial but have been found to be lazy, indifferent, or migratory."[31] Samoans had more promising ways to gain their living—by cutting copra or by joining the colonial service as soldiers and clerks. According to this list of skilled workers in Tutuila, white and Black carpenters from the U.S. mainland continued to arrive in Tutuila under contract, relieving some of the labor shortage.[32] These newly arrived contract workers complicated colonial hierarchies of race and status. If African American construction workers faced racial discrimination at home, their U.S. citizenship elevated their status among Samoan and Melanesian workers in Tutuila. As seen from Pago Pago harbor, U.S. labor history at the turn of the twentieth century looks more complex.

Racial hierarchies shaped Underwood's perception of the relative skills of the workers. The three good or very good carpenters were probably white Americans, while two mixed-race carpenters were described as "fair." Given Underwood's racialized choice of words, the other "so-called carpenters" were local Samoans who did not meet the governor's expectations. The fact that Underwood characterized them as "lazy, indifferent, or migratory" has to be seen in connection with long-standing racial stereotypes about Samoan indolence. According to the idea of Native indolence, Samoans, like other colonized people at the time, were lazy, unreliable, and inconstant workers who could not be tasked with complex and long-term labor projects. Colo-

nial officials in nearby German Samoa similarly portrayed Samoans as living in a tropical paradise in which work was superfluous.[33] Around the same
time, the government newspaper in German Samoa observed, with uncon-
cealed schadenfreude, that U.S. Navy officials could not motivate Samoans
to work for them. According to the newspaper, even the fuelwood needed for
the warship stationed in Pago Pago had to be imported from Apia.[34]

In contrast to these racialized notions of labor, Samoans had developed a
complex system of constructing houses. Samoan carpenters were organized
into craft guilds, mirroring family structures with apprentices (*tufuga fa'i
fale*) and master builders (*matai tufuga fa'i fale*). Carpentry was a hereditary
profession, but apprentices had to prove their worth in order to be elected to
the guild in their home districts.[35] Master builders received their title through
seniority and practical experience. Around 1900, between fifty and seventy
master builders lived in Samoa, leading their own craft guilds. Master carpenters, who were able to make durable houses and canoes, enjoyed a status
similar to *matai* and were allowed to drink *kava* right after them.

The construction of a Samoan house was a major challenge of organizing
labor and material. For the duration of the construction (an average of nine
months for a medium-sized house), carpenters and their apprentices moved
into their patrons' homes and received food and accommodations in return
for their services. A mutual and sacred contract was entered into between a
carpenter and a *matai*, whose family had to cut and transport wood for the
house to be constructed.[36] The reciprocal expectations of labor, food, and accommodations in exchange for the construction skills of the carpenter team
had to be honored by both sides, otherwise a construction project might easily be abandoned halfway. Samoan carpenters thus had considerable if un-
spoken control over their work process, payment, and personal dignity.[37]

This form of organizing construction labor—including strikes, the taboo-
ing of employers, and the expectation of immediate rewards—distinguished
Samoa from other Polynesian societies.[38] Samoan carpenters proved flexible
enough to adapt their long-standing traditions to the changing times. When
copra prices plunged dramatically after World War I, the carpenter guild departed from tradition and decided to loosen the requirement of lavish feasts
during the construction process. As a result, Samoan clients could better afford the heavy expenses involved in the building of a new house, and the
construction business soon picked up again.[39]

Communal construction projects, based on reciprocity and respect, clashed with the public works policies of German and American colonial officials. Given their efficient system of organizing labor that guaranteed a steady income and high social status, Samoan carpenters did not depend on joining the construction projects of the U.S. Navy. Dismissive comments, such as those by Underwood, provided evidence for this simple fact. In any case, colonial administrators in both American and German Samoa relied on Samoan carpenters to build the necessary material infrastructure. Despite such negative views of Samoan work skills, Samoan carpenters successfully built a new church house for the London Missionary Society in 1902, a lumber shed and boathouse in Tutuila in 1906, and a new hospital in Moto'otua in 1912.[40]

Samoans and Americans were not the only workers in Tutuila. The naval administration also employed a number of "colored laborers" in construction projects. These might have been African American workers under contract for the navy but were more likely migrants from other parts of the Pacific, such as Niue, Vanuatu, the Solomon Islands, and New Guinea. The 1903 census also listed a dozen "Asians," eight of whom worked on the station ship, and five "Africans" (or African Americans), four of whom worked on the station ship.[41] Since the 1870s, thousands of migrants from Melanesia and other parts of Polynesia had been coming to Upolu to work on copra and cocoa plantations. In the early 1900s, some were finding their way to neighboring Tutuila in search of work and freedom from the harsh discipline on large-scale plantations in German Samoa. Overall, navy officials preferred workers from Niue over those from other parts of the Pacific but still found them to be not "very profitable."[42]

In contrast to German Samoa, there were no Chinese workers in American Samoa at the beginning of the twentieth century. Since the 1880s, anti-immigration legislation had excluded Chinese migrants from entering several states on the U.S. West Coast and Hawai'i.[43] The Chinese Exclusion Act, passed by Congress in 1882, also applied to U.S. territories, such as American Samoa. In 1910, Governor John F. Parker made this legal bar to Chinese migrants explicit: "There are no Chinese inhabitants [in American Samoa]," he noted, "the Chinese Exclusion Act having been declared by the High Court to be in force at this Station."[44] Given this hostile climate toward immigration from China, navy officials in Tutuila had few alternatives but to rely on workers from other parts of the Pacific.

In November 1904, a group of Samoan government officials asked Governor Underwood why "colored laborers in the employ of the government" did not pay more than two dollars in taxes, even though they were using large amounts of money from the government. Samoan leaders were concerned that the tax burden was not equally distributed among the inhabitants of American Samoa and petitioned the naval government to increase taxes on foreign workers. Underwood defended the status quo by arguing that these workers did not receive "the same benefits and advantages from the government that Samoans do."[45] As guest workers, the Melanesians and non-Samoan Polynesians who lived and worked in Tutuila helped expand U.S. colonial rule and therefore aroused the anger of Samoan taxpayers.

The debate about the collection and proper use of tax revenue foreshadowed one of the major complaints of the anti-colonial Mau movement in the early 1920s, when Mau leaders would accuse U.S. Navy officials even more directly of misusing the funds collected from Samoan taxpayers. The Samoan petition to raise taxes on foreign workers also pointed to the limits of inter-racial and interclass solidarity. If racial hierarchies shaped the perception of U.S. Navy officials, Samoan leaders entertained their own prejudices and animosities. While construction workers developed a sense of shared exploitation regardless of race, Samoan government officials were motivated by a different kind of class consciousness. As members of the colonial administration, Samoan government officials shared with their white American colleagues a top-down perspective on labor management. But at the same time, Samoan government officials realized that non-Samoan construction workers helped entrench U.S. Navy rule over the islands. Samoans who joined the colonial administration were acutely aware of other workers in the service of U.S. colonialism but grew blind to the class exploitation they all shared.

Protests against colonial rule revolved not only around claims over people and their labor power but also around claims over their lands. On one of the navy maps, the land fill on which the coal sheds were erected was marked as "reclaimed land." This act of reclamation had two sides: on the one hand, the coal sheds were erected on a man-made fill that "reclaimed" land from the ocean with soil from a nearby cut in the hills. On the other hand, the material act of reclamation of land had a symbolic dimension. Together with the wharf, copra shed, storehouse, and other buildings erected on this reclaimed

Figure 13. Flag Raising Day, Fagatogo, Tutuila, April 17, 1900.

National Archives and Records Administration, Washington, DC, RG 80, file 3931, box 34.

land, the coal sheds represented the basis for U.S. claims on Tutuila. Hence, the reclaiming of "native" lands to build a coaling station linked the construction of material infrastructure to U.S. political and military claims on the islands at large. A photograph portraying Flag Raising Day on April 17, 1900, provides visual evidence of the intertwined nature of reclamation.

As the photograph (Figure 13) shows, the official flag-raising ceremony took place right on top of the cut from which the soil for the land fill was drawn. Participants in the ceremony had filed up Sogelau Hill in Fagatogo before the Stars and Stripes went up. Below the ceremony, scores of Samoan workers and their American supervisors momentarily ceased their busy activities and watched the spectacle above. Most were dressed in white shirts and black *lava lavas,* and some were holding umbrellas to protect themselves against the sun. The angle of the photograph draws a straight line of vision from the wharf's steel bars at sea level, across the cable-car tracks where the backs of workers reinforce the view upward, to the top of the cut. There, a group of navy officials and Samoan dignitaries congregate, having just raised the U.S. flag, which towers over everything. Land reclamation, the photograph's perspective suggests, merged seamlessly with U.S. claims over Tutuila's land and its people. Indeed, the photographer stood on the very steel bars on which the new wharf would soon be erected. His panoramic vision would not have been possible without this part of the construction process having preceded his shot. When the flag-raising ceremony had come to an end, workers resumed cutting away the front of Sogelau Hill to fill in the harbor reef. By reclaiming land, the U.S. Navy and its local workers turned the soil of Tutuila's coastal hills into additional space to be colonized.[46]

This visual representation of U.S. claims over Tutuila offered a limited view of the protracted struggles on the ground. As on the U.S. mainland at the time, strikes were not uncommon among workers in Tutuila. In late August 1905, for example, Melanesian and Polynesian workers employed by the naval government went on strike over reduced wages. On August 23, 1905, Governor C. B. T. Moore received orders from the Navy Department to cut the wages of government laborers from $1 to $0.80 per day. When Moore announced this wage cut to begin September 1, the government workers united and adopted a resolution to quit work. Their task at the time was to add another land fill to the east of Swimming Point. Due to lack of blasting powder, material for the fill had to be broken out by hand—an arduous task that might have contributed to the workers' decision to strike.[47]

Striking against the threatened wage cut bound the Samoan workers closer to their colleagues from other parts of the Pacific. As Moore noted in his 1905 report to Washington, "nearly all of the people employed are not natives of the American islands."[48] A 1906 report contradicted Moore's claim, noting that Samoan workers, not other Pacific Islanders, had struck and had "continued in their refusal to work for nearly a month."[49] Most likely, the group of strikers consisted of workers from both Samoa and other islands. Non-Samoan Pacific Islanders, in particular, resisted the proposed wage cut because they had come to Tutuila for the express purpose of earning cash. In a defiant act, these labor migrants from Micronesia and Melanesia had crossed the recently drawn colonial boundary between German and American Samoa in search for better employment. In doing so, they defined their own version of Oceanian globality.

Governor Moore's reaction to the workers' challenge to government authority was soft-spoken but firm. Moore informed the workers that they would "not be permitted to remain idle about this island" and would be treated as vagrants if they did not find other employment.[50] At the same time, he reassured the workers that they would not be forced to work for $0.80 a day, but that those who were willing to continue with reduced wages would be protected by the government. Moore defended the reduced daily wage as "sufficient" but also hinted at the possibility of reintroducing the old daily wage of $1, if necessary.[51] The Navy Department in Washington and its representatives in Tutuila were testing the waters for saving labor costs.

The workers themselves did not budge for several months. In October 1905, Moore reported that the labor situation had straightened itself out. Even though he failed to mention any details, it is safe to assume from his choice of words that the workers finally caved in and accepted the wage cuts. A new deck for the coal dock was being laid, Moore announced, and new quarters for the officers were about to be completed as well.[52] Despite their courageous stand against the wage cut, the Melanesian and Polynesian laborers were back at work. When the second major fill was completed in 1906, they had moved more than 270,000 cubic feet of earth.[53]

As the 1905 strike showed, the infrastructure workscape posed unique problems for worker solidarity. Because most construction projects in Samoa lasted only weeks or months, workers had less time to develop deeper bonds of solidarity than they would have on plantations, where contracts ran three years or longer. In American Samoa, the U.S. Navy recruited skilled workers from the mainland to lead the construction projects. And since there were few other workers available, Samoans did most of the manual labor in Tutuila. Both the limited length of labor projects and the mixed racial composition of the workforce made organized resistance against low pay and bad working conditions more difficult than in other workscapes. Beyond the naval station in Pago Pago, construction workers also reshaped Samoa's transport links on land and sea.

Island Pathways

Like all Pacific Islanders, the people who settled Samoa three millennia ago were master navigators. Samoans are descendants of Oceanian seafarers who had successfully sailed thousands of miles through unknown seas, from Southeast Asia into the island Pacific. European explorers, such as Louis-Antoine de Bougainville, recognized this proud Samoan heritage by naming the group Navigator Islands in 1768.[54] Samoans regularly rowed and sailed in between their islands as well as to neighboring island groups in Fiji, Tonga, Tuvalu, Tokelau, and Niue. Samoans who joined American whaling ships and Christian missionaries in the 1830s journeyed even farther. Their far-flung travels combined trade with politics and cultural exchange. Samoans who went on *malaga* to visit friends, relatives, and political allies living in remote villages and on neighboring islands maintained personal ties and often forged new ones.

The formal division of Samoa in 1900 interrupted long-standing links between Savai'i and Upolu in the west and Tutuila and the Manu'a Islands to the east. The new colonial boundary between German and American Samoa turned what used to be a short journey by boat into a border crossing with considerable personal and political risks.[55] For the longest time, Samoans had been following established paths on and between their home islands. The Samoan word for "path"—*ala*—applies to both land and sea, as in *alāva'a*, a well-defined boat track within the coastal reef—or, more generally, a shipping lane. Expert Samoan navigators knew these safe pathways through the reef through inherited tradition and personal experience and, at high tide or during bad weather, used their knowledge to steer their boats safely through the reef.

Rudimentary roads hugged the coastlines of all Samoan islands, passable by foot all year round. Samoans knew the best way to get from one village to another, in both good and bad weather. With the introduction of draft animals such as horses, oxen, and mules for commercial agriculture, these footpaths appeared outdated to enterprising Euro-American officials, plantation owners, and traders. Since the 1860s, the only major roads in Samoa were those leading to large foreign-owned plantations. Probably the most important of these plantation roads stretched from Apia all the way to one of the major DHPG plantations in Mulifanua, twenty miles to the west. The Mulifanua road and others were built by the Micronesian and Melanesian workers of the DHPG, beginning in the 1880s. By 1893, small trucks were running on these plantation roads, carrying crops, tools, and food.[56] Access to market became so important in Upolu that plantation lands with connection to roads sold for almost double than those without.[57] After 1900, old *ala* came under pressure on both land and sea, even as Samoans kept using their well-worn pathways. The main ports in Apia and Pago Pago were at the center of this rewiring of Samoa.[58]

Besides accommodating military and commercial ships, German and American colonial officials pursued an active policy of constructing roads. In the spirit of internal improvements on the U.S. mainland throughout the nineteenth century, constructing new roads—as well as improving and extending existing ones—was designed to facilitate the transportation of cash crops to global markets.[59] Consequently, most roads that were newly built or extended before 1900 followed established trade routes or connected foreign plantations to ports. The port of Apia became increasingly important as an entrepôt for export goods, such as copra and cocoa, as well as imported goods, such as foodstuffs and manufactures. Similar centripetal forces turned Pago Pago harbor into a commercial hub on which most roads in Tutuila converged. Both German and American colonial officials pushed ahead with the expansion of the road system for yet another reason. With decades of violent internal and imperial conflicts still fresh in their minds, colonial officials hoped to use the improved transportation and communication infrastructure, centered on roads and ships, in case of military emergencies. Better roads and more regular visits from warships meant more power for the few white men on the islands.

Since the days of the tridominium, German consuls in Apia were complaining about the lack of investment in roadbuilding.[60] Given the relative weakness of the tripartite government in general, this was hardly a surprise. The only workers who could be forced to build roads were either plantation workers on contract for the DHPG or prisoners. In 1893, the municipal council of Apia encouraged police sergeant Friedrich Marquardt to use prisoners for public works.[61] Two years later, Marquardt would step down from his office as police chief to organize the second Samoan ethnographic show tour, together with his brother Carl. As supervisor of prisoners engaged in roadwork, Marquardt must have learned a thing or two about managing workers.

In 1894, a number of imprisoned Samoan *matai* in Upolu were hired by Euro-American settlers to build a mile-long road leading to the boundary of the municipality of Apia. Following Samoan custom, the *matai* were fed by their employers and delegated the hard labor to relatives. As U.S. consul William Blacklock commented in disbelief, the *matai,* who were actually serving prison sentences, "appeared to be having a real good time, and were always laughing and joking, and enjoying themselves generally." According to Blacklock, the prisoners "used to knock off work every afternoon about three o'clock and go for a bathe in the river before returning to the jail for the night."[62] Through the 1890s, high-ranking Samoans were able to escape the disciplinary measures, including manual labor, by resorting to traditions of cooperative work gangs. As Blacklock's tone indicates, Euro-American officials were desperate for a more forceful approach to roadwork.

After 1900, officials in both colonies complained about the difficulties they faced motivating Samoans to build and expand roads. German colonial officials even bribed Samoan villages with wagons to make them widen their narrow paths.[63] In August 1901, residents of Matautu in Savai'i were forced to build roads for a new plantation. To punish vocal opposition to the German takeover in Savai'i, Governor Solf ordered the arrest of six leading orators and had them removed to Upolu to perform roadwork. Part of the initial opposition in Matautu for which the leaders were punished was the residents' refusal to build roads for a new plantation in the area. Unlike the imprisoned *matai* from 1894, the exiled orators from Savai'i could not rely on relatives to assist them with the hard labor.[64]

Only a few months after this incident, U.S. officials in Tutuila faced similar difficulties with the building of roads. In November 1901, Rear Admiral Silas Casey stressed the importance of building roads to link isolated villages but cautioned against the labor costs necessary to do so: "The Samoans," he explained, "are satisfied with their narrow tracks, and when called upon to make the roads wider they expect the Government to compensate them for their work." To finance the construction of roads, Casey suggested raising the import duties to 10 percent and taxing Samoans "in labor for their share of the expense."[65]

Fair compensation for such hard manual labor as building and maintaining roads remained a crucial point of controversy between colonial officials and workers. In June 1902, the Samoan government, which retained considerable authority over local matters, ordered a group of Samoan road workers to strike for better pay and food. According to the German construction supervisor Friedrich Stünzner, a Samoan police officer from Mulinu'u appeared one morning and, in the name of Lauaki and all Samoan village councilors (faipule), called on his fellow Samoans to stop working. Stünzner reassured the workers of the colonial administration's protection, but the police officer countered that the Samoan government would throw everyone who went to work in jail. The threat of jail convinced the Samoan road workers, who all left their posts soon afterward.[66]

Lack of adequate food was Lauaki's official complaint, but the workers' reluctance to leave work cast doubt on the legitimacy of his claim. According to their German boss, who had a vested interest in keeping the roadwork going, each Samoan worker received four pieces of biscuit with tea at 8 a.m. and three-quarters of canned meat, bananas, and rice at noon. In the evenings, they were given no food because they went home to eat. Samoan workers employed in roadwork, Stünzner claimed, had so much food that they passed on two pieces of biscuit and rice to their relatives. To give out more food, he objected, would be "an outrage" and would only help feed the inhabitants of Mulinu'u at the expense of the German colonial administration.[67] Stünzner's interpretation of the strike turned out to be correct. Lauaki and the other Samoan faipule soon apologized, and the road workers took up their labor tasks again. During Solf's absence, acting governor Heinrich Schnee tried to avoid further disaffection and punished none of the strikers. Samoan government officials, led by Lauaki, merely wanted to siphon off more food for themselves.[68]

There is one additional piece of evidence that Samoans ever worked voluntarily in road construction in German Samoa. From July to November 1909, a number of Samoans joined the roadwork for daily wages of 2 marks ($0.50) in cash and 75 pfennigs ($0.19) for food. The Samoan workers likely made an exception to their dislike for roadwork because a long drought had led to a shortage of food.[69] Like their German counterparts in Upolu, U.S. officials in Tutuila found that unpaid roadwork sparked little interest among Samoans.[70] If they worked on roads at all, Governor Sebree noted, a whole village "works at it, say for one or two days, or perhaps a week, and then the people rest for a week."[71] Instead of maintaining roads, as Euro-American officials wanted, Samoans maintained long-standing labor practices based on cooperation and need.

Given the difficulties of forcing Samoans to work on roads, the administrations in German and American Samoa sought out other workers. In German Samoa, it was mostly Chinese and even a few white men who were employed in roadwork. Other Samoan and Chinese prisoners were forced to clean administration buildings and neighboring properties.[72] In the fall of 1904, the German colonial administration opened new barracks for the Chinese workers under government contract, including beds for forty workers and overseers, a storeroom, and a separate kitchen.[73] By the end of 1907, six of the Chinese workers applied to the colonial administration for a one-year extension of their labor contracts under the condition that they were allowed more opium.[74] Two years later, Stünzner's successor as road construction supervisor seemed to have gotten along with his Chinese workers just fine. In a report to the governor, he requested to use parts of his fund to purchase gifts for Chinese holidays in order to "give the Chinese a treat."[75]

Major roads on foreign-owned plantations were usually maintained by plantation workers themselves, such as the Chinese workers on Richard Deeken's plantation in Tapatapao.[76] Both German and American colonial administrations also forced prisoners to build roads. As during the construction of the U.S. coaling station in Tutuila, convict laborers for the German Samoan government transported soil and rocks on a light trolley placed on a movable streetcar line that extended over three thousand feet. According to a U.S. consul report from 1908, the Samoan and Chinese prisoners were "not so satisfactory as contract labor."[77] Free labor ideology thrived among U.S. diplomats at a time when forms of unfree labor dominated most of the global countryside. In reality, however, prisoners also worked for the U.S. naval government in Tutuila, building roads and loading copra.[78]

Samoan and Chinese workers who were looking for casual employment adapted to the changing economic circumstances and chose the kind of labor that would earn them the most cash. Chinese workers hired by the German colonial administration could earn between 15 and 25 marks ($3.75–$6.25) a month, including food. Most Chinese workers built and maintained roads, while others kept the custom docks free from sand.[79] In 1913, the German colonial administration hired an average of forty Chinese workers at a time, thirty of whom built roads, while the rest served as crafters and wagoners.[80] Samoan day laborers received up to 3 marks ($0.75) a day, without food. In times of high copra prices, Samoans either cut more copra on their own plantations or joined Melanesian, Micronesian, and Chinese workers on Euro-American plantations. As German colonial officials did not fail to notice, Samoans usually preferred plantation labor over roadwork.[81]

The slow pace of roadwork was a constant source of frustration for U.S. naval officials. In 1907, a mere three miles of new roads were built, while repairs due to heavy rains and resulting landslides were needed.[82] A 1908 report indicated that no trail in Tutuila was passable for artillery except by mule and complained about the lack of local guides.[83] "Each native," a report from a visiting U.S. warship found, "knows the trails in the immediate vicinity of his village, and some of the main trails, but was easily lost a little distance from home. There did not seem to be any one with a comprehensive knowledge of all the means of communication in the Island and it is most important for purpose of defense that there should be."[84] The report concluded with a recommendation to train Samoan guides as part of the *fita fita* guard. A few years later, the pace of roadwork in Tutuila had picked up. In 1910, workers built nine miles of new roads and repaired an additional eight and a half miles of existing roads. They also reinforced a number of bridges with Australian hardwood and blasted out boat passages through reefs with dynamite.[85] The use of blasting powder radically transformed the centuries-old network of boat tracks.

Yet the building of infrastructure still proceeded too slowly for U.S. Navy officials. In 1911, Governor William M. Crose laconically summarized the state of roadwork in Tutuila: "There are no roads in Tutuila which would be dignified by that name in the United States."[86] The roads, he lamented, were little more than trails, mainly because Samoans refused to work on road construction unless they were paid for all their work.[87] Out of frustration with this perceived lack of progress in roadbuilding, Crose required Samoan villages to furnish labor for the construction of roads in October 1911. For roads with "public utility," half of the labor cost was to be carried by the naval government, which also provided materials for blasting and bridge building. For roads of mere "local importance," the naval government was to offer only building materials. Samoans who refused to perform roadwork could be fined double the daily wage for each day missed or even thrown in jail for four days.[88] Since prisoners could be legally coerced to work for the colonial administration, this draconian provision turned the building of roads into a regime of forced labor. The system did not, however, have the intended effect. In 1921, Governor Waldo A. Evans introduced a special road tax of $2.25 to pay for the construction and maintenance of roads. Prisoners who were detailed to roadwork still went out in gangs every day but had new help in the form of a ten-ton road roller and a three-ton Denby truck.[89]

The construction of roads pitted colonial officials and workers against one another in particular ways. For Samoans, used to their own ways of moving around their home islands, roadwork seemed hardly necessary and unnecessarily hard. If not forced to as a form of punishment, Samoan workers only engaged in roadwork when other options for earning cash were unavailable. And yet to say that roadbuilding helped discipline Samoan communities to colonial control is to tell only half the story.[90] As in other areas of colonial life, Samoan workers proved creative in adapting this form of hard manual labor to existing practices, such as cooperative work groups and occasional wage labor. For the Chinese workers employed by the German colonial administration, building and maintaining roads was merely another, if more physically demanding, form of contract labor. There is little evidence to reconstruct the role of Micronesian and Melanesian workers in roadbuilding, probably because most continued to work on plantations throughout their contracts. With the help of these workers, a network of roads crisscrossed northwestern Upolu by 1914, the most densely integrated part of the Samoan islands. But travel on the islands remained slow; the sixteen-mile round trip from the U.S. naval station in Fagatogo to Leone still took a whole day in 1920.[91] By that time, Samoa had become entangled in interimperial struggles to draw the colonial periphery into global communication networks.

Telegraphic Imperialism in German Samoa

The first years of the twentieth century were dominated by the "telegraphic imperialism" of major imperial powers.[92] After decades of political wrangling and several interimperial conferences, the British cable across the Pacific was finally completed in December 1902. Stretching from Vancouver via Fanning Island (3,200 miles, the longest distance between two cable stations anywhere in the world) and Fiji to Auckland, the British cable completed the so-called All-Red Line, which linked the major British colonies around the world. Now cabling Sydney from London via the Pacific took only an hour (instead of a day) and cost half the price.[93] It took similarly heated debates and backroom dealings before the U.S. cable from San Francisco via Honolulu reached Manila on July 4, 1903. In masking the crucial financial backing from British telegraph companies, the opening of the U.S. cable on such a symbolic date encapsulated the general shift from economic to imperial considerations in the building of communication lines at the turn of the twentieth century.[94]

The German Empire was the third major player in the race for laying cables across the Pacific. Increasingly uneasy with its dependence on British lines, German officials planned their own lines that would connect Berlin with its far-flung colonies in China, New Guinea, and Samoa. A unique joint venture, the German-Dutch Telegraph Company eventually installed a cable from Menado in the Dutch East Indies via Yap to Shanghai in the fall of 1905.[95] Now Germany, too, had its own submarine cables in the Pacific. In addition, German navy officials attempted to compensate for the relative lack of cables vis-à-vis Great Britain by investing in the new technology of wireless radio.[96]

While the telegraph bound together remote British, German, and U.S. colonies, it also deepened the technological gap between colonizers and the colonized. In German Samoa, as in other colonies, the colonized had little to no access to the new technological wonders. Far from being an engine of peace and progress for everyone, as the evangelists of technology had claimed for half a century, the telegraph and its successors had different effects on the lives of colonized people around the globe. More than ten thousand miles from Berlin, the German colony of Samoa posed considerable challenges for officials trying to keep their superiors at home informed of local developments. German consuls in Apia had been complaining about the lack of adequate communication lines with Berlin since the 1860s, and these complaints intensified as other colonial powers began to compete for control over Samoa in the last quarter of the nineteenth century.

Although Samoa remained relatively isolated from the rest of the world until the beginning of the twentieth century, the communication revolution transformed life on the islands themselves. By the 1880s, local mail service had taken off in Samoa. Between 1885 and 1900, New Zealand–born photographer John Davis ran the post office in Apia. And in September 1886, the German steamer *Lübeck* from the shipping company Norddeutscher Lloyd started regular mail service from Sydney to Apia and Tonga.[97] As the islands remained contested among Germany, Great Britain, and the United States, so did their postal service. Only after the raising of the German flag in 1900 did the mail system further expand. Before 1909, seven additional post offices had opened throughout Upolu and Savai'i. The imperial post office in Apia delivered letters twice every three weeks along the north coast of Upolu and around Savai'i.[98] The mail carriers were initially drawn from the Samoan *fita fita* guard. Later on, two Samoans were selected by a *matai* and paid a respectable monthly salary of 48 marks ($12) by the German government.[99] The two Samoan assistants who worked in the German post office continued to do so right up to World War I, but then refused their services to the New Zealand military administration.

At the beginning of the twentieth century, steamships brought news and mail to Europe and the United States from Samoa roughly every three weeks. Mail packages to Germany were sent to either Bremen or Naples via Sydney through ships of the Norddeutscher Lloyd (a voyage of 47 days). Alternatively, letters to Europe could be sent via Pago Pago to San Francisco through the Oceanic Steamship Company via Vancouver (41 days).[100] The Samoa Shipping & Trading Company ran the steamer *Maori* from Apia to Pago Pago twice every three weeks until the start of the world war, when the German ship *Staatssekretär Solf* took over.[101]

Sending telegrams from or to Samoa posed even more difficult challenges. Before the wireless station opened in German Samoa in 1914, telegrams from Samoa were carried by ship to one of the nearest cable stations in Suva, Fanning Island, or Auckland via local agents. The *Samoanische Zeitung* ran regular ads offering the services of the Pacific Cable Board to customers in Apia. Telegrams would be sent from the British cable station on Fanning Island through a local agent at the International Hotel, a Mr. Easthope, who happened to be the owner of the hotel. Customers were advised that the Oceanic's steamer called at Fanning Island four days after leaving Pago Pago, and the telegram could then be sent on to basically anywhere in the world. If a passing ship did not lay anchor at port, Samoan couriers would sometimes swim out into the bay to deliver the mail.

Telegrams to Samoa had to be sent to one of these stations first and then on to Samoa as standard mail through one of the steamship lines. This complicated procedure contrasted sharply with the almost instant connection that British colonies such as nearby Fiji or the U.S.-occupied Philippines enjoyed, forcing military planners to look for alternatives. To this end, German colonial officials opened a local telegraph system on the two main islands of Upolu and Savai'i in 1906.[102] In fall 1906, Apia and neighboring plantations were connected by telephone.[103] By 1914, more than 150 stations were in operation, stretching over a hundred miles across the islands.[104] Despite the small number of people living on the islands, they attracted considerable traffic. Plans for a further extension of the local telegraph system, from Apia to the western tip of the island in Mulifanua, were thwarted by the onset of the war. There is little evidence on who used these local telegraph lines, but it seems likely that white European settlers as well as visitors to Samoa accounted for the overwhelming majority of telegrams sent through these domestic lines.[105]

German colonial officials were alert to the necessity of having faster communication lines to their distant colonies in the Pacific. Following a rebellion on the Micronesian island of Ponape in the winter of 1910, which resulted in the deaths of seven German officials and more than two dozen Micronesians, German military officials demanded better and faster access to Berlin as well as between colonies. The connection to the Imperial German Navy station in Kiaochow in China was seen as particularly crucial in case of another military emergency. Newspapers in both Germany and Samoa began lobbying extensively for a cable or wireless connection after the Ponape rebellion, and they redoubled their efforts in 1912.

A Berlin newspaper complained in January 1913 that "the news coverage reaching the German colonies still remains in dire straits and the German colonial newspapers are still dependent on Reuter [sic] telegrams, which often times carry reports hostile to Germany." The article went on to say that Samoa was the most isolated of all German colonies. To illustrate Samoa's isolation, the newspaper reported that the promotion of former governor Solf to colonial secretary had reached Samoa only by way of a newspaper from New Zealand.[106] In response to this article, the *Samoanische Zeitung* in Apia explained the archipelago's isolation and confirmed that the *Auckland Weekly News,* which arrived with the Union Steamship line, had, in fact, brought the news of Solf's recall to Berlin. News from Germany arrived via cable from Fiji, the article elaborated, usually three days after the publication of the weekly Samoan newspaper. That is why the newspaper could publish important news even before the official cable arrived in Samoa. Despite this privileged access to information, the Samoan newspaper concluded with a passionate critique of the island's far-from-splendid isolation from the rest of the world: "Three weeks we are totally cut off from the world, without receiving any message, and what we are then able to read in a colonial newspaper that is relevant for us, is very scant. Samoa should finally be linked to the rest of the world by cable or wireless just like New Guinea."[107] By 1913, the long-standing calls for better integration of Samoa into the global communications network became increasingly hard to ignore for German decision makers.[108]

While plans for a wireless chain had been discussed in Berlin for some time, the German Colonial Office did not begin making more specific plans until the fall of 1909. Technical problems, especially the high degree of atmospheric interference close to the equator, delayed the introduction of wireless radio stations throughout the Pacific. It took until spring 1912 before a subsidiary of the German-Dutch Telegraph Company was granted a concession to build wireless stations along a strategic line running from Kiaochow to Yap, Rabaul, Nauru, and Samoa.[109] Germany was not alone in realizing the benefits of the new wireless technology to circumvent British hegemony in submarine cables. Around the same time, the U.S. Congress provided $1.5 million for the establishment of a chain of high-powered radio stations in the Panama Canal Zone, California, Hawai'i, Guam, American Samoa, and the Philippines. The first station, built in record time near Honolulu, opened in August 1912.[110]

Meanwhile, the newly founded German South Seas Company for Wireless Telegraphy, together with the leading German wireless company, Telefunken, sent an expedition to Samoa in April 1912 to begin planning a wireless station. Solf pulled the bureaucratic levers in Berlin to secure a state subsidy and speed up the construction process.[111] From a purely technical standpoint, a wireless station in Samoa had the additional advantage of connecting easily with the British station in Fiji, around seven hundred miles to the southwest, and from there, with the British cable, to Australia and New Zealand as well as to Canada. But the strategic advantages of an independent wireless chain in case of war were dominant in the minds of German officials. Apart from the wireless station in Kiaochow, which had been in operation since 1906, additional German stations in the Pacific opened in Yap and Nauru in December 1913.

Construction of the station in the hills of Tafaigata, five miles southwest of Apia, began in earnest in the summer of that year. German chief engineer Richard Hirsch had arrived in Apia in May 1913 and had purchased a piece of land for the station. Next, Hirsch directed Samoan and Chinese workers to build a six-mile-long small-gauge railway to transport machines and tower parts uphill.[112] A self-made locomotive carried the construction material for nearly three miles to the bottom of the hill, where workers had to drag and push it uphill the rest of the way. Given this arduous task, an acute labor shortage slowed down the project. In response, the German government had to pay the mostly unskilled workers 3 marks ($0.75) a day, more than double the usual rate for contract laborers at the time.

Initially, only a dozen Chinese contract laborers worked to clear the underbrush and carry material to the construction site.[113] The Chinese contingent was soon enlarged to twenty-eight, and forty additional workers from various Pacific islands joined them shortly afterward. The German construction team was highly conscious of potential conflict among the multiracial labor force. In reports to his employer Telefunken in Berlin, Hirsch claimed that the "proper treatment" of the workers helped avert more violent conflicts or even the intervention of colonial troops. As an example, he cited animosities between Chinese workers from Shanghai and others from Hong Kong. In response to such internal conflicts, Hirsch argued, rigorous racial segregation and "lots of patience" were needed.[114] German officials had to rely on every available worker to perform the physically demanding construction labor. Racial segregation of the workforce was both a response to real interracial conflict and a testament to the danger of revolt against difficult work conditions. As in the construction of the U.S. naval station in Tutuila, the building of the wireless station in Upolu came at a price for the Chinese, Melanesian, and Samoan workers.

Samoan laborers cut down trees around the construction site, but German authorities were not satisfied with their performance and introduced task work to ensure faster progress. The newly arrived chief engineer Hirsch quickly imbibed the racial stereotypes of Samoans pervasive among white European settlers: "The Samoan," he noted, "represents the strange type of the gentleman savage; good manners, wonderful grandezza, and pyramidal laziness."[115] Yet the radio tower in Apia was built by workers who gave the lie to the selective gaze of their colonizers.

The labor shortage was exacerbated by the poor health of workers and bosses alike. While the latest transport of Chinese workers had recently arrived in Apia, it had to be put under quarantine due to cases of smallpox. The new Chinese workers could thus not immediately be used for building the station. To finish the construction, Hirsch eventually leased laborers from German planters on specially designed and costly contracts.[116] At its high point, twelve tons of heavy construction material was transported from port to work site each day. Work conditions were hard. Samoan and Chinese workers suffered from the heat and tropical diseases. No fewer than 28 out of a total workforce of 174 were affected by inflammatory wounds on their feet and had to stop working. For their part, German engineers and staff suffered from dysentery and fever. The enduring labor shortage even forced Telefunken back in Berlin to ask the Colonial Office to hire prison laborers.[117]

In dire straits because of depressed natural rubber prices, the Samoa-Kautschuk-Compagnie (SKC) offered the German government fifty Chinese laborers in May 1914. Equally short of cash, Governor Schultz forwarded the offer to Telefunken, which he thought could make good use of the additional workers in the final stretch of finishing the radio tower. Eventually, twenty-seven Chinese laborers were picked up at the company's headquarters, transported to the construction site, and paid 32 marks ($8) a month, all courtesy of the German government.[118] This state-sponsored labor assistance program demonstrated how important the wireless station was for the German colonial administration in Samoa. After months of excruciating labor in the tropical heat, the station was finally completed on June 30, 1914.[119] Across the channel, the U.S. wireless radio station had opened just days before on an 850-foot-high mountain ridge overlooking Pago Pago harbor.[120]

As the exploitation of this diverse crew of colonial workers showed, the making of empire was a daunting physical task, borne by those who rarely

Figure 14. Telefunken wireless radio station, Apia, 1914. Willy Schmidt and Hans Werner, eds., *Geschichte der deutschen Post in den Kolonien und im Ausland* (Leipzig: Konkordia-Verlag, 1939), opp. 321. Widener Library, Harvard University.

saw the fruits of their toils. The labor conditions tolerated by the German-run telegraph company belied the dominant self-representation of imperial communication lines as a means of peace and progress for everyone. If colonial officials had to weigh their desire for increased access to information with security concerns over telegraph lines in foreign hands, they also had to rely on the colonized to build these new means of communication. As the history of German Samoa shows, the telegraph did not bring peace and progress but rather the opposite: the first message that the newly built wireless station received from Berlin was news that war had erupted in Europe.

On August 29, 1914, just a month into the hostilities, troops from Great Britain and New Zealand occupied German Samoa. They encountered no resistance from the German authorities. Governor Schultz had been staying night and day at the new wireless station waiting for news from Europe. The initial plan to completely destroy the station was eventually abandoned, not the least because German officials believed that Samoans "saw the [four-hundred-foot tall] station tower as a visible sign of the Emperor's power."[121] Thus, when British forces arrived in Samoa, German engineers removed some vital parts to disable the wireless station, as under no circumstances could the newly built German wireless station fall into enemy hands. In an attempt to rebuild the big tower, the British caused the explosion of one of its giant wheels, which tore through the station roof and further damaged the tower. A Samoan bystander lost his leg in the accident.[122] New parts had to be imported, and the entire station had to be slowly rebuilt.[123] As one U.S. official reported, the wireless station in Apia had ceased operations on August 22, 1914.[124] Throughout the war, British and New Zealand occupation forces had to rely on their cable link in Fiji to communicate with London. Meanwhile, German mail service and local telegraph lines within Samoa, now under British censorship, continued uninterrupted throughout the war.

Even though the Germans gave up their colony without a fight, Samoa had been at the center of interimperial competition in the Pacific for decades. Communication networks played a crucial part in this clash of empires over a group of islands thousands of miles from London, Berlin, and Washington. As it turned out, the cable that would bring peace and progress to Samoa brought mostly hardship for the people who built it. And its completion was followed in short order by a world war that, in the eyes of most Samoans, replaced one colonial power with another.

• • •

At the turn of the twentieth century, German and American officials justified their colonial presence in Samoa by promising to bring modern technology and global trade. As latecomers to the colonial scramble, both empires leveraged their growing industrial power to pursue their civilizing missions around the world, including in the South Pacific. In this context, infrastructure and those who built it gained in importance. If colonial officials saw the building of infrastructure as a way to increase their control over people, workers in Samoa seized the new opportunities that came with such construction projects. On the one hand, Samoan workers welcomed an additional avenue for earning cash, which had become increasingly important as a way to purchase manufactured goods, pay taxes, and contribute to churches. The 1905 strike by workers engaged in the construction of the U.S. naval station in Tutuila was one in a series of conflicts highlighting the crucial issue of fair wages. On the other hand, the building and improvement of infrastructure, such as roads, ports, and storage buildings, served not only the interests of foreign traders and military officials but also home-grown initiatives, such as the Samoan copra cooperatives. With more frequent shipping connections to markets in Europe, Australia, and the United States, Samoan copra producers gained greater economic clout, if not real political autonomy. And even if these new means of connection were largely outside the control of islanders themselves, they offered new and more regular ways of interacting with the wider Pacific world and beyond.[125]

In these and other ways, the hard labor of grading roads and carrying steel bars became a crucible for worker solidarity. The diverse group of workers who built the colonial infrastructure created structures of solidarity that tied them closer together. Construction workers helped lay the material foundations of colonial globality but, in doing so, also fashioned their own version of Oceanian globality.

5

MEDIATORS

According to a famous Samoan proverb, the pathway to leadership is through service ('*O le ala i le pule o le tautua*). Samoan *matai* are expected to serve their family, village, and country by providing resources; honoring the family name; fundraising for building projects; and giving skillful speeches.[1] These four types of service (*tautua*) are crucial factors in determining which family members receive *matai* titles and, thus, a pathway to leadership and authority. But with the onset of coconut colonialism in the late nineteenth century, Samoan understandings of service began to change. As colonial administrators created new demand for service labor—ranging from soldiers to translators and nurses—Samoans incorporated these new avenues to service leadership into their existing social system (*fa'a matai*). In doing so, Samoan service workers became crucial intermediaries who molded the demands of colonial globality into their own version of Oceanian globality.

Colonial service jobs represented the white-collar counterparts to the more physically exacting labor on plantations and roads. At the same time, service workers faced similar challenges in their jobs and found similar ways to confront them. As with sustainable farming and ethnographic performing, most workers in the service economy, particularly those in the police force and in health care, were native Samoans. Except for female nurses, Samoan men had better chances for social advancement in the colonial service. Service workers performed the crucial work of mediating between Samoan and Euro-American interests, values, and knowledge. Trained by colonial officials to "enlighten" their fellow islanders, Samoan mediators reshaped this paternalistic logic according to their own goals and the needs of their community.

In the process, they reshaped Samoa's relationship with the wider world according to their Oceanian values and emerged as leaders in the islands' struggle for greater self-determination.

What distinguished the colonial service from other workscapes was its deep link to colonial power. Nobody worked closer to the governors of German and American Samoa than did their personal attendants, interpreters, and cooks. This physical, and sometimes emotional, proximity to powerful colonial officials afforded service workers a privileged position in the circulation of knowledge and decision making in Samoa. While the native guards in both German and American Samoa were small in number and had mostly representative functions, members nevertheless received basic training in firearms and military discipline, which lent them prestige and led to military careers for generations of Samoans to come. Likewise, nurses in both colonies were the first Samoans to receive extended training in medical care, which also offered opportunities to travel and learn. With their training and expertise, these nurses would remain powerful members of their communities long after World War I. Besides a handful of domestic workers, nurses were the first female wage earners in Samoa, upsetting the long-standing gendered labor system. For the first time, Samoan women commanded control over their own cash.

The most striking feature of the colonial service workforce was the prominent role that mixed-race people played in it. Unlike on plantations, descendants of Euro-American and Samoan parents were overrepresented in jobs that involved intercultural and multilingual skills such as translators, interpreters, and government clerks. Drawing on their biracial and bicultural family backgrounds, service workers of mixed-race descent occupied crucial intermediary positions in Samoa. Colonial administrators depended on them to translate, interpret, and mediate between colonial policy and local circumstances. At the same time, many workers in other occupations found their mixed-race colleagues in government offices and hospitals to be important sources of information. With such influence, service workers needed to keep the trust of both sides. Exploring the ways in which colonial intermediaries, such as the service workers in Samoa, navigated this contradictory world offers insights into the workings of coconut colonialism.[2]

Samoan Warriors

As early as the mid-nineteenth century, security was one of the major concerns of the Euro-American colonizers in Samoa. For centuries, supporters of leading *matai* competing for the succession of titles were usually well-armed with clubs and knives and knew how to wield them. Beginning in the 1860s, many Samoans purchased Western-made firearms, especially rifles, in exchange for land titles. Selling land for arms undermined Samoan society while also increasing the overall military prowess of Samoans. As a consequence, even before German, British, and American diplomats agreed on tripartite rule over the municipality of Apia in 1889, the disarmament of Samoan soldiers had become a top priority.

Parallel to the efforts to reduce Samoan firepower, a municipal police force was established in 1888 to maintain "peace and order" in the commercial center of Apia, where virtually all Europeans and Americans resided.[3] By the summer of 1888, fourteen young Samoan men, all from powerful families, had enlisted for a two-year term and received Prussian infantry training by Captain Eugen Brandeis. Rifles and ammunition for the new police force were on their way from Germany.[4] After the division of the islands into German and American Samoa in 1900, both colonial administrations were quick to establish their own Samoan security forces, in the image of the police force during the tridominium. Thus, the Fitafita Guard was born.

In American Samoa, one of Commandant Tilley's first requests to the Navy Department was for permission to enlist Samoans as landsmen in the U.S. Navy. In 1900, he was authorized to enlist fifty-eight men for four years. Guard members were equipped as infantry, had one three-inch landing gun, and were trained by a U.S. Marine sergeant "in infantry drill, in boat drill, and *to a certain extent* with the field gun."[5] The qualification "to a certain extent" revealed the limits of trust U.S. Navy officials were willing to extend to their Samoan orderlies. Too much combat expertise, they feared, could backfire.

Most members of the Fitafita Guard (*fitafita* means "soldier") were sons of *matai* and took immense pride in their official capacity. Similarities to the emphasis on etiquette and discipline in Samoan culture certainly accounted for part of the attraction to the newly established guard. Serving in

Figure 15. Nelson Huron (U.S. Marine Corps) with Fitafita Guard, c. 1924–1925.
Records of the United States Marine Corps, General Photographic File, NARA-CP, RG 127-G, box 17, no. 60.

the Fitafita Guard offered considerable prestige in Samoan society, not the least because it conformed to the ideal of service to the community. In that sense, colonial officials and Samoan leaders agreed, guardsmen set an example for other Samoan youth.[6] Their uniforms made visible the merging of American and Samoan culture in the guard as a whole: a turkey-red cap, a white cotton undershirt with a sash of the same turkey-red color, and a white *lava lava* banded at the hem with rows of stripes denoting the soldier's rank.[7] True to Samoan custom, the Fitafita did not wear shoes.[8] According to a U.S. Navy captain in Tutuila, the Samoan soldiers' "gorgeous uniform, the fact of being real soldiers (fita fita), drilling like the 'papalangi' [sic] or foreigners, and best of all getting $16.00 per month & ration has made them aristocrats."[9] With their display of muscular masculinity, the Samoan soldiers fulfilled one of the stereotypes Euro-American audiences expected when they came to see Samoan men in ethnographic shows.

Another major incentive to join the guard was the good pay. Membership in the Fitafita Guard offered a welcome source of cash for individual soldiers and their extended families.[10] Into the 1930s, service in the Fitafita Guard was one of the best-paid jobs available to American Samoans. The money they spent in local stores and the navy commissary also helped fuel economic growth on the islands. In 1901, a landsman in the guard received $25 a month and a coxswain in one of the navy tugboats even made $35 a month.[11] Upon visiting Tutuila in the fall of 1901, Rear Admiral Silas Casey, commander in chief of the U.S. Navy in the Pacific, was so impressed by the guard that he recommended raising their pay to match that of regular U.S. Marines.[12] At least in pay, Samoan soldiers became the equals of their American colleagues.

Though the guard was initially set up to maintain order and enforce court decisions, its tasks diversified as colonial administrations spread their control over the islands. In American Samoa, guardsmen began to help with construction projects in addition to protecting navy buildings. But because the Fitafita Guard remained small in number, the navy's captain of the watch continued to be necessary to guard government property, particularly at night.[13] Apart from these duties, the guardsmen provided the crew for the governor's barge with twelve rowers and a coxswain.[14]

From early on, the Fitafita Guard assumed another service function: musical entertainment. In 1902, two U.S. Navy musicians were sent to Tutuila to teach the guardsmen how to organize a band and perform music.[15] The new U.S. naval station band consisted of seventeen pieces, and to the delight of the locals, the performers quickly mastered the instruments.[16] After 1905, the band gave public concerts twice a week from a brand-new bandstand, which they had built themselves.[17] Within the prestige-laden guard, the band members emerged as the true "aristocrats of American Samoa."[18] As the Fitafita band showed, Samoans were engaged in performative labor not only abroad but also at home. To be fair, the kind of American military music the Samoan band members played on duty had little else in common with the call-and-response songs troupe members performed at Chicago's world's fair.

The ranks of the Fitafita Guard continued to swell in the early years of U.S. rule, so much so that new barracks had to be built to house them. The old barracks, constructed by members of the guard themselves, consisted of a concrete building made from native lime and rock. As a 1906 report indicated, the walls of the old barracks were crumbling from age and tropical climate and had turned soft and mushy. Moreover, the old barracks also served as the naval station prison, which stretched its capacity. Navy officials in Tutuila requested funds for new barracks to be made with Oregon pine, redwood, iron roofing, and concrete walls. In the new building, there would also be space for a separate room for the station band.[19] As soon as the funds were granted, the guardsmen went to work. All in all, they broke more than fifty-four hundred cubic feet of rock for the barracks. Except for some portions of carpenter work, members of the guard performed all the labor.[20] Following a few months of delays, the new barracks were completed in November 1908. According to the official report, the barracks were "in every way most satis factory, dry and cool."[21] Upon completion, guard members officially moved into the two-story structure, with an arched Mission Revival–style veranda facing the parade ground. To accommodate Samoan custom, though, many of the guard members were allowed to sleep at home with their families.[22] In any case, the fathers of the guardsmen, most of them high-ranking *matai,* must have been proud of their sons. The feast that followed the dedication ceremony was one of the largest ever held in Samoa, with guests consuming more than twenty-five thousand items of food.

The Fitafita Guard did not always enjoy such unqualified support among civilian Samoans. Especially early on, there were several reports of violent clashes between guardsmen and other Samoans living in Tutuila. In the summer of 1903, Tafito and Pau, two Samoan men from Fagalogo, attacked a member of the guard against whom they had a grievance. They were stopped by the police and thrown into prison. At that time, the old guard barracks still housed the naval station prison, which put the two violators face to face with the colleagues of the attacked guard. "Whilst in their cells," a newspaper article noted, "they were set upon and ill-treated in a most disgraceful manner by several of the Fita Fitas, who were on guard at the gaol." For their conduct, five guardsmen received prison sentences with hard labor for terms ranging from one month to two years. In addition, they were all dismissed from the guard. Tafito and Pau themselves were sentenced to four months imprisonment each for their physical attack on the guard. The article concluded with a dire warning: "It is to be hoped that this will be a lesson to the Fita Fitas, as their behavior towards both whites and natives has been—to say the least—very aggressive."[23] As this example showed, the guardsmen who were tasked with keeping order on the island needed to be disciplined themselves from time to time.

Other members of the guard, however, were models in military discipline and loyalty. During his time as governor from 1915 to 1919, John M. Poyer employed a personal attendant and bodyguard: Talalotu. In the recollections of Poyer's daughter, "No more military man ever stood at salute than the Governor's orderly, Talalotu [who] followed the Governor at a respectful distance, whenever he left the house, and wore a dagger in his belt."[24] Talalotu was so close to the Poyer family that he named his first son after his boss, John Martin Poyer, and his second son after the governor's private secretary, Luther Williams Cartwright. Rumor had it that after the Poyers had left Tutuila in 1919, Talalotu even named his third son after the governor's daughter, Mary Porter Poyer, as a sign of his loyalty.[25] Even accounting for a whiff of colonial nostalgia on Poyer's part, Talalotu's dedication to his job as a guardsman and orderly to the U.S. governor seems indisputable. Samoan service workers like Talalotu frequently developed a deep sense of loyalty to their employers, who in turn depended on them to run their administrative business. And as isolated episodes of violence against local civilians demonstrated, the Fitafita Guard in American Samoa was a crucial pillar of the colonial administration.

Forty miles to the west, in German Samoa, the colonial administration established a similar Samoan guard, also naming them Fitafita. A contingent

Figure 16. Members of the Fitafita in German Samoa, n.d. Bildarchiv der Deutschen Kolonialgesellschaft, Universitätsbibliothek Frankfurt am Main (042-0245-56).

of Samoan government soldiers was recruited only months after the raising of the German flag in 1900. Mataʻafa Iosefo had pushed the new German administration to enlist Samoan soldiers, hoping it would increase Samoan influence (including his own) on colonial decision-making.[26] As in American Samoa, the German Samoan Fitafita were mainly tasked with maintaining order on the streets and guarding government buildings, including their own four Samoan *fales*. Two Samoan Fitafita, Paulo and Toʻo, worked as personal security guards for Governor Solf and his family. Over time, the Fitafita assumed other service functions, such as delivering mail, rowing boats, and driving carriages. Some Samoan leaders, like Iosefo, thought that the guard was too small in number. In a letter to Solf from August 1901, Iosefo derided the Fitafita as "a mere dancing-class for the pleasure and enjoyment of the Samoan people."[27] For Mataʻafa Iosefo and other leaders, Samoan participation in the colonial service increased their own influence over the colonial administration.

By 1905, the German administration was employing thirty-one regular soldiers for 20 marks ($5) per month, six privates for 24 marks ($6) per month, two corporals for 30 marks ($7.50) per month, and one sergeant for 60 marks ($15) per month.[28] In addition to their salaries, the soldiers received a daily provision allowance of 80 pfennigs ($0.20) and, on public holidays, even free cake. Compared to other wage labor accessible to Samoans at the time, the monthly salary of the Fitafita in German Samoa was relatively low, but the job was steady and safe, with opportunities to advance within the ranks to earn more money and status. Most importantly, serving as a Fitafita conferred considerable prestige in Samoan society and offered access to the most powerful officials in the colony. This was the bargain of collaboration for Samoan soldiers.[29]

Governor Solf had to defend even these moderate expenditures against attacks from the German colonialist press and a group of settlers around Deeken, who wanted the Samoan guards replaced by soldiers from German New Guinea.[30] Both long-established settlers and Solf agreed that replacing the Samoan Fitafita with Melanesian soldiers would incite racial prejudice among Samoans and endanger the safety of the colony.[31] Solf's trust in his Samoan soldiers had limits, however. When a military confrontation with Lauaki's followers appeared imminent in early 1909, the governor ordered the German police commissioner to secretly remove all firing pins from Fitafita rifles.[32] A dispatch of sixty Melanesian soldiers from German New Guinea was called in to protect the colony. Even though the Melanesian soldiers did not see direct combat, calls to permanently replace the Samoan Fitafita resurfaced in the aftermath of Lauaki's rebellion. Perhaps precisely because they were never really needed, the Samoan Fitafita continued to enjoy official support.[33] Apart from this exceptional intervention and repeated calls for a permanent deployment, German Samoa remained the only German colony in the Pacific without a Melanesian police force right through the end of German rule in 1914. On the one hand, a more muscular security presence would have undermined Governor Solf's policy of salvage colonialism, which relied on nonviolent coercion. On the other hand, the German navy's Asiatic Squadron in Kiaochow was only two weeks away from Samoa in case of military contingencies. For their part, the veterans of the native guard were proud of their service and held regular meetings in their own Fitafita club in Matautu.[34]

After their three-year enlistment term, Fitafita who spoke good English could join the German Samoan police force as *leoleo* (police). Thus, the Fitafita became a training ground for other security services in the colony. The *leoleo* dated back to the days of the tridominium and were kept on duty after

1900 to ensure the safety of Euro-Americans in Apia. Soon thereafter, they were tasked with safeguarding the new government jail in Vaimea. In 1902, only seven *leoleo* worked for the German colonial administration.[35] Four years later, their number had increased to twenty-two. After 1903, the Samoan *leoleo* received an additional mandate: supervising the newly arrived Chinese contract laborers. Given the expanding commercial plantation agriculture in Upolu and Savai'i, the Samoan police officers came to play a more direct role in entrenching colonial power on the islands. Their new supervising role on plantations eventually led to clashes with Chinese workers. Although the Samoan police officers and soldiers never saw direct combat, they were essential to the security and prosperity of the colony.

Conflicts between Samoan police officers and Chinese workers were common. In November 1905, a Chinese worker by the name of Ah Che was struck by Fatu, a Samoan police officer, for not wearing his identification badge. According to Fatu's testimony, he had encountered Che on the street without his required identification number. When he had tried to arrest him and force him to jail, Che resisted, prompting Fatu to push him. A witness report contradicted Fatu's story and confirmed Che's version that he was directly hit by Fatu in front of the jail. Moreover, in an evaluation by his employer, Fatu was described as "generally quite useful, but tending to violent acts." Although German colonial officials did rely on Samoan police officers to keep plantation workers in check, they did not tolerate excessive punishment meted out by them. The following month, Fatu was fined 20 marks ($5) by the German Imperial Court for abusing Che.[36] Here, as in the flogging of workers by plantation owners, the colonial state's monopoly on violence was at stake. And even though Samoan police officers, like Fatu, were technically part of the colonial administration, Chinese workers could expect legal protection, not the least because of their crucial importance for the economic future of the colony.

In the following years, German plantation owners repeatedly asked the colonial administration in Apia to send Samoan Fitafita to maintain order on their plantations.[37] In February 1910, SSG manager Zwingenberger wrote to Solf to send him three Fitafita to protect his SSG employees against attacks by Chinese workers.[38] Clashes between Samoan Fitafita and Chinese workers culminated in 1914 in a much-publicized shoot-out that cost four Fitafita and three German plantation owners their lives. On February 8, 1914, a group of four young Samoan Fitafita—Ao, Faalili, Fili, and Sefo—went to watch an American Western movie in the new cinema in Apia. Two years earlier, Harry J. Moors, impresario of two Samoan ethnographic show troupes, had introduced screenings of American cowboy pictures and British war films to the town hall in Apia, exciting Samoan youth and exasperating colonial officials alike.[39] After the movie had ended, the four adolescents proceeded to a plantation hut where a group of Chinese workers were gambling. There, they got into an argument, stole money from the workers, and destroyed the gambling den.[40] To make their escape, they also stole horses, rifles, and three hundred cartridges from the apartment of a German police officer. When a group of German plantation employees confronted them, the Samoan "cowboys," as they were described in the press, immediately opened fire, killing a German plantation manager and his overseer.

In response, Governor Schultz recruited a group of Samoan police officers, Samoan civilians, and German settlers to hunt the runaways down. On February 11, 1914, they found them hiding in a hut in Malie. High noon was close. As it later became clear, Samoan bystanders had tried to intervene to stop the battle, but the four shooters had told them to go away. They wanted to die this way, they boasted, killing as many "slave-makers" as possible.[41] After a dramatic shoot-out that lasted four hours, Sefo and another young German volunteer, Otto Hellige, were killed, while Faalili and Fili were lynched by several of the Samoan hunters, led by Saga. Only Ao survived, heavily wounded, and was hanged two days later in the government jail in Vaimea.[42]

As colonial officials in both Samoas blamed the bad influence of "cowboy pictures" being shown in Apia for this "killing spree," the deeper fault lines that the fatal shoot-out laid bare were conveniently ignored. Conflicts between Samoan Fitafita and Chinese workers were a direct consequence of the divide-and-rule strategy pursued by the German colonial administration. Samoans, Melanesians, and Chinese were racially segregated on plantations and even in hospitals, making cross-racial solidarity more difficult. The native guard was one of the most segregated colonial institutions. Offering steady pay and social prestige, the guard was open only to Samoans, not to Chinese or Melanesian migrant workers. The number of Samoan police officers actually increased in proportion to the number of Chinese workers arriving in Samoa. Tensions between Samoan soldiers and Chinese workers on plantations were further exacerbated because both competed for the favors

of Samoan women. At the same time, Samoan government employees were
voicing their dislike of intimate relationships between Chinese men and
Samoan women. Moreover, Samoans blamed the Chinese newcomers for
rising crime rates on their islands.

The timing of the shoot-out turned out to be no coincidence. The following day, the Samoan Fitafita were scheduled to receive a public warning about
their repeated attacks on Chinese workers.[43] With official sanctions loom-
ing, the Samoan youngsters seized the last opportunity for independent
action. For his part, Governor Schultz used the fatal events to dissolve the
Samoan Fitafita altogether. Only the oldest and longest-serving members
were transferred to other service jobs within the administration. However,
when New Zealand troops occupied German Samoa just a few months later,
many of the former Fitafita and *leoleo* reenlisted with the new colonial power
in town.[44]

As this violent episode showed, cross-racial conflicts could easily spill over
into outright resistance to the German employers of Chinese workers and to
the colonial presence as a whole. Far from being a mere "decorative adjunct"
to the colonial administration, Samoan soldiers, if tested, did not shirk from
using their military training even against the German settlers they were
meant to protect.[45] The seeds of racial conflict sown by colonial officials had
come back to haunt them.

Between Worlds: The Adventures of Charles T. Taylor

Since the days of the tridominium, Samoans had worked for the German,
British, and American diplomatic representations as clerks, translators, interpreters, and aides. Le Mamea, for instance, worked as English-Samoan
interpreter for the tripartite government and joined his half brother Te'o Tuvale as a member of the ethnographic show troupe touring through Germany
in 1900. Tuvale had actually apprenticed as an assistant clerk in Le Mamea's
office since 1878 and, after his return from Germany, was hired by Imperial
Court judge Heinrich Schnee as a clerk. Tuvale later became Governor Solf's
secretary and interpreter. One of Tuvale's sons, Atoa Te'o Tuvale, followed in
his father's footsteps in the colonial service and became chief interpreter of
Western Samoa's Legislative Assembly after independence in 1962.[46]

Another long-serving government clerk was Meisake, who began his career in 1879 as undersecretary of state for the Samoan government. He went on to work as a clerk and interpreter for several German consuls in the 1880s and 1890s before moving to the governor's office in 1900. Not long after, Meisake asked Solf for a pay raise, but the governor declined. According to Solf, Meisake then threatened to leave for Tutuila and work for the U.S. naval administration. Meisake said he was sick of German tightfistedness. Meisake did not act on his threat and never switched employers. In any case, Meisake's insistence on a fair wage for his long work experience showed that Samoan service workers knew what they were worth.[47]

The number of Samoan and Chinese government employees soared after 1900, as the German and American colonial administrations needed more and more local help in their daily operations. Speeches needed to be translated, letters needed to be filed, and floors needed to be swept. Beyond the colonial administration buildings, Samoans and Chinese were employed as plantation inspectors, tax collectors, teachers, boat crew, and runners.[48] Among the first three hundred Chinese workers who arrived in Apia in April 1903 were seven overseers, along with four domestic workers and four noncontracted artisans.[49] The German administration soon began hiring several Chinese workers for its customs office and construction department.[50] By 1908, more than sixty Chinese contract laborers were working for the German administration, most in road construction and in the hospital.[51] The two chief clerks in the Chinese commissioner's office—Lau Ah Mau and Wang Ah Kau—received the highest salaries of all: 60 marks ($15) a month.[52] Even though the German agent Wandres had relied on Chinese interpreters on his recruiting trips to China, no official Chinese interpreter worked for the colonial administration in German Samoa until 1912. In May of that year, Tsang Shin Lun was hired for 300 marks ($75) a month to interpret and translate between Chinese and English.[53]

Translation work became one of the most important services Samoan government employees could offer. Le Mamea, Tuvale, and Meisake had been trailblazers in this regard. Governor Solf acquired conversational Samoan and could understand most of the spoken language, but legal regulations and especially official speeches demanded a command of formal Samoan beyond his reach. To bridge the language gap, the German administration hired

Figure 17. Group including Wilhelm Solf, Charles T. Taylor (standing behind Solf's left shoulder), Charles H. Mills, and Mataʻafa Iosefo at Mulinuʻu, 1903.
Alexander Turnbull Library, Wellington, New Zealand (PAColl-6001-45).

translators and interpreters who were native Samoans and had learned German and English. This requirement made Samoans of mixed-race descent ideal candidates for these positions. Their daily labor routines included office work, translating official correspondence and legislation, and interpreting speeches given by the governor and other high-ranking colonial officials. Similar to Samoan performers in ethnographic shows, service workers were engaged in a particular kind of performative labor. One of the most influential and longest-serving interpreters in German Samoa was Charles T. Taylor.

Born in 1871 to a shipbuilder from Liverpool and a Samoan mother in Motoʻotua, just outside Apia, the young Charles grew up speaking both English and Samoan. Among his Samoan friends he was known as Sale, while most Euro-American settlers called him Charley. When it became public that Charles's father was already married to a woman in New Zealand, he deserted his son and moved back there. To avoid the disgrace of illegitimate birth, a German family in Upolu adopted Taylor, who became fluent in German. At the age of fifteen, Taylor's gift for languages was discovered by the British consul in Apia, who in 1886 hired him to be his official interpreter. This job marked the beginning of Taylor's long and productive career at the center of the linguistic melting pot that was German Samoa.

His position as interpreter at the British consulate in Apia offered Taylor other opportunities as well. When Henry Adams and John La Farge arrived in Samoa in the fall of 1890, Taylor became their personal interpreter, and it was through him that the famous American visitors gained access to Samoan culture. Without Taylor's linguistic assistance, La Farge would not have been able to learn about Samoan myths, nor would he have been able to reach some of the remote villages in which he drew his famous sketches. Adams acknowledged Taylor's important mediating role in his letters, recalling that "our boy Charley" translated Samoan sermons.[54] Adams's paternalistic tone reveals the ambiguous relationship Taylor had to negotiate with his employer, veering between intimacy and condescension.[55]

While Taylor was working as an interpreter for the British consulate, he also clerked in the store of Harry J. Moors, the American trader who had brought a Samoan troupe to the world's fair in Chicago in 1893. It was likely Moors who introduced Taylor to another famous visitor to Samoa: Robert Louis Stevenson. The world-renowned Scotsman had come to Samoa in December 1889 to escape the obligations of a star author and strengthen his weak physical frame. Moors, a good friend of Stevenson's, recalled that it was Taylor who first taught Samoan to Stevenson. Always the ironist, Stevenson referred to his teacher as "Charlie Taylor—the sesquipedalian young half-caste."[56] After Stevenson passed away in 1894, Taylor continued the poet's efforts to translate Samoan poetry into English with the help of Australian journalist William F. Whyte.[57] Taylor also became more outspoken about his deceased boss. In an article for the *Samoa Times* from February 1895, Taylor accused Stevenson of providing guns to the supporters of Tamasese Lealofi I in their war against the German-backed Malietoa Laupepa. A month later, Taylor was sentenced to three months in jail for slander.[58]

After his release from jail, Taylor's life quieted down when he married Tipesa Timaio, who was from a respected Samoan family from Savai'i. Among other odd jobs, Taylor worked as a boatbuilder.[59] In 1900, the British consulate in Apia closed and Taylor had to find a new job. It did not take long before the new German administration secured Taylor's services. Taylor's considerable experience, together with his ability to speak German—the increasingly dominant language in town—made him an important asset to the administration. Taylor became not only government interpreter at the Samoan High Court but also office clerk and Governor Solf's personal interpreter.[60] These were busy days for the thirty-year-old man.

For young and gifted Samoans like Taylor, the colonial world opened up new possibilities far beyond their home. Since Taylor had proved himself a valuable interpreter both to Solf and to the administration at large, the governor decided to send him to the birthplace of his adoptive parents: Germany. Taylor must have been thrilled at this opportunity. To be sure, Solf did not have Taylor's personal happiness in mind when he made the decision to send him almost ten thousand miles away. Following a similar logic to sending Samoan performers to Europe, Solf hoped that such a long and expensive journey would impress upon the minds of Samoans that the German Empire was a cultural and military powerhouse. For his part, Taylor wanted to go to Germany mostly to improve his German language skills. Yet apart from these practical considerations, Samoan service workers like Taylor seized every opportunity for travel with heartfelt conviction. A desire for learning and going on *malaga* to see the world combined to make such trips alluring to Samoans.

In November 1901, Taylor embarked on his weeks-long trip to Germany, calling at Sydney before passing through the Suez Canal to reach the northern German port city of Bremerhaven. From there, he traveled on by train to Witzenhausen, just south of the famous university city Göttingen in central Germany. In this small town, he enrolled in the German Colonial School Wilhelmshof, which had opened only three years before his arrival. Founded by German colonialists, industrialists, and missionaries, the Colonial School offered practical training to German officials and colonial subjects in plantation agriculture, handiwork, and other skills useful in the German colonies.[61] As a rule, the school accepted students only between the ages of seventeen and twenty-seven, but when Taylor arrived, he was already over thirty years old. Solf's political influence and personal friendship with the school's first director and former Protestant pastor, Ernst Albert Fabarius, had likely opened the door.

At school, Taylor took primarily German classes together with courses on office management. Taylor did not participate in the more physically demanding curriculum, such as agricultural courses, partly because Solf had warned the school's head teacher ahead of Taylor's arrival that he, like many other "half-castes," could not withstand too much physical exertion.[62] According to Solf, Taylor also exhibited "a heavily Samoan imagination."[63] Ignorant of his boss's comments, Taylor wrote to Solf about his daily schedule at the school and even asked the governor for additional money to buy gifts for his fellow students.[64] Not coincidentally, Solf was on home leave in Germany when Taylor was attending the Colonial School, and he kept in regular touch with him through the mail. Taylor's monthly salary was suspended while he was in Germany, but Solf sent him money from his personal pocket.[65] Fearing what Taylor might do with his own money, Solf held fast to his policy of protecting Samoans from the dangers of Euro-American capitalism far away from Samoa.

In one of his letters to Solf from June 1902, Taylor told him about his visit to the nearby Wartburg, where Martin Luther had translated the New Testament from ancient Greek into German nearly four centuries earlier. Visiting this landmark site in German history, Taylor might have felt a sense of kinship with the brave German founder of Protestantism from the sixteenth century. After all, not only were they both Protestants and independent thinkers, but they were also crucial mediators between worlds. If Luther translated the New Testament in a record ten weeks, Taylor did his part by sending Solf translations of letters he had requested even while both stayed in Germany. In his letter to Solf, Taylor described his visit to Wartburg and Luther's parlor merely as a famous place to tell his friends about back in Samoa. But to a curious man like Taylor, the historical link between these two translators must have been obvious.[66]

Shortly after his Wartburg visit, Taylor and Solf briefly met in person in the famous spa town of Bad Kissingen. In a letter after their meeting, Solf expressed his disappointment in Taylor for not taking his mission in Germany as seriously as he should. Solf told Taylor not only to learn how to speak German but "to feel and think German" as well.[67] Solf continued with this surprising advice for a mixed-race Samoan like Taylor: "In the future, try not to be three-quarters Samoan and one-quarter German, but rather seek to be three-quarters German and one-quarter Samoan."[68] Partly fueled by disappointment in Taylor's progress, Solf urged his interpreter to develop the kind of cross-cultural empathy that his own system of indirect rule in Samoa rested on. Solf's curt command revealed the simple fact that he depended on Taylor's translating and interpreting skills to be an effective governor.

Taylor himself cultivated this sort of cross-cultural intimacy with Solf when he addressed his employer as "my dear Governor" and "my dear master" in his letters.[69] True to Solf's call for transcending his Samoan roots to become more "German," Taylor added the following comment to his translated letters for Solf: "I understand all what you wish to say, just from your glance."[70] The fact that Taylor wrote this sentence in English did little to distract from his sincere effort as a professional translator to think himself into the mind of his German boss. To be sure, the relationship between service workers such as Taylor and their superiors was different from the relationship between, for example, a Chinese plantation worker and his employer. Translation work implied a degree of familiarity and even intimacy between worker and employer unimaginable and unnecessary in other workscapes. In what could be lost in translation, those who did the translating found their power.

Taylor's wish to be near Solf was inextricably linked to his desire to see the world. After their meeting in Bad Kissingen, Taylor asked Solf if he could visit him in Berlin, the empire's capital and biggest city. To Taylor's chagrin, Solf rejected Taylor's wish because, as he explained to him in a letter, such a big city as Berlin would be a danger for Taylor without proper guidance.[71] Apparently, Solf did not want to assume direct responsibility for Taylor beyond sending him some pocket money, for it could not have been Taylor's lack of German that would have made a trip to Berlin impossible. Solf further justified his decision by reassuring Taylor that he had only his best interests for his "colonial career" in mind.[72]

Taylor himself had different plans. He not only wanted to visit Berlin but wanted to see other parts of the world as well. Months before his scheduled return to Samoa, Taylor had already asked Solf to change his original ticket from Bremen to Apia via Sydney. Solf must have told Taylor about his plans to return to Samoa through the United States in order to make some diplomatic visits along the way. Desperate to accompany his boss to the United States, Taylor asked, "Couldn't I go with you, Mr. Governor, via America? That way, I could see more of the world."[73] Again, Solf declined.

Upon his return to Samoa, Taylor continued working as Solf's interpreter, but he was not alone anymore. During Taylor's absence, another Samoan had taken over the duties of government interpreter: Afamasaga Maua (Saga for short). Saga had joined the municipal police force in the 1890s, remaining in office after Germany took control in 1900. As Taylor's substitute, Saga did such an excellent job that Solf promoted him to be official translator. While there is no evidence that Saga actively ousted Taylor during his stay in Germany, Saga clearly seized his chance. In February 1903, Solf made Saga his private secretary and advisor on Samoan matters. As Solf's most trusted aide, Saga used his great personal influence to calm tensions during Lauaki's Mau a Pule in 1908.[74] Saga and Taylor likely shared responsibilities in translating and interpreting for the colonial administration for a few years. In early August 1911, a tragic accident cut Taylor's remarkable journey short: he fell from his horse, which he kept to "expedite the orders of Your Excellency," and fractured his skull. Taylor, who was just forty years old, died from his injuries. Shortly after, Solf was recalled from Apia to become secretary in the Colonial Office in Berlin. By that time, an increasing number of Samoans had followed Taylor's and Saga's lead in joining the ranks of the colonial service.

Taio Tolo and the Campaign for Samoan Equality

In the years leading up to World War I, more than a dozen Samoans were employed in the German administration. Compared to other German colonies, particularly in Africa, more systematic efforts to integrate colonized people into the German administration came relatively late to Samoa.[75] Funded by the head tax, a new government school opened in 1908 to offer training to young Samoan men in military discipline, practical skills, and the German language. Virtually all graduates entered government service as interpreters, clerks, and artisans. To provide further training, particularly talented students were sent to Germany or other German colonies from time to time.

When Rear Admiral Erich Gühler, commander of the German East Asian Fleet, visited Samoa in August 1910, he was so impressed by the government school that he took two of its Samoan students with him. At the German-controlled shipyard in Qingdao, they would be trained as carpenters and locksmiths, as was the rule with young men from Saipan. The opportunity to travel to China was tempting to many Samoan students: "The interest was extraordinary," Gühler noted with a bit of surprise, "everybody wanted to come along."[76] Samoan apprentices in distant China gave colonial globality their own flavor. Over the course of the following year, more and more young Samoans went on to learn basic German and entered government jobs as interpreters, clerks, drawing assistants, and medical assistants. As Governor Schultz, Solf's successor, reported back to Berlin, the Samoan employees saved the colonial administration money compared to hiring Europeans.[77] By early 1914, there were fifteen Samoans employed by the German colonial administration.

Although they had some of the best-paying jobs available to Samoans at the time, the government employees were far from satisfied. On February 5, 1914, virtually all of the Samoan government employees congregated at the government hospital in Moto'otua for a secret meeting. The meeting was organized by one of Taylor's successors in the office of government interpreter: Taio Tolo. Two days earlier, Taio had sent around a letter to his fellow government employees in which he announced the "secret conference" and asked his colleagues to indicate their interest in attending. Taio elaborated that the meeting would not involve official matters but rather be an open discussion among the Samoan employees about "their relations to the Germans."[78] As main organizer, Taio signed his own name first at the bottom of the circular letter in the name of the "high *fono* (council meeting)." That way, Taio firmly embedded the planned meeting within Samoan tradition and raised the stakes for participation. All of the fifteen Samoan employees signed the letter indicating their intention to participate in the meeting. One of them was Sepulona, Taio's brother, an assistant doctor at the government hospital. It was likely Sepulona who suggested his workplace as an appropriate place to meet. Open since 1912, the government hospital was located at some distance from the other government buildings and a busy place, where a get-together of such a large number of Samoan government employees would attract less attention.

At the meeting, eleven of the fifteen original signatories were present: Taio Tolo, Atimalala, Sepulona, Sofeni, Hanipale, Ma'a Anae, Tauvela, Mago, Maiuu, Tasi, and Paniani. As noted in the official *fono* report, written by Paniani, both Kenape and Ma'a had excused their absence. Why the other two employees who had signed the circular letter did not attend the meeting is not known. Besides the interpreter Taio, who was elected chair of the meeting, five of the attendees were clerks, three—including Sepulona—were assistant doctors, and one worked in the post office. As their first act, the members signed an oath in which they swore to uphold their votes in the meeting. The *fono* members then proceeded to debate several topics that agitated their minds, following a set agenda.[79]

First, Taio raised the question of why the Germans and Samoans were not equal. By then, it would have become clear to all Samoan employees present why their meeting had to be kept secret. Paniani, who worked at the post office, was the first to chime in. He complained that he and his fellow Samoan post office clerks were not treated well by the Europeans. From the European point of view, Paniani claimed, the Samoan employees were "like servants or black contract laborers, so to speak."[80] The assistant doctors Atimalala and Sepulona both confirmed Paniani's impressions by elaborating on their own experiences in the government hospital.

After these complaints, Taio himself intervened. The real reason why the Europeans were treating the Samoans so badly, he argued, was that the Samoans were still living in "ignorance." To make his case, Taio pointed to other island groups whose inhabitants were "waking up" after several of the local islanders had been sent to Europe for their education.[81] Stressing the lack of educational opportunities in German Samoa, Taio averred: "All schools in Samoa are entirely insufficient; that way, we cannot gain the education which is necessary to be equal to the Germans, except when a number of students was to be sent to Europe for training."[82] Hanipale immediately supported Taio's proposal by reminding the *fono* members that Taio himself would be traveling soon to Germany to improve his German there. This training program, Hanipale opined, should be expanded so that more than one Samoan student could travel abroad every year. Confronted with his upcoming study trip to Germany, Taio asked the meeting to refrain from discussing his travel plans until his departure. Taio was probably afraid his Germany trip would be in danger if his superiors learned about the secret meeting. Beside these practical considerations, it was good Samoan etiquette to keep the debate about German-Samoan relations as impersonal and relevant to the other members as possible. Taio concluded his comment by emphasizing the good for Samoa as a whole: "May it come about that many will travel to Germany to be taught there in different schools so that something fruitful will emerge for this group of islands, not for the physical well-being of the individual or of his family, but for the whole of Samoa."[83]

Try as he might, it was not easy for Taio to distract from the fact that it was he who was chosen to go to Germany for language training. His position as government interpreter, which put him in close contact with the governor, made him an important asset to the colonial administration and a likely candidate for further training. Like Taylor more than a decade earlier, Taio had a crucial intermediary position in the transmission of colonial power in Samoa. If Taylor had been an innovator as intercultural mediator and multilingual genius, Taio learned how to use his privileged place in the colonial labor hierarchy to organize his fellow workers for plans bigger than himself.

In contrast to the mixed-race Taylor, Taio and his fellow conspirers in Moto'otua came from leading Samoan families. More than half of the *fono* members under Taio's leadership had fathers who had worked in the colonial service.[84] Family pedigree and racial purity were significant for Taio and his supporters, so they crossed out the signature of one of the original signatories two weeks after the meeting, citing his mixed-race background.[85] Taio himself was well-aware that the leaders of anti-colonial resistance in other parts of the Pacific world were often workers in the colonial service who had received a metropolitan education. As Taio prepared to follow in Taylor's footsteps and take a trip to Germany, he was also pursuing an education to become a leader of his people against his teachers.

After debating the strained relations between Samoans and Germans, the meeting moved on to other topics. Several members sharply criticized the practice of Samoan women living with Chinese men and demanded a law banning this form of cohabitation. In response, Taio called for more caution and argued that an official ban would not be appropriate because the Chinese consul would object.[86] As this debate from early 1914 showed, interracial sex continued to be a contentious issue between Samoans and Chinese long after the first arrival of Chinese workers in 1903. The final topic returned the discussion to labor relations between Samoans and Europeans. Tasi complained about the fact that Samoans were prohibited from working as assistants in European-owned trade stores outside Apia. Tasi argued that if this ban were not lifted, "no schools would be needed anymore for the Samoans because they would have no opportunity to usefully apply the things they had learned."[87] Education, at home and abroad, was a major concern for the Samoan elite.

At the end of the meeting, Taio reminded all attendees to keep the proceedings secret, especially from friends, relatives, and acquaintances. This was particularly important because people in Samoa were widely known for gossip and slander, Taio elaborated. Taio, for one, was well aware of the danger the *fono* members were facing: "Even if everything is right what we have done, it would still be perceived as a 'revolt' against the government."[88] He closed the meeting by calling on his fellow Samoans to be "united" and "with true patriotism true and honest to one another."[89] Together with the oath the attendees had sworn at the beginning of the meeting, Taio's call for patriotic unity was a significant step toward a more aggressive and coordinated front against colonial rule. Born among highly educated Samoans employed by the colonial administration, this spirit of "revolt," in Taio's prescient phrase, would only grow stronger after New Zealand took over the islands from the German Empire. Those closest to colonial power grew closer to one another and appointed themselves leaders of the anti-colonial movement of the 1920s.

As the discussions at their secret meeting showed, Taio and his followers saw themselves as the enlightened avant-garde among their less-educated compatriots. Like the *ilustrados* in the colonial Philippines, Samoan government employees such as Taio and Taylor before him used their multilingualism and travel experiences to define themselves as a cosmopolitan elite ready to challenge their colonial rulers.[90] Forged in the crucible of colonial service, this emerging young elite not only contested colonial rule from outside but also challenged older structures of authority within Samoan society.

When it eventually came to light, senior Samoan government employees saw Taio's secret *fono* as an attempt to undermine their own influence.[91] One of them was Taylor's successor as government interpreter, Saga. His impressive career climbing the ranks of the colonial service turned Saga into one of the most influential and best-paid Samoans of his generation. By April 1912, he was earning 180 marks ($45) a month.[92] Confronted with Taio's secret *fono*, Saga saw his own considerable influence in danger. After all, forty-one-year-old Saga was the governor's official spokesperson and Taio merely his junior colleague as government interpreter. Perhaps Taio reminded Saga of his own rise out of Taylor's shadow. Moreover, Taio's father, Tolo, was also employed by the colonial administration, which made Taio's actions seem even more subversive. Further complicating the generational conflicts was the fact that the meeting's elected secretary was one of Saga's own sons: Paniani. To repair his public reputation and strengthen his position as top government advisor, Saga called on Governor Schultz to award him a German medal.[93] But the onset of the war robbed him of this symbolic reassurance. Like many Samoan Fitafita, Saga did not hesitate to join the New Zealand military administration after August 1914 as inspector of the Samoan police.[94]

Earlier challenges to colonial rule—such as Lauaki's rebellion, which Saga helped to disperse, and the copra cooperative movement—sat uneasily with the experiences and demands of government interpreters and medical assistants such as Taio and his brother Sepulona. In many ways, their demands for equal treatment and opportunity posed a more fundamental challenge to German colonial rule over Samoa. Their proximity to and implication with colonial power made Samoan government employees more likely but also more ambivalent allies in the fight against colonialism. And beyond these tensions in Samoan society, the interests of workers from other Pacific islands and China were not easy to reconcile with Samoan demands for more political and economic self-determination.

It took a few months after the *fono* in February 1914 before colonial authorities in German Samoa found out about it. At the end of April 1914, Schultz received confidential information from Samoan sources that a group of young Samoans had held a secret meeting to discuss, among other things, their status vis-à-vis their white employers.[95] The group, Schultz was informed, had kept written records of their meeting. Schultz immediately ordered a search of Taio's desk, where the circular letter and the meeting report were found. For better and for worse, Taio sat too close to the governor. Schultz especially appreciated having written evidence for the secret meeting because it prevented Taio and his followers from denying or embellishing their plans.

Having learned about the meeting, Schultz did not bother to go through the German Empire's legal process to punish the offenders. Instead, the governor used his own considerable discretionary powers to deal with Taio and his followers in, as he called it, an "administrative fashion."[96] He summarily dismissed Taio, his personal interpreter and aide, and declared that he would be sent to German New Guinea. There, "far away from home, family, and peers," Schultz explained, Taio would have a few years "to think about what is proper for him."[97] Like other Samoan leaders before him, Taio was sentenced to exile in another German colony, which was also the home of many Melanesian workers who had gone the other way to work on Samoan plantations.

Schultz was fully aware of the link between Taio's planned educational trip to the German heartland and his exile to a remote part of the German Empire. To justify his harsh decision, Schultz recalled that the German tour of Tamasese's troupe in 1910 had been pushed through against an official ban precisely because of the desired "educational and political effect" on the visitors. According to Schultz, a similar effect was to be expected from Taio's upcoming visit to Germany. Given the circumstances, however, Taio's trip to Germany had to be changed into a trip to New Guinea.[98] In the last moment, Taio was saved by the outbreak of world war, which shifted the administration's priorities. Ships were suddenly needed for the war, leaving none available to send a former Samoan government employee into exile in New Guinea.

Taio's brother Sepulona fared relatively better. He, too, was dismissed, but with the possibility of reemployment. Schultz thought that in contrast to Taio, Sepulona had a "modest and obedient" personality and thus deserved a second chance. All other *fono* attendees were denied a scheduled pay raise and were severely reprimanded. On top of the governor's sanctions, the Samoan government employees were strongly censured by their own fathers, many of whom—including Saga—were veterans of the colonial service themselves. Challenges to colonial structures of authority intersected with challenges to familial structures of authority as fathers saw their families' access to lucrative and prestigious government jobs in jeopardy. This next generation of Samoan government workers had come to question their loyalty to their employers and just as importantly to their fathers.

The Education of Miss Pepe

Health care was the third major branch of the colonial service in Samoa. Women provided the overwhelming majority of medical workers in Samoa. In traditional Samoan culture, women were expected to be the emotional and spiritual centers of their families. According to this gendered division of family labor, women were tasked with healing, nurturing, and comforting family members. As guardians of the sacred covenant among brothers and sisters (*feagaiga*), women played a role in Samoan society that prepared them for professional careers in nursing.[99] Virtually all female healers learned their skills from their mothers or other female relatives.[100] Medical knowledge was thus passed on through matrilineal lines.

Euro-American concepts of health invaded Samoa in the same way that diseases, like the flu, had done.[101] With the arrival of British missionaries in 1830, Euro-American medical beliefs and practices were introduced in Samoa. In travel reports, visitors frequently lauded Samoans for their personal hygiene, though some ridiculed them for their frequent baths. In addition to the influence of Euro-American missionaries, Samoan medicine borrowed from Melanesian and Chinese workers who came to the islands.[102] Samoan healers (*fofō*) adopted those medical practices that proved most effective in treating illness, such as maintaining better hygiene and incorporating new plant substances into their repertoire. As a result, pre-contact Samoan medicine was not replaced but rather expanded by Euro-American ideas on health. In contrast to German and New Zealand–occupied Samoa, the U.S. naval administration in Tutuila pursued an active policy of suppressing traditional healing practices it deemed "unscientific" and dangerous to Samoan health. However, despite a law that required Samoan healers to be registered and prohibited anyone else from providing medical treatment under heavy penalty, U.S. health officials did not succeed in eradicating long-standing medical beliefs and practices among Samoans.[103]

Because the expansion of Euro-American medicine into Samoan villages required the formal consent of *matai* and the general support of Samoans, a medical division of labor emerged: illnesses deemed of Samoan origin were treated with Samoan medicine, whereas new illnesses introduced by Euro-Americans demanded treatment according to Euro-American medicine.[104] This pragmatic syncretism intensified after the flu pandemic in 1918–19, which both undermined the legitimacy of Samoan medicine and removed an entire generation of older Samoan leaders who had defended it.[105] Yet as late as the 1970s, Samoan nurses remained open to folk medicine and shared a belief in the supernatural causes of many illnesses.[106]

Despite different approaches to Samoan medicine, colonial officials in both German and American Samoa established hospitals to promote hygiene among Samoans and improve the general health of the population. In German Samoa, the government hospital consisted of separate units segregated according to race. Beginning in 1903, a hospital for Europeans provided services for white settlers only, whereas smaller so-called barracks cared for the Chinese and Samoans.[107] The official name of "barracks"—as in the military barracks that housed the Fitafita Guard—clearly indicated a racial hierarchy in medical care, with considerably fewer resources and services available to Chinese and Samoan patients. Prices for bandages and drugs reflected differences in purchasing power. While Europeans had to pay 2 marks ($0.50) for medical supplies, others paid only half, and poor patients nothing at all.[108] Medical personnel followed the racial segregation of patients. In the hospital for Europeans, only white nurses and doctors were allowed to work. On top of their monthly salary, white nurses received free accommodations, electricity, food, and laundry.[109] Only in the lavatories did European patients encounter one of the three Chinese attendants.[110] Apart from the government hospital, the DHPG paid its own doctor, Dr. Zieschank, to care for its Melanesian and Chinese plantation workers. To address the increasing demand for medical care for Samoans, a new government hospital opened in Apia in 1912.

Graduates of Papauta Girls' School, the first four Samoan students—Mere Natapu, Nela Sopoaga, Vailima, and Naoafioga—were between twelve and fourteen years old when they started nursing school. Their basic medical training included nursing skills such as temperature taking, sponging, measuring blood pressure, and applying dressings. Many of these skills, such as how to nurse babies or how to keep things clean, proved useful beyond the hospital. If colonial officials had hoped for precisely this transmission of hygienic norms and skills into wider Samoan society, many Samoan families undoubtedly benefited from having a trained nurse in their midst.

As the first generation of nurses recalled decades later, the work environment in the government hospital was marked by rigid racial hierarchies. The white nurses and doctors were in charge of the hospital and commanded the respect of their Samoan colleagues. Often, it was difficult for the Samoan nurses to voice their opinions about a patient, let alone disagree with their white bosses. The relationship between white and Samoan nurses in the government hospital thus mirrored the relationship between colonizers and the colonized more broadly. Samoan nurses took their time to learn how to speak

Figure 18. Government hospital in Apia, 1912.
Hospital, Apia. From the album Samoa, c. 1918, by Alfred James Tattersall. Te Papa (O.041863).

with greater confidence, but their white superiors took even longer to listen to their concerns.[111]

The unequal work environment had devastating consequences for the people living in Upolu and Savai'i at the end of World War I. While Samoa was free of malaria—a formidable obstacle to Euro-American colonization in other parts of the world—a virus more common in Europe and North America proved all the more dangerous to Samoans: the H1N1, or "Spanish," influenza. Trailing the destruction and malnutrition of World War I, the flu spread across the world like a bushfire in the fall of 1918. Sailing from Auckland on October 31 and arriving in Apia on November 7, the steamer SS *Talune* brought with it good news about the armistice in Europe as well as several flu-infected passengers, who would spell bad news for Western Samoa. When the pandemic rapidly spread throughout Upolu and Savai'i, the New

Zealand military administration failed in quarantining the islands, leading to the death of over one-fifth of the total population in a matter of weeks.[112]

Among the many Samoan casualties was forty-five-year-old Saga, the powerful interpreter and government spokesperson. Saga's proximity to colonial power could not save his life. Ta'isi O. F. Nelson lost his mother, his four-year-old and only son, and several other family members.[113] Indeed, the flu killed so many *matai*, church leaders, and other community leaders that it represented a deep break with the Samoan past and brought a new generation into power.[114] While Colonel Robert Logan blamed "ill-disciplined" Samoan nurses for this human disaster and refused outside help, his counterpart in American Samoa, Commander Poyer, managed to prevent the virus from entering, resulting in no casualties.[115] A strict quarantine enforced by Samoans who patrolled the shores to keep unwanted visitors from Upolu away and a good portion of luck kept the flu away from Tutuila. Partly in response to this drastic difference in colonial governance, Samoan leaders in Western Samoa in January 1919 presented a petition to Robert Ward Tate, the new civil administrator, demanding unification with American Samoa.[116]

Around the time the government hospital opened in Apia, similar plans were being made in neighboring American Samoa. The government hospital in Apia served as the explicit model. In February 1911, Governor William Crose asked the secretary of the navy for permission to erect a native hospital and several dispensaries. Prior to that, the U.S. Navy employed doctors and medical staff for its own personnel, offering medical assistance to Samoans only in cases of emergency. In 1909, two Samoan hospital corpsmen began duty at the naval hospital, but there was still no place to go for Samoan patients.[117] Crose complained about an acute lack of adequate health services for Samoans in Tutuila and linked the proposed hospital to the overall navy policy toward Samoans: "The Samoans do not yet realize the necessity of health measures, of medical treatment, and their gradual education must be continued."[118] As Crose's comment showed, providing medical care to Samoans was not an act of selflessness by colonial administrators but rather was linked to "educating" Samoans in the ways of Western civilization.

To finance the new hospital and dispensaries, Crose suggested that they charge the Samoans whenever possible—a radical departure from the free health care Samoans received in the German colony. U.S. Navy officials simply had fewer financial resources than their German counterparts, partly due to differences in the metropolitan health-care systems.[119] In April 1911, the Navy Department granted permission under the condition that no additional expenses would be involved.[120] Hence, Samoans financed and built the new hospital on their own. The following year, the first hospital for Samoan patients opened in the village of Malaloa, known to locals as the Annex due to its location next to the naval station in Fagatogo. In the beginning, the hospital staff included two American hospital corpsmen, an untrained female nurse, and a janitor.[121] Soon thereafter, the first two branch dispensaries opened in Tutuila, and two more were added to serve the outlying districts and Manu'a.[122] Operated by navy hospital corpsmen and Samoan assistants, the dispensaries offered free medical treatment and supplies to Samoans, whereas the hospital remained a pay-as-you-go institution.[123]

It took another two years before more concrete plans for the training of Samoan medical staff materialized. In July 1913, Navy Surgeon C. J. Ely requested two navy nurses to come to Tutuila to train Samoan women as nurses and educate them about hygiene and "feminine care."[124] Due to the remoteness of some villages in Tutuila, Ely noted, getting Samoan patients to the central hospital at the naval station in Pago proved difficult. Local and early diagnosis would improve the health situation drastically. "If we get the right people and train them properly," the navy surgeon explained, "they will engender in the minds of Samoans respect for the fly, mosquito and intestinal parasites and a realization of the necessity of latrines and pure water."[125] In Ely's view, the presence of trained white female nurses and an additional two to three student Samoan nurses would induce Samoan women to seek medical care before it was too late.[126] In response to Ely's report, the Navy Department ordered the establishment of a training school for nurses in American Samoa, hoping that the "scope of the instruction will not be beyond the comprehension of the native women."[127] At the time, the U.S. Navy operated similar training schools for local nurses in Guam, Hawai'i, the Philippines, and Haiti.[128] American Samoa would be the latest—if smaller—addition to the expanding archipelago of medical training under U.S. auspices.

On February 23, 1914, a little over two weeks after Taio's secret *fono* in the government hospital in Apia, the Training School for Samoan Nurses opened in Tutuila. The hospital consisted of three large houses for patients from each of the three districts, and an additional three small *fales* for the *matai* of each district. Since the hospital lacked waste disposal, nurses had to climb down a steep hill to empty and wash the bedpans in the ocean.[129] Regulations at the hospital reflected Samoan life. Because the hospital did not supply food, patients had friends deliver it directly to their mats.[130]

The first class of student nurses consisted of four young Samoan women— Anna, Cora, Winnie, and India.[131] Due to concerns about the intellectual capabilities of Samoan women, the students initially received only elementary instruction in medicine and hygiene. They learned the names and uses of hospital utensils, such as the thermometer, before receiving basic lessons in anatomy and physiology.[132] Despite (or perhaps because of) these low expectations, the apprentices were "much interested in the work."[133] As in Upolu, the two-year training emphasized practical skills in providing first aid and dressing wounds but also included lessons in housekeeping, such as cleaning, cooking, and cutting grass.[134] In effect, the daily labor tasks of the Samoan nurses resembled those of domestic workers: mopping floors, cleaning bedpans, and making beds.[135]

Samoan women were attracted to the nursing school mainly because it offered a career outside the traditional Samoan labor system but was still compatible with community service and family care. The school was so attractive that Samoan women from Savai'i and Upolu flocked to it.[136] Graduates of the training school were among the only Samoan women at the time who earned their own cash. (Only a handful of domestic workers hired by navy officials or Euro-American traders had an independent cash income in Tutuila.) While undergraduate nurses received only $2.50 a month, graduates made $15.00 a month.[137] In addition to their monthly salaries, the naval administration provided free uniforms, food, quarters, and electric lighting to the Samoan nurses.[138]

The interest of the Samoan nurses in training might have had something to do with the enthusiasm of their teachers. In 1908, the U.S. Navy had established the Navy Nurse Corps, whose first twenty graduate nurses were known as the "Sacred Twenty."[139] Two of the first graduates, Mary Humphrey and Corinne Anderson, arrived in Tutuila from San Francisco in October 1913 to assume their assignments as superintendent and assistant of the new training school.[140] As dedicated teachers, Humphrey and Anderson

Figure 19. Grace Pepe on U.S.S. *Sonoma* on her way to Mare Island, California, June 23, 1919. Author's collection.

compiled a "Care Procedure Book" to guide their Samoan students.[141] At the same time, Humphrey complained that most Samoan student nurses spoke little English even after years of missionary school.[142] Despite these challenges, the first class graduated in November 1916 to great fanfare. The new chief nurse, Ada Pendleton, awarded "large class pins of gold, with an attractive design in red and blue enamel," to the nurses and treated them to a month-long holiday trip to Apia.[143] Among the first graduates of the training school was Grace Pepe.

With her great enthusiasm and quick wit, Pepe excelled in school. De-scribed as "a young Samoan of unusual mental development" by a navy of-ficial, Pepe clearly exceeded all paternalistic expectations of the navy men in charge.[144] Along with fellow nurses Initia and Feiloaiga, Pepe was a graduate of the Atauloma Girls School, established by the London Missionary Society (LMS) in 1900. Before becoming a feeder for the nursing school, the all-girls school prepared its graduates to be the wives of LMS pastors. For example,

Initia and her pastor husband Nemaia served the LMS at Lawes College in Papua New Guinea.[145] As in other colonies at the time, caring for souls went hand in hand with caring for bodies.

Partly in response to the crowded nurses' quarters, the chief nurse, Hannah Workman, created a new program for the student nurses in 1919. The Samoan nurses, including Pepe, rotated between training in primary nursing in the main hospital and periods of service in outlying districts. As a result, the Samoan nurses learned how to cooperate with white navy medical officers and nurses and also developed a greater sense of enthusiasm for their work. To honor the general success of the training school, the navy surgeon general assigned "Miss Grace Pepe" to the naval hospital at Mare Island, northeast of San Francisco, for further training.[146] Pepe's training trip to the U.S. mainland had explicit didactic purposes: "It is hoped that the reports which Miss Pepe will take back to her beloved island will result in a greater interest for nursing and welfare work among the native Samoan girls and through this medium it is believed that improved conditions, particularly for the women and children, will develop in the island."[147]

If the U.S. Navy had its own motives, Pepe relished the opportunity to travel.[148] Like Taylor and Tuvale before her, Pepe followed in the footsteps of generations of Samoans on the move. Unlike Taylor and Tuvale, however, Pepe was a woman. Apart from the female members of ethnographic show troupes, Pepe was one of the first women from Tutuila to venture out to the U.S. mainland. Together with her male counterparts in the Fitafita Guard, Pepe's stay on Mare Island initiated a wave of Samoan migration linked to the U.S. armed forces that has continued into the present. Traveling Samoans, like Pepe, shaped their own versions of Oceanian globality.

Although never officially enlisted, Pepe was such an important civilian employee that she deserved further training, paid for by the U.S. Navy. In his request to transfer Pepe to Mare Island, the chief of the Navy Bureau of Medicine and Surgery called her "an apt pupil and an exceptionally good nurse."[149] She was assigned to the naval hospital on Mare Island "to supplement the training she has already received with a wider clinical experience in a large hospital."[150] Two members of the Navy Nurse Corps who were scheduled to return to the mainland after duty in Tutuila accompanied Pepe on her journey into an unknown world. By June 1919, Pepe was officially registered as a skilled laborer at Mare Island Naval Hospital with a monthly salary of $30.[151]

As unfamiliar as San Francisco must have been to Pepe, she had moved from one island under navy control to another. Mare Island had been purchased by the U.S. Navy in 1852 for use as a shipyard. By 1910, two giant dry docks had been erected, together with other facilities, including a naval hospital. Hence, the navy's infrastructure and personnel were, to some extent, familiar to Pepe. She had seen American men in uniform before in Tutuila, and the inside of a hospital had by then become second nature. And yet the dimensions of navy life that Pepe encountered on Mare Island were mind-boggling. Although fifty years old at the time of Pepe's stay, the Mare Island Naval Hospital with its 250 beds and freight elevator could not be compared with the modest Samoan hospital at home in Tutuila.[152] Likewise, the sheer number of personnel at the U.S. Navy's main base on the West Coast dwarfed the minuscule navy presence in Pago Pago.

Little is known about Pepe's daily routines in the Bay Area. Most of her days on Mare Island were probably dedicated to medical training, the original purpose for her trip. As a civilian employee, Pepe was free to leave the navy installations on Mare Island, and she might have made occasional visits to San Francisco while in training. To gain additional experience in a large hospital, Pepe also received training at the Children's Hospital in downtown San Francisco.[153] Given its distance to Mare Island, Pepe likely stayed either at the hospital's nurses' quarters or in an apartment nearby during her stint there. After half a year on the U.S. mainland, Pepe returned to Tutuila in early 1920.[154]

Upon her return, Pepe kept traveling. Eager to put her newly gained medical knowledge and experience into practice, she traveled from village to village in Tutuila, handing out medicines and "lecturing on various health topics."[155] Together with the other Samoan nurses assigned to different districts in Tutuila, Pepe instructed villagers in public hygiene and infant care. The handful of district nurses also kept a comprehensive record of their work and sent back reports on all births and deaths in the districts.[156] Pepe usually stayed at local missions, where she was provided with food.[157] Her long-standing connection to the LMS provided Pepe with the infrastructure she needed to do her job. Soon thereafter, she was appointed chief nurse. By 1924, the Training School for Samoan Nurses from which Pepe had graduated represented, in the eyes of one navy official, "one of the chief educational features" of American Samoa.[158]

Samoan nurses like Pepe had to navigate their way through treacherous waters. On the one hand, the first generation of Samoan nurses was trained by the colonial administrations to educate their fellow islanders in "proper" sanitation and "enlightened" health practices. From the colonialist viewpoint, health education was essential in making colonized people "modern" and manageable subjects.[159] In this version of the U.S. civilizing mission, the policing of unhealthy practices and potentially insurgent practices were two sides of the same coin.[160] Over time, colonial officials came to depend on public hygiene to enforce the "good" behavior of their Samoan subjects. As late as 1924, U.S. Navy officials complained about the lack of Samoan doctors practicing Western medicine. "As practical doctors," a navy official suggested, "these educated Samoans would do much toward eliminating the Samoan Witch, or Devil Doctor, now causing so much harm with his bad practices and Samoan Medicines."[161] Christian missionaries had been complaining about Samoan "superstition" ever since their arrival in 1830, but in fact Samoan medical beliefs and practices had many things in common with the Euro-American medicine practiced by missionaries.[162]

On the other hand, Samoan nurses reinterpreted this paternalistic logic according to their own needs. Pepe and the other graduates of the Training School for Samoan Nurses in Tutuila fought to be active participants in the politics of colonial care. Some Samoan villages selected women for training in Euro-American medicine who were already known and respected as *fofō*.[163] Out of earshot of her teachers, Pepe used her American education in anatomy and physiology to complement and expand her knowledge of Samoan popular medicine. Pepe and Samoan nurses like her were creative bricoleurs who recombined elements of Samoan and Euro-American medicine into a new and effective mixture in the service of their community.[164] In their everyday encounters with villagers, Samoan nurses became healers who cared for the physical and psychological wounds inflicted by coconut colonialism.

Like other service workers employed as police soldiers or interpreters, the Samoan nurses became crucial intermediaries and powerful political actors. Samoan women who worked as traditional healers and district nurses became leading members of the women's health committees founded in the early 1920s under New Zealand civil administration. Modeled on the societies of wives of *matai* and orators (*faletua ma tausi*), these committees included the influential women of a village, such as the wives of *matai,* and were usually led by the pastor's wife. Dressed in bright uniforms, committee members worked with fellow villagers to promote public health practices, particularly childcare, hygiene, and sanitation.[165] In doing so, women's health committee members and district nurses who served in Samoan villages gained political influence over matters beyond medicine. They became crucial intermediaries who bridged the worlds of Samoan and Euro-American medicine and, in the process, amassed political capital that they could use to challenge outside claims on Samoan society more generally.[166] Not surprisingly, experienced members of the women's health committees emerged as the leaders of the Mau movement that challenged New Zealand rule over Western Samoa, including its increasing threat to Samoan self-determination in health care.[167]

When New Zealand troops occupied German Samoa in August 1914, over four hundred Samoan officials were kept in office from the days of the German administration.[168] Since their salaries were provided by the head tax levied on Samoans, the Samoan service workers enjoyed a considerable degree of autonomy, especially in local matters. Desperate to reduce the costs of military occupation and rein in the perceived "excesses" of the German period, military administrator Logan uncoupled the head tax income from the financing of the Samoan administration officials and started using the funds for other purposes as well. In doing so, he threatened not only the cherished privileges of the Samoan service workers but also, and more importantly, Samoan self-determination at large.[169] Together with the flu pandemic in the fall of 1918, Logan's aggressive restructuring of the Samoan colonial service inspired the anti-colonial Mau movement that would grip the islands in the early 1920s. Anti-colonial resistance became effective precisely at the moment when colonial rulers ran out of willing collaborators.[170]

• • •

Work in the colonial service left an ambivalent legacy for Samoans for decades to come. On the one hand, service jobs in the security, administrative, and health sectors offered new opportunities to learn skills and earn cash. Many Samoans appreciated these avenues for professional advancement, which in many cases served both individual interests and those of their families. Samoan nurses, like Grace Pepe, acquired crucial nursing skills, which they then used to improve the general health of their families and Samoan society as a whole. Similarly, members of the Fitafita Guard and police officers in both German and American Samoa leveraged their military training to gain social status and launch successful careers. As the Samoan proverb suggests, the pathway to leadership did go through service. On the other hand, colonial service still remained service to the colonial administrations. While new possibilities arose with the Euro-American colonial presence, the new service jobs remained limited in terms of the lack of choice and decision-making power on the job. For example, Samoan police officers supervised Chinese plantation workers, and government interpreters like Charles T. Taylor translated Governor Solf's speeches into Samoan. Nonetheless, for some families, service work in successive administrations became a tradition. Le Mamea, his half brother Te'o Tuvale, and then Tuvale's son, Atoa, all worked as government interpreters, from the colonial period into Samoan independence. In the end, service also provided a pathway from colonial control to self-government.

It was precisely their precarious position between colonizer and colonized, foreign and local, outside and inside, that made workers in the colonial service so indispensable for both sides. If colonialists depended on Indigenous intermediaries to a greater extent, the fewer resources they received from the metropole, then colonial Samoa is a good case in point.[171] Despite their powerful positions, the actual experiences of service workers in Samoa were far more complex. Governor Solf's British Samoan interpreter Charles T. Taylor, for instance, had a delicate job that cannot be understood as either collaboration or resistance. Service workers like Taylor were torn not only between the demands of their jobs and the interests of their people but also between their own Oceanian aspirations and the limits colonial globality imposed on them.

EPILOGUE
Samoa and the World

Before the break of dawn on December 28, 1929, the Samoan Mau movement came head to head with the New Zealand administration. At 5:15 a.m. that Saturday morning, around three hundred Mau members gathered for what began as a peaceful procession around Apia Bay to protest abuses by New Zealand officials. Fed up with years of Mau civil disobedience, colonial administrator Stephen Allen dispatched military police to arrest Mau supporters for nonpayment of taxes. Before the first sun rays lit up Apia Bay, a brawl had erupted. At 6:20 a.m., New Zealand military police opened fire on the marching Samoans with rifles and two Lewis machine guns, last used in France during World War I. The Samoans, who had only their clubs, knives, and fists, dispersed in all directions. In just fifteen minutes, several Samoan leaders, including Tupua Tamasese Lealofi III, were fatally shot, and more than fifty Samoans were wounded. All told, eleven Samoans and one New Zealand constable died in the brutal escalation, which would come to be enshrined in Samoan history as Black Saturday. In response, Allen moved to outlaw the Mau and began harassing and arresting supporters. As many male Mau members went into hiding, the women's Mau—including many members of the women's committees—carried on the torch of resistance.[1]

Years of tensions between Samoans and the New Zealand administration had led up to that fateful day. When New Zealand took over German Samoa during World War I, the lives of most Samoans were unaffected. That would change dramatically in November 1918, when military administrator Robert Logan allowed the New Zealand steamer SS *Talune* to dock in Apia with several passengers who were infected with influenza. After Samoa's most deadly disease outbreak, which killed one out of five islanders, the traumatized survivors rightfully blamed the New Zealand administration for not having done enough to prevent the spread of the pandemic.

In spite of this mismanagement, Western Samoa became a mandated territory of New Zealand under the permanent mandate system of the newly founded League of Nations in 1921. The new civil administration kept many of the German policies in place but also sought to expand control by banning the exchange of fine mats and introducing a medical tax. Administrator Richardson also sought to individualize landholdings and appoint members of the Fono of Faipule, and even went so far as to banish a young Tupua Tamasese Lealofi III to Savai'i for refusing to remove a hibiscus hedge from his property. These drastic actions sparked the resistance of many *matai,* who saw their economic and political authority undermined. Beginning in the mid-1920s, Samoans and European settlers lobbied the New Zealand civil administration for greater political, economic, and cultural self-determination.

No single Samoan was more involved in putting Western Samoa on the trajectory for national self-determination than Ta'isi O. F. Nelson. Like many of his fellow anti-colonial activists, Nelson was of mixed-race background and spoke several languages. Throughout his life, Nelson straddled the worlds separating his personal and economic interests in his native Samoa and the competing agendas of Euro-American empires in the South Pacific. As a former office worker for the largest German trading company in Samoa, who had become one of the wealthiest Pacific Islanders of his time, Nelson personified the contradictions of the colonial world. On the one hand, his rise to political power was at least partly based on his success as a savvy businessman who seized the new opportunities created by the arrival of outlanders, rising demand for tropical fruit and foreign goods, and long-distance shipping lines. As the son of a Swedish father and Samoan mother, Nelson was ideally situated to take advantage of the cultural and commercial contact zone that emerged around the harbor of Apia. On the other hand, Nelson competed with European and American businesses that were deeply entangled with colonial interests. Nowhere was this more evident than with Nelson's own first employer, the DHPG. In 1908, Nelson had supported Lauaki's Mau a Pule and its campaign to restore Samoan political and economic self-determination in the face of German colonization. As he confronted coconut colonialism, Nelson realized early on that economic power would have to rest on greater political self-determination for his home islands. By traveling across Samoa and later across the world, Nelson became a tireless advocate for Samoan independence against colonial systems of control.

Nelson and other Samoans used the League of Nations to make a case against what they perceived as abuses by the New Zealand administration. In her recent study of the mandate system, Susan Pedersen argued that Samoans "mounted what was probably the most protracted, well-organized, and impressive campaign for self-determination of any mandated territory."[2] As early as 1921, Samoans sent a petition to the British king George V to remove the New Zealand mandate over the former German colony. In 1926, more than eight thousand Samoans signed a petition to the League of Nations complaining about Richardson's abuses, including restrictions on *malaga,* waste of tax revenue, and the appointment of *fono* members. Signed by virtually all Samoan men on Upolu and Savai'i, the 1926 petition not only highlighted encroachments on Samoan rights on a world stage but also aligned with long-standing Samoan deliberative practices.[3] Unwilling to take Samoan grievances seriously, Richardson responded by calling for military police and warships to restore order on the islands.

To channel their dissatisfaction, Samoans founded a movement under the banner of O le Mau (The Opinion) in March 1927. Following in the footsteps of Pullack's 'Oloa and Lauaki's Mau a Pule a generation earlier, the Mau of the 1920s united Samoans with mixed-race Samoans and Euro-American settlers in a powerful coalition. Chanting "*Samoa mo Samoa*" (Samoa for the Samoans), Mau members reappropriated Richardson's original deferral of self-determination into a rallying cry for full-scale decolonization. The Mau movement managed to enlist widespread support among Samoan *matai,* who were themselves angry about attacks on their traditional privileges, including their right to go on *malaga* and receive titles. Besides public demonstrations and petitions, Mau followers boycotted government schools, refused to pay their taxes, and even organized their own police force. Peaceful noncooperation and civil disobedience were their main strategies of resistance.[4]

Throughout the 1920s, Samoans continued sending petitions to the Permanent Mandates Commission, the prime minister of New Zealand, the British king, and the U.S. president to protest against violations of their economic, political, and cultural autonomy. All of them were politely declined, outright dismissed, or simply ignored. Tellingly, the European members of the Permanent Mandates Commission in Geneva discounted the Mau petitions by blaming cunning and troublesome "half-castes" like Nelson for inciting an "impressionable people."[5] In 1928, Nelson himself traveled ten thousand miles to Geneva to make the case for Samoan self-determination at the League of Nations, the newly established international body designed to protect the interests of national and ethnic communities. Members of the Permanent Mandates Commission refused to receive Nelson officially, but a commissioner did meet with him in private, to little effect.[6]

Even if self-determination for mandated territories remained more rhetoric than reality, Nelson and other anti-colonial leaders used the League to make a case for the formal end of colonialism. Experienced navigators of the world of empire, Samoans deftly internationalized their local struggle for self-determination on the global stage.[7] Nelson returned from Geneva only to be exiled to New Zealand in January 1929. One of the most vocal and influential supporters of Samoan self-determination thus was not in Apia on Black Saturday. Nelson would not return to Samoa until May 1933, only to be banished again for sedition the following March, this time for ten years. After a new Labor government in Wellington shortened his sentence, Nelson returned triumphantly to Samoa in July 1936. Eight years later, Nelson quietly passed away surrounded by his closest family members. Thus, when Samoan independence finally arrived on January 1, 1962, Nelson would not be around to see that momentous event, which he had done so much to bring about. But Nelson's dedication to Samoa would outlive the man himself. Ta'isi O. F. Nelson's grandson, Tupua Tamasese Tupuola Ta'isi Efi, would serve as prime minister of Western Samoa (1976–1982) and later as cohead of state (2007–2017).

In neighboring American Samoa, a Mau movement of its own formed in 1920 to protest against the excesses of navy rule. When it became known that government officials had embezzled government funds, Samoan leaders, with the help of American critics of navy rule, organized a public campaign against those abuses. Tensions were exacerbated by the fact that most U.S. officials in American Samoa were members of the U.S. Navy, a hierarchical organization based on a strict chain of command and regular job rotation. American Samoans organized a copra boycott and practically shut down the naval government, which depended on the taxes drawn from the sale of copra. In contrast to the New Zealand administration's reaction in Western Samoa, Governor Waldo A. Evans exonerated some of the accused protesters and created a more transparent native tax fund, which reassured many followers of the Mau. Most Samoans resumed cutting copra soon thereafter.[8] Yet the Mau movement persisted and spread throughout American Samoa during the 1920s, evolving into a watchdog of the navy.[9] As in Western Samoa, the Mau in American Samoa involved members of women's committees, which had been set up in 1919 to improve public health in the villages. Among them was a nurse by the name of Grace Pepe. In the end, the Mau movement in American Samoa turned out to be less violent and extensive than its counterpart in Western Samoa. Both anti-colonial movements, however, were driven by similar complaints about the benefits of colonial rule and inspired one another.[10] More broadly, struggles for greater self-determination in both Western and American Samoa revealed the international origins of anti-colonial nationalism in the 1920s.

• • •

The emergence of a more direct and sustained anti-colonial movement like the Mau gave the earlier labor protests deeper meaning. As this book has shown, Samoan resistance against coconut colonialism—Euro-American control over tropical islands to extract their resources—began well before the 1920s.[11] From the repeated violent clashes in the second half of the nineteenth century onward, Samoans fought against colonial domination, without succeeding in completely banishing its impact on their lives. As the German and U.S. Navy administrations expanded following partition in 1900, Samoans struggled to maintain control over their political, economic, and cultural practices. Beginning in 1904, Samoan copra cooperatives challenged the monopoly of Euro-American traders in both colonies. A few years later, Lauaki posed a serious threat to the legitimacy of the German colonial administration by organizing copra boycotts and vying for the support of U.S. warships. Throughout the period, workers on commercial plantations, in construction, and in the colonial service voiced their dissatisfaction with their employers. They protested against inadequate food, poor working conditions, and low pay. In doing so, they reached across racial divides to fellow workers from other Pacific islands and China and also fostered ties to increasingly powerful mixed-race Samoans. Economic boycotts continued throughout the 1920s.[12] In Tutuila as well, conflicts over just compensation for construction work outlasted the 1905 strike and helped fuel the Mau movement. In a letter from November 1921, a Samoan *matai* from Tutuila complained about the labor conditions in roadwork: "Sometimes we get paid and other times we do not. . . . These Navy men are putting this work without compensation upon us and we do not like it or them."[13] For Samoans, complaints against unpaid hard labor and resistance to U.S. colonial rule were closely intertwined. By enlarging the circle of solidarity and insisting on economic self-determination, the working people of Samoa helped prepare the coordinated challenge to outlander rule by the Mau movement.

Nelson, who dedicated his life to Samoan self-determination in a still-colonial world, continued the world enlargement pursued by an earlier generation of working people in Samoa. As the title of O'Brien's biography suggests, Nelson was a smart navigator (*Tautai*) of the political, economic, and cultural crosscurrents of his time. Yet in his successes and his failures, Nelson followed in the wake of countless earlier navigators of perhaps lesser fame but no less importance. As this book has shown, Samoa's diverse working people at the turn of the twentieth century were the innovators of a specifically Oceanian form of globality. On plantations and on tour, Samoans found common cause with Chinese migrant workers and fellow Pacific Islanders, which allowed them to link their own struggles against Euro-American coconut colonialism to decolonization movements around the world. Samoans of mixed-race descent, such as interpreter Charles T. Taylor, played an important part in mediating local and global encounters around culture, language, and work. Later on, Nelson and his fellow Mau leaders made use of these earlier travels and travails to challenge outlander rule in more direct ways. In Samoa as elsewhere, decolonization was a cultural and political movement that depended on movements across spatial and racial boundaries. And more often than not, it was through their lived experiences across different workscapes that Samoans engaged with the meaning of colonialism.

• • •

Besides recovering the labor roots of decolonization in Samoa, *Coconut Colonialism* offers new insights for scholars of globalization and capitalism. First, the Samoan case throws into sharp relief the important role of workers in the making of globalization. Samoans and migrants from around the Pacific forged new connections with one another and the wider world because and in spite of colonial regimes of difference. As Samoa was drawn into the orbit of Euro-American empires at the turn of the twentieth century, the islands' working people extended their networks and interests outward, into the Pacific and beyond. In the process, workers in Samoa remade the colonial form of globality imposed on them in their own Oceanian image. With their wide-ranging *malaga,* Samoans collapsed distinctions between the local and the global and became important actors in the globalization of their home islands. Samoans of mixed-race descent, such as Taylor and Nelson, played important roles in mediating between colonizers and the colonized, often blurring clear-cut lines between these categories. Through traveling and meeting fellow Pacific Islanders around the world, these globe-trotting Samoans also grew increasingly aware of shared struggles against colonial exploitation.

Second, the story of Samoa's relationship with the world, as traced in this book, offers a fresh take on the history of globalization. The conventional narrative about globalization emphasizes the role of the powerful in shaping the inevitable economic integration of our planet: explorers sailed the ocean blue, colonial officials established law and order, and trade soon followed the flag. In contrast to this triumphalist account of globalization, this account of Samoa at the turn of the twentieth century presents a more complicated picture. Globalization, as seen from the South Pacific, was a decidedly local and remarkably intimate affair that pitted Pacific Islanders against Euro-American outlanders, workers against capitalists, even fathers against sons. Many of the central features of Samoa's globalization at the start of the twentieth century are familiar to readers at the dawn of the twenty-first century: cash crop production and its attendant ecological costs, unfree forms of migration and plantation labor, and the resilience of ordinary people in the face of colonialism and capitalism. As this study has argued, working people—diverse, mobile, and politically astute—were powerful participants in the struggle over the globalization of Samoa. By telling the stories of Samoans on the move, this book presents a neglected history of our global yet tenaciously unequal present. Given ongoing debates about the costs and benefits of globalization today, historians may do well to recall its contested character as well as its deep colonial roots.

Third, the experience of workers in colonial Samoa was typical of the past (and present) work under capitalism more generally. The expansion of cash crop agriculture around coconuts posed particular challenges to Samoan farmers as well as to the thousands of contract workers who came to the islands. Conflicts arose over difficult working conditions, greedy Euro-

American agents, and the role of colonial administrations in the copra economy. If tropical fruits, like the coconut, were important drivers of colonization in Samoa and in the wider Pacific, they also shaped the contours of resistance to global capitalism. Because Samoan producers were successful in defending much of their land base from outlanders, they were able to maintain food sovereignty—the foundation for sustained military and political power. In this regard, Samoans had different experiences under Euro-American colonialism than did Hawaiians.[14] Besides holding on to their land base for sustainable farming, Samoans creatively adapted the world of export copra to their own needs and values. Although short lived, copra cooperatives in both German and American Samoa posed challenges to the economic hegemony of outlanders and questioned the very legitimacy of colonial rule over the islands. By launching copra cooperatives, Samoans proved themselves savvy participants in the expanding global copra trade.

Fourth and finally, the Pacific deserves more scholarly attention as one of the major postemancipation commodity frontier zones, characterized by globally traded cash crops and unfree labor migration. Beginning in the mid-nineteenth century, Samoa became part of a plantation belt that spanned the tropics, from the Caribbean to Africa to the South Pacific. This tropical plantation complex was dominated by export-oriented monocrop production, with varying degrees of mechanization and industrialization. Indeed, plantation labor in tropical colonies helped fuel industrial capitalism in the metropoles.[15] The advancing commodification of the global countryside was enabled by the building of crucial pieces of infrastructure, linking plantation islands such as Samoa to metropolitan markets. Hundreds of workers who built the roads, docks, and port facilities of Samoa made the circulation of commodities, ships, and migrants possible in the first place. While new shipping links enabled new kinds of global travel, such as Nelson's trip to Geneva, colonial administrators in German and American Samoa used long-distance steamships for gunboat diplomacy and exiling uncooperative islanders. Plantations also brought together different labor regimes, ranging from Indigenous producers and day laborers to small Euro-American settlers and large trading companies to migrant contract workers from around the Pacific. As historians of agricultural capitalism have argued, the confluence of different systems of unfree labor enabled global cash crop markets to flourish.[16] With its multiracial migrant labor force often divided against itself and subject to increasingly strict discipline, the tropical plantation complex carried the seeds of today's global division of labor. Then as now, consumers of tropical fruit like coconuts in markets in the Global North remain far removed from the conditions of production in the Global South. Focusing on copra plantation workers in colonial Samoa reveals the hidden human costs of capitalist agriculture.

• • •

Epeli Hauʻofa has reminded scholars of the Pacific that "we cannot read our histories without knowing how to read our landscapes (and seascapes)."[17] As this book has shown, neither can we understand the history of colonial Samoa without knowing how to read its different workscapes. Like other colonized peoples, Samoans experienced Euro-American colonialism and capitalism primarily through work. Because the labor question dominated the logic of Euro-American empire builders in Samoa and elsewhere, workscapes emerged as central arenas of colonial contestation. How Samoa's workers related to one another and to their employers was fundamentally shaped by the environmental and social contexts in which they operated. Opportunities to build forms of community and trust were generally greatest within specific workscapes. Plantation workers shared similar tasks in similar natural environments and spent the entire day in the company of fellow workers. Despite differences in size, crop, and location, most foreign-owned plantations in Samoa established rigid lines of authority and work schedules. Faced with similar forms of exploitation, plantation workers found similar ways to resist. Some Melanesian plantation workers joined Samoan church services in villages bordering their plantation workscapes. Others, like the Chinese plantation workers, leveraged the power of their home government to improve their work conditions.

While community building was easiest *within* specific workscapes, conflicts among workers emerged *between* different workscapes. Plantation owners and colonial officials pursued a strategy of divide-and-control aimed at preventing worker solidarity through racial segregation. Thus, Samoan men were hired by colonial administrations to police Melanesian and Chinese workers on plantations. Fueled by fears of interracial sexual encounters and crime, this colonial policy of confrontation led to several outbreaks of violence between Samoans and migrant laborers. Racial tensions between

Samoans and Chinese continued into World War I, when New Zealand annexed German Samoa.

Despite these tensions, the most effective forms of resistance against coconut colonialism emerged out of attempts to transcend the division of labor. Workers who moved between workscapes were in the best position to challenge the demands of the colonizers. Chinese plantation workers knew that a handful of fellow migrants to Samoa were employed in other occupations, such as cooking and interpreting. When a group of Chinese workers filed a petition protesting the cruelty of their German plantation owner, they had already consulted with the governor's personal cook and Chinese interpreter at the Imperial Court. By making connections across workscapes, workers in Samoa exposed the interdependence of different kinds of labor and were better able to resist exploitation. From plantations to the governor's office, workers in Samoa used the particular dynamics of their workscapes to imagine an Oceanian future beyond coconut colonialism.

• • •

At the dawn of the twenty-first century, coconuts and coconut products line the shelves of grocery stores from Auckland to Amsterdam. Copra production, which brought thousands of workers to Samoa at the turn of the twentieth century, remains one of the mainstays of Samoan agriculture. Smaller copra farmers in Samoa, however, face stiff competition from bigger suppliers in the Philippines and Indonesia. Looking for a lucrative niche, some enterprising Samoans have specialized in producing and exporting coconut oil to customers in Polynesian communities overseas.[18] Meanwhile, Australian and New Zealand farmers are recruiting Pacific Islanders, including Samoans, to work on their orchards and vineyards.[19] Now, as then, islanders on the move are reshaping Oceania and the world beyond.

NOTES

Introduction

1. AGCA 6051 / 0127 IA 19, personal file, Charles T. Taylor, 1900–14, ANZ Wellington.

2. Solf to Taylor, July 8, 1902, NAS, IG 14 F4 IA 19.

3. Solf to Taylor, July 4, 1902, NAS, IG 14 F4 IA 19.

4. Taylor to Solf, May 17, 1902, NAS, IG 14 F4 IA 19.

5. In his description of Samoan traveling parties, German Navy doctor and amateur ethnologist Augustin Krämer called Samoans *"reiselustig"* ("fond of traveling" or "travel-happy"). Damon Salesa, "'Travel-Happy' Samoa: Colonialism, Samoan Migration and a 'Brown Pacific,'" *New Zealand Journal of History* 37, no. 2 (2003): 174.

6. R. C. Green and Janet M. Davidson, *Archaeology in Western Samoa,* vol. 2 (Auckland: Auckland Institute and Museum, 1974), 247.

7. Salesa, "'Travel-Happy' Samoa," 175.

8. Ibid., 174.

9. Sa'iliemanu Lilomaiava-Doktor, "Beyond 'Migration': Samoan Population Movement (*Malaga*) and the Geography of Social Space (*Vā*)," *Contemporary Pacific* 21, no. 1 (2009): 22.

10. Salesa, "'Travel-Happy' Samoa," 175.

11. Ibid., esp. 184.

12. Malama Meleisea and Penelope Schoeffel Meleisea, *Lagaga: A Short History of Western Samoa* (Suva, Fiji: University of the South Pacific, 1987), 45. On Sio Vili and the Tahitian Mamaia movement, see Rhys Richards, "The Decision to *Lotu*: New Perspectives from Whaling Records on the Sources and Spread of Christianity in Samoa," *Pacific Studies Journal* 17, no. 1 (1994): 29–44; Lowell D. Holmes, "Cults, Cargo, and Christianity: Samoan Responses to Western Religion," *Missiology: An International Review* 8, no. 4 (1980): 478–480.

13. Meleisea and Schoeffel Meleisea, *Lagaga*, 45.

14. James W. Davidson, *Samoa mo Samoa: The Emergence of the Independent State of Western Samoa* (Oxford: Oxford University Press, 1967), 38; Paul M.

Kennedy, *The Samoan Tangle: A Study in Anglo-German-American Relations, 1878–1900* (Dublin: Irish University Press, 1974), 6.

15. The coconut still awaits a global commodity history in the vein of Sidney Mintz's on sugar. Sidney W. Mintz, *Sweetness and Power: The Place of Sugar in Modern History* (New York: Viking Press, 1985). For a popular account, with many anecdotes but little historical analysis, see Robin Laurance, *Coconut: How the Shy Fruit Shaped the World* (Stroud, UK: History Press, 2019).

16. Malama Meleisea, *The Making of Modern Samoa: Traditional Authority and Colonial Administration in the History of Western Samoa* (Suva, Fiji: Institute of Pacific Studies of the University of the South Pacific, 1987), 1. According to Meleisea, "foreign involvement [in Samoa] was . . . often based on a false assumption about which faction was the 'legitimate' claimant to the monarchy." Meleisea and Schoeffel Meleisea, *Lagaga,* 99.

17. Nicholas Thomas, *Islanders: The Pacific in the Age of Empire* (New Haven, CT: Yale University Press, 2010), 281.

18. Edwin P. Hoyt, *The Typhoon That Stopped a War* (New York: D. McKay, 1968).

19. Holger Droessler, "Colonialism by Deferral: Samoa under the Tridominium, 1889–1899," in *Rethinking the Colonial State,* ed. Søren Rud and Søren Ivarsson, Political Power and Social Theory 33 (Bingley, UK: Emerald, 2017), 203–224.

20. Joseph Kennedy, *The Tropical Frontier: America's South Sea Colony* (Mangilao, Guam: Micronesian Area Research Center, 2009).

21. Michael J. Field, *Mau: Samoa's Struggle against New Zealand Oppression* (Wellington, NZ: Reed, 1984). On the Mau movement in American Samoa, see David A. Chappell, "The Forgotten Mau: Anti-Navy Protest in American Samoa, 1920–1935," *Pacific Historical Review* 69, no. 2 (2000): 235–236.

22. Epeli Hau'ofa, "Our Sea of Islands," in *A New Oceania: Rediscovering Our Sea of Islands,* ed. Epeli Hau'ofa, Vijay Naidu, and Eric Waddell (Suva: University of the South Pacific, 1993), 2–16.

23. Thomas, *Islanders,* 3, 13.

24. Kealani Cook, *Return to Kahiki: Native Hawaiians in Oceania* (Cambridge: Cambridge University Press, 2018), 95–125.

25. Naval War Board (Rear Adm. Montgomery Sicard, Capt. Alfred T. Mahan, Capt. A. S. Crowninshield) to Sec. of the Navy John D. Long, August 13–30, 1898, NARA-DC, RG 45, entry 372.

26. Eric Williams, *Capitalism and Slavery* (Chapel Hill: University of North Carolina Press, 1944); Eric Hobsbawm, *Industry and Empire: From 1750 to the Present Day* (New York: Weidenfeld & Nicholson, 1968); Kenneth Pomeranz, *The Great Divergence: China, Europe, and the Making of the Modern World Economy* (Princeton: Princeton University Press, 2000); Prasannan Parthasarathi, "The Great Divergence," *Past and Present* 176, no. 1 (2002): 275–293; Orlando Patterson, *The Confounding Island: Jamaica and the Postcolonial Predicament* (Cambridge, MA: Harvard University Press, 2019).

27. For an excellent example, see Katerina M. Teaiwa, *Consuming Ocean Island: Stories of People and Phosphate from Banaba* (Bloomington: Indiana University Press, 2015). On settler capitalism in Samoa, see Cluny and La'avasa Macpherson, *The Warm Winds of Change: Globalisation in Contemporary Samoa* (Auckland: Auckland University Press, 2009), 39, 108–115.

28. By "globalization," I mean the development, concentration, and increasing importance of worldwide political, economic, and cultural integration. See Jürgen Osterhammel and Niels P. Petersson, *Globalization: A Short History* (Princeton: Princeton University Press, 2005), 26.

29. Recent studies from the so-called new history of capitalism include Noam Maggor, *Brahmin Capitalism: Frontiers of Wealth and Populism in America's First Gilded Age* (Cambridge, MA: Harvard University Press, 2017); Sven Beckert, *Empire of Cotton: A Global History* (New York: Knopf, 2014); Walter Johnson, *River of Dark Dreams: Slavery and Empire in the Cotton Kingdom* (Cambridge, MA: Harvard University Press, 2013); Richard White, *Railroaded: The Transcontinentals and the Making of Modern America* (New York: Norton, 2011).

30. Recent studies of labor and capitalism in the Pacific include JoAnna Poblete, *Balancing the Tides: Marine Practices in American Sāmoa* (Honolulu: University of Hawai'i Press, 2020); JoAnna Poblete, *Islanders in the Empire: Filipino and Puerto Rican Laborers in Hawai'i* (Urbana: University of Illinois Press, 2014); Gregory Rosenthal, *Beyond Hawai'i: Native Labor in the Pacific World* (Berkeley: University of California Press, 2018); Gregory T. Cushman, *Guano and the Opening of the Pacific World: A Global Ecological History* (Cambridge: Cambridge University Press, 2013); Gerald Horne, *The White Pacific: U.S. Imperialism and Black Slavery in the South Seas after the Civil War* (Honolulu: University of Hawai'i Press, 2007).

31. Beckert, *Empire of Cotton,* esp. 340–378.

32. Kris Manjapra, "Plantation Dispossessions: The Global Travel of Agricultural Racial Capitalism," in *American Capitalism: New Histories,* ed. Sven Beckert and Christine Desan (New York: Columbia University Press, 2019), 361–387.

33. On commodity frontiers, see Jason W. Moore, "Sugar and the Expansion of the Early Modern World-Economy: Commodity Frontiers, Ecological Transformation, and Industrialization," *Review (Fernand Braudel Center)* 23, no. 3 (2000): 409–433; Ulbe Bosma, *The Making of a Periphery: How Island Southeast Asia Became a Mass Exporter of Labor* (New York: Columbia University Press, 2019); Casey Lurtz, *From the Grounds Up: Building an Export Economy in Southern Mexico* (Palo Alto, CA: Stanford University Press, 2019).

34. For the case of cotton cultivators in German Togo, see Beckert, *Empire of Cotton,* 371.

35. On asking big questions in another small place, see Charles Joyner, *Down by the Riverside: A South Carolina Slave Community* (Urbana: University of Illinois Press, 1984). On the importance of the labor question for decolonization in Africa, see Fredrick Cooper, *Decolonization and African Society: The Labor Question in French and British Africa* (Cambridge: Cambridge University Press, 1996).

36. On bridging the study of social experience and cultural practices in labor history, see Daniel E. Bender, "Sensing Labor: The Stinking Working-Class after the Cultural Turn," in *Rethinking U.S. Labor History: Essays on the Working-Class Experience, 1756–2009,* ed. Donna T. Haverty-Stacke and Daniel J. Walkowitz (New York: Continuum, 2010), 256–257.

37. Ronald Takaki, *Pau Hana: Plantation Life and Labor in Hawaiʻi, 1835–1920* (Honolulu: University of Hawaiʻi Press, 1983); Poblete, *Islanders in the Empire.*

38. Andrews's conceptualization of a workscape derives from his study of the relationships between mine workers and the non-human environment in early twentieth-century Colorado. See Thomas G. Andrews, *Killing for Coal: America's Deadliest Labor War* (Cambridge, MA: Harvard University Press, 2008), 125. G. Samantha Rosenthal has also used the concept to analyze the circum-Pacific work sites of Hawaiians. See Rosenthal, *Beyond Hawaiʻi,* 106.

39. On the roots of the Mau movement in earlier labor struggles, see Malama Meleisea, *O Tama Uli: Melanesians in Western Samoa* (Suva, Fiji: University of the South Pacific, 1980), 48.

40. Kennedy, *Samoan Tangle.*

41. On imperial webs of exchange in New Zealand / Aotearoa, see Tony Ballantyne, *Entanglements of Empire: Missionaries, Māori, and the Question of the Body* (Durham: Duke University Press, 2014), 24.

42. Davidson, *Samoa Mo Samoa.*

43. Richard P. Gilson, *Samoa 1830 to 1900: The Politics of a Multi-Cultural Community* (Oxford: Oxford University Press, 1970).

44. Malama Meleisea, "The Last Days of the Melanesian Labour Trade in Western Samoa," *Journal of Pacific History* 11, no. 2 (1976): 126–132; Meleisea, *O Tama Uli.*

45. Doug Munro and Stewart Firth, "Samoan Plantations: The Gilbertese Laborers' Experience, 1867–1896," in *Plantation Workers: Resistance and Accommodation,* ed. Brij V. Lal, Doug Munro, and Edward D. Beechert (Honolulu: University of Hawaiʻi Press, 1993), 101–127; Nancy Tom, *The Chinese in Western Samoa, 1875–1985: The Dragon Came from Afar* (Apia: Western Samoa Historical and Cultural Trust, 1986); Featunaʻi Ben Liuaʻana, "Dragons in Little Paradise: Chinese (Mis-) Fortunes in Samoa, 1900–1950," *Journal of Pacific History* 32, no. 1 (1997): 29–48.

46. Patricia O'Brien, *Tautai: Sāmoa, World History, and the Life of Taʻisi O. F. Nelson* (Honolulu: University of Hawaiʻi Press, 2017).

47. This book rides on a wave of recent scholarship on Pacific Islanders in motion. On decolonization in the Pacific, see Tracey Banivanua-Mar, *Decolonisation and the Pacific: Indigenous Globalisation and the Ends of Empire* (Cambridge: Cambridge University Press, 2016). On interracialism in New Zealand and Samoa, see Damon Salesa, *Racial Crossings: Race, Intermarriage, and the Victorian British Empire* (Oxford: Oxford University Press, 2011). On American Samoa, see Poblete, *Balancing the Tides;* JoAnna Poblete, "Bridging Indigenous and Immigrant Strug-

gles: A Case Study of American Samoa," *American Quarterly* 62, no. 3 (2010): 501–522. On Hawai'i, see Cook, *Return to Kahiki;* Rosenthal, *Beyond Hawai'i;* David A. Chang, *The World and All the Things upon It: Native Hawaiian Geographies of Exploration* (Minneapolis: University of Minnesota Press, 2016); Poblete, *Islanders in the Empire;* Adria L. Imada, *Aloha America: Hula Circuits through the U.S. Empire* (Durham, NC: Duke University Press, 2012); Jean Barman and Bruce McIntyre Watson, *Leaving Paradise: Indigenous Hawaiians in the Pacific Northwest, 1787–1898* (Honolulu: University of Hawai'i Press, 2006); David A. Chappell, *Double Ghosts: Oceanian Voyagers on Euroamerican Ships* (Armonk, NY: M.E. Sharpe, 1997). On Micronesia, see K. M. Teaiwa, *Consuming Ocean Island;* Keith L. Camacho, *Cultures of Commemoration: The Politics of War, Memory, and History in the Mariana Islands* (Honolulu: University of Hawai'i Press, 2011); Vicente M. Diaz, *Repositioning the Missionary: Rewriting the Histories of Colonialism, Native Catholicism, and Indigeneity in Guam* (Honolulu: University of Hawai'i Press, 2010); Teresia K. Teaiwa, "bikinis and other s / pacific n / oceans," *Contemporary Pacific* 6, no. 1 (1994): 87–109.

48. Frank Jacobs, "The Border That Stole 500 Birthdays," *New York Times Opinionator,* July 31, 2012, https://opinionator.blogs.nytimes.com/2012/07/31/the-border-that-stole-500-birthdays.

49. Salesa, "'Travel-Happy' Samoa," 176.

50. David Armitage and Alison Bashford, eds., *Pacific Histories: Ocean, Land, People* (New York: Palgrave Macmillan, 2014).

51. Hermann Hiery is one of the leading experts on Germany's history in the South Pacific, including Samoa. See Hermann Hiery, *Das Deutsche Reich in der Südsee (1900–1921): Eine Annährung an die Erfahrungen verschiedener Kulturen* (Göttingen: Vandenhoeck & Ruprecht, 1995); Hermann Hiery, ed., *Die Deutsche Südsee, 1884–1914: Ein Handbuch* (Paderborn: Ferdinand Schöningh, 2001). On German women in the Pacific, see Livia Loosen, *Deutsche Frauen in den Südsee-Kolonien des Kaiserreichs: Alltag und Beziehungen zur Indigenen Bevölkerung, 1884–1919* (Bielefeld: Transcript, 2014). For a sociological approach to German colonialism, including a section on Samoa, see George Steinmetz, *The Devil's Handwriting: Precoloniality and the German Colonial State in Qingdao, Samoa, and Southwest Africa* (Chicago: University of Chicago Press, 2007). On embedding the German colonial empire in global history, see Sebastian Conrad, "Rethinking German Colonialism in a Global Age," *Journal of Imperial and Commonwealth History* 41, no. 4 (2013): 543–566. On Samoa in colonial discourse, see Gabriele Förderer, *Koloniale Grüße aus Samoa: Eine Diskursanalyse von deutschen, englischen und US-amerikanischen Reisebeschreibungen aus Samoa von 1860–1916* (Bielefeld: Transcript, 2017); Thomas Schwarz, *Ozeanische Affekte: Die literarische Modellierung Samoas im kolonialen Diskurs* (Berlin: TEIA—Internet Akademie und Lehrbuch Verlag, 2013). For an overview of American Samoan history, see J. Kennedy, *Tropical Frontier.* On U.S. colonialism and the law, see Kirisitina G. Sailiata, "The

Samoan Cause: Colonialism, Culture, and the Rule of Law" (PhD thesis, University of Michigan, 2014).

52. For an overview of scholarship on U.S. imperialism and labor, see Julie Greene, "The Labor of Empire: Recent Scholarship on U.S. History and Imperialism," *Labor: Studies in Working-Class History of the Americas* 1, no. 2 (2004): 113–129. See also Greene's *The Canal Builders: Making America's Empire at the Panama Canal* (New York: Penguin Press, 2009). Other influential works include Jana K. Lipman, *Guantánamo: A Working-Class History Between Empire and Revolution* (Berkeley: University of California Press, 2009); Andrew Zimmerman, *Alabama in Africa: Booker T. Washington, the German Empire, and the Globalization of the New South* (Princeton: Princeton University Press, 2010); Daniel E. Bender and Jana K. Lipman, eds., *Making the Empire Work: Labor and United States Imperialism* (New York: New York University Press, 2015). On the role of labor in the German colonies, see Minu Haschemi Yekani, *Koloniale Arbeit: Rassismus, Migration und Herrschaft in Tansania (1885–1914)* (Frankfurt am Main: Campus Verlag, 2019); Felix Axster, "Arbeit an der 'Erziehung zur Arbeit' oder: die Figur des guten deutschen Kolonisators," in *"Deutsche Arbeit": Kritische Perspektiven auf ein ideologisches Selbstbild,* ed. Felix Axster and Nikolas Lelle, 226–251 (Göttingen: Wallstein Verlag, 2018); Sebastian Conrad, "'Kulis' nach Preußen? Mobilität, chinesische Arbeiter und das deutsche Kaiserreich, 1890–1914," *Comparativ* 13, no. 4 (2003): 80–95.

53. As early as the 1960s, Herbert Gutman argued that nonwhite, non-U.S.-born workers were central to the making of the American working class. See Gutman's *Work, Culture, and Society in Industrializing America: Essays in American Working-Class and Social History* (New York: Alfred A. Knopf, 1976). Closer to Samoa, Ronald Takaki has traced the multiracial composition of Hawai'i's working class. See his *Pau Hana: Plantation Life and Labor in Hawai'i, 1835–1920* (Honolulu: University of Hawai'i Press, 1983). Other important works on Pacific labor include Poblete, *Islanders in the Empire;* Kornel S. Chang, *Pacific Connections: The Making of the U.S.-Canadian Borderlands* (Berkeley: University of California Press, 2012); Moon-Ho Jung, *Coolies and Cane: Race, Labor, and Sugar in the Age of Emancipation* (Baltimore: Johns Hopkins University Press, 2006).

1. Coconuts

This chapter draws on Holger Droessler, "Copra World: Coconuts, Plantations, and Cooperatives in German Samoa," *Journal of Pacific History* 53, no. 4 (November 2018): 417–435.

1. David C. Pitt, *Tradition and Economic Progress in Samoa: A Case Study of the Role of Traditional Social Institutions in Economic Development* (Oxford: Clarendon Press, 1970), 200.

2. Robert W. Franco, *Samoan Perceptions of Work: Moving Up and Moving Around* (New York: AMS Press, 1991), 63.

3. Richard Deeken, *Manuia Samoa! Samoanische Reiseskizzen und Beobachtungen* (Oldenburg: G. Stalling, 1901), 156. Quoted in Peter Mühlhäusler, "Samoan Plantation Pidgin English and the Origin of New Guinea Pidgin," *Papers in Pidgin and Creole Linguistics* 1 (1978): 70; Darrell T. Tryon and Jean-Michel Charpentier, *Pacific Pidgins and Creoles: Origins, Growth and Development* (Berlin: Mouton de Gruyter, 2004), 245.

4. For a detailed description of Samoan material culture, see Peter H. Buck (Te Rangi Hiroa), *Samoan Material Culture* (Honolulu: Bishop Museum, 1930), 551.

5. Franco, *Samoan Perceptions of Work,* 63.

6. Ibid., 59.

7. Buck, *Samoan Material Culture,* 550.

8. William T. Pritchard, *Polynesian Reminiscences; or, Life in the South Pacific Islands* (London: Chapman and Hall, 1866), 170.

9. Franco, *Samoan Perceptions of Work,* 61.

10. R. F. Watters, "Cultivation in Old Samoa," *Economic Geography* 34, no. 4 (1958): 348.

11. Augustin Krämer, *Die Samoa-Inseln: Entwurf einer Monographie mit besonderer Berücksichtigung Deutsch-Samoas* (Stuttgart: E. Schweizerbart, 1902–3), 143.

12. On Samoan baskets, see Buck, *Samoan Material Culture,* 189–208.

13. Krämer, *Samoa-Inseln,* 89.

14. Ibid., 129.

15. On land alienation and the Samoan civil wars, see Malama Meleisea, *The Making of Modern Samoa: Traditional Authority and Colonial Administration in the History of Western Samoa* (Suva: Institute of Pacific Studies of the University of the South Pacific, 1987), 21–45.

16. Ibid., 31.

17. Kurt Schmack, *J. C. Godeffroy & Sohn, Kaufleute zu Hamburg: Leistung und Schicksal eines Welthandelshauses* (Hamburg: Broschek, 1938), 112.

18. Doug Munro and Stewart Firth, "Samoan Plantations: The Gilbertese Laborers' Experience, 1867–1896," in *Plantation Workers: Resistance and Accommodation,* ed. Brij V. Lal, Doug Munro, and Edward D. Beechert (Honolulu: University of Hawai'i Press, 1993), 103.

19. James W. Davidson, *Samoa mo Samoa: The Emergence of the Independent State of Western Samoa* (Oxford: Oxford University Press, 1967), 45. On the effects of the U.S. Civil War on global cotton production, see Sven Beckert, "Emancipation and Empire: Reconstructing the Worldwide Web of Cotton Production in the Age of the American Civil War," *American Historical Review* 109, no. 5 (2004): 1405–1438.

20. Schmack, *J. C. Godeffroy & Sohn,* 145.

21. Gordon R. Lewthwaite, "Land, Life and Agriculture to Mid-Century," in *Western Samoa: Land, Life, and Agriculture in Tropical Polynesia,* ed. James W.

Fox and Kenneth B. Cumberland (Christchurch, NZ: Whitcombe & Tombs, 1962), 143–144; Stewart Firth, "German Recruitment and Employment of Labourers in the Western Pacific before the First World War" (PhD thesis, University of Oxford, 1973), 61; Franco, *Samoan Perceptions of Work*, 149.

22. Gregory T. Cushman, *Guano and the Opening of the Pacific World: A Global Ecological History* (Cambridge: Cambridge University Press, 2013), 101–102.

23. Davidson, *Samoa mo Samoa*, 46.

24. Ibid.

25. Pitt, *Tradition and Economic Progress*, 110.

26. On Samoans' land consciousness, see Felix M. Keesing, *Modern Samoa: Its Government and Changing Life* (London: G. Allen & Unwin, 1934), 273.

27. Davidson, *Samoa mo Samoa*, 64.

28. Keesing, *Modern Samoa*, 260–280; Meleisea, *Making of Modern Samoa*, 45.

29. Robert H. Stauffer, *Kahana: How the Land Was Lost* (Honolulu: University of Hawai'i Press, 2003).

30. Keesing, *Modern Samoa*, 273–275.

31. Line-Noue Memea Kruse, *The Pacific Insular Case of American Sāmoa: Land Rights and Law in Unincorporated U.S. Territories* (London: Palgrave Macmillan, 2018).

32. *Afakasi* is the Samoan transliteration of the English "half-caste." On mixed-race Samoans, see Damon Salesa, "Half-Castes between the Wars: Colonial Categories in New Zealand and Samoa," *New Zealand Journal of History* 34, no. 1 (2000): 98–116; Damon Salesa, "'Troublesome Half-Castes': Tales of a Samoan Borderland" (MA thesis, University of Auckland, 1997). See also Meleisea, *Making of Modern Samoa*, 156, 175–176, 179.

33. Patricia O'Brien, *Tautai: Sāmoa, World History, and the Life of Ta'isi O. F. Nelson* (Honolulu: University of Hawai'i Press, 2017), 14.

34. Ibid.

35. Susan Pedersen, *The Guardians: The League of Nations and the Crisis of Empire* (Oxford: Oxford University Press, 2015), 173.

36. George Steinmetz, *The Devil's Handwriting: Precoloniality and the German Colonial State in Qingdao, Samoa, and Southwest Africa* (Chicago: University of Chicago Press, 2007), 309. On Stevenson in Samoa, see Ann C. Colley, *Robert Louis Stevenson and the Colonial Imagination* (Aldershot: Ashgate, 2004).

37. Solf to Passarge, October 29, 1906, BArch, N 1053 / 28.

38. Buck, *Samoan Material Culture*, 544.

39. Keesing, *Modern Samoa*, 30.

40. German Consulate to Foreign Office-Colonial Office, May 30, 1900, BArch, R 1001 / 2540.

41. Pitt, *Tradition and Economic Progress*, 19.

42. Rose to Hohenlohe-Schillingsfürst, April 12, 1898, BArch, R 1001 / 2540.

43. Around 1900, 1 U.S. dollar was equivalent to 4 German marks or 4 shillings British sterling. The equivalents of all subsequent currencies are given in U.S. dollars.

44. Franz Reinecke, *Samoa* (Berlin: W. Süsserott, 1902), 201.

45. Pitt, *Tradition and Economic Progress,* 20.

46. Keesing, *Modern Samoa,* 295. On the impact of Christian missionaries on Samoan politics, see Featunaʻi Ben Liuaʻana, *Samoa Tulaʻi: Ecclesiastical and Political Face of Samoa's Independence, 1900–1962* (Apia: Malua Printing Press, 2001).

47. Jocelyn Linnekin, "Fine Mats and Money: Contending Exchange Paradigms in Colonial Samoa," *Anthropological Quarterly* 64, no. 1 (1991): 2. Before 1900, different kinds of specie were circulating in Samoa, including American, Mexican, and Chilean dollars, as well as German marks. See also Damon Salesa, "'Travel-Happy' Samoa: Colonialism, Samoan Migration and a 'Brown Pacific,'" *New Zealand Journal of History* 37, no. 2 (2003): 172.

48. Linnekin, "Fine Mats and Money," 7.

49. Keesing, *Modern Samoa,* 330–331.

50. *Auckland Evening Post,* October 19, 1914.

51. On Samoan mats, see Buck, *Samoan Material Culture,* 209–227, 275–281.

52. The word *ʻaumāga* translates into "the strength of the village." Malama Meleisea and Penelope Schoeffel Meleisea, *Lagaga: A Short History of Western Samoa* (Suva: University of the South Pacific, 1987), 28.

53. Penelope Schoeffel, "Daughters of Sina: A Study of Gender, Status and Power in Western Samoa" (PhD thesis, Australian National University, 1979), 435.

54. Ibid., 39.

55. Caroline Ralston, "Women Workers in Samoa and Tonga in the Early Twentieth Century," in *Labour in the South Pacific,* edited by Clive Moore, Jacqueline Leckie, and Doug Munro (Townsville: James Cook University of Northern Queensland, 1990), 68.

56. The biggest exception were the Coe sisters. Damon Salesa, "Emma and Phoebe: 'Weavers of the Border,'" *Journal of the Polynesian Society* 123, no. 2 (2014): 145–167. On Emma Coe, see Robert W. Robson, *Queen Emma: The Samoan-American Girl Who Founded an Empire in 19th Century New Guinea* (Sydney: Pacific Publications, 1971).

57. Ralston, "Women Workers in Samoa and Tonga," 71.

58. Ibid., 73.

59. Fofo I. F. Sunia, ed., *The Women of American Samoa, 1900–2000: A Hundred Years of Development and Achievements* (Pago-Pago: Amerika Samoa Humanities Council, 2005), 96.

60. Siapo.com, accessed May 20, 2021, siapo.com/kolone-leoso.html; siapo.com /mary-pritchard.html.

61. Schoeffel, "Daughters of Sina," chaps. 9 and 10.

62. In the German colonies in Africa as well as in German New Guinea, colonized people were forced to work for plantation owners and the colonial administration. Arthur Gordon's indirect rule in nearby British Fiji inspired the German administration in Samoa. Meleisea, *Making of Modern Samoa*, xi. On the British Empire as a model for Solf, see Peter J. Hempenstall and Paula T. Mochida, *The Lost Man: Wilhelm Solf in German History* (Wiesbaden: Harrassowitz, 2005), 95.

63. I borrow the term *salvage colonialism* from historical sociologist George Steinmetz's meticulous study *Devil's Handwriting*, 317–341. As Steinmetz points out (355), Solf leveraged his substantial ethnographic capital as an expert on Samoan culture to integrate the conflicting interests of non-German settlers, missionaries, and his colonial administration. George Steinmetz, *The Devil's Handwriting: Precoloniality and the German Colonial State in Qingdao, Samoa, and Southwest Africa* (Chicago: University of Chicago Press, 2007). On German ethnographers as salvage colonialists, see Harry Liebersohn, "Coming of Age in the Pacific: German Ethnography from Chamisso to Krämer," in *Worldly Provincialism: German Anthropology in the Age of Empire*, ed. H. Glenn Penny and Matti Bunzl (Ann Arbor: University of Michigan Press, 2003), 31–46. On Solf's salvage colonialism as a pragmatic choice rather than a principled decision, see Peter J. Hempenstall, "Indigenous Resistance to German Rule in the Pacific Colonies of Samoa, Ponape and New Guinea, 1884 to 1914" (PhD thesis, University of Oxford, 1973), 269; Evelyn Wareham, *Race and Realpolitik: The Politics of Colonisation in German Samoa* (Frankfurt am Main: Peter Lang, 2002), 157. Significantly, the DHPG supported Solf's policy in exchange for continued access to cheap laborers from Melanesia. Firth, "German Recruitment," 314.

64. Lloyd Osbourne, introduction to *Samoa under the Sailing Gods*, by Newton A. Rowe (London: Putnam, 1930), xii.

65. On perceptions of work in German Samoa, see Jürgen Schmidt, "Arbeit und Nicht-Arbeit im 'Paradies der Südsee': Samoa um 1890 bis 1914," *Arbeit—Bewegung—Geschichte* 15, no. 2 (2016): 7–25. On Germans' visions of their Pacific colonies, see Holger Droessler, "Germany's El Dorado in the Pacific: Metropolitan Representations and Colonial Realities, 1884–1914," in *Imperial Expectations and Realities: El Dorados, Utopias, and Dystopias*, ed. Andrekos Varnava (Manchester: Manchester University Press, 2015), 105–124.

66. *Samoanische Zeitung*, April 23, 1904. Commentators even speculated about deporting captured Herero fighters to German Samoa. *Samoanische Zeitung*, July 16, August 6, 1904.

67. Marcel van der Linden, *Workers of the World: Essays Toward a Global Labor History* (Leiden: Brill, 2008), 34.

68. Rose to Hohenlohe-Schillingsfürst, August 30, 1896, BArch, R 1001 / 2539.

69. Buck, *Samoan Material Culture*, 546.

70. Biermann to Caprivi, April 30, 1894, BArch, R 1001 / 2539.

71. Solf, "Notizen zur Landwirtschaft," BArch, N 1053 / 6, p. 292.

72. Schmack, *J. C. Godeffroy & Sohn*, 291.

73. Total copra output in German Samoa rose by 23 percent, from 7,792 tons in 1899 to 9,634 tons in 1913. Keesing, *Modern Samoa*, 300, 303.

74. Peter J. Hempenstall, *Pacific Islanders under German Rule: A Study in the Meaning of Colonial Resistance* (Canberra: Australian National University Press, 1978), 70.

75. Richard P. Gilson, *Samoa 1830 to 1900: The Politics of a Multi-Cultural Community* (Oxford: Oxford University Press), 406.

76. Keesing, *Modern Samoa*, 260.

77. Hempenstall, *Pacific Islanders under German Rule*, 53.

78. Firth, "German Recruitment," 242.

79. DHPG Business Report 1907, StAH, 621-1 / 14, p. 25.

80. Keesing, *Modern Samoa*, 293.

81. Ibid., 328.

82. Linnekin, "Fine Mats and Money," 7.

83. Salesa, "'Travel-Happy' Samoa," 175.

84. In 1902, the DHPG operated a total of ten copra kilns in German Samoa: five kilns in Mulifanua, three kilns in Vaitele, and two kilns in Vailele. Reinecke, *Samoa*, 194, 196, 198.

85. L. M. Fischel, *Copra Market Report* (London: 1927).

86. Firth, "German Recruitment," 61.

87. Reinecke, *Samoa*, 206.

88. Supf to Imperial Colonial Office, September 7, 1907, BArch, R 1001 / 7991.

89. Hanssen to Solf, December 3, 1907, BArch, R 1001 / 7991, pp. 9–10.

90. Pitt, *Tradition and Economic Progress*, 197.

91. Reinecke, *Samoa*, 206.

92. For cash-strapped colonial officials, head taxes raised funds for the colonial administration and, at the same time, promised to secure a constant supply of labor to produce exports.

93. Rose to Hohenlohe-Schillingsfürst, April 20, 1897, BArch, R 1001 / 2540.

94. Keesing, *Modern Samoa*, 487.

95. For a discussion of a similar logic in Hawai'i, see Ronald T. Takaki, *Pau Hana: Plantation Life and Labor in Hawai'i, 1835–1920* (Honolulu: University of Hawai'i Press, 1983), 73.

96. Firth, "German Recruitment," 244. DHPG manager Riedel recounted that Samoans earned 3–4 marks ($0.75–$1.00) per day, while their labor was not worth more than 1 mark ($0.25) per day. Otto Riedel, *Der Kampf um Deutsch-Samoa: Erinnerungen eines Hamburger Kaufmanns* (Berlin: Deutscher Verlag, 1938), 83.

97. Heimrod to J. S. Williams, October 27, 1904, NARA-CP, RG 84, vol. 52.

98. SSG Business Reports 1905, 1906, BArch, R 1001 / 2493.

99. SSG Business Report 1907, BArch, R 1001 / 2494.

100. SSG Business Report 1911, BArch, R 1001 / 2496.

101. Upolu-Cacao-Kompagnie, BArch, R 1001 / 2499.

102. Report on SPG, March 30, 1914, BArch, R 1001 / 2500.

103. Firth, "German Recruitment," 247.

104. Franco, *Samoan Perceptions of Work,* 180.

105. German Consulate to Foreign Office-Colonial Office, May 30, 1900, BArch, R 1001 / 2540.

106. Iosefo to Solf, June 25, 1903, BArch, R 1001 / 3063, p. 81. For a published version of the petition, see Arthur J. Knoll and Hermann Hiery, eds., *The German Colonial Experience: Select Documents on German Rule in Africa, China, and the Pacific, 1884–1914* (Lanham, MD: University Press of America, 2010), 189–191.

107. Iosefo to Solf, June 25, 1903, BArch, R 1001 / 3063, p. 81.

108. Ibid.

109. Franco, *Samoan Perceptions of Work,* 184–185.

110. Knappe to Foreign Office, November 9, 1886, BArch, R 1001 / 2926.

111. Biermann to Caprivi, March 20, 1893, BArch, R 1001 / 2926, p. 14.

112. Krüger to DHPG headquarters Apia, March 9, 1893, BArch, R 1001 / 2926.

113. Papalu to Stübel, August 3, 1889, NARA-CP, RG 84, vol. 61; Stübel to Foreign Office, August 13, 1889, BArch, R 1001 / 2926.

114. Stübel to Foreign Office, September 12, 1889, BArch, R 1001 / 2926, p. 11.

115. Stübel to Foreign Office, October 8, 1889, BArch, R 1001 / 2926.

116. Biermann to Caprivi, March 20, 1893, BArch, R 1001 / 2926.

117. DHPG to German Consulate Apia, August 15, 1895, BArch, R 1001 / 2926.

118. Blacklock to Chief Justice Ide, May 5, 1896, NARA-CP, RG 84, vol. 51.

119. Rose to Hohenlohe-Schillingsfürst, April 12, 1898, BArch, R 1001 / 2540.

120. The global struggle over land ownership is explored in Andro Linklater, *Owning the Earth: The Transforming History of Land Ownership* (London: Bloomsbury, 2013).

121. Building on E. P. Thompson's ideas on the moral economy of peasants, historian Karl Jacoby has coined the term "moral ecology" in *Crimes against Nature: Squatters, Poachers, Thieves, and the Hidden History of American Conservation* (Berkeley: University of California Press, 2001), 3.

122. Despite these complaints, a growing number of mixed-race Samoans found employment as traders in the 1890s. In 1895, the DHPG alone employed four mixed-race Samoans in its trading stores, including a young Ta'isi O. F. Nelson. List of DHPG Employees in 1895, BArch, R 1001 / 2478.

123. Firth, "German Recruitment," 245.

124. Lewthwaite, "Land, Life and Agriculture," 149.

125. Keesing, *Modern Samoa,* 315.

126. Hempenstall, *Pacific Islanders under German Rule,* 43.

127. Ibid., 225n36.

128. Ibid., 44.

129. Firth, "German Recruitment," 258.

130. On cotton cooperatives, see Sven Beckert, *Empire of Cotton: A Global History* (New York: Knopf, 2014), 338.

131. O'Brien, *Tautai,* 25.

132. Oloa-Kompagnie, BArch, R 1001 / 3064, pp. 92–94.

133. Schultz to Solf, February 2, 1905, BArch, N 1053 / 132, p. 25.

134. Ibid., 28.

135. Hempenstall, *Pacific Islanders under German Rule,* 44.

136. Ibid., 45.

137. Ibid.

138. Ibid., 46.

139. Keesing, *Modern Samoa,* 87.

140. Saleimoa Vaai, *Samoa Faamatai and the Rule of Law* (Apia: National University of Samoa, 1999), 93.

141. Hempenstall, *Pacific Islanders under German Rule,* 48–49.

142. An armada of brand-new battleships was sent around the world by President Theodore Roosevelt to showcase the U.S. Navy's new blue-water capabilities, passing by Pago Pago on August 1, 1908. One of the main reasons Roosevelt sent the fleet around the world was to back up legal bars to Japanese immigration to the United States. On Lauaki and the fleet visit, see ibid., 56.

143. Statement by Lauaki to Williams, February 27, 1909, BArch, N 1053 / 30, p. 148.

144. O'Brien, *Tautai,* 27.

145. Peter Hempenstall interprets the Mau a Pule as the "rearguard action" of a traditionalist group of talking chiefs around Lauaki, attempting but failing to revive their political power. Hempenstall, *Pacific Islanders under German Rule,* 56.

146. A few years later, Apolosi Nawai founded the Viti Trading Company in nearby Fiji, in a similar quest for greater economic autonomy. For his activism, Nawai was twice sent into exile by the British colonial administration. Brij V. Lal, *Broken Waves: A History of the Fiji Islands in the Twentieth Century* (Honolulu: University of Hawai'i Press, 1992), 48–54; Timothy J. Macnaught, *The Fijian Colonial Experience: A Study of the Neotraditional Order under British Colonial Rule Prior to World War II* (Canberra: Australian National University, 1982), 75–92.

147. "Petition Forwarded by Certain Residents of Western Samoa on the 4th February 1910 to the High President of the German Parliament in Berlin," appended to *1927 Report of Visit by Hon. W. Nosworthy, Minister of External Affairs to Mandated Territory of Western Samoa* (Wellington: Government Printer, 1927), 46. For an analysis, see O'Brien, *Tautai,* 27–29.

148. Peter J. Hempenstall and Noel Rutherford, *Protest and Dissent in the Colonial Pacific* (Suva: Institute of Pacific Studies of the University of the South Pacific, 1984), 32.

149. *Toeaina* means "elders" in Samoan. On the Toeaina Club, see Davidson, *Samoa mo Samoa,* 110–111; Mary Boyd, "Coping with Samoan Resistance after the 1918 Influenza Epidemic: Colonel Tate's Problems and Perplexities," *Journal of Pacific History* 15, no. 3 (1980): 160–174; Meleisea, *Making of Modern Samoa,* 116; Hermann Hiery, *The Neglected War: The German South Pacific and the Influence of World War I* (Honolulu: University of Hawai'i Press, 1995), 168, 178–179.

150. Vaai, *Samoa Faamatai,* 106.

151. Lewthwaite, "Land, Life and Agriculture," 161; O'Brien, *Tautai,* 35; Hempenstall and Rutherford, *Protest and Dissent,* 32.

152. Sebree to Asst. Sec. of the Navy, August 9, 1902, NARA-DC, RG 80, file 3931, box 35, item 347, p. 4.

153. Keesing, *Modern Samoa,* 341.

154. Crose to Sec. of the Navy, July 14, 1911, NARA-DC, RG 80, file 3931, box 40, p. 7.

155. Stronach to Gov., June 30, 1914, NARA-SB, RG 284, MF T1182, roll 1.

156. Stearns to Sec. of the Navy, July 21, 1914, NARA-DC, RG 80, file 3931, box 42, p. 20.

157. Stronach to Gov., June 30, 1914, NARA-SB, RG 284, MF T1182, roll 1.

158. Stronach to Gov., July 1, 1915, NARA-SB, RG 284, MF T1182, roll 1.

159. Noble to Gov., July 1, 1919, NARA-SB, RG 284, MF T1182, roll 1.

160. Noble to Gov., August 1, 1920, NARA-SB, RG 284, MF T1182, roll 1.

161. Keesing, *Modern Samoa,* 341.

162. Ibid., 491.

2. Planters

1. Solf to District Judge, April 10, 1904, ANZ Wellington, SAMOA-BMO, Series 4, box 73, T40/1904, vol. 1, p. 3.

2. "Urteil gegen Richard Deeken," June 16, 1904, BArch, R 1001/2320, p. 139.

3. The first eighty-one Gilbertese Islanders were forcibly recruited in 1867. Doug Munro and Stewart Firth, "Samoan Plantations: The Gilbertese Laborers' Experience, 1867–1896," in *Plantation Workers: Resistance and Accommodation,* ed. Brij V. Lal, Doug Munro, and Edward D. Beechert (Honolulu: University of Hawai'i Press, 1993), 103.

4. Ibid., 104–106.

5. By the late 1870s, men received $2 per month, usually payable in tobacco, plus rations, while women and children made $1. Ibid., 123n18.

6. Of the total 4,857 workers, 2,250 were from the Gilbert Islands (46%), 1,201 from the New Hebrides (25%), 693 from New Britain and New Ireland (14%), 618 from the Solomon Islands (13%), and 95 from the Caroline Islands (2%). Stübel to Bismarck, January 27, 1886, BArch, R 1001/2316.

7. Munro and Firth, "Samoan Plantations," 114–115.

8. For a detailed discussion of the origins of labor recruitment before 1900, see Stewart Firth, "German Recruitment and Employment of Labourers in the Western Pacific before the First World War" (PhD thesis, University of Oxford, 1973), 24–84.

9. Hahl to Imperial Colonial Office, November 16, 1913, BArch, R 1001 / 2313.

10. Between 1900 and 1913, the average price of Pacific copra in Europe almost doubled. S. Firth, "German Recruitment," 135.

11. Estimate based on reports in "Kontrolle über die melanesischen Kontraktarbeiter," NAS, IDO 4 F2 II 4, vol. 1.

12. During the years of German rule in Samoa, the DHPG paid out an average dividend of 21 percent. S. Firth, "German Recruitment," 242.

13. For a succinct summary of the debates about importing Chinese workers to German Samoa, see Stewart Firth, "Governors versus Settlers: The Dispute over Chinese Labour in German Samoa," *New Zealand Journal of History* 11, no. 2 (1977): 155–179.

14. Report by Wandres, May 20, 1903, BArch, R 1001 / 2319.

15. Moors to Solf, *Samoanische Zeitung,* April 4, 1903, BArch, R 1001 / 2319.

16. Nancy Tom, *The Chinese in Western Samoa, 1875–1985: The Dragon Came from Afar* (Apia: Western Samoa Historical and Cultural Trust, 1986), 36. Hans Mosolff, *Die chinesische Auswanderung: Ursachen, Wesen und Wirkungen* (Rostock: Carl Hinstorffs Verlag, 1932), 405–448.

17. Ibid., 21–37.

18. Philip A. Kuhn, *Chinese among Others: Emigration in Modern Times* (Lanham, MD: Rowman & Littlefield, 2008); Ching-Hwang Yen, *Coolies and Mandarins: China's Protection of Overseas Chinese during the Late Ch'ing Period, 1851–1911* (Singapore: Singapore University Press, 1985).

19. Walton Look Lai, "Asian Contract and Free Migrations to the Americas," in *Coerced and Free Migration: Global Perspectives,* ed. David Eltis (Stanford: Stanford University Press, 2002), 229–258.

20. Overall, family remittances by Chinese workers in Samoa remained relatively low. In 1912, they amounted to 7 percent of total wages paid. See also Hermann Hiery, "Die deutsche Verwaltung Samoas, 1900–1914," in *Die Deutsche Südsee 1884–1914: Ein Handbuch,* ed. Hermann Hiery (Paderborn: Ferdinand Schöningh, 2001), 672.

21. Solf to District Judge, April 10, 1904, ANZ Wellington, SAMOA-BMO, Series 4, box 73, T40 / 1904, vol. 1, pp. 3–4.

22. Adam McKeown, *Chinese Migrant Networks and Cultural Change: Peru, Chicago, Hawaii, 1900–1936* (Chicago: University of Chicago Press, 2001), esp. chap. 2; see also his *Melancholy Order: Asian Migration and the Globalization of Borders* (New York: Columbia University Press, 2008).

23. Featuna'i Ben Liua'ana, "Dragons in Little Paradise: Chinese (Mis-) Fortunes in Samoa, 1900–1950," *Journal of Pacific History* 32, no. 1 (1997): 29–48;

A. S. Noa Siaosi, "Catching the Dragon's Tail: The Impact of the Chinese in Samoa" (MA thesis, University of Canterbury, 2010); Tom, *Chinese in Western Samoa.*

24. Evelyn Wareham, *Race and Realpolitik: The Politics of Colonisation in German Samoa* (Frankfurt am Main: Peter Lang, 2002), 111.

25. Erich Langen, "Deutsch-Samoa," *Jahrbuch über die deutschen Kolonien* 5 (1912): 219.

26. John La Farge, *Reminiscences of the South Seas* (Garden City: Doubleday, Page, 1912), 97.

27. *The Cyclopedia of Samoa, Tonga, Tahiti, and the Cook Islands* (Papakura: R. McMillan, 1983), 3. In addition to the 258 Germans, 106 British, 35 Americans, and several other Europeans, there were around 815 "half-castes" and more than 33,000 Samoans in German Samoa in 1906. Wareham, *Race and Realpolitik,* 177.

28. Hiery, "Die deutsche Verwaltung Samoas," 670–671.

29. Ibid., 672.

30. Munro and Firth, "Samoan Plantations," 101.

31. Augustin Krämer, *Die Samoa-Inseln: Entwurf einer Monographie mit besonderer Berücksichtigung Deutsch-Samoas* (Stuttgart: E. Schweizerbart, 1902–3), 138. On the DHPG plantation in Mulifanua, Deeken noted a tree distance of ten meters (33 feet). Richard Deeken, *Manuia Samoa! Samoanische Reiseskizzen und Beobachtungen* (Oldenburg: G. Stalling, 1901), 151.

32. "Mulifanua-Pflanzungen," table no. 5, *Ländereien und Pflanzungen der Deutschen Handels- und Plantagen-Gesellschaft der Südsee-Inseln zu Hamburg in Samoa: Uebersichtskarten und Ansichten,* 1900, Commerzbibliothek Hamburg.

33. Otto Riedel, *Der Kampf um Deutsch-Samoa: Erinnerungen eines Hamburger Kaufmanns* (Berlin: Deutscher Verlag, 1938), 89.

34. Franz Reinecke, *Samoa* (Berlin: W. Süsserott, 1902), 206; Kurt Schmack, *J. C. Godeffroy & Sohn, Kaufleute zu Hamburg: Leistung und Schicksal eines Welthandelshauses* (Hamburg: Broschek, 1938), 280.

35. Krause and Marggraff to SSG, September 19, 1904, BArch, R 1001/2492, p. 159.

36. Ibid.

37. Each Chinese worker was guaranteed a daily supply of thirty-two ounces of rice, ten ounces of salted fish or meat, and ten ounces of vegetables. "Chinesische Angelegenheiten," *Samoanische Zeitung,* May 9, 1903, BArch, R 1001/2319, p. 161. Melanesian workers followed a similar work schedule. Malama Meleisea, *O Tama Uli: Melanesians in Western Samoa* (Suva: Institute of Pacific Studies of the University of the South Pacific, 1980), 27.

38. Ibid., 17.

39. Ibid., 27.

40. "Chinesische Angelegenheiten," 161. By comparison, Chinese workers on Peruvian cotton plantations in the 1870s received 1.5 pounds of rice a day. Vin-

cent C. Peloso, *Peasants on Plantations: Subaltern Strategies of Labor and Resistance in the Pisco Valley, Peru* (Durham, NC: Duke University Press, 1999), 23.

41. Müller to Imperial Court, April 20, 1905, NAS, IDC-3 F2 III 2b, vol. 4.

42. *Samoanische Zeitung*, February 1, 1902.

43. "Chinesische Angelegenheiten," 161.

44. Riedel, *Kampf um Deutsch-Samoa*, 188.

45. "Zur Chinesen-Einfuhr," *Samoanische Zeitung*, May 9, 1903, BArch, R 1001/2319, p. 159.

46. Meleisea, *O Tama Uli*, 27.

47. Samoan plantation pidgin emerged during the 1880s on the large DHPG plantations in Vailele, Vaitele, and Mulifanua. While DHPG workers recruited from Melanesia were the principal speakers of Samoan plantation pidgin, their white and mixed-race employers, white labor recruiters, and Samoans living close to the plantations also used this new language. Chinese workers did not use Samoan plantation pidgin but a form of Samoan pidgin. Peter Mühlhäusler, "Samoan Plantation Pidgin English and the Origins of New Guinea Pidgin: An Introduction," *Journal of Pacific History* 11, no. 2 (1976): 122–123; Peter Mühlhäusler, "Samoan Plantation Pidgin English and the Origin of New Guinea Pidgin," *Papers in Pidgin and Creole Linguistics* 1 (1978): 75.

48. Riedel, *Kampf um Deutsch-Samoa*, 68.

49. Meleisea, *O Tama Uli*, 15.

50. Riedel, *Kampf um Deutsch-Samoa*, 85.

51. In 1907, the DHPG plantation in Mulifanua employed 40 horses and 120 donkeys to help workers with transporting copra. *Cyclopedia of Samoa*, 82.

52. Rose to Hohenlohe-Schillingsfürst, April 12, 1898, BArch, R 1001/2540; DHPG Business Report, 1902–03, BArch, R 1001/6522, p. 710.

53. Riedel, *Kampf um Deutsch-Samoa*, 85.

54. Reinecke, *Samoa*, 204–205; Kenneth B. Cumberland, "Plantation Agriculture," in *Western Samoa: Land, Life, and Agriculture in Tropical Polynesia*, ed. James W. Fox and Kenneth B. Cumberland (Christchurch, NZ: Whitcombe & Tombs, 1962), 251.

55. Riedel, *Kampf um Deutsch-Samoa*, 85.

56. Mary Poyer Kniskern, *Life in Samoa from 1915 to 1919* (USA: Self-published, 1993), 10.

57. Deeken, *Manuia Samoa!*, 151–152.

58. Riedel, *Kampf um Deutsch-Samoa*, 185.

59. Robert W. Franco, *Samoan Perceptions of Work: Moving Up and Moving Around* (New York: AMS Press, 1991), 148; Felix M. Keesing, *Modern Samoa: Its Government and Changing Life* (London: G. Allen & Unwin, 1934), 301.

60. For an extended analysis of environmental changes on Samoan plantations, see Holger Droessler, "Changes on the Plantation: An Environmental History of Colonial Samoa, 1880–1920," in *Migrant Ecologies: Environmental Histories of the*

Pacific, ed. James Beattie, Edward Melillo, and Ryan T. Jones (Honolulu: University of Hawai'i Press, forthcoming).

61. Business Report 1907, StAH, 621-1 / 14, p. 26.

62. Ibid.

63. Solf to AA-KA, May 24, 1903, BArch, R 1001 / 2319.

64. Identification badges were common in other plantation economies at the time. On sugar plantations in Hawai'i, for example, workers had to wear "bangos." Ronald T. Takaki, *Pau Hana: Plantation Life and Labor in Hawai'i, 1835–1920* (Honolulu: University of Hawai'i Press, 1983), 54.

65. Liua'ana, "Dragons in Little Paradise," 32.

66. "Chinesische Angelegenheiten," 161.

67. Reinecke, *Samoa,* 194. Riedel, *Kampf um Deutsch-Samoa,* 86. *Mulifanua* literally means "land's end" or "land's bottom" in Samoan.

68. Meleisea, *O Tama Uli,* 18.

69. *Samoanische Zeitung,* May 2, 1903, BArch, R 1001 / 2319.

70. Meleisea, *O Tama Uli,* 15.

71. Mühlhäusler, "Samoan Plantation Pidgin English" (1978), 80.

72. Riedel, *Kampf um Deutsch-Samoa,* 83.

73. S. Firth, "German Recruitment," 257. In the early 1900s, Melanesian workers on DHPG plantations earned 1.35 marks ($0.34) a day. Riedel, *Kampf um Deutsch-Samoa,* 187.

74. Meleisea, *O Tama Uli,* 15.

75. Asenati Liki, "Women as Kin: Working Lives, Living Work and Mobility among Samoan *Teine uli,"* in *Oceanian Journeys and Sojourns: Home Thoughts Abroad,* ed. Judith A. Bennett (Dunedin: Otago University Press, 2015), 126–159. See also Mühlhäusler, "Samoan Plantation Pidgin English" (1976), 123.

76. Overall, more than six thousand New Guineans went to work in Samoa between 1879 and 1913. Mühlhäusler, "Samoan Plantation Pidgin English" (1976), 125. Between 1887 and 1912, 5,285 workers were recruited from the Bismarck Archipelago and the German Solomon Islands to work on DHPG plantations in Samoa. S. Firth, "German Recruitment," 327.

77. Mühlhäusler, "Samoan Plantation Pidgin English" (1978), 109.

78. Stübel to Bismarck, July 23, 1886, BArch, R 1001 / 2316. The first plantation in German New Guinea, started by a British trader in 1885, employed 150 North Solomon Islanders who had previously worked in German Samoa. Mühlhäusler, "Samoan Plantation Pidgin English" (1976), 125.

79. Meleisea, *O Tama Uli,* 10. As Meleisea notes, the workers are referred to by their Samoan names. Their Melanesian names were not recorded.

80. Ibid., 35.

81. In colonial Hawai'i, too, "plantations made so little distinction between work site and home that managerial regulation reached into the private sphere."

Gary Y. Okihiro, *Pineapple Culture: A History of the Tropical and Temperate Zones* (Berkeley: University of California Press, 2009), 142–143.

82. According to an 1883 health report by Donald Ross, a British surgeon in Apia, Samoan workers were better cared for than those in Fiji or Queensland. Stübel to Bismarck, January 27, 1886, BArch, R 1001/2316. On working conditions in Queensland, see Adrian Graves, *Cane and Labour: The Political Economy of the Queensland Sugar Industry, 1862–1906* (Edinburgh: Edinburgh University Press, 1993).

83. Trutz von Trotha, "'One for Kaiser': Beobachtungen zur politischen Soziologie der Prügelstrafe am Beispiel des 'Schutzgebietes Togo,'" in *Studien zur Geschichte des deutschen Kolonialismus in Afrika: Festschrift zum 60. Geburtstag von Peter Sebald,* ed. Peter Heine and Ulrich van der Heyden (Pfaffenweiler: Centaurus, 1995), 527. After a scandal, Governor Hahl outlawed the flogging of Chinese workers in German New Guinea in January 1903. Stewart Firth, *New Guinea under the Germans* (Carlton: Melbourne University Press, 1983), 116; Andreas Steen, "Germany and the Chinese Coolie: Labor, Resistance, and the Struggle for Equality, 1884–1914," in *German Colonialism Revisited: African, Asian, and Oceanic Experiences,* ed. Nina Berman, Klaus Mühlhahn, and Patrice Nganang (Ann Arbor: University of Michigan Press, 2014), 149.

84. Reinecke, *Samoa,* 198.

85. Liua'ana, "Dragons in Little Paradise," 32n19.

86. S. Firth, "German Recruitment," 259.

87. Mühlhäusler, "Samoan Plantation Pidgin English" (1978), 72; S. Firth, "German Recruitment," 259.

88. Liua'ana, "Dragons in Little Paradise," 38.

89. Meleisea, *O Tama Uli,* 10, 27.

90. Harry J. Moors, "Theodore Weber," *Samoa Times,* November 14, 1924.

91. *Samoanische Zeitung,* July 3, 1909, BArch, R 1001/2338.

92. Steen, "Germany and the Chinese Coolie," 152.

93. S. Firth, "German Recruitment," 261.

94. German Consulate Fukien to RKA, May 3, 1907, BArch, R 1001/2323.

95. Report by Lin Shu Fen, enclosed to Rex to Bülow, July 20, 1908, BArch, R 1001/2323.

96. S. Firth, "German Recruitment," 264.

97. AA to Chinese Legate Berlin, September 13, 1911, BArch, R 1001/2328.

98. Schultz to RKA, February 10, 1913, BArch, R 1001/2328.

99. Wareham, *Race and Realpolitik,* 119.

100. Lin to Mitchell, May 28, 1912, NARA-CP, RG 84, vol. 77. As Lin did not fail to mention a year later, the United States officially recognized the new Chinese Republic on May 2, 1913.

101. S. Firth, "Governors versus Settlers," 168.

102. Meleisea, *O Tama Uli,* 42.

103. Keesing, *Modern Samoa,* 313–314.

104. Michael J. Field, *Mau: Samoa's Struggle against New Zealand Oppression* (Wellington: Reed, 1984), 13.

105. Ibid., 11.

106. L. P. Leary, *New Zealanders in Samoa* (London: W. Heinemann, 1918), 90.

107. Hermann Hiery, *The Neglected War: The German South Pacific and the Influence of World War I* (Honolulu: University of Hawai'i Press, 1995), 167.

108. Field, *Mau,* 31.

109. Liua'ana, "Dragons in Little Paradise," 34.

110. Franco, *Samoan Perceptions of Work,* 152.

111. Tom, *Chinese in Western Samoa,* 36.

112. Keesing, *Modern Samoa,* 357.

113. Liua'ana, "Dragons in Little Paradise," 44.

114. James C. Scott, *Weapons of the Weak: Everyday Forms of Peasant Resistance* (New Haven: Yale University Press, 1985).

115. Chin to Schultz, July 24, 1911, BArch, R 1001 / 2327, p. 7.

116. Meleisea, *O Tama Uli,* 43.

117. Mühlhäusler, "Samoan Plantation Pidgin English" (1978), 86.

118. Meleisea, *O Tama Uli,* 35.

119. Ibid.

120. Ibid.

121. Ibid., 10.

122. Unnamed soldier's letter, ANZ Wellington, War Archives, Samoan Expeditionary Force, Series 210 / 3 / 12.

123. James N. Bade, ed., *Karl Hanssen's Samoan War Diaries, August 1914–May 1915: A German Perspective on New Zealand's Military Occupation of German Samoa* (Frankfurt am Main: Peter Lang, 2011), 79–80.

124. La Farge, *Reminiscences of the South Seas,* 262. Toward the end of his stay in Samoa, La Farge recounted the story of a Samoan man who had allegedly been killed and eaten by Solomon Islander runaways after he survived a shipwreck off Manono Island. Even though La Farge cast some doubt on the veracity of the incident, it becomes clear that he—in accordance with dominant Euro-American perceptions of the time—saw Polynesians as the more beautiful and "civilized" race vis-à-vis the darker-skinned Melanesians. La Farge, *Reminiscences of the South Seas,* 283–286.

125. Krüger to DHPG headquarters Apia, March 9, 1893, BArch, R 1001 / 2926.

126. Ibid.

127. "Register, German Chinese Commissioner, 1913–1932," ANZ Wellington, SAMOA-BMO Series 2, box 3, item 12.

128. *Samoanische Zeitung,* June 4, 1904, 1.

129. At the same time, escapes from plantations also functioned as a safety valve, letting off steam and allowing the system of labor exploitation to continue relatively undisturbed. For a similar argument on sugar plantations in Hawai'i, see Takaki, *Pau Hana,* 151.

130. Tilley to Asst. Sec. of the Navy, February 1, 1901, NARA-DC, RG 80, file 3931, box 34, pp. 263–264.

131. Joseph Kennedy, "The Wild Man of Samoa: A Tale from the Graveyard of Strangers," *Natural History* (February 2004).

132. Tilley to Asst. Sec. of the Navy, February 1, 1901, NARA-DC, RG 80, file 3931, box 34, pp. 263–264.

133. Robert Louis Stevenson, *A Footnote to History: Eight Years of Trouble in Samoa* (New York: Charles Scribner's Sons, 1892), 32.

134. Pollock to Sec. of the Navy, June 23, 1923, NARA-DC, RG 80, file 3931, box 37.

135. Ibid.

136. J. Kennedy, "Wild Man of Samoa."

137. Ibid.

3. Performers

1. Adria L. Imada, *Aloha America: Hula Circuits through the U.S. Empire* (Durham, NC: Duke University Press, 2012), 95.

2. David Ciarlo, *Advertising Empire: Race and Visual Culture in Imperial Germany* (Cambridge, MA: Harvard University Press, 2011), 25–64.

3. Bernth Lindfors, ed., *Africans on Stage: Studies in Ethnological Show Business* (Bloomington: Indiana University Press, 1999).

4. In recent years, scholars of ethnographic shows have increasingly focused on the experiences of the performers themselves. See David Beck, *Unfair Labor? American Indians and the 1893 World's Columbian Exposition in Chicago* (Lincoln: University of Nebraska Press, 2019); Sadiah Qureshi, *Peoples on Parade: Exhibitions, Empire, and Anthropology in Nineteenth-Century Britain* (Chicago: University of Chicago Press, 2011); Anne Dreesbach, *Gezähmte Wilde: Die Zurschaustellung "exotischer" Menschen in Deutschland, 1870–1940* (Frankfurt am Main: Campus, 2005); Roslyn Poignant, *Professional Savages: Captive Lives and Western Spectacle* (New Haven: Yale University Press, 2004); Hilke Thode-Arora, *Für fünfzig Pfennig um die Welt: Die Hagenbeckschen Völkerschauen* (Frankfurt am Main: Campus, 1989); Robert W. Rydell, *All the World's a Fair: Visions of American Empire at American International Expositions, 1876–1916* (Chicago: University of Chicago Press, 1984). Hilke Thode-Arora's exhibition volume, *From Samoa with Love? Samoan Travelers in Germany, 1895–1911: Retracing the Footsteps* (Munich: Hirmer, 2014) includes several chapters on Samoan performers in what she refers

to as "ethnic shows" in Germany but has little to say about performances in the United States. On the Samoan village in Chicago, see Mandy Treagus, "The South Seas Exhibit at the Chicago World's Fair, 1893," in *Oceania and the Victorian Imagination: Where All Things Are Possible,* ed. Richard D. Fulton and Peter H. Hoffenberg (Burlington, VT: Ashgate, 2013), 52–57.

5. Between 1875 and 1914, more than three hundred ethnographic shows— so-called *Völkerschauen*—toured through Germany alone. Among many others, the tours included Native Americans, "Eskimos," Nubians, Togolese, Herero, Dahomeyans, and Singhalese. Thode-Arora, *Für fünfzig Pfennig um die Welt,* 168–178.

6. Sierra A. Bruckner, "The Tingle-Tangle of Modernity: Popular Anthropology and the Cultural Politics of Identity in Imperial Germany" (PhD thesis, University of Iowa, 1999), 364–365.

7. Poignant, *Professional Savages,* 77–110.

8. Damon Salesa, "Misimoa: An American on the Beach," *Common-Place* 5, no. 2 (2005), http://commonplace.online / article / misimoa-an-american-on-the-beach; Damon Salesa, "'Travel-Happy' Samoa: Colonialism, Samoan Migration and a 'Brown Pacific,'" *New Zealand Journal of History* 37, no. 2 (2003): 171–188.

9. Imada makes a similar argument about the Hawaiian hula dancers who entered into performance contracts because they "gave them a chance to earn a decent living, tour the powerful country that had colonized theirs, and increase their individual prestige and fame." Imada, *Aloha America,* 114.

10. *San Francisco Chronicle,* August 19, 1889.

11. *Watkins Express,* August 29, 1889.

12. *Brooklyn Daily Eagle,* September 20, 1889, 4.

13. Thode-Arora, *From Samoa with Love,* 108.

14. "New York City–Review of the Week: Koster & Bial's," *New York Clipper,* October 26, 1889, 551.

15. Poignant, *Professional Savages,* 199.

16. *Samoa Times,* August 15, 1891, 2.

17. Thode-Arora, *From Samoa with Love,* 89.

18. *Kölnische Volkszeitung,* April 26, 1890.

19. Christopher B. Balme, *Pacific Performances: Theatricality and Cross-Cultural Encounter in the South Seas* (New York: Palgrave Macmillan, 2007), 128. On panoptikums in imperial Germany, see Ciarlo, *Advertising Empire,* 81–87.

20. Andrew Zimmerman, *Anthropology and Antihumanism in Imperial Germany* (Chicago: University of Chicago Press, 2001), 18–19.

21. See Stephen J. Gould, *The Mismeasure of Man* (New York: W. W. Norton, 1981).

22. Balme, *Pacific Performances,* 129.

23. Interracial romances were common at ethnographic exhibitions. See, for instance, Thode-Arora, *Für fünfzig Pfennig,* 115–117, 168–178.

24. *Samoa Times,* October 18, 1890, 2.

25. *Samoa Times,* August 15, 1891, 2.

26. Poignant, *Professional Savages,* 200.

27. Ibid.

28. Roslyn Poignant, "Captive Aboriginal Lives: Billy, Jenny, Little Toby and Their Companions," in *Captive Lives: Australian Captivity Narratives,* ed. Kate Darian-Smith, Roslyn Poignant, and Kay Schaffer (London: University of London, 1993), 52.

29. *Samoa Times,* August 15, 1891, 2.

30. Joseph Theroux, "Rediscovering 'H.J.M.,' Samoa's 'Unconquerable' Harry Moors," *Pacific Islands Monthly* 52, no. 8 (1981): 51.

31. Joseph Theroux, "H.J.M.: Showman, Author, Farmer, and Crusading Politician," *Pacific Islands Monthly* 52, no. 9 (1981): 59.

32. Mabeu to Blacklock, February 27, 1893, NARA-CP, RG 84, vol. 44.

33. *Samoa Weekly Herald,* December 30, 1893.

34. Salesa, "Misimoa."

35. A newspaper article noted that Moors had originally intended to recruit twenty-five Samoans. *Samoa Times,* February 25, 1892.

36. *Samoa Times,* May 13, 1893, 3.

37. Harry J. Moors, "Some Recollections of Early Samoa," *Samoa Times,* August 7, 1925, 3; Salesa, "Misimoa"; J. C. Furnas, *Anatomy of Paradise: Hawaii and the Islands of the South Seas* (New York, NY: W. Sloane Associates, 1948), 419.

38. Furnas, *Anatomy of Paradise,* 419.

39. Moors, "Some Recollections of Early Samoa," *Samoa Times,* July 4, 1924, 3; Moors, "Some Recollections of Early Samoa," *Samoa Times,* August 14, 1925, 3.

40. The fair's official guidebook recommended visiting the Midway after the White City. Rydell, *All the World's a Fair,* 62.

41. Burton Benedict, "The Anthropology of World's Fairs," in *The Anthropology of World's Fairs: San Francisco's Panama Pacific International Exposition of 1915* (Berkeley, CA: Lowie Museum of Anthropology, 1983), 49–50. According to Furnas, Bloom said that "for reasons best known to himself, he does not care to discuss the Samoans' career at the Fair." Furnas, *Anatomy of Paradise,* 419n2.

42. Rydell, *All the World's a Fair,* 47–48. On the role of world's fairs in contemporary U.S. debates on immigration and imperialism, see Matthew Frye Jacobson, *Barbarian Virtues: The United States Encounters Foreign Peoples at Home and Abroad, 1876–1917* (New York: Hill & Wang, 2000). On the ethnographic gaze at world's fairs, see Alison Griffiths, *Wondrous Difference: Cinema, Anthropology, and Turn-of-the-Century Visual Culture* (New York: Columbia University Press, 2002), 46–85. On Hagenbeck's role in organizing animal and ethnographic shows, see Thode-Arora, *Für fünfzig Pfennig,* 115–117.

43. Contract with Leigh S. Lynch, October 30, 1891, Chicago History Museum, World's Columbian Exposition, Concession Agreements, vol. 1, "Villages of the Dutch East India Settlements," p. 1.

44. Ewan Johnston, "'Polynesien in der Plaisance': Das samoanische Dorf und das Theater der Südseeinseln auf der Weltausstellung in Chicago, 1893," *Comparativ* 9, no. 5/6 (1999): 95.

45. Benjamin C. Truman, *History of the World's Fair, Being a Complete and Authentic Description of the Columbian Exposition from Its Inception* (Chicago: Mammoth, 1893), 572; Furnas, *Anatomy of Paradise*, 419.

46. *Photographs of the World's Fair: An Elaborate Collection of Photographs of the Buildings, Grounds and Exhibits of the World's Columbian Exposition, with a Special Description of the Famous Midway Plaisance* (Chicago: Werner, 1894), 351.

47. Gabriele Dürbeck, *Stereotype Paradiese: Ozeanismus in der deutschen Südseeliteratur, 1815–1914* (Tübingen: Niemeyer, 2007); Gabriele Dürbeck, "Samoa als inszeniertes Paradies: Völkerausstellungen um 1900 und die Tradition der Populären Südseeliteratur," in *Die Schau des Fremden: Ausstellungskonzepte zwischen Kunst, Kommerz und Wissenschaft*, ed. Cordula Grewe (Stuttgart: Steiner, 2006), esp. 73–78; Rod Edmond, *Representing the South Pacific: Colonial Discourse from Cook to Gauguin* (Cambridge: Cambridge University Press, 1997); Margaret Jolly, "From Point Venus to Bali Ha'i: Eroticism and Exoticism in Representations of the Pacific," in *Sites of Desire, Economies of Pleasure: Sexualities in Asia and the Pacific*, ed. Lenore Manderson and Margaret Jolly (Chicago: University of Chicago Press, 1997), 99–122.

48. "Samoan Surprises," *Daily Inter Ocean*, June 14, 1893, supp.

49. Adams and La Farge even grew tired of the obligatory dances when they visited Samoa in 1890. It is not known if Adams avoided the Samoan Village in Chicago for that reason. Henry Adams, *The Education of Henry Adams* (Boston: Houghton Mifflin, 1918), chap. 22; John La Farge, *Reminiscences of the South Seas* (Garden City: Doubleday, Page, 1912).

50. Balme, *Pacific Performances*, 144. A parallel development turned the hula into a metonymy of Hawaiian culture. Imada, *Aloha America*, 13.

51. For an overview of the collection held at the Library of Congress, see Dorothy Sara Lee, ed., *The Federal Cylinder Project: A Guide to Field Cylinder Collections in Federal Agencies*, vol. 8, *Early Anthologies* (Washington, DC: Library of Congress, 1984).

52. *Photographs of the World's Fair*, 313.

53. Imada, *Aloha America*, 71.

54. In the 1890s, nonwhite plantation laborers in Hawai'i were earning an average of $12 a month, but white performers in dime museums and similar entertainment venues in the United States could make up to $2,000 a month. Imada, *Aloha America*, 75.

55. On the gender dimensions of colonialism in the Pacific, see Jolly, "From Point Venus to Bali Ha'i"; Teresia K. Teaiwa, "bikinis and other s/pacific n/oceans," *Contemporary Pacific* 6, no. 1 (1994): 87–109.

56. Imada, *Aloha America*, 95.

57. Kini interview, quoted in ibid.

58. "Had a Novel Feast," *Daily Inter Ocean,* September 7, 1893, 1.

59. Imada, *Aloha America,* 95.

60. Just six years before Chicago, Hawaiian diplomats negotiated a treaty with Malietoa Laupepa to launch a Polynesian Confederacy to counter Euro-American colonialism. According to Kealani Cook, strong opposition by German officials in Samoa and *haole* settlers in Hawai'i can be read as indirect evidence of the confederacy's power. Kealani Cook, *Return to Kahiki: Native Hawaiians in Oceania* (Cambridge: Cambridge University Press, 2018), 159. On the Polynesian Confederacy, see also Gerald Horne, *The White Pacific: U.S. Imperialism and Black Slavery in the South Seas after the Civil War* (Honolulu: University of Hawai'i Press, 2007), 118–123.

61. On the Christchurch exhibition, see Amiria J. M. Henare, *Museums, Anthropology and Imperial Exchange* (Cambridge: Cambridge University Press, 2005), 220–227. On Polynesian exchanges at the exhibition, see Ewan Johnston, "Reinventing Fiji at 19th-Century and Early 20th-Century Exhibitions," *Journal of Pacific History* 40, no. 1 (2005): 36–37. In 1906, a Samoan mixed-race trader by the name of Sam Meredith applied for permission to bring a Samoan troupe to the Christchurch exhibition, but the German Colonial Office rejected the request, probably due to fears of excessive Anglo-Saxon influence. Thode-Arora, *From Samoa with Love,* 139.

62. Nichols to Putnam, November 21, 1893, Field Museum, World's Columbian Exposition Collections, Anthropology Department.

63. Moors, "Some Recollections of Early Samoa." *Samoa Times,* July 4, 1924, 3.

64. Theroux, "H.J.M.: Showman," 59.

65. Thode-Arora, *From Samoa with Love,* 93.

66. In 1899, Carl Marquardt published an early study of Samoan tattooing. Carl Marquardt, *Die Tätowirung beider Geschlechter in Samoa* (Berlin: D. Reimer, 1899).

67. Carl Marquardt, *Der Roman der Samoanerinnen und die Geschäftspraxis des Berliner Passage-Panoptikums* (Berlin: Selbstverlag, 1897), 26.

68. Thode-Arora, *From Samoa with Love,* 95.

69. Ibid., 93.

70. Ibid., 113.

71. Ibid., 93.

72. Ibid., 197.

73. *Vossische Zeitung,* September 19, 1895.

74. Thode-Arora, *From Samoa with Love,* 99.

75. Ibid., 207.

76. Ibid., 99.

77. Balme, *Pacific Performances,* 130; Dürbeck, "Samoa als inszeniertes Paradies," 83.

78. On July 5, 1896, alone, over twenty-one thousand people visited the zoo, prompting city officials to add extra trams. *Frankfurter Zeitung,* July 7, 1896, 1.

79. *Kleine Presse,* July 1, 1896.

80. "Die Samoanertruppe im Wasser," *Frankfurter Zeitung,* July 12, 1896, 1.

81. *Kleine Presse,* July 15, 1896.

82. "Samoa in Frankfurt," *Frankfurter Zeitung,* July 10, 1896, 1.

83. "Samoa in Frankfurt," *Frankfurter Zeitung,* July 8, 1896, 3.

84. Ibid.; "Samoa in Frankfurt," *Frankfurter Zeitung,* July 10, 1896, 1.

85. Victor Turner and Edith Turner, "Performing Ethnography," *Drama Review* 26, no. 2 (1982): 48.

86. Marquardt, *Der Roman der Samoanerinnen,* 4–5.

87. Thode-Arora, *From Samoa with Love,* 111.

88. Marquardt, *Der Roman der Samoanerinnen,* 20.

89. Ibid., 4.

90. Dreesbach, *Gezähmte Wilde,* 171.

91. Marquardt, *Der Roman der Samoanerinnen,* 11.

92. Thode-Arora, *From Samoa with Love,* 111.

93. Ibid., 201. One particularly motivated Berliner traveled to Copenhagen after seeing Fai's portrait and offered her a golden bracelet. Ibid., 106.

94. "Aus dem Zoologischen Garten," *Frankfurter Zeitung,* August 14, 1897, 3.

95. Eric Ames, *Carl Hagenbeck's Empire of Entertainments* (Seattle: University of Washington Press, 2008), 91; Thode-Arora, *Für fünfzig Pfennig,* 168–178.

96. "Aus dem Zoologischen Garten," *Kleine Presse,* August 13, 1897, 4. In a series of ethnographic shows touring Europe during the 1890s, Gumma was cast as the "chief warrior-queen" of a corps of African "Amazons." On the Amazon shows, see Bruckner, "Tingle-Tangle of Modernity," 278–280; Ciarlo, *Advertising Empire,* 95–99. It is not known whether Gumma had already been part of the Dahomeyan Village at the World's Columbian Exposition in Chicago in 1893, where she might have encountered a Samoan troupe for the first time. On the Dahomeyan Village on the Midway, see Robert W. Rydell, "'Darkest Africa': African Shows at America's World's Fairs, 1893–1940," in *Africans on Stage: Studies in Ethnological Show Business,* ed. Bernth Lindfors (Bloomington: Indiana University Press, 1999), 136–142.

97. "Aus dem Zoologischen Garten," *Kleine Presse,* August 13, 1897, 4.

98. Ibid.

99. Gumma had extensive experience selling her photographs—group pictures for 1 mark ($0.25) and bare-breasted solo portraits for 2 marks ($0.50)—to German audiences. Nigel Rothfels, *Savages and Beasts: The Birth of the Modern Zoo* (Baltimore: Johns Hopkins University Press, 2002), 134.

100. "Bratfest bei den Samoanern," *Frankfurter General-Anzeiger,* August 13, 1897, 2.

101. Thode-Arora, *From Samoa with Love,* 110.

102. *Samoa Weekly Herald,* January 1, 1898.

103. Thode-Arora, *From Samoa with Love,* 95, 112.

104. Ibid., 113.

105. Ibid., 117.

106. Peggy Fairbairn-Dunlop, *Tamaitai Samoa: Their Stories* (Suva: Institute of Pacific Studies, University of the South Pacific, 1996), 25.

107. Thode-Arora, *From Samoa with Love,* 121.

108. Ibid.

109. Balme, *Pacific Performances,* 132–133.

110. Alexander C. T. Geppert, *Fleeting Cities: Imperial Expositions in Fin-de-Siècle Europe* (New York: Palgrave Macmillan, 2010), 48.

111. Thode-Arora, *From Samoa with Love,* 120–121.

112. Ibid., 121; Balme, *Pacific Performances,* 133.

113. Thode-Arora, *From Samoa with Love,* 127.

114. Ibid.

115. "Samoaner in Frankfurt," *Frankfurter Zeitung,* June 20, 1901, 2.

116. On the politics of collecting ethnographic objects in imperial Germany, see H. Glenn Penny, *Objects of Culture: Ethnology and Ethnographic Museums in Imperial Germany* (Chapel Hill: University of North Carolina Press, 2002).

117. Thode-Arora, *From Samoa with Love,* 126; Ames, *Carl Hagenbeck's Empire,* 98–102; Dreesbach, *Gezähmte Wilde,* 275; Bruckner, "Tingle-Tangle of Modernity," 375–424.

118. Harald Sippel, "Rassismus, Protektionismus oder Humanität? Die gesetzlichen Verbote der Anwerbung von 'Eingeborenen' zu Schaustellungszwecken in den deutschen Kolonien," in *Kolonialausstellungen: Begegnungen mit Afrika?,* ed. Robert Debusmann and János Riesz (Frankfurt am Main: IKO-Verlag für interkulturelle Kommunikation, 1995), 56–57.

119. Ibid., 62.

120. This critique of ethnographic shows came especially from German missionary societies. Bruckner, "Tingle-Tangle of Modernity," 390–403.

121. Balme, *Pacific Performances,* 131–132; Bruckner, "Tingle-Tangle of Modernity," 407.

122. Alexander Honold, "Der Exot und sein Publikum: Völkerschau in der Kolonialzeit," in *Rassenmischehen, Mischlinge, Rassentrennung: Zur Politik der Rasse im deutschen Kolonialreich,* ed. Frank Becker (Stuttgart: Franz Steiner, 2004), 374.

123. Bruckner, "Tingle-Tangle of Modernity," 422. Carl Marquardt himself reacted to the ban by exporting ethnographic objects from Samoa to museums around the world, using local contacts through his brother and sister-in-law. Thode-Arora, *From Samoa with Love,* 54.

124. Thode-Arora, *From Samoa with Love,* 127.

125. *Samoanische Zeitung,* March 29, 1902.

126. Thode-Arora, *From Samoa with Love*, 129.

127. Ibid.

128. Ibid.

129. Ibid., 130.

130. Jose D. Fermin, *1904 World's Fair: The Filipino Experience* (Quezon City: University of the Philippines Press, 2004), 151.

131. Ibid., 1–4; Christopher A. Vaughan, "Ogling Igorots: The Politics and Commerce of Exhibiting Cultural Otherness, 1898–1913," in *Freakery: Cultural Spectacles of the Extraordinary Body*, ed. Rosemarie G. Thomson (New York: New York University Press, 1996), 223–224. On the racial politics of the fair, see Paul Kramer, "Making Concessions: Race and Empire Revisited at the Philippine Exposition, St. Louis, 1901–1905," *Radical History Review* 73, no. 1 (1999): 75–114.

132. Rydell, *All the World's a Fair*, 163.

133. On the "polyglot" Pike, see Nancy J. Parezo and Don Fowler, *Anthropology Goes to the Fair: The 1904 Louisiana Purchase Exposition* (Lincoln: University of Nebraska Press, 2007), 234–265.

134. Adam McKeown, *Melancholy Order: Asian Migration and the Globalization of Borders* (New York: Columbia University Press, 2008), 241.

135. Mark Bennitt, ed., *History of the Louisiana Purchase Exposition, Comprising the History of the Louisiana Territory, the Story of the Louisiana Purchase and a Full Account of the Great Exposition, Embracing the Participation of the States and Nations of the World, and Other Events of the St. Louis World's Fair of 1904* (St. Louis: Universal Exposition, 1905), 722.

136. Underwood to Asst. Sec. of the Navy, July 10, 1903, NARA-DC, RG 80, 3931, box 35, p. 8.

137. Furnas, *Anatomy of Paradise*, 420.

138. *Century Magazine*, quoted in Furnas, *Anatomy of Paradise*, 420.

139. Richard Harding Davis, quoted in ibid., 421.

140. *Samoanische Zeitung*, October 22, 1904, 2.

141. Furnas, *Anatomy of Paradise*, 420.

142. Ibid.

143. Ibid., 421.

144. Bennitt, *History of the Louisiana Purchase Exposition*, 481.

145. Furnas, *Anatomy of Paradise*, 421.

146. Ibid.

147. Balme, *Pacific Performances*, 133.

148. Thode-Arora, *From Samoa with Love*, 140. In contrast to African ethnographic shows at the time, the Samoan shows emphasized traits Samoans shared with their German colonizers. Balme, *Pacific Performances*, 132; Jutta Steffen-Schrade, "Samoaner im Frankfurter Zoo," in *Talofa! Samoa, Südsee: Ansichten und Einsichten*, ed. Gerda Kroeber-Wolf and Peter Mesenhöller (Frankfurt am Main: Museum für Völkerkunde, 1998), 382.

149. Balme, *Pacific Performances*, 134; Dreesbach, *Gezähmte Wilde*, 275.

150. Thode-Arora, *From Samoa with Love*, 140.

151. "Ausführung von Eingeborenen zum Zwecke der Schaustellung," NAS, IG-24 F2.

152. Thode-Arora, *From Samoa with Love*, 141.

153. Ibid., 142; Dürbeck, "Samoa als inszeniertes Paradies," 92.

154. Thode-Arora, *From Samoa with Love*, 141–142.

155. Riedel, *Kampf um Deutsch-Samoa*, 219; Balme, *Pacific Performances*, 134; Thode-Arora, *From Samoa with Love*, 145.

156. Thode-Arora, *From Samoa with Love*, 145.

157. Ibid., 144. Buffalo Bill's Wild West Show was the most popular ethnographic show at the time in Europe. Robert W. Rydell and Rob Kroes, *Buffalo Bill in Bologna: The Americanization of the World, 1869–1922* (Chicago: University of Chicago Press, 2005). Germans in particular were fascinated by Karl May's adventure novels, which featured heroic Native Americans. H. Glenn Penny, *Kindred by Choice: Germans and American Indians since 1800* (Chapel Hill: University of North Carolina Press, 2013); Ames, *Carl Hagenbeck's Empire*, 107–115.

158. Riedel, *Kampf um Deutsch-Samoa*, 219.

159. Ibid.

160. Ibid.

161. In Breslau, Tamasese took a trip in the airship *Parseval*, which, like him, traveled on to the Oktoberfest in Munich. Asked if he was scared during his daring flight, Tamasese mixed Samoan bravado with the nonchalance of an experienced tourist on a grand tour through Europe: "Scared! Why should I be? If white men are too afraid to go up in airships, why should we Samoans be? No one will say, surely, that we are cowards. . . . There is no more courage needed to go on an airship than to go on an ordinary ship or a train." *Sydney Morning Herald*, November 9, 1911.

162. Ernst von Destouches, *Die Jahrhundertfeier des Münchener Oktoberfestes: Gedenkbuch* (Munich: Lindauer, 1912), 44.

163. Gabriel to Ansprenger, September 11, 1910, StdAM, Oktoberfest, no. 114.

164. Anne Dreesbach, "'Neu! Grösste Sehenswürdigkeit! Neu! Zum ersten Male in München!' Exotisches auf dem Münchner Oktoberfest zwischen 1890 und 1911," in *"Gleich hinterm Hofbräuhaus waschechte Amazonen": Exotik in München um 1900*, ed. Anne Dreesbach and Helmut Zedelmaier (Munich: Dölling und Galitz, 2003), 23, 27.

165. Destouches, *Die Jahrhundertfeier des Münchener Oktoberfestes*, 79.

166. Riedel, *Kampf um Deutsch-Samoa*, 219–220.

167. Thode-Arora, *From Samoa with Love*, 169.

168. L. P. Leary, *New Zealanders in Samoa* (London: W. Heinemann, 1918), 110.

169. Thode-Arora, *From Samoa with Love*, 173.

170. Riedel, *Kampf um Deutsch-Samoa*, 220. Riedel's memory was undoubtedly skewed by the colonial revisionism that came to dominate Weimar and

Nazi Germany. Florian Krobb and Elaine Martin, eds., *Weimar Colonialism: Discourses and Legacies of Post-Imperialism in Germany after 1918* (Bielefeld: Aisthesis, 2014).

171. *Sydney Morning Herald,* November 9, 1911.

172. Ibid.

173. Balme, *Pacific Performances,* 123.

174. *Sydney Morning Herald,* November 9, 1911.

175. Thode-Arora, *From Samoa with Love,* 168.

176. According to family memory, Pu'emalo also found a Singer sewing machine on tour, which she proudly brought back with her to Samoa. Ibid., 177.

177. For an analysis of the fair's imperial and gender dimensions, see Sarah J. Moore, *Empire on Display: San Francisco's Panama-Pacific International Exposition of 1915* (Norman: University of Oklahoma Press, 2013). On the Panama-Pacific International Exposition in general, see Abigail M. Markwyn, *Empress San Francisco: The Pacific Rim, the Great West, and California at the Panama-Pacific International Exposition* (Lincoln: University of Nebraska Press, 2014).

178. Personal Name File: "Schneidewind," NARA-CP, RG 350; Vaughan, "Ogling Igorots," 228.

179. General Classified Files, No. 13431-56, 13431-71, NARA-CP, RG 350.

180. Claire Prentice, *The Lost Tribe of Coney Island: Headhunters, Luna Park, and the Man Who Pulled Off the Spectacle of the Century* (Boston: New Harvest, 2014), 320.

181. The male members were Onesai, Sete, Mutu, Sale, Tasali, Taa, Taaviliga, Leasio, Umu, Tetame, Setu, Tui, and Peti. The female members were Yui, Tulima, Nellie, Faasala, Faapusa, Veve, Tauvali, Faapepe, Sema, Vaaia, and Feteai. NARA-DC, RG 85, A3422 Passenger Lists of Vessels Arriving at Honolulu, Hawai'i, vol. 84, p. 218.

182. Alone among U.S. passport holders today, American Samoans are U.S. nationals rather than full U.S. citizens. As such, they are not, for example, allowed to vote in presidential elections or hold federal office.

183. Naval commanders and visitors alike stressed the increased importance of American Samoa after the opening of the Panama Canal. Stearns to Sec. of the Navy, July 21, 1914, NARA-DC, RG 80, file 3931, box 42, p. 16; Charles B. Davenport, Edwin Conklin, Richard Ely, and Edward C. Franklin to President Wilson, December 15, 1914, NARA-DC, RG 80, file 3931, box 43, p. 3.

184. The Joy Zone in San Francisco helped visitors forget the less joyful events in that other zone surrounding the Panama Canal. For an account of the workers who built the canal, see Julie Greene, *The Canal Builders: Making America's Empire at the Panama Canal* (New York: Penguin Press, 2009).

185. Laura Ingalls Wilder to Almanzo Wilder, September 4, 1915, in Roger L. MacBride, ed., *West from Home: Letters of Laura Ingalls Wilder to Almanzo Wilder, San Francisco, 1915* (New York: Harper & Row, 1974), 39.

186. Ibid., 40.

187. Bryan to Connick, April 18, 1915, Bancroft Library, University of California, Berkeley, Panama-Pacific International Exposition Records, carton 63, folder 46.

188. Frank M. Todd, *The Story of the Exposition, Being the Official History of the International Celebration Held at San Francisco in 1915 to Commemorate the Discovery of the Pacific Ocean and the Construction of the Panama Canal,* vol. 2 (New York: G. P. Putnam's Sons, 1921), 352.

189. Imada, *Aloha America,* 95.

190. "The Forbidden City at the Exposition," *San Francisco Chronicle,* May 2, 1915, supp.

191. In spring 1915, the Somali performers staged a labor stoppage after their employer failed to pay their wages. Fair organizers, with the help of immigration officials, deported the Somali workers to Angel Island. Markwyn, *Empress San Francisco,* 224–225.

192. Moore, *Empire on Display,* 181–189.

193. Greene, *Canal Builders,* 363–365.

194. Imada, *Aloha America,* 19.

195. Ibid., 76.

196. Ibid., 75. Rydell argues that Africans onstage at U.S. world's fairs also "turned showcases of empire into theaters of resistance." Rydell, "'Darkest Africa,'" 136. For a related account that interprets stage performance as an avenue for mobility and creating community, see Jayna Brown, *Babylon Girls: Black Women Performers and the Shaping of the Modern* (Durham: Duke University Press, 2008), esp. 15, 108.

4. Builders

1. On German–American naval competition, see Dirk Bönker, *Militarism in a Global Age: Naval Ambitions in Germany and the United States before World War I* (Ithaca, NY: Cornell University Press, 2012); Jan Rüger, *The Great Naval Game: Britain and Germany in the Age of Empire* (Cambridge: Cambridge University Press, 2007).

2. Tirpitz to Bülow, October 11, 1899, quoted in Edgar T. S. Dugdale, ed., *German Diplomatic Documents, 1871–1914,* vol. 3, *The Growing Antagonism (1898–1910)* (New York: Harper, 1928), 73.

3. Daniel R. Headrick, *The Tools of Empire: Technology and European Imperialism in the Nineteenth Century* (Oxford: Oxford University Press, 1981).

4. On the role of infrastructure in U.S. colonial state formation, see Justin F. Jackson, "Roads to American Empire: U.S. Military Public Works and Capitalist Transitions, 1898–1934," *Journal of Historical Sociology* 33, no. 1 (2020): 116–133; Colin D. Moore, *American Imperialism and the State, 1893–1921* (Cambridge: Cambridge University Press, 2017); Alfred W. McCoy and Francisco A. Scarano, eds., *Colonial*

Crucible: Empire in the Making of the Modern American State (Madison: University of Wisconsin Press, 2009). On German infrastructure plans in Africa, see Dirk van Laak, *Imperiale Infrastruktur: Deutsche Planungen für die Erschließung Afrikas, 1880–1960* (Paderborn: Ferdinand Schöningh, 2004). On railways in German Southwest Africa, see Julio Decker, "Lines in the Sand: Railways and the Archipelago of Colonial Territorialization in German Southwest Africa, 1897–1914," *Journal of Historical Geography* 70 (2020): 74–87.

5. According to Michael Adas, claims of technological superiority have formed the basis of the U.S. civilizing mission since European settlement. Michael Adas, *Dominance by Design: Technological Imperatives and America's Civilizing Mission* (Cambridge, MA: Harvard University Press, 2006). On settler colonization in North America as a political technology, see Paul Frymer, *Building an American Empire: The Era of Territorial and Political Expansion* (Princeton, NJ: Princeton University Press, 2017). Likewise, German colonial officials sought to remodel the Chinese city of Qingdao to demonstrate their technological superiority. See Agnes Kneitz, "German Water Infrastructure in China: Colonial Qingdao, 1898–1914," *NTM* 24, no. 4 (2016): 422.

6. Jackson, "Roads to American Empire," 118; Decker, "Lines in the Sand," 76. On commercial shipping in Oceania, see Frances Steel, *Oceania under Steam: Sea Transport and the Cultures of Colonialism, c. 1870–1914* (Manchester: Manchester University Press, 2011).

7. On the workers who built the Panama Canal, see Julie Greene, *The Canal Builders: Making America's Empire at the Panama Canal* (New York: Penguin Press, 2009). On workers in the Suez Canal Zone, see Valeska Huber, *Channelling Mobilities: Migration and Globalisation in the Suez Canal Region and Beyond, 1869–1914* (Cambridge: Cambridge University Press, 2013), esp. 105–138.

8. For a more detailed account, see Holger Droessler, "Whose Pacific? U.S. Security Interests in American Samoa from the Age of Empire to the Pacific Pivot," *Pacific Asia Inquiry* 4, no. 1 (Fall 2013): 58–65. On the importance of coal in late nineteenth-century America, see Paul Shulman, *Coal and Empire: The Birth of Energy Security in Industrial America* (Baltimore: Johns Hopkins University Press, 2015).

9. Paul M. Kennedy, *The Samoan Tangle: A Study in Anglo-German-American Relations, 1878–1900* (Dublin: Irish University Press, 1974), 143.

10. Department of State, *Foreign Relations of the United States, 1899* (Washington, DC: Government Printing Office, 1901), 638. For Tripp's memoirs of Samoa, see Bartlett Tripp, *My Trip to Samoa* (Cedar Rapids, IA: The Torch Press, 1911).

11. USS *California* to Commander in Chief, U.S. Pacific Fleet, November 1908, NARA-DC, RG 38, box 1083, N-1-b, Reg.-No. 1374, p. 8.

12. The harbor in Saluafata, twelve miles east of Apia, offered better protection but was considerably smaller. Saleaula in Savai'i was the best harbor on the island but provided little protection and was a poor holding ground. British Foreign

Office, Historical Section, *Former German Possessions in Oceania* (London: HM Stationery Office, 1920), 35–36.

13. McAdoo to Sec. of State, December 30, 1896, NARA-CP, RG 84, vol. 21.

14. Cridler to Shade, December 14, 1897, NARA-CP, RG 84, vol. 22.

15. Cridler to Osborn, August 5, 1898, NARA-CP, RG 84, vol. 22.

16. Ibid.

17. 1904 Report of Expenditures and Estimates, NARA-DC, RG 71, entry 56, vol. 94, p. 71.

18. Greene, *Canal Builders,* 16.

19. At the time, the biggest U.S. battleships could carry around two thousand tons of coal. Norman Friedman, *U.S. Battleships: An Illustrated Design History* (London: Arms and Armour Press, 1986), 104.

20. Tilley to Sec. of the Navy, February 23, 1900, NARA-DC, RG 80, file 3931, box 34.

21. Report on Native Government by Secretary of Native Affairs, E. W. Gurr, November 18, 1901, NARA-DC, RG 80, file 3931, box 35.

22. Tilley to Sec. of the Navy, February 23, 1900, NARA-DC, RG 80, file 3931, box 34.

23. Sebree to Asst. Sec. of the Navy, December 24, 1901, NARA-DC, RG 80, file 3931, box 34.

24. Bloch to Sebree, November 2, 1902, NARA-DC, RG 80, file 3931, box 35, p. 2.

25. 1908 Report of Expenditures and Estimates, NARA-DC, RG 71, entry 56, vol. 106.

26. 1903 Report of Expenditures and Estimates, NARA-DC, RG 71, entry 56, vol. 90, p. 10.

27. 1905 Report of Expenditures and Estimates, NARA-DC, RG 71, entry 56, vol. 97.

28. Ibid., 20.

29. 1902 Report of Expenditures and Estimates, NARA-DC, RG 71, entry 56, vol. 83.

30. *Samoanische Zeitung,* August 8, 1903, 5.

31. Underwood to Asst. Sec. of the Navy, November 24, 1903, NARA-DC, RG 80, file 3931, box 35, p. 2.

32. At the time, American carpenters in Tutuila earned between $3.50 and $4.00 a day. Report on Native Government by Secretary of Native Affairs, E. W. Gurr, November 18, 1901, NARA-DC, RG 80, file 3931, box 35.

33. Many German settlers claimed that Samoans did not need to work because of the bounty of their islands. See, for example, Frieda Zieschank, *Ein Jahrzehnt in Samoa, 1906–1916* (Leipzig: E. Haberland, 1918), 96.

34. *Samoanische Zeitung,* March 19, 1904, 3.

35. E. S. C. Handy and Willowdean C. Handy, *Samoan House Building, Cooking, and Tattooing* (Honolulu: Bishop Museum, 1924), 15.

36. Robert W. Franco, *Samoan Perceptions of Work: Moving Up and Moving Around* (New York: AMS Press, 1991), 80.

37. John B. Stair, *Old Samoa; or, Flotsam and Jetsam from the Pacific Ocean* (London: Religious Tract Society, 1897), 157.

38. Buck speculates about the foreign origins of the Samoan system, which required the immediate provision of food and payment to carpenters. Peter H. Buck (Te Rangi Hiroa), *Samoan Material Culture* (Honolulu: Bishop Museum, 1930), 679.

39. Handy and Handy, *Samoan House Building,* 17.

40. 1906 Report of Expenditures and Estimates, NARA-DC, RG 71, entry 56, vol. 100, p. 4.

41. Census of 1903, NARA-SB, RG 284, MF T1182, roll 4.

42. Moore to True, August 6, 1906, NARA-DC, RG 80, file 3931, box 36.

43. Alexander Saxton, *The Indispensable Enemy: Labor and the Anti-Chinese Movement in California* (Berkeley: University of California Press, 1971).

44. Parker to Asst. Sec. of the Navy, March 9, 1910, NARA-DC, RG 80, file 3931, box 38.

45. Questions by Native Government Officials, November 22, 1904, NARA-DC, RG 80, file 3931, box 36, p. 1.

46. In 1900, the U.S. Navy owned sixteen acres of Tutuila's total land area of thirty-five thousand acres. By 1903, that area had doubled to thirty-eight acres. Memo on Samoan Islands by Bureau of Equipment, February 6, 1900, NARA-DC, RG 80, file 3931, box 34; 1903 Report of Expenditures and Estimates, NARA-DC, RG 71, entry 56, vol. 90.

47. 1906 Report of Expenditures and Estimates, NARA-DC, RG 71, entry 56, vol. 100.

48. Moore to Asst. Sec. of the Navy, August 28, 1905, NARA-DC, RG 80, file 3931, box 36, no. 184, p. 3.

49. 1906 Report of Expenditures and Estimates, NARA-DC, RG 71, entry 56, vol. 100, p. 16.

50. Moore to Asst. Sec. of the Navy, August 28, 1905, NARA-DC, RG 80, file 3931, box 36, no. 184, p. 3. At the same time, U.S. officials also used vagrancy laws to discipline workers in the fully incorporated states and in the Panama Canal Zone. Greene, *Canal Builders,* 62, 139–140.

51. Moore to Asst. Sec. of the Navy, August 28, 1905, NARA-DC, RG 80, file 3931, box 36, no. 184, p. 3.

52. Moore to Asst. Sec. of the Navy, October 9, 1905, NARA-DC, RG 80, file 3931, box 36.

53. 1906 Report of Expenditures and Estimates, NARA-DC, RG 71, entry 56, vol. 100.

54. Sylvia Masterman, *The Origins of International Rivalry in Samoa, 1845–1884* (London: G. Allen & Unwin, 1934), 14.

55. Damon Salesa, "'Travel-Happy' Samoa: Colonialism, Samoan Migration and a 'Brown Pacific,'" *New Zealand Journal of History* 37, no. 2 (2003): 183.

56. Biermann to Caprivi, May 23, 1893, BArch, R 1001 / 2539.

57. *Samoanische Zeitung,* March 26, 1904.

58. Salesa, "'Travel-Happy' Samoa," 174.

59. On roadbuilding in the fully incorporated United States at the turn of the twentieth century, see I. B. Holley Jr., *The Highway Revolution, 1895–1925: How the United States Got Out of the Mud* (Durham, NC: Carolina Academic Press, 2008); Howard L. Preston, *Dirt Roads to Dixie: Accessibility and Modernization in the South, 1885–1935* (Knoxville: University of Tennessee Press, 1991).

60. For these reports, see BArch, R 1001 / 2539.

61. *Samoa Times,* December 23, 1893.

62. Blacklock to Asst. Sec. of State, May 22, 1894, NARA-CP, RG 84, vol. 5, p. 166.

63. British Foreign Office, *Former German Possessions in Oceania,* 35.

64. Felix M. Keesing, *Modern Samoa: Its Government and Changing Life* (London: G. Allen & Unwin, 1934), 84.

65. Report on Pago Pago by Casey to Sec. of the Navy, November 19, 1901, NARA-DC, RG 38, box 1086, N-5-a, Reg.-No. 02 / 39, p. 4.

66. Stünzner to Schnee, June 18, 1902, BArch, N 1053 / 25, p. 33.

67. Ibid., p. 34.

68. Note by Schnee, July 8, 1902, BArch, N 1053 / 25, p. 35.

69. Report by Brenner, December 17, 1909, NAS, IG 4 F3 I 4a, vol. 1.

70. Underwood to Asst. Sec. of the Navy, July 10, 1903, NARA-DC, RG 80, file 3931, box 35, p. 5.

71. Sebree to Asst. Sec. of the Navy, August 9, 1902, NARA-DC, RG 80, file 3931, box 35, item 347, p. 6.

72. Annual Report 1910 / 11, BArch, RD 15 / 2.

73. *Samoanische Zeitung,* November 26, 1904, 1.

74. List of Chinese Workers Employed by the Government, December 9, 1907, NAS, IG 4 F3 I 4a, vol. 1.

75. Report by Brenner, December 17, 1909, NAS, IG 4 F3 I 4a, vol. 1.

76. DSG to AA-KA, November 21, 1904, BArch, R 1001 / 2484.

77. Parkhouse to Asst. Sec. of State, August 27, 1908, NARA-CP, RG 84, vol. 8, January 8, 1904–December 1, 1908, p. 339.

78. Dwyer to Parker, September 17, 1909, NARA-DC, RG 80, file 3931, box 38, p. 6.

79. Annual Report 1910 / 11, BArch, RD 15 / 2, p. 186.

80. Annual Report 1913 / 14, BArch, R 1001 / 6523.

81. Annual Report 1910 / 11, BArch, RD 15 / 2, p. 186.

82. Parker to Sec. of the Navy, July 25, 1908, NARA-DC, RG 80, file 3931, box 37, p. 4.

83. Myers (USS *West Virginia*) to Commander in Chief, U.S. Pacific Fleet, October 29, 1908, NARA-DC, RG 38, box 1083, N-1-b, Reg.-No. 1374.

84. Report on Fortifications and Defenses (USS *California*) to Commander in Chief, U.S. Pacific Fleet, November 1908, NARA-DC, RG 38, box 1083, N-1-b, Reg.-No. 1374, p. 15.

85. Crose to Sec. of the Navy, July 14, 1911, NARA-DC, RG 80, file 3931, box 40, p. 6.

86. Ibid., 5.

87. Ibid., 6.

88. "Act concerning Construction and Maintenance of Roads," October 17, 1911, NARA-DC, RG 80, file 3931, box 41.

89. Annual report by Evans, July 1, 1921, NARA-DC, RG 80, file 3931, box 36, p. 6.

90. Keesing, *Modern Samoa*, 298.

91. Amerika Samoa Humanities Council, *A History of American Samoa* (Honolulu: Bess Press, 2009), 187.

92. Deep Kanta Lahiri Choudhury, *Telegraphic Imperialism: Crisis and Panic in the Indian Empire, 1830–1920* (New York: Palgrave Macmillan, 2010).

93. Hugh Barty-King, *Girdle Round the Earth: The Story of Cable and Wireless and Its Predecessors to Mark the Group's Jubilee, 1929–1979* (London: Heinemann, 1979), 142.

94. Daniel R. Headrick, *The Invisible Weapon: Telecommunications and International Politics, 1851–1945* (Oxford: Oxford University Press, 1991), 101. On telegraph lines and globalization, see Roland Wenzlhuemer, *Connecting the Nineteenth-Century World: The Telegraph and Globalization* (Cambridge: Cambridge University Press, 2013); Simone Müller, *Wiring the World: The Social and Cultural Creation of Global Telegraph Networks* (New York: Columbia University Press, 2016).

95. Headrick, *Invisible Weapon*, 109.

96. Heidi J. S. Evans, "'The Path to Freedom'? Transocean and German Wireless Telegraphy, 1914–1922," *Historical Social Research* 35, no. 1 (2010): 213. On building a wireless network as a colonial form of German *Weltpolitik*, see Heidi J. S. Tworek, *News from Germany: The Competition to Control World Communications, 1900–1945* (Cambridge, MA: Harvard University Press, 2019), 51.

97. Willy Schmidt and Hans Werner, eds., *Geschichte der deutschen Post in den Kolonien und im Ausland* (Leipzig: Konkordia-Verlag, 1939), 347.

98. British Foreign Office, *Former German Possessions in Oceania*, 32.

99. AA-KA, "Postwesen—Samoa," BArch, R 1001 / 2686.

100. British Foreign Office, *Former German Possessions in Oceania*, 32.

101. Heimrod to Williams, October 27, 1904, NARA-CP, RG 84, vol. 52.

102. Around the same time, there were fourteen telephones in operation in Tutuila. 1905 Report of Expenditures and Estimates, NARA-DC, RG 71, entry 56, vol. 97.

103. Heimrod to Asst. Sec. of State, July 23, 1907, NARA-CP, RG 84, vol. 8.

104. British Foreign Office, *Former German Possessions in Oceania,* 33.

105. Schmidt and Werner, *Geschichte der deutschen Post,* 351–353.

106. *Die Post,* January 17, 1913.

107. *Samoanische Zeitung,* April 6, 1913, 2.

108. On German efforts to circumvent British news agencies, see Tworek, *News from Germany,* 45–69.

109. *Elektrotechnische Zeitschrift,* September 19, 1912, 990.

110. Hugh G. J. Aitken, *The Continuous Wave: Technology and American Radio, 1900–1932* (Princeton, NJ: Princeton University Press, 1985), 137. For a general account with no specific reference to Samoa, see Jonathan R. Winkler, *Nexus: Strategic Communications and American Security in World War I* (Cambridge, MA: Harvard University Press, 2008).

111. British Foreign Office, *Former German Possessions in Oceania,* 41.

112. Plans for a light railway connecting Apia to the west coast of Upolu were never realized. Ibid., 32.

113. Annual Report 1913–14, BArch, R 1001 / 6523.

114. Hirsch to Telefunken Berlin, August 25, 1913, BArch, Files of the Imperial Post Office, no. 15376.

115. Ibid.

116. Telefunken to Imperial Post Office, August 15, 1913, BArch, Files of the Imperial Post Office, no. 15376.

117. Telefunken to Imperial Post Office, March 23, 1914, BArch, Files of the Imperial Post Office, no. 15377.

118. Tecklenburg to Vogel (SKC), May 2, 1914, NAS, IG 135 F2 I4a, vol. 3.

119. Reinhard Klein-Arendt, "Die Nachrichtenübermittlung in den deutschen Südseekolonien," in *Die Deutsche Südsee, 1884–1914: Ein Handbuch,* ed. Hermann Hiery (Paderborn: Ferdinand Schöningh, 2001), 191–192.

120. Initially, communications with Honolulu were still unreliable, but a stronger transmitter set soon resolved this technical issue. Stearns to Sec. of the Navy, July 8, 1914, NARA-DC, RG 80, file 3931, box 42.

121. Schmidt and Werner, *Geschichte der deutschen Post,* 356.

122. Reinhard Klein-Arendt, *Kamina ruft Nauen! Die Funkstellen in den deutschen Kolonien, 1904–1918* (Köln: W. Herbst, 1996), 262.

123. Schmidt and Werner, *Geschichte der deutschen Post,* 356.

124. Bullard to Navy Dep., September 28, 1914, NARA-DC, RG 80, file 3931, box 43.

125. Salesa, "'Travel-Happy' Samoa," 184. For a similar argument about the constrained agency of Maori, see Tony Ballantyne, *Entanglements of Empire: Missionaries, Māori, and the Question of the Body* (Durham, NC: Duke University Press, 2014), 257.

5. Mediators

1. Tanuvasa Tofaeono Tavale, *Tautua 'ese'ese NCEA Samoan: Vāega Lua* (Auckland: Fuelavelave Press, 2013), 6–12.

2. On the social history of colonial intermediaries in Africa, see Benjamin N. Lawrance, Emily Lynn Osborn, and Richard L. Roberts, "African Intermediaries and the 'Bargain' of Collaboration," in *Intermediaries, Interpreters, and Clerks: African Employees in the Making of Colonial Africa,* ed. Benjamin N. Lawrance, Emily Lynn Osborn, and Richard L. Roberts (Madison: University of Wisconsin Press, 2006), 7.

3. Becker to Bismarck, January 9, 1888, BArch, R 1001 / 2673, p. 3.

4. Fritze to Admiralty, August 13, 1888, BArch, R 1001 / 2673, p. 28.

5. Report on American Samoa by Colby, March 30, 1924, NARA-DC, RG 38, box 1084, N-1-b, Reg.-No. 17336-A, Annex No. 1, "Naval Station," p. 24 (emphasis added).

6. Felix M. Keesing, *Modern Samoa: Its Government and Changing Life* (London: G. Allen & Unwin, 1934), 133, 347.

7. Capt. Edward J. Dorn, August 24, 1900, Edward John Dorn Papers, Manuscript Division, Library of Congress, box 3, General Correspondence, 1900.

8. Mary Poyer Kniskern, *Life in Samoa from 1915 to 1919* (USA: Self-published, 1993), 8.

9. Capt. Edward J. Dorn, August 24, 1900, Edward John Dorn Papers, Manuscript Division, Library of Congress, box 3, General Correspondence, 1900.

10. Toetu Faaleava, *"Fitafita:* Samoan Landsmen in the United States Navy, 1900–1951" (PhD thesis, University of California, Berkeley, 2003).

11. Casey to Sec. of the Navy, November 19, 1901, NARA-DC, RG 38, box 1086, N-5-a, Reg.-No. 02 / 39.

12. Ibid.

13. 1906 Report of Expenditures and Estimates, NARA-DC, RG 71, entry 56, vol. 100, p. 78.

14. Report on American Samoa by Colby, March 30, 1924, NARA-DC, RG 38, box 1084, N-1-b, Reg.-No. 17336-A, Annex No. 1, "Naval Station," p. 24.

15. Tuala Sevaaetasi, "The Fitafita Guard and Samoan Military Experience," in *Remembering the Pacific War,* ed. Geoffrey M. White (Honolulu: Center for Pacific Islands Studies, University of Hawai'i at Manoa, 1991), 182.

16. Kniskern, *Life in Samoa,* 8.

17. 1905 Report of Expenditures and Estimates, NARA-DC, RG 71, entry 56, vol. 97, p. 6.

18. Keesing, *Modern Samoa,* 347.

19. 1906 Report of Expenditures and Estimates, NARA-DC, RG 71, entry 56, vol. 100, p. 58.

20. 1908 Report of Expenditures and Estimates, NARA-DC, RG 71, entry 56, vol. 106, p. 6.

21. 1909 Report of Expenditures and Estimates, NARA-DC, RG 71, entry 56, vol. 109.

22. Report on American Samoa by Colby, March 30, 1924, NARA-DC, RG 38, box 1084, N-1-b, Reg.-No. 17336-A, Annex No. 1, "Naval Station," p. 24.

23. *Samoanische Zeitung,* August 8, 1903, p. 3, BArch, R 1001 / 2320.

24. Kniskern, *Life in Samoa,* 8.

25. Ibid.

26. Hermann Hiery, "Die Polizei im deutschen Samoa: Deutsche Hoffnungen und samoanische Erwartungen," in *Barrieren und Zugänge: Die Geschichte der europäischen Expansion,* ed. Thomas Beck, Marília dos Santos Lopes, and Christian Rödel (Wiesbaden: Harrassowitz Verlag, 2004), 269.

27. Mata'afa to Solf, August 13, 1901, NAS, quoted in ibid., 270.

28. Basic Guidelines for Pay and Provisions for Police Force, April 1, 1905, BArch, R 1001 / 2673, p. 33.

29. Ronald Robinson, "Non-European Foundations of European Imperialism: Sketch for a Theory of Collaboration," in *Studies in the Theory of Imperialism,* ed. Roger Owen and Bob Sutcliffe (London: Longman, 1972), 121.

30. Solf to AA-KA, January 31, 1904, BArch, N 1053 / 25, vol. 6, 91904, p. 16.

31. "Die schwarze Schutztruppe," *Samoanische Zeitung,* May 8, 1909.

32. *Koloniale Zeitschrift* 11 (1910): 196.

33. In stark contrast to Indigenous soldiers in other German colonies, such as the Askari troops in German East Africa, the Samoan Fitafita never saw direct combat. On the Askari, see Michelle R. Moyd, *Violent Intermediaries: African Soldiers, Conquest, and Everyday Colonialism in German East Africa* (Athens: Ohio University Press, 2014).

34. Coerper to Wilhelm II, May 16, 1909, BArch, R 1001 / 2673, p. 37.

35. "Name List of Policemen, Apia," April 18, 1902, NAS, quoted in Hiery, "Die Polizei im deutschen Samoa," 266.

36. Moors to Imperial Court, November 27, 1905, NAS, IDC-3 F1 III 1b, vol. 2.

37. Schultz to RKA, September 24, 1910, BArch, R 1001 / 2495.

38. Zwingenberger to Solf, February 1, 1910, BArch, R 1001 / 2495.

39. Hiery, "Die Polizei im deutschen Samoa," 271.

40. A report by U.S. naval governor Mitchell in Tutuila told a different story about the events. According to Mitchell, the four Samoan men had been gambling with the Chinese workers but had been caught and sentenced to jail. After the guards had succeeded in escaping from jail, they returned to the Chinese makeshift casino and took their revenge. Perhaps they blamed one of their Chinese gambling colleagues for revealing their presence in the den. Mitchell to Stearns, February 10–11, 1914, NARA-DC, RG 80, file 3931, box 42.

41. Report by Kruse, February 18, 1914, NAS, quoted in Hiery, "Die Polizei im deutschen Samoa," 273n29.

42. On the Samoan cowboy shoot-out as renegade history, see Damon Salesa, "Cowboys in the House of Polynesia," *Contemporary Pacific* 22, no. 2 (2010): 330–331.

43. Report by Pusch, February 15, 1914, ANZ Wellington, Archives of the German Colonial Administration, 6051, quoted in Hiery, "Die Polizei im deutschen Samoa," 273n30.

44. Löhneysen to Bernstorff, September 30, 1914, BArch, R 1001/2624, p. 87.

45. Peter J. Hempenstall, "Indigenous Resistance to German Rule in the Pacific Colonies of Samoa, Ponape and New Guinea, 1884 to 1914" (PhD thesis, University of Oxford, 1973), 274.

46. Hilke Thode-Arora, ed., *From Samoa with Love? Samoan Travelers in Germany, 1895–1911: Retracing the Footsteps* (Munich: Hirmer, 2014), 127.

47. Solf, "Ten-Year Program," BArch, R 1001/4789.

48. Budget for Samoa, 1901, BArch, RD 15/12.

49. Report by Wandres, May 20, 1903, BArch R, 1001/2319.

50. "List of Chinese Workers Employed by the Government," December 9, 1907, NAS, IG 4 F3 I 4a, vol. 1.

51. "List of Chinese Workers Employed by the Government," February 1908, NAS, IG 4 F3 I 4a, vol. 1.

52. Ibid.

53. "Personal Files concerning the Chinese Interpreter Tsang Shin Lin," NAS, IG 14 F6 IA 101, vol. 1.

54. J. C. Levenson, ed., *The Letters of Henry Adams*, vol. 3 (Cambridge, MA: Belknap Press of Harvard University Press, 1982), 354.

55. Besides Taylor, Adams and La Farge also depended on the help of their Japanese attendant Awoki, who compiled a dictionary of Samoan names and words for his employers. To La Farge's dismay, it was Awoki who received "the truest affection and good-will" of the Samoans: "We are too far up and too white, and cannot play." John La Farge, *Reminiscences of the South Seas* (Garden City, NY: Doubleday, Page, 1912), 80, 279.

56. Harry J. Moors, *With Stevenson in Samoa* (Boston: Small, Maynard, 1910), 107.

57. Ibid., 109. Born in Australia, Whyte visited Samoa and Tonga as coeditor of the *New Zealand Herald*. Following in Moors's footsteps, Whyte went on to tour the United States with a Maori troupe in 1910.

58. Samoan Supreme Court decision, March 21, 1895, BArch, R 1001/2549, p. 16.

59. Richard Deeken, *Manuia Samoa! Samoanische Reiseskizzen und Beobachtungen* (Oldenburg: G. Stalling, 1901), 238.

60. *Samoanisches Gouvernements-Blatt* 3, no. 21 (1903), BArch, RD 224-2/3/4.

61. Torben Gülstorff, "Vom Wilhelmshof in die Fremde: Einblicke in die Lehre vom Eigenen und Fremden an der Kolonialschule Witzenhausen—Ansätze eines interkulturellen Lernens?" *Öt Kontinens,* no. 2010 (2011): 399.

62. Solf to Weber, April 29, 1902, NAS, IG 14 F4 IA 19.

63. Solf to Weber, June 8, 1902, NAS, IG 14 F4 IA 19.

64. Taylor to Solf, May 17, 1902, NAS, IG 14 F4 IA 19.

65. Solf to AA-KA, February 27, 1902, NAS, IG 14 F4 IA 19.

66. Taylor to Solf, June 19, 1902, NAS, IG 14 F4 IA 19.

67. Solf to Taylor, July 4, 1902, NAS, IG 14 F4 IA 19.

68. Ibid.

69. Taylor to Solf, June 19, 1902, NAS, IG 14 F4 IA 19.

70. Ibid.

71. Solf to Taylor, July 8, 1902, NAS, IG 14 F4 IA 19.

72. Solf to Taylor, July 4, 1902, NAS, IG 14 F4 IA 19.

73. Taylor to Solf, May 17, 1902, NAS, IG 14 F4 IA 19.

74. Peter J. Hempenstall, *Pacific Islanders under German Rule: A Study in the Meaning of Colonial Resistance* (Canberra: Australian National University Press, 1978), 60.

75. Hermann Hiery, *Das Deutsche Reich in der Südsee (1900–1921): Eine Annährung an die Erfahrungen verschiedener Kulturen* (Göttingen: Vandenhoeck & Ruprecht, 1995), 298.

76. Gühler to Wilhelm II, September 7, 1910, BArch, R 1001 / 2760.

77. Schultz to RKA, June 7, 1914, BArch, R 1001 / 2760.

78. Letter by Taio Tolo, February 2, 1914, enclosure to Schultz to RKA, June 7, 1914, BArch, R 1001 / 2760. For a published account of the meeting, see Arthur J. Knoll and Hermann J. Hiery, eds., *The German Colonial Experience: Select Documents on German Rule in Africa, China, and the Pacific, 1884–1914* (Lanham, MD: University Press of America, 2010), 491–492.

79. Reflecting their intermediary positions, Taio and his followers combined Samoan and German elements in their meeting. On the one hand, the meeting was modeled on a Samoan *fono* in which leading *matai* convened to discuss important matters, the most important of which were made binding by an oath. On the other hand, some of the formal elements of the meeting betrayed the influence of an education in German administration: the meeting minutes, the election of a chair and secretary, and the agenda of topics to be discussed. Hiery, *Deutsche Reich in der Südsee,* 298–299.

80. Report by Taio Tolo and Paniani, February 5, 1914, enclosure to Schultz to RKA, June 7, 1914, BArch, R 1001 / 2760, p. 4.

81. Taio might have been thinking of the so-called Sokeh rebellion on the Micronesian island of Ponape or the anti-colonial movement led by Apolosi Nawai in nearby Fiji.

82. Report by Taio Tolo and Paniani, February 5, 1914, enclosure to Schultz to RKA, June 7, 1914, BArch, R 1001 / 2760, pp. 4–5.

83. Ibid., 5.

84. Schultz to RKA, June 7, 1914, BArch, R 1001 / 2760, p. 175.

85. Letter by Taio Tolo, February 2, 1914, enclosure to Schultz to RKA, June 7, 1914, BArch, R 1001 / 2760.

86. Report by Taio Tolo and Paniani, February 5, 1914, enclosure to Schultz to RKA, June 7, 1914, BArch, R 1001 / 2760, p. 7.

87. Ibid.

88. Ibid., 8.

89. Ibid.

90. On the *ilustrados,* see Michael Cullinane, *Ilustrado Politics: Filipino Elite Responses to American Rule, 1898–1908* (Quezon City: Ateneo de Manila University Press, 2003).

91. Schultz to Solf, May 5, 1914, BArch, N 1053 / 132.

92. Despite this generous salary, Saga still had to borrow additional money from the government to feed his large family. Solf continued to grant direct loans to Saga, even though Euro-American government employees had complained and despite a regulation that had explicitly banned European traders from offering loans to Samoans. Hiery, "Die Polizei im deutschen Samoa," 267.

93. Schultz to Solf, May 5, 1914, BArch, N 1053 / 132.

94. Hermann Hiery, *The Neglected War: The German South Pacific and the Influence of World War I* (Honolulu: University of Hawai'i Press, 1995), 168.

95. Perhaps Schultz received the tip through the connections of his personal attendant Fatu, whom he had adopted as a five-year-old boy. Erich Schultz-Ewerth, *Erinnerungen an Samoa* (Berlin: A. Scherl, 1926), 146–148.

96. Schultz to RKA, June 7, 1914, BArch, R 1001 / 2760, p. 175.

97. Ibid.

98. Ibid., 177.

99. Lesley Barclay et al., *Samoan Nursing: The Story of Women Developing a Profession* (St. Leonards: Allen & Unwin, 1998), 140. For a detailed account of Samoan views on illness, see Penelope Schoeffel, "Daughters of Sina: A Study of Gender, Status and Power in Western Samoa" (PhD thesis, Australian National University, 1979), chap. 8.

100. Schoeffel, "Daughters of Sina," 390.

101. Kerri A. Inglis, "Disease and the 'Other': The Role of Medical Imperialism in Oceania," in *Native Diasporas: Indigenous Identities and Settler Colonialism in the Americas,* ed. Gregory D. Smithers and Brooke N. Newman (Lincoln: University of Nebraska Press, 2014), 405.

102. Cluny Macpherson and La'avasa Macpherson, *Samoan Medical Belief and Practice* (Auckland: Auckland University Press, 1990), 72–73.

103. Keesing, *Modern Samoa,* 387. British officials in India pursued a similar policy of suppressing local healing traditions by passing the Medical Practitioners Registration Act in 1912. Harald Fischer-Tiné, *Pidgin-Knowledge: Wissen und Kolonialismus* (Zürich: Diaphanes, 2013), 48.

104. Macpherson and Macpherson, *Samoan Medical Belief,* 89.

105. Ibid., 58. A similar process of syncretization occurred in Guam. Anne Perez Hattori, *Colonial Dis-Ease: U.S. Navy Health Policies and the Chamorros of Guam, 1898–1941* (Honolulu: University of Hawai'i Press, 2004), 153.

106. Schoeffel, "Daughters of Sina," 392.

107. At the same time, Governor Solf and his wife Hanna benefited from a global division of domestic labor in their own residence in Vailima. A young Chinese woman by the name of Amah attended to Hanna Solf and her son Lagi. And a young Somali man, Juma bin Khamissi, worked as the governor's personal attendant. On Amah, see Johanna Solf, Personal Diary, September 7, 1908–September 7, 1909, Private Archive, Eugen Solf, Kronberg, p. 18. On Juma, see Solf to Fries, March 12, 1903, NAS, IG 79 F4; Peter J. Hempenstall and Paula T. Mochida, *The Lost Man: Wilhelm Solf in German History* (Wiesbaden: Harrassowitz, 2005), 64.

108. *Samoanisches Gouvernements-Blatt* 3, no. 42 (1905), BArch RD 224-2 / 3 / 4.

109. Ibid.

110. *The Cyclopedia of Samoa, Tonga, Tahiti, and the Cook Islands* (Papakura, NZ: R. McMillan, 1983), 66.

111. Ibid., 4.

112. In Western Samoa, more than 8,500 people (22% of the total population) died of the flu. Over 675,000 Americans succumbed to the virus, representing 0.5 percent of the total population. Worldwide, the Spanish flu claimed the lives of more than 50 million people, or 3 percent of the total world population. Sandra M. Tomkins, "The Influenza Epidemic of 1918–19 in Western Samoa," *Journal of Pacific History* 27, no. 2 (1992): 181–197; Alfred W. Crosby, *America's Forgotten Pandemic: The Influenza of 1918,* 2nd ed. (Cambridge: Cambridge University Press, 2003), 203–263.

113. Malama Meleisea, *The Making of Modern Samoa: Traditional Authority and Colonial Administration in the History of Western Samoa* (Suva, Fiji: Institute of Pacific Studies of the University of the South Pacific, 1987), 174–175; James W. Davidson, *Samoa mo Samoa: The Emergence of the Independent State of Western Samoa* (Oxford: Oxford University Press, 1967), 94.

114. Keesing, *Modern Samoa,* 96–97. For similar social effects following earlier flu outbreaks, see Macpherson and Macpherson, *Samoan Medical Belief,* 56.

115. "Epidemic Commission," *Samoa Times,* June 21, 1919, 4.

116. Hiery, *Neglected War,* 177.

117. Kress to Kellogg, July 1, 1924, NARA-DC, RG 80, file 3931, box 38, pp. 6–7.

118. Crose to Sec. of the Navy, February 3, 1911, NARA-DC, RG 80, file 3931, box 39, p. 2.

119. Free health care was part of Bismarck's social imperialism directed against the German left in the 1880s. On the concept of social imperialism, see Hans-Ulrich Wehler, *Das Deutsche Kaiserreich, 1871–1918* (Göttingen: Vandenhoeck & Ruprecht, 1973).

120. Navy Department to Crose, April 4, 1911, NARA-DC, RG 80, file 3931, box 39.

121. Ryan, "The Samoan Hospital," June 30, 1926, NHHC, Navy Nurse Corps Records.

122. Keesing, *Modern Samoa*, 386.

123. In 1914, Governor Parker asked for permission to enlist a couple of young Samoan men as apprentice seamen to work in the navy dispensaries, but the Navy Department denied his request. Parker to Surgeon-General, December 6, 1914; Braisted to Navy Dept., January 25, 1915, NARA-DC, RG 52, box 451, file 126237. In 1916, a group of six Samoan Fitafita commenced medical duty in the outlying dispensaries. Kress to Kellogg, July 1, 1924, NARA-DC, RG 80, file 3931, box 38, pp. 6–7.

124. Ely to Stokes, July 31, 1913, NARA-DC, RG 52, box 449, file 126156, p. 1.

125. Ibid.

126. Ibid., 2.

127. Stokes to Sec. of the Navy, August 26, 1913, NARA-DC, RG 52, box 449, file 126156.

128. Susan H. Godson, *Serving Proudly: A History of Women in the U.S. Navy* (Annapolis: Naval Institute Press, 2001), 49–51. On biomedical interventions in the U.S.-occupied Philippines, see Warwick Anderson, *Colonial Pathologies: American Tropical Medicine, Race, and Hygiene in the Philippines* (Durham, NC: Duke University Press, 2006). On U.S. Navy health policy in Guam, which had more similarities to American Samoa, see Hattori, *Colonial Dis-Ease.*

129. Humphrey, "Letters from Navy Nurses," *American Journal of Nursing* 15, no. 9 (1915): 760.

130. Ibid., 761.

131. Ely to Surgeon-General, April 7, 1914, NARA-DC, RG 52, box 449, file 126156.

132. Humphrey, "Letters from Navy Nurses," 762.

133. Ely to Surgeon-General, April 7, 1914, NARA-DC, RG 52, box 449, file 126156.

134. Report on American Samoa by Colby, March 30, 1924, NARA-DC, RG 38, box 1084, N-1-b, Reg.-No. 17336-A, Annex No. 1, "Naval Station," p. 16.

135. In this regard, the experiences of Samoan nurses were similar to those of their counterparts in Guam. Hattori, *Colonial Dis-Ease*, 144.

136. Barclay et al., *Samoan Nursing*, 12.

137. Report on American Samoa by Colby, March 30, 1924, NARA-DC, RG 38, box 1084, N-1-b, Reg.-No. 17336-A, Annex No. 1, "Naval Station," p. 16.

138. Ibid.

139. Godson, *Serving Proudly,* 40–42.

140. Stokes to Stearns, September 9, 1913, NHHC, Feeney Notebooks, folder 8, box 24.

141. "Care Procedure Book, Samoan Hospital," NHHC, Navy Nurse Corps Records, folder 2, box 17.

142. Humphrey, "Letters from Navy Nurses," 761.

143. Lenah S. Higbee, "Letters from Navy Nurses," *American Journal of Nursing* 17, no. 3 (1916): 248.

144. *Annual Report of the Surgeon General, U.S. Navy, Chief of the Bureau of Medicine and Surgery to the Secretary of the Navy for the Fiscal Year 1919* (Washington, DC: Government Printing Office, 1919), 13.

145. John Garrett, *Where Nets Were Cast: Christianity in Oceania since World War II* (Suva: Institute of Pacific Studies, University of the South Pacific, 1997), 21.

146. *Annual Report of the Surgeon General, 1919,* 12–13.

147. Ibid., 13.

148. For a similar emphasis on the travel opportunities for health professionals in Guam, see Hattori, *Colonial Dis-Ease,* 8.

149. Braisted to Sec. of the Navy, April 18, 1919, NARA-DC, RG 52, box 367, file 124942.

150. Ibid.

151. Ibid.

152. Arnold S. Lott, *A Long Line of Ships: Mare Island's Century of Naval Activity in California* (Annapolis: United States Naval Institute, 1954), 102.

153. *Annual Report of the Surgeon General, 1919,* 13.

154. *Annual Report of the Surgeon General, 1920,* 746.

155. NARA-DC, RG 80, file 3931, box 36, p. 6.

156. Report on American Samoa by Colby, March 30, 1924, NARA-DC, RG 38, box 1084, N-1-b, Reg.-No. 17336-A, Annex No. 1, "Naval Station," p. 16.

157. Report on American Samoa by Colby, March 30, 1924, NARA-DC, RG 38, box 1084, N-1-b, Reg.-No. 17336-A, Annex No. 1, "Naval Station," p. 11.

158. Kress to Kellogg, July 1, 1924, NARA-DC, RG 80, file 3931, box 38, p. 7.

159. For a similar argument on the U.S.-occupied Philippines, see Anderson, *Colonial Pathologies.*

160. On counterinsurgency policing in the U.S.-occupied Philippines, see Alfred W. McCoy, *Policing America's Empire: The United States, the Philippines, and the Rise of the Surveillance State* (Madison: University of Wisconsin Press, 2009).

161. Kress to Kellogg, July 1, 1924, NARA-DC, RG 80, file 3931, box 38, pp. 6–7.

162. Macpherson and Macpherson, *Samoan Medical Belief,* 63.

163. Ibid., 81.

164. For the use of Claude Lévi-Strauss's concept of bricolage to describe Samoan medical practitioners, see Malama Meleisea, "Review: *Samoan Medical Belief and Practice* by Cluny Macpherson and La'avasa Macpherson," *Journal of the Polynesian Society* 105, no. 2 (1996): 259.

165. Keesing, *Modern Samoa,* 382.

166. Penelope Schoeffel, "Dilemmas of Modernization in Primary Health Care in Western Samoa," *Social Science and Medicine* 19, no. 3 (1984): 210–211.

167. Keesing, *Modern Samoa,* 394.

168. Report by Logan, October 27, 1914, ANZ Wellington, Governor-General of New Zealand, Series 21 / 1.

169. Hiery, *Neglected War,* 163–164.

170. Robinson, "Non-European Foundations of European Imperialism," 138.

171. Ibid., 122.

Epilogue

1. On Black Saturday, see Michael J. Field, *Mau: Samoa's Struggle against New Zealand Oppression* (Wellington, NZ: Reed, 1984), 147–159.

2. Susan Pedersen, *The Guardians: The League of Nations and the Crisis of Empire* (Oxford: Oxford University Press, 2015), 169.

3. Ibid., 189. Samoan petitions for outside assistance began in the mid-nineteenth century. Fellow Polynesians in Hawai'i also sent petitions against U.S. annexation to Congress and the president in the 1890s. See Noenoe K. Silva, *Aloha Betrayed: Native Hawaiian Resistance to American Colonialism* (Durham, NC: Duke University Press, 2004).

4. On the Mau as a movement for greater Samoan autonomy, see Kilifoti Sisilia Eteuati, "Evaevaga a Samoa: Assertion of Samoan Autonomy, 1920–1936" (PhD thesis, Australian National University, 1982). For an overview, see Malama Meleisea, *The Making of Modern Samoa: Traditional Authority and Colonial Administration in the History of Western Samoa* (Suva, Fiji: Institute of Pacific Studies of the University of the South Pacific, 1987), 126–147.

5. Patricia O'Brien, *Tautai: Sāmoa, World History, and the Life of Ta'isi O. F. Nelson* (Honolulu: University of Hawai'i Press, 2017), 180.

6. Pedersen, *Guardians,* 180.

7. On anti-colonial "worldmaking" by Black internationalists, see Adom Getachew, *Worldmaking After Empire: The Rise and Fall of Self-Determination* (Princeton, NJ: Princeton University Press, 2019).

8. David A. Chappell, "The Forgotten Mau: Anti-Navy Protest in American Samoa, 1920–1935," *Pacific Historical Review* 69, no. 2 (2000): 235–236.

9. Ibid., 251.

10. Ibid., 232.

11. See also Featunaʻi Ben Liuaʼana, "Dragons in Little Paradise: Chinese (Mis-) Fortunes in Samoa, 1900–1950," *Journal of Pacific History* 32, no. 1 (1997): 44.

12. Felix M. Keesing, *Modern Samoa: Its Government and Changing Life* (London: G. Allen & Unwin, 1934), 303–304; Chappell, "Forgotten Mau," 249.

13. Ripley to Harding, December 30, 1921, NARA-DC, RG 80, file 3931, box 34, pp. 23–24.

14. Haunani-Kay Trask, *From a Native Daughter: Colonialism and Sovereignty in Hawaiʻi* (Monroe, ME: Common Courage Press, 1993); Silva, *Aloha Betrayed;* Ronald T. Takaki, *Pau Hana: Plantation Life and Labor in Hawaiʻi, 1835–1920* (Honolulu: University of Hawaiʻi Press, 1983).

15. Sidney W. Mintz, *Sweetness and Power: The Place of Sugar in Modern History* (New York: Viking Press, 1985). On the Plantationocene, see Donna Haraway et al., "Anthropologists Are Talking—about the Anthropocene," *Ethnos* 81, no. 3 (2016): 556.

16. Andrew Zimmerman, *Alabama in Africa: Booker T. Washington, the German Empire, and the Globalization of the New South* (Princeton, NJ: Princeton University Press, 2010), 152.

17. Epeli Hauʻofa, "Pasts to Remember," in *We Are the Ocean: Selected Works* (Honolulu: University of Hawaiʻi Press, 2008), 73.

18. Toaga Alefosio and April K. Henderson, "On Skin and Bone: Samoan Coconut Oil in Indigenous Practice," *Journal of Pacific History* 53, no. 4 (2018): 397–416.

19. John Connell, "Temporary Labour Migration in the Pacific," in *Migration and Development: Perspectives from Small States,* ed. Wonderful Hope Khonje (London: Commonwealth Secretariat, 2015), 60–91.

BIBLIOGRAPHY

Primary Sources

ARCHIVES

Germany

Bundesarchiv, Berlin-Lichterfelde, Germany (BArch)
    R 1001 Reichskolonialamt
    RD 15 / 2 Jahresberichte über die Entwicklung der deutschen Schutzgebiete
Bundesarchiv, Koblenz, Germany (BArch)
    N 1053 Nachlass Solf
Commerzbibliothek Hamburg, Germany
Private Archive, Eugen Solf, Kronberg, Germany
    Johanna Solf, Personal Diary, September 7, 1908–September 7, 1909
Staatsarchiv Hamburg, Germany (StAH)
    DHPG records
Stadtarchiv Munich, Germany (StdAM)

New Zealand

Alexander Turnbull Library, Wellington, New Zealand (ATL Wellington)
Archives New Zealand, Wellington, New Zealand (ANZ Wellington)
    Archives of the German Colonial Administration (AGCA)
    Samoa, British Military Occupation (SAMOA-BMO)
    War Archives, Samoan Expeditionary Force

Samoa

National Archives Samoa, Malifa, Samoa (NAS)
    German Colonial Administration Records
Nelson Memorial Public Library, Apia, Samoa

United States

Bancroft Library, University of California, Berkeley, USA
    Panama-Pacific International Exposition Records

Chicago History Museum, Chicago, USA

Field Museum, Chicago, USA

Library of Congress, Washington, DC, USA
    Edward John Dorn Papers

National Archives and Records Administration, College Park, USA (NARA-CP)
    RG 84 Records of the Foreign Service Posts of the Department of State
    RG 350 Bureau of Insular Affairs

National Archives and Records Administration, San Bruno, USA (NARA-SB)
    RG 284 Records of the Government of American Samoa

National Archives and Records Administration, Washington, DC, USA (NARA-DC)
    RG 38 Records of the Office of the Chief of Naval Operations
    RG 45 Naval Records Collection of the Office of Naval Records and Library
    RG 52 Records of the Bureau of Medicine and Surgery
    RG 71 Records of the Bureau of Yards and Docks
    RG 80 General Records of the Department of the Navy
    RG 85 Records of the Immigration and Naturalization Service

Naval History and Heritage Command, Washington, DC, USA (NHHC)
    Navy Nurse Corps Records

PUBLISHED SOURCES

Adams, Henry. *The Education of Henry Adams.* Boston: Houghton Mifflin, 1918.

Annual Report of the Surgeon General, U.S. Navy, Chief of the Bureau of Medicine and Surgery to the Secretary of the Navy for the Fiscal Year 1919. Washington, DC: Government Printing Office, 1919.

Annual Report of the Surgeon General, U.S. Navy, Chief of the Bureau of Medicine and Surgery to the Secretary of the Navy for the Fiscal Year 1920. Washington, DC: Government Printing Office, 1920.

Arnold, C. D., and H. D. Higinbotham. *Official Views of the World's Columbian Exposition.* Chicago: Chicago Photo-Gravure, 1893.

Bade, James N., ed. *Karl Hanssen's Samoan War Diaries, August 1914–May 1915: A German Perspective on New Zealand's Military Occupation of German Samoa.* Frankfurt am Main: Peter Lang, 2011.

Bennitt, Mark, ed. *History of the Louisiana Purchase Exposition, Comprising the History of the Louisiana Territory, the Story of the Louisiana Purchase and a*

Full Account of the Great Exposition, Embracing the Participation of the States and Nations of the World, and Other Events of the St. Louis World's Fair of 1904. St. Louis, MO: Universal Exposition, 1905.

British Foreign Office, Historical Section. *Former German Possessions in Oceania.* London: HM Stationery Office, 1920.

Churchill, Llewella P. *Samoa 'Uma: Where Life Is Different.* London: Forest and Stream, 1902.

The Cyclopedia of Samoa, Tonga, Tahiti, and the Cook Islands. Papakura, NZ: R. McMillan, 1983. First printed 1907 by McCarron, Stewart (Sydney).

Deeken, Richard. *Manuia Samoa! Samoanische Reiseskizzen und Beobachtungen.* Oldenburg: G. Stalling, 1901.

Department of State. *Foreign Relations of the United States, 1899.* Washington, DC: Government Printing Office, 1901.

Destouches, Ernst von. *Die Jahrhundertfeier des Münchener Oktoberfestes: Gedenkbuch.* Munich: Lindauer, 1912.

Dugdale, Edgar T. S., ed. *German Diplomatic Documents, 1871–1914.* Vol. 3, *The Growing Antagonism (1898–1910).* New York: Harper, 1928.

Ebert, Paul. *Südsee-Erinnerungen.* Leipzig: K. F. Koehler, 1924.

Ehlers, Otto. *Samoa: Die Perle der Südsee.* Berlin: Hermann Paetel, 1895.

Fischel, L. M. *Copra Market Report.* London: 1927.

Higbee, Lenah S. "Letters from Navy Nurses." *American Journal of Nursing* 17, no. 3 (1916): 248–249.

Humphrey. "Letters from Navy Nurses." *American Journal of Nursing* 15, no. 9 (1915): 760–763.

Kniskern, Mary Poyer. *Life in Samoa from 1915 to 1919.* USA: Self-published, 1993.

Krämer, Augustin. *Die Samoa-Inseln: Entwurf einer Monographie mit besonderer Berücksichtigung Deutsch-Samoas.* Stuttgart: E. Schweizerbart, 1902–3.

La Farge, John. *Reminiscences of the South Seas.* Garden City, NY: Doubleday, Page, 1912.

Leary, L. P. *New Zealanders in Samoa.* London: W. Heinemann, 1918.

Levenson, J. C., ed. *The Letters of Henry Adams.* Vol. 3. Cambridge, MA: Belknap Press of Harvard University Press, 1982.

MacBride, Roger L., ed. *West from Home: Letters of Laura Ingalls Wilder to Almanzo Wilder, San Francisco, 1915.* New York: Harper & Row, 1974.

"Mandated Territory of Western Samoa (Report of Visit by Hon. W. Nosworthy, Minister of External Affairs)." *Appendix to the Journals of the House of Representatives.* 1927. Session 1, A-4B.

Marquardt, Carl. *Der Roman der Samoanerinnen und die Geschäftspraxis des Berliner Passage-Panoptikums.* Berlin: Selbstverlag, 1897.

———. *Die Tätowirung beider Geschlechter in Samoa.* Berlin: D. Reimer, 1899.

Moors, Harry J. *With Stevenson in Samoa.* Boston: Small, Maynard, 1910.

Photographs of the World's Fair: An Elaborate Collection of Photographs of the Buildings, Grounds and Exhibits of the World's Columbian Exposition, with a Special Description of the Famous Midway Plaisance. Chicago: Werner, 1894.

Pritchard, William T. *Polynesian Reminiscences; or, Life in the South Pacific Islands.* London: Chapman and Hall, 1866.

Reinecke, Franz. *Samoa.* Berlin: W. Süsserott, 1902.

Riedel, Otto. *Der Kampf um Deutsch-Samoa: Erinnerungen eines Hamburger Kaufmanns.* Berlin: Deutscher Verlag, 1938.

Schultz-Ewerth, Erich. *Erinnerungen an Samoa.* Berlin: A. Scherl, 1926.

Stair, John B. *Old Samoa; or, Flotsam and Jetsam from the Pacific Ocean.* London: Religious Tract Society, 1897.

Stevenson, Margaret, and Marie C. Balfour. *Letters from Samoa, 1891–1895.* London: Methuen, 1906.

Stevenson, Robert Louis. *A Footnote to History: Eight Years of Trouble in Samoa.* New York: Charles Scribner's Sons, 1892.

Todd, Frank M. *The Story of the Exposition, Being the Official History of the International Celebration Held at San Francisco in 1915 to Commemorate the Discovery of the Pacific Ocean and the Construction of the Panama Canal.* New York: G. P. Putnam's Sons, 1921.

Tripp, Bartlett. *My Trip to Samoa.* Cedar Rapids, IA: Torch Press, 1911.

Truman, Benjamin C. *History of the World's Fair, Being a Complete and Authentic Description of the Columbian Exposition from Its Inception.* Chicago: Mammoth, 1893.

Turner, George. *Samoa: A Hundred Years Ago and Long Before.* London: Macmillan, 1884.

Zieschank, Frieda. *Ein Jahrzehnt in Samoa, 1906–1916.* Leipzig: E. Haberland, 1918.

NEWSPAPERS AND MAGAZINES

Auckland Evening Post
Brooklyn Daily Eagle
Daily Inter Ocean
Die Post
Elektrotechnische Zeitschrift
Fiji Times
Frankfurter General-Anzeiger
Frankfurter Zeitung
Jahrbuch über die deutschen Kolonien
Kleine Presse
Kölnische Volkszeitung
Koloniale Zeitschrift

Mid-Pacific Magazine
New York Clipper
Samoa News
Samoa Times
Samoa Weekly Herald
Samoanische Zeitung
Samoanisches Gouvernements-Blatt
San Francisco Chronicle
Sydney Morning Herald
Vossische Zeitung
Watkins Express

Secondary Literature

Adas, Michael. *Dominance by Design: Technological Imperatives and America's Civilizing Mission.* Cambridge, MA: Harvard University Press, 2006.

Aitken, Hugh G. J. *The Continuous Wave: Technology and American Radio, 1900–1932.* Princeton, NJ: Princeton University Press, 1985.

Alefosio, Toaga, and April K. Henderson. "On Skin and Bone: Samoan Coconut Oil in Indigenous Practice." *Journal of Pacific History* 53, no. 4 (2018): 397–416.

Amerika Samoa Humanities Council. *A History of American Samoa.* Honolulu: Bess Press, 2009.

Ames, Eric. *Carl Hagenbeck's Empire of Entertainments.* Seattle: University of Washington Press, 2008.

Anderson, Warwick. *Colonial Pathologies: American Tropical Medicine, Race, and Hygiene in the Philippines.* Durham, NC: Duke University Press, 2006.

Andrews, Thomas G. *Killing for Coal: America's Deadliest Labor War.* Cambridge, MA: Harvard University Press, 2008.

Appadurai, Arjun. *Modernity at Large: Cultural Dimensions of Globalization.* Minneapolis: University of Minnesota Press, 1996.

Armitage, David, and Alison Bashford, eds. *Pacific Histories: Ocean, Land, People.* New York: Palgrave Macmillan, 2014.

Axster, Felix. "Arbeit an der 'Erziehung zur Arbeit' oder: die Figur des guten deutschen Kolonisators." In *"Deutsche Arbeit": Kritische Perspektiven auf ein ideologisches Selbstbild,* edited by Felix Axster and Nikolas Lelle, 226–251. Göttingen: Wallstein Verlag, 2018.

Ballantyne, Tony. *Entanglements of Empire: Missionaries, Māori, and the Question of the Body.* Durham, NC: Duke University Press, 2014.

Balme, Christopher B. *Pacific Performances: Theatricality and Cross-Cultural Encounter in the South Seas.* New York: Palgrave Macmillan, 2007.

Banivanua-Mar, Tracey. *Decolonisation and the Pacific: Indigenous Globalisation and the Ends of Empire.* Cambridge: Cambridge University Press, 2016.

Barclay, Lesley, Jennifer Fenwick, Faamanatu Nielson, Barbara Poston-Anderson, Pele Stowers, and Jennifer Wilkinson. *Samoan Nursing: The Story of Women Developing a Profession.* St. Leonards, UK: Allen & Unwin, 1998.

Barman, Jean, and Bruce McIntyre Watson. *Leaving Paradise: Indigenous Hawaiians in the Pacific Northwest, 1787–1898.* Honolulu: University of Hawai'i Press, 2006.

Barty-King, Hugh. *Girdle Round the Earth: The Story of Cable and Wireless and Its Predecessors to Mark the Group's Jubilee, 1929–1979.* London: Heinemann, 1979.

Beck, David. *Unfair Labor? American Indians and the 1893 World's Columbian Exposition in Chicago.* Lincoln: University of Nebraska Press, 2019.

Beckert, Sven. "Emancipation and Empire: Reconstructing the Worldwide Web of Cotton Production in the Age of the American Civil War." *American Historical Review* 109, no. 5 (2004): 1405–1438.

———. *Empire of Cotton: A Global History.* New York: Alfred A. Knopf, 2014.

Bell, Leonard. "Eyeing Samoa: People, Places and Spaces in Photographs of the Late 19th and Early 20th Centuries." In *Tropical Visions in an Age of Empire,* edited by Felix Driver and Luciana Martins, 156–174. Chicago: University of Chicago Press, 2005.

Bender, Daniel E. "Sensing Labor: The Stinking Working-Class after the Cultural Turn." In *Rethinking U.S. Labor History: Essays on the Working-Class Experience, 1756–2009,* edited by Donna T. Haverty-Stacke and Daniel J. Walkowitz, 243–265. New York: Continuum, 2010.

Bender, Daniel E., and Jana K. Lipman, eds. *Making the Empire Work: Labor and United States Imperialism.* New York: New York University Press, 2015.

Benedict, Burton. "The Anthropology of World's Fairs." In *The Anthropology of World's Fairs: San Francisco's Panama Pacific International Exposition of 1915,* edited by Burton Benedict, 1–66. Berkeley, CA: Lowie Museum of Anthropology, 1983.

Bönker, Dirk. *Militarism in a Global Age: Naval Ambitions in Germany and the United States before World War I.* Ithaca, NY: Cornell University Press, 2012.

Bosma, Ulbe. *The Making of a Periphery: How Island Southeast Asia Became a Mass Exporter of Labor.* New York: Columbia University Press, 2019.

Boyd, Mary. "Coping with Samoan Resistance after the 1918 Influenza Epidemic: Colonel Tate's Problems and Perplexities." *Journal of Pacific History* 15, no. 3 (1980): 155–174.

Brown, Jayna. *Babylon Girls: Black Women Performers and the Shaping of the Modern.* Durham, NC: Duke University Press, 2008.

Bruckner, Sierra A. "The Tingle-Tangle of Modernity: Popular Anthropology and the Cultural Politics of Identity in Imperial Germany." PhD thesis, University of Iowa, 1999.

Buck, Peter H. (Te Rangi Hiroa). *Samoan Material Culture*. Honolulu: Bishop Museum, 1930.

Camacho, Keith L. *Cultures of Commemoration: The Politics of War, Memory, and History in the Mariana Islands*. Honolulu: University of Hawai'i Press, 2011.

Chang, David A. *The World and All the Things upon It: Native Hawaiian Geographies of Exploration*. Minneapolis: University of Minnesota Press, 2016.

Chang, Kornel S. *Pacific Connections: The Making of the U.S.-Canadian Borderlands*. Berkeley: University of California Press, 2012.

Chappell, David A. *Double Ghosts: Oceanian Voyagers on Euroamerican Ships*. Armonk, NY: M. E. Sharpe, 1997.

———. "The Forgotten Mau: Anti-Navy Protest in American Samoa, 1920–1935." *Pacific Historical Review* 69, no. 2 (2000): 217–260.

Ciarlo, David. *Advertising Empire: Race and Visual Culture in Imperial Germany*. Cambridge, MA: Harvard University Press, 2011.

Colley, Ann C. *Robert Louis Stevenson and the Colonial Imagination*. Aldershot, UK: Ashgate, 2004.

Connell, John. "Temporary Labour Migration in the Pacific." In *Migration and Development: Perspectives from Small States,* edited by Wonderful Hope Khonje, 60–91. London: Commonwealth Secretariat, 2015.

Conrad, Sebastian. "'Kulis' nach Preußen? Mobilität, chinesische Arbeiter und das deutsche Kaiserreich, 1890–1914." *Comparativ* 13, no. 4 (2003): 80–95.

———. "Rethinking German Colonialism in a Global Age." *Journal of Imperial and Commonwealth History* 41, no. 4 (2013): 543–566.

Cook, Kealani. *Return to Kahiki: Native Hawaiians in Oceania*. Cambridge: Cambridge University Press, 2018.

Cooper, Fredrick. *Decolonization and African Society: The Labor Question in French and British Africa*. Cambridge: Cambridge University Press, 1996.

Corbey, Raymond. "Ethnographic Showcases, 1870–1930." *Cultural Anthropology* 8, no. 3 (1993): 338–369.

Crosby, Alfred W. *America's Forgotten Pandemic: The Influenza of 1918*. 2nd ed. Cambridge: Cambridge University Press, 2003.

Cullinane, Michael. *Ilustrado Politics: Filipino Elite Responses to American Rule, 1898–1908*. Quezon City: Ateneo de Manila University Press, 2003.

Cumberland, Kenneth B. "Plantation Agriculture." In *Western Samoa: Land, Life, and Agriculture in Tropical Polynesia,* edited by James W. Fox and Kenneth B. Cumberland, 239–265. Christchurch, NZ: Whitcombe & Tombs, 1962.

Cushman, Gregory T. *Guano and the Opening of the Pacific World: A Global Ecological History*. Cambridge: Cambridge University Press, 2013.

Davidson, James W. *Samoa mo Samoa: The Emergence of the Independent State of Western Samoa*. Oxford: Oxford University Press, 1967.

Decker, Julio. "Lines in the Sand: Railways and the Archipelago of Colonial Territorialization in German Southwest Africa, 1897–1914." *Journal of Historical Geography* 70 (October 2020): 74–87.

Diaz, Vicente M. *Repositioning the Missionary: Rewriting the Histories of Colonialism, Native Catholicism, and Indigeneity in Guam.* Honolulu: University of Hawai'i Press, 2010.

Dreesbach, Anne. *Gezähmte Wilde: Die Zurschaustellung "exotischer" Menschen in Deutschland, 1870–1940.* Frankfurt am Main: Campus, 2005.

———. "'Neu! Grösste Sehenswürdigkeit! Neu! Zum ersten Male in München!' Exotisches auf dem Münchner Oktoberfest zwischen 1890 und 1911." In *"Gleich hinterm Hofbräuhaus waschechte Amazonen": Exotik in München um 1900,* edited by Anne Dreesbach and Helmut Zedelmaier, 9–33. Munich: Dölling und Galitz, 2003.

Droessler, Holger. "Changes on the Plantation: An Environmental History of Colonial Samoa, 1880–1920." In *Migrant Ecologies: Environmental Histories of the Pacific,* edited by James Beattie, Edward Melillo, and Ryan T. Jones. Honolulu: University of Hawai'i Press, forthcoming.

———. "Colonialism by Deferral: Samoa under the Tridominium, 1889–1899." In *Rethinking the Colonial State,* edited by Søren Rud and Søren Ivarsson, 203–224. Political Power and Social Theory 33. Bingley, UK: Emerald, 2017.

———. "Copra World: Coconuts, Plantations, and Cooperatives in German Samoa." *Journal of Pacific History* 53, no. 4 (November 2018): 417–435.

———. "Germany's El Dorado in the Pacific: Metropolitan Representations and Colonial Realities, 1884–1914." In *Imperial Expectations and Realities: El Dorados, Utopias, and Dystopias,* edited by Andrekos Varnava, 105–124. Manchester: Manchester University Press, 2015.

———. "Whose Pacific? U.S. Security Interests in American Samoa from the Age of Empire to the Pacific Pivot." *Pacific Asia Inquiry* 4, no. 1 (Fall 2013): 58–65.

Dürbeck, Gabriele. "Samoa als inszeniertes Paradies: Völkerausstellungen um 1900 und die Tradition der Populären Südseeliteratur." In *Die Schau des Fremden: Ausstellungskonzepte zwischen Kunst, Kommerz und Wissenschaft,* edited by Cordula Grewe, 69–94. Stuttgart: Steiner, 2006.

———. *Stereotype Paradiese: Ozeanismus in der deutschen Südseeliteratur, 1815–1914.* Tübingen: Niemeyer, 2007.

Edmond, Rod. *Representing the South Pacific: Colonial Discourse from Cook to Gauguin.* Cambridge: Cambridge University Press, 1997.

Eteuati, Kilifoti Sisilia. "Evaevaga a Samoa: Assertion of Samoan Autonomy, 1920–1936." PhD thesis, Australian National University, 1982.

Evans, Heidi J. S. "'The Path to Freedom'? Transocean and German Wireless Telegraphy, 1914–1922." *Historical Social Research* 35, no. 131 (2010): 209–233.

Faaleava, Toetu. "*Fitafita*: Samoan Landsmen in the United States Navy, 1900–1951." PhD thesis, University of California, Berkeley, 2003.

Fairbairn-Dunlop, Peggy. *Tamaitai Samoa: Their Stories.* Suva, Fiji: Institute of Pacific Studies, University of the South Pacific, 1996.

Faleomavaega, Eni F. H. *Navigating the Future: A Samoan Perspective on U.S.-Pacific Relations.* Carson, CA: KIN Publications, 1995.

Fermin, Jose D. *1904 World's Fair: The Filipino Experience.* Quezon City: University of the Philippines Press, 2004.

Field, Michael J. *Mau: Samoa's Struggle against New Zealand Oppression.* Wellington, NZ: Reed, 1984.

Firth, Raymond. *Primitive Polynesian Economy.* London: G. Routledge & Sons, 1939.

Firth, Stewart. "German Recruitment and Employment of Labourers in the Western Pacific before the First World War." PhD thesis, University of Oxford, 1973.

———. "Governors versus Settlers: The Dispute over Chinese Labour in German Samoa." *New Zealand Journal of History* 11, no. 2 (1977): 155–179.

———. *New Guinea under the Germans.* Carlton: Melbourne University Press, 1983.

Fischer-Tiné, Harald. *Pidgin-Knowledge: Wissen und Kolonialismus.* Zurich: Diaphanes, 2013.

Förderer, Gabriele. *Koloniale Grüße aus Samoa: Eine Diskursanalyse von deutschen, englischen und US-amerikanischen Reisebeschreibungen aus Samoa von 1860–1916.* Bielefeld: Transcript, 2017.

Fox, James W., and Kenneth B. Cumberland, eds. *Western Samoa: Land, Life, and Agriculture in Tropical Polynesia.* Christchurch, NZ: Whitcombe & Tombs, 1962.

Franco, Robert W. *Samoan Perceptions of Work: Moving Up and Moving Around.* New York: AMS Press, 1991.

Friedman, Norman. *U.S. Battleships: An Illustrated Design History.* London: Arms and Armour Press, 1986.

Frymer, Paul. *Building an American Empire: The Era of Territorial and Political Expansion.* Princeton, NJ: Princeton University Press, 2017.

Furnas, J. C. *Anatomy of Paradise: Hawaii and the Islands of the South Seas.* New York: W. Sloane Associates, 1948.

Garrett, John. *Where Nets Were Cast: Christianity in Oceania since World War II.* Suva, Fiji: Institute of Pacific Studies, University of the South Pacific, 1997.

Geppert, Alexander C. T. *Fleeting Cities: Imperial Expositions in Fin-de-Siècle Europe.* New York: Palgrave Macmillan, 2010.

Getachew, Adom. *Worldmaking after Empire: The Rise and Fall of Self-Determination.* Princeton, NJ: Princeton University Press, 2019.

Gilson, Richard P. *Samoa 1830 to 1900: The Politics of a Multi-Cultural Community.* Oxford: Oxford University Press, 1970.

Godson, Susan H. *Serving Proudly: A History of Women in the U.S. Navy.* Annapolis: Naval Institute Press, 2001.

Gould, Stephen J. *The Mismeasure of Man.* New York: W. W. Norton, 1981.

Grattan, F. J. H. *An Introduction to Samoan Custom.* Apia: Samoa Printing & Publishing, 1948.

Graves, Adrian. *Cane and Labour: The Political Economy of the Queensland Sugar Industry, 1862–1906.* Edinburgh: Edinburgh University Press, 1993.

Green, R. C., and Janet M. Davidson. *Archaeology in Western Samoa.* Vol. 2. Auckland: Auckland Institute and Museum, 1974.

Greene, Julie. *The Canal Builders: Making America's Empire at the Panama Canal.* New York: Penguin Press, 2009.

———. "The Labor of Empire: Recent Scholarship on U.S. History and Imperialism." *Labor: Studies in Working-Class History of the Americas* 1, no. 2 (2004): 113–129.

Griffiths, Alison. *Wondrous Difference: Cinema, Anthropology, and Turn-of-the-Century Visual Culture.* New York: Columbia University Press, 2002.

Gülstorff, Torben. "Vom Wilhelmshof in die Fremde: Einblicke in die Lehre vom Eigenen und Fremden an der Kolonialschule Witzenhausen—Ansätze eines interkulturellen Lernens?" *Öt Kontinens,* no. 2010 (2011): 395–412.

Gutman, Herbert. *Work, Culture, and Society in Industrializing America: Essays in American Working-Class and Social History.* New York: Alfred A. Knopf, 1976.

Handy, E. S. C., and Willowdean C. Handy. *Samoan House Building, Cooking, and Tattooing.* Honolulu: Bishop Museum, 1924.

Haraway, Donna, Noboru Ishikawa, Scott F. Gilbert, Kenneth Olwig, Anna L. Tsing, and Nils Bubandt. "Anthropologists Are Talking—about the Anthropocene." *Ethnos* 81, no. 3 (2016): 535–564.

Haschemi Yekani, Minu. *Koloniale Arbeit: Rassismus, Migration und Herrschaft in Tansania (1885–1914).* Frankfurt am Main: Campus Verlag, 2019.

Hattori, Anne Perez. *Colonial Dis-Ease: U.S. Navy Health Policies and the Chamorros of Guam, 1898–1941.* Honolulu: University of Hawai'i Press, 2004.

Hau'ofa, Epeli. "Our Sea of Islands." In *A New Oceania: Rediscovering Our Sea of Islands,* edited by Epeli Hau'ofa, Vijay Naidu, and Eric Waddell, 2–16. Suva, Fiji: University of the South Pacific, 1993.

———. "Pasts to Remember." In *We Are the Ocean: Selected Works,* 60–79. Honolulu: University of Hawai'i Press, 2008.

Headrick, Daniel R. *The Invisible Weapon: Telecommunications and International Politics, 1851–1945.* Oxford: Oxford University Press, 1991.

———. *The Tools of Empire: Technology and European Imperialism in the Nineteenth Century.* Oxford: Oxford University Press, 1981.

Hempenstall, Peter J. "Indigenous Resistance to German Rule in the Pacific Colonies of Samoa, Ponape and New Guinea, 1884 to 1914." PhD thesis, University of Oxford, 1973.

———. *Pacific Islanders under German Rule: A Study in the Meaning of Colonial Resistance.* Canberra: Australian National University Press, 1978.

Hempenstall, Peter J., and Paula T. Mochida. *The Lost Man: Wilhelm Solf in German History*. Wiesbaden: Harrassowitz, 2005.

Hempenstall, Peter J., and Noel Rutherford. *Protest and Dissent in the Colonial Pacific*. Suva, Fiji: Institute of Pacific Studies of the University of the South Pacific, 1984.

Henare, Amiria J. M. *Museums, Anthropology and Imperial Exchange*. Cambridge: Cambridge University Press, 2005.

Hiery, Hermann. *Bilder aus der deutschen Südsee: Fotografien, 1884–1914*. Paderborn: Ferdinand Schöningh, 2005.

———. *Das Deutsche Reich in der Südsee (1900–1921): Eine Annährung an die Erfahrungen verschiedener Kulturen*. Göttingen: Vandenhoeck & Ruprecht, 1995.

———, ed. *Die Deutsche Südsee, 1884–1914: Ein Handbuch*. Paderborn: Ferdinand Schöningh, 2001.

———. "Die deutsche Verwaltung Samoas, 1900–1914." In *Die Deutsche Südsee 1884–1914: Ein Handbuch,* edited by Hermann Hiery, 649–675. Paderborn: Ferdinand Schöningh, 2001.

———. "Die Polizei im deutschen Samoa: Deutsche Hoffnungen und samoanische Erwartungen." In *Barrieren und Zugänge: Die Geschichte der europäischen Expansion,* edited by Thomas Beck, Marília dos Santos Lopes, and Christian Rödel, 266–273. Wiesbaden: Harrassowitz Verlag, 2004.

———. *The Neglected War: The German South Pacific and the Influence of World War I*. Honolulu: University of Hawai'i Press, 1995.

Hinsley, Curtis M. "The World as Marketplace: Commodification of the Exotic at the World's Columbian Exposition, Chicago, 1893." In *Exhibiting Cultures: The Poetics and Politics of Museum Display,* edited by Ivan Karp and Steven D. Lavine, 344–365. Washington, DC: Smithsonian Institution Press, 1991.

Hobsbawm, Eric. *Industry and Empire: From 1750 to the Present Day*. New York: Weidenfeld & Nicholson, 1968.

Holley, I. B., Jr., *The Highway Revolution, 1895–1925: How the United States Got Out of the Mud*. Durham, NC: Carolina Academic Press, 2008.

Holmes, Lowell D. "Cults, Cargo, and Christianity: Samoan Responses to Western Religion." *Missiology: An International Review* 8, no. 4 (1980): 471–487.

———. *Samoan Village*. New York: Holt, Rinehart and Winston, 1974.

Honold, Alexander. "Der Exot und sein Publikum: Völkerschau in der Kolonialzeit." In *Rassenmischehen, Mischlinge, Rassentrennung: Zur Politik der Rasse im deutschen Kolonialreich,* edited by Frank Becker, 357–375. Stuttgart: Franz Steiner, 2004.

Horne, Gerald. *The White Pacific: U.S. Imperialism and Black Slavery in the South Seas after the Civil War*. Honolulu: University of Hawai'i Press, 2007.

Hoyt, Edwin P. *The Typhoon That Stopped a War*. New York: D. McKay, 1968.

Huber, Valeska. *Channelling Mobilities: Migration and Globalisation in the Suez Canal Region and Beyond, 1869–1914.* Cambridge: Cambridge University Press, 2013.

Imada, Adria L. *Aloha America: Hula Circuits through the U.S. Empire.* Durham, NC: Duke University Press, 2012.

Inglis, Kerri A. "Disease and the 'Other': The Role of Medical Imperialism in Oceania." In *Native Diasporas: Indigenous Identities and Settler Colonialism in the Americas,* edited by Gregory D. Smithers and Brooke N. Newman, 385–409. Lincoln: University of Nebraska Press, 2014.

Jackson, Justin F. "Roads to American Empire: U.S. Military Public Works and Capitalist Transitions, 1898–1934." *Journal of Historical Sociology* 33, no. 1 (2020): 116–133.

Jacobson, Matthew Frye. *Barbarian Virtues: The United States Encounters Foreign Peoples at Home and Abroad, 1876–1917.* New York: Hill & Wang, 2000.

Jacoby, Karl. *Crimes against Nature: Squatters, Poachers, Thieves, and the Hidden History of American Conservation.* Berkeley: University of California Press, 2001.

Johnson, Walter. *River of Dark Dreams: Slavery and Empire in the Cotton Kingdom.* Cambridge, MA: Harvard University Press, 2013.

Johnston, Ewan. "'Polynesien in der Plaisance': Das samoanische Dorf und das Theater der Südseeinseln auf der Weltausstellung in Chicago, 1893." *Comparativ* 9, no. 5/6 (1999): 89–102.

———. "Reinventing Fiji at 19th-Century and Early 20th-Century Exhibitions." *Journal of Pacific History* 40, no. 1 (2005): 23–44.

Jolly, Margaret. "From Point Venus to Bali Ha'i: Eroticism and Exoticism in Representations of the Pacific." In *Sites of Desire, Economies of Pleasure: Sexualities in Asia and the Pacific,* edited by Lenore Manderson and Margaret Jolly, 99–122. Chicago: University of Chicago Press, 1997.

Jones, Christopher F. *Routes of Power: Energy and Modern America.* Cambridge, MA: Harvard University Press, 2014.

Joyner, Charles. *Down by the Riverside: A South Carolina Slave Community.* Urbana: University of Illinois Press, 1984.

Jung, Moon-Ho. *Coolies and Cane: Race, Labor, and Sugar in the Age of Emancipation.* Baltimore: Johns Hopkins University Press, 2006.

Keesing, Felix M. *Modern Samoa: Its Government and Changing Life.* London: G. Allen & Unwin, 1934.

Kennedy, Joseph. *The Tropical Frontier: America's South Sea Colony.* Mangilao, Guam: Micronesian Area Research Center, 2009.

———. "The Wild Man of Samoa: A Tale from the Graveyard of Strangers." *Natural History,* February 2004.

Kennedy, Paul M. *The Samoan Tangle: A Study in Anglo-German-American Relations, 1878–1900.* Dublin: Irish University Press, 1974.

Klein-Arendt, Reinhard. "Die Nachrichtenübermittlung in den deutschen Süd-seekolonien." In *Die Deutsche Südsee, 1884–1914: Ein Handbuch,* edited by Hermann Hiery, 177–197. Paderborn: Ferdinand Schöningh, 2001.

———. *Kamina ruft Nauen! Die Funkstellen in den deutschen Kolonien, 1904–1918.* Köln: W. Herbst, 1996.

Kneitz, Agnes. "German Water Infrastructure in China: Colonial Qingdao, 1898–1914." *NTM* 24, no. 4 (2016): 421–450.

Knoll, Arthur J., and Hermann J. Hiery, eds. *The German Colonial Experience: Select Documents on German Rule in Africa, China, and the Pacific, 1884–1914.* Lanham, MD: University Press of America, 2010.

Kramer, Paul. "Making Concessions: Race and Empire Revisited at the Philippine Exposition, St. Louis, 1901–1905." *Radical History Review* 73, no. 1 (1999): 75–114.

Krobb, Florian, and Elaine Martin, eds. *Weimar Colonialism: Discourses and Legacies of Post-Imperialism in Germany after 1918.* Bielefeld: Aisthesis, 2014.

Kroeber-Wolf, Gerda, and Peter Mesenhöller, eds. *Talofa! Samoa, Südsee: Ansichten und Einsichten.* Frankfurt am Main: Museum für Völkerkunde, 1998.

Kuhn, Philip A. *Chinese among Others: Emigration in Modern Times.* Lanham, MD: Rowman & Littlefield, 2008.

Laak, Dirk van. *Imperiale Infrastruktur: Deutsche Planungen für die Erschließung Afrikas, 1880–1960.* Paderborn: Ferdinand Schöningh, 2004.

Lahiri Choudhury, Deep Kanta. *Telegraphic Imperialism: Crisis and Panic in the Indian Empire, 1830–1920.* New York: Palgrave Macmillan, 2010.

Lai, Walton Look. "Asian Contract and Free Migrations to the Americas." In *Coerced and Free Migration: Global Perspectives,* edited by David Eltis, 229–258. Stanford: Stanford University Press, 2002.

Lal, Brij V. *Broken Waves: A History of the Fiji Islands in the Twentieth Century.* Honolulu: University of Hawai'i Press, 1992.

Lal, Brij V., Doug Munro, and Edward D. Beechert, eds. *Plantation Workers: Resistance and Accommodation.* Honolulu: University of Hawai'i Press, 1993.

Langen, Erich. "Deutsch-Samoa." *Jahrbuch über die deutschen Kolonien* 5 (1912).

Laurance, Robin. *Coconut: How the Shy Fruit Shaped the World.* Stroud, UK: History Press, 2019.

Lawrance, Benjamin N., Emily Lynn Osborn, and Richard L. Roberts. "African Intermediaries and the 'Bargain' of Collaboration." In *Intermediaries, Interpreters, and Clerks: African Employees in the Making of Colonial Africa,* edited by Benjamin N. Lawrance, Emily Lynn Osborn, and Richard L. Roberts, 3–34. Madison: University of Wisconsin Press, 2006.

Lee, Dorothy Sara, ed. *The Federal Cylinder Project: A Guide to Field Cylinder Collections in Federal Agencies.* Vol. 8, *Early Anthologies.* Washington, DC: Library of Congress, 1984.

Lehman, F. K., and David J. Herdrich. "On the Relevance of Point Field for Spatiality in Oceania." In *Representing Space in Oceania: Culture in Language and*

Mind, edited by Giovanni Bennardo, 179–197. Canberra: Australian National University Press, 2002.

Lewthwaite, Gordon R. "Land, Life and Agriculture to Mid-Century." In *Western Samoa: Land, Life, and Agriculture in Tropical Polynesia,* edited by James W. Fox and Kenneth B. Cumberland, 130–176. Christchurch, NZ: Whitcombe & Tombs, 1962.

Liebersohn, Harry. "Coming of Age in the Pacific: German Ethnography from Chamisso to Krämer." In *Worldly Provincialism: German Anthropology in the Age of Empire,* edited by H. Glenn Penny and Matti Bunzl, 31–46. Ann Arbor: University of Michigan Press, 2003.

Liki, Asenati. "Women as Kin: Working Lives, Living Work and Mobility among Samoan *Teine uli.*" In *Oceanian Journeys and Sojourns: Home Thoughts Abroad,* edited by Judith A. Bennett, 126–159. Dunedin, NZ: Otago University Press, 2015.

Lilomaiava-Doktor, Sa'iliemanu. "Beyond 'Migration': Samoan Population Movement (*Malaga*) and the Geography of Social Space (*Vā*)." *Contemporary Pacific* 21, no. 1 (2009): 1–32.

Linden, Marcel van der. *Workers of the World: Essays toward a Global Labor History.* Leiden: Brill, 2008.

Lindfors, Bernth, ed. *Africans on Stage: Studies in Ethnological Show Business.* Bloomington: Indiana University Press, 1999.

Linklater, Andro. *Owning the Earth: The Transforming History of Land Ownership.* London: Bloomsbury, 2013.

Linnekin, Jocelyn. "Fine Mats and Money: Contending Exchange Paradigms in Colonial Samoa." *Anthropological Quarterly* 64, no. 1 (1991): 1–13.

Lipman, Jana K. *Guantánamo: A Working-Class History between Empire and Revolution.* Berkeley: University of California Press, 2009.

Liua'ana, Featuna'i Ben. "Dragons in Little Paradise: Chinese (Mis-) Fortunes in Samoa, 1900–1950." *Journal of Pacific History* 32, no. 1 (1997): 29–48.

———. *Samoa Tula'i: Ecclesiastical and Political Face of Samoa's Independence, 1900–1962.* Apia: Malua Printing Press, 2001.

Lockwood, Brian A. *Samoan Village Economy.* Oxford: Oxford University Press, 1971.

Loosen, Livia. *Deutsche Frauen in den Südsee-Kolonien des Kaiserreichs: Alltag und Beziehungen zur Indigenen Bevölkerung, 1884–1919.* Bielefeld: Transcript, 2014.

Lott, Arnold S. *A Long Line of Ships: Mare Island's Century of Naval Activity in California.* Annapolis: United States Naval Institute, 1954.

Lurtz, Casey. *From the Grounds Up: Building an Export Economy in Southern Mexico.* Stanford: Stanford University Press, 2019.

Macnaught, Timothy J. *The Fijian Colonial Experience: A Study of the Neotraditional Order under British Colonial Rule Prior to World War II.* Canberra: Australian National University, 1982.

Macpherson, Cluny, and La'avasa Macpherson. *Samoan Medical Belief and Practice.* Auckland: Auckland University Press, 1990.

———. *The Warm Winds of Change: Globalisation in Contemporary Samoa.* Auckland: Auckland University Press, 2009.

Maggor, Noam. *Brahmin Capitalism: Frontiers of Wealth and Populism in America's First Gilded Age.* Cambridge, MA: Harvard University Press, 2017.

Manjapra, Kris. "Plantation Dispossessions: The Global Travel of Agricultural Racial Capitalism." In *American Capitalism: New Histories,* edited by Sven Beckert and Christine Desan, 361–387. New York: Columbia University Press, 2019.

Markwyn, Abigail M. *Empress San Francisco: The Pacific Rim, the Great West, and California at the Panama-Pacific International Exposition.* Lincoln: University of Nebraska Press, 2014.

Masterman, Sylvia. *The Origins of International Rivalry in Samoa, 1845–1884.* London: G. Allen & Unwin, 1934.

McCoy, Alfred W. *Policing America's Empire: The United States, the Philippines, and the Rise of the Surveillance State.* Madison: University of Wisconsin Press, 2009.

McCoy, Alfred W., and Francisco A. Scarano, eds. *Colonial Crucible: Empire in the Making of the Modern American State.* Madison: University of Wisconsin Press, 2009.

McKeown, Adam. *Chinese Migrant Networks and Cultural Change: Peru, Chicago, Hawaii, 1900–1936.* Chicago: University of Chicago Press, 2001.

———. *Melancholy Order: Asian Migration and the Globalization of Borders.* New York: Columbia University Press, 2008.

Meleisea, Malama. "The Last Days of the Melanesian Labour Trade in Western Samoa." *Journal of Pacific History* 11, no. 2 (1976): 126–132.

———. *The Making of Modern Samoa: Traditional Authority and Colonial Administration in the History of Western Samoa.* Suva, Fiji: Institute of Pacific Studies of the University of the South Pacific, 1987.

———. *O Tama Uli: Melanesians in Western Samoa.* Suva, Fiji: Institute of Pacific Studies of the University of the South Pacific, 1980.

———. "Review: *Samoan Medical Belief and Practice* by Cluny Macpherson and La'avasa Macpherson." *Journal of the Polynesian Society* 105, no. 2 (1996): 259–261.

Meleisea, Malama, and Penelope Schoeffel Meleisea. *Lagaga: A Short History of Western Samoa.* Suva, Fiji: University of the South Pacific, 1987.

Memea Kruse, Line-Noue. *The Pacific Insular Case of American Sāmoa: Land Rights and Law in Unincorporated U.S. Territories.* London: Palgrave Macmillan, 2018.

Mintz, Sidney W. *Sweetness and Power: The Place of Sugar in Modern History.* New York: Viking Press, 1985.

Moore, Colin D. *American Imperialism and the State, 1893–1921*. Cambridge: Cambridge University Press, 2017.

Moore, Jason W. "Sugar and the Expansion of the Early Modern World-Economy: Commodity Frontiers, Ecological Transformation, and Industrialization." *Review (Fernand Braudel Center)* 23, no. 3 (2000): 409–433.

Moore, Sarah J. *Empire on Display: San Francisco's Panama-Pacific International Exposition of 1915*. Norman: University of Oklahoma Press, 2013.

Morlang, Thomas. *Askari und Fitafita: 'Farbige' Söldner in den deutschen Kolonien*. Berlin: Links, 2008.

Mosolff, Hans. *Die chinesische Auswanderung: Ursachen, Wesen und Wirkungen*. Rostock: Carl Hinstorffs Verlag, 1932.

Moyd, Michelle R. *Violent Intermediaries: African Soldiers, Conquest, and Everyday Colonialism in German East Africa*. Athens: Ohio University Press, 2014.

Mühlhäusler, Peter. "Samoan Plantation Pidgin English and the Origin of New Guinea Pidgin." *Papers in Pidgin and Creole Linguistics* 1 (1978): 67–119.

———. "Samoan Plantation Pidgin English and the Origins of New Guinea Pidgin: An Introduction." *Journal of Pacific History* 11, no. 2 (1976): 122–125.

Müller, Simone. *Wiring the World: The Social and Cultural Creation of Global Telegraph Networks*. New York: Columbia University Press, 2016.

Munro, Doug, and Stewart Firth. "Samoan Plantations: The Gilbertese Laborers' Experience, 1867–1896." In *Plantation Workers: Resistance and Accommodation,* edited by Brij V. Lal, Doug Munro, and Edward D. Beechert, 101–127. Honolulu: University of Hawai'i Press, 1993.

O'Brien, Patricia. *Tautai: Sāmoa, World History, and the Life of Ta'isi O. F. Nelson*. Honolulu: University of Hawai'i Press, 2017.

Okihiro, Gary Y. *Pineapple Culture: A History of the Tropical and Temperate Zones*. Berkeley: University of California Press, 2009.

O'Meara, J. Tim. *Samoan Planters: Tradition and Economic Development in Polynesia*. Orlando: Holt, Rinehart and Winston, 1990.

Osbourne, Lloyd. Introduction to *Samoa under the Sailing Gods,* by Newton A. Rowe, xi–xiv. London: Putnam, 1930.

Osterhammel, Jürgen, and Niels P. Petersson, *Globalization: A Short History*. Princeton, NJ: Princeton University Press, 2005.

Paisley, Fiona. *Glamour in the Pacific: Cultural Internationalism and Race Politics in the Women's Pan-Pacific*. Honolulu: University of Hawai'i Press, 2009.

Parezo, Nancy J., and Don Fowler. *Anthropology Goes to the Fair: The 1904 Louisiana Purchase Exposition*. Lincoln: University of Nebraska Press, 2007.

Parthasarathi, Prasannan. "The Great Divergence." *Past and Present* 176, no. 1 (2002): 275–293.

Patterson, Orlando. *The Confounding Island: Jamaica and the Postcolonial Predicament*. Cambridge, MA: Harvard University Press, 2019.

Pedersen, Susan. *The Guardians: The League of Nations and the Crisis of Empire*. Oxford: Oxford University Press, 2015.

Peloso, Vincent C. *Peasants on Plantations: Subaltern Strategies of Labor and Resistance in the Pisco Valley, Peru.* Durham, NC: Duke University Press, 1999.

Penny, H. Glenn. *Kindred by Choice: Germans and American Indians since 1800.* Chapel Hill: University of North Carolina Press, 2013.

———. *Objects of Culture: Ethnology and Ethnographic Museums in Imperial Germany.* Chapel Hill: University of North Carolina Press, 2002.

Pitt, David C. *Tradition and Economic Progress in Samoa: A Case Study of the Role of Traditional Social Institutions in Economic Development.* Oxford: Clarendon Press, 1970.

Poblete, JoAnna. *Balancing the Tides: Marine Practices in American Sāmoa.* Honolulu: University of Hawai'i Press, 2020.

———. "Bridging Indigenous and Immigrant Struggles: A Case Study of American Samoa." *American Quarterly* 62, no. 3 (2010): 501–522.

———. *Islanders in the Empire: Filipino and Puerto Rican Laborers in Hawai'i.* Urbana: University of Illinois Press, 2014.

Poignant, Roslyn. "Captive Aboriginal Lives: Billy, Jenny, Little Toby and Their Companions." In *Captive Lives: Australian Captivity Narratives,* edited by Kate Darian-Smith, Roslyn Poignant, and Kay Schaffer, 35–57. London: University of London, 1993.

———. *Professional Savages: Captive Lives and Western Spectacle.* New Haven, CT: Yale University Press, 2004.

Pomeranz, Kenneth. *The Great Divergence: China, Europe, and the Making of the Modern World Economy.* Princeton, NJ: Princeton University Press, 2000.

Prentice, Claire. *The Lost Tribe of Coney Island: Headhunters, Luna Park, and the Man Who Pulled Off the Spectacle of the Century.* Boston: New Harvest, 2014.

Preston, Howard L. *Dirt Roads to Dixie: Accessibility and Modernization in the South, 1885–1935.* Knoxville: University of Tennessee Press, 1991.

Qureshi, Sadiah. *Peoples on Parade: Exhibitions, Empire, and Anthropology in Nineteenth-Century Britain.* Chicago: University of Chicago Press, 2011.

Ralston, Caroline. "Women Workers in Samoa and Tonga in the Early Twentieth Century." In *Labour in the South Pacific,* edited by Clive Moore, Jacqueline Leckie, and Doug Munro, 67–77. Townsville: James Cook University of Northern Queensland, 1990.

Richards, Rhys. "The Decision to *Lotu:* New Perspectives from Whaling Records on the Sources and Spread of Christianity in Samoa." *Pacific Studies Journal* 17, no. 1 (1994): 29–44.

Robinson, Ronald. "Non-European Foundations of European Imperialism: Sketch for a Theory of Collaboration." In *Studies in the Theory of Imperialism,* edited by Roger Owen and Bob Sutcliffe, 117–140. London: Longman, 1972.

Robson, Robert W. *Queen Emma: The Samoan-American Girl Who Founded an Empire in 19th Century New Guinea.* Sydney: Pacific Publications, 1971.

Rosenthal, Gregory. *Beyond Hawai'i: Native Labor in the Pacific World*. Berkeley: University of California Press, 2018.

Rothfels, Nigel. *Savages and Beasts: The Birth of the Modern Zoo*. Baltimore: Johns Hopkins University Press, 2002.

Rowe, Newton A. *Samoa under the Sailing Gods*. London: Putnam, 1930.

Rüger, Jan. *The Great Naval Game: Britain and Germany in the Age of Empire*. Cambridge: Cambridge University Press, 2007.

Rydell, Robert W. *All the World's a Fair: Visions of American Empire at American International Expositions, 1876–1916*. Chicago: University of Chicago Press, 1984.

———. "'Darkest Africa': African Shows at America's World's Fairs, 1893–1940." In *Africans on Stage: Studies in Ethnological Show Business*, edited by Bernth Lindfors, 135–155. Bloomington: Indiana University Press, 1999.

Rydell, Robert W., and Rob Kroes. *Buffalo Bill in Bologna: The Americanization of the World, 1869–1922*. Chicago: University of Chicago Press, 2005.

Sailiata, Kirisitina G. "The Samoan Cause: Colonialism, Culture, and the Rule of Law." PhD thesis, University of Michigan, 2014.

Salesa, Damon. "Cowboys in the House of Polynesia." *Contemporary Pacific* 22, no. 2 (2010): 330–348.

———. "Emma and Phoebe: 'Weavers of the Border.'" *Journal of the Polynesian Society* 123, no. 2 (2014): 145–167.

———. "Half-Castes between the Wars: Colonial Categories in New Zealand and Samoa." *New Zealand Journal of History* 34, no. 1 (2000): 98–116.

———. "Misimoa: An American on the Beach." *Common-Place* 5, no. 2 (2005). http://commonplace.online / article / misimoa-an-american-on-the-beach.

———. *Racial Crossings: Race, Intermarriage, and the Victorian British Empire*. Oxford: Oxford University Press, 2011.

———. "'Travel-Happy' Samoa: Colonialism, Samoan Migration and a 'Brown Pacific.'" *New Zealand Journal of History* 37, no. 2 (2003): 171–188.

———. "'Troublesome Half-Castes': Tales of a Samoan Borderland." MA thesis, University of Auckland, 1997.

Saxton, Alexander. *The Indispensable Enemy: Labor and the Anti-Chinese Movement in California*. Berkeley: University of California Press, 1971.

Schmack, Kurt. *J. C. Godeffroy & Sohn, Kaufleute zu Hamburg: Leistung und Schicksal eines Welthandelshauses*. Hamburg: Broschek, 1938.

Schmidt, Jürgen. "Arbeit und Nicht-Arbeit im 'Paradies der Südsee': Samoa um 1890 bis 1914." *Arbeit—Bewegung—Geschichte* 15, no. 2 (2016): 7–25.

Schmidt, Willy, and Hans Werner, eds. *Geschichte der deutschen Post in den Kolonien und im Ausland*. Leipzig: Konkordia-Verlag, 1939.

Schoeffel, Penelope. "Daughters of Sina: A Study of Gender, Status and Power in Western Samoa." PhD thesis, Australian National University, 1979.

———. "Dilemmas of Modernization in Primary Health Care in Western Samoa." *Social Science and Medicine* 19, no. 3 (1984): 209–216.

Schwarz, Thomas. *Ozeanische Affekte: Die literarische Modellierung Samoas im kolonialen Diskurs.* Berlin: TEIA—Internet Akademie und Lehrbuch Verlag, 2013.

Scott, James C. *Weapons of the Weak: Everyday Forms of Peasant Resistance.* New Haven, CT: Yale University Press, 1985.

Sevaaetasi, Tuala. "The Fitafita Guard and Samoan Military Experience." In *Remembering the Pacific War,* edited by Geoffrey M. White, 181–184. Honolulu: Center for Pacific Islands Studies, University of Hawai'i at Manoa, 1991.

Shore, Bradd. "Sexuality and Gender in Samoa: Conceptions and Missed Conceptions." In *Sexual Meaning: The Cultural Construction of Gender and Sexuality,* edited by Sherry B. Ortner and Harriet Whitehead, 192–215. Cambridge: Cambridge University Press, 1981.

Shulman, Paul. *Coal and Empire: The Birth of Energy Security in Industrial America.* Baltimore: Johns Hopkins University Press, 2015.

Siaosi, A. S. Noa. "Catching the Dragon's Tail: The Impact of the Chinese in Samoa." MA thesis, University of Canterbury, 2010.

Silva, Noenoe K. *Aloha Betrayed: Native Hawaiian Resistance to American Colonialism.* Durham, NC: Duke University Press, 2004.

Sippel, Harald. "Rassismus, Protektionismus oder Humanität? Die gesetzlichen Verbote der Anwerbung von 'Eingeborenen' zu Schaustellungszwecken in den deutschen Kolonien." In: *Kolonialausstellungen: Begegnungen mit Afrika?,* edited by Robert Debusmann and János Riesz, 43–64. Frankfurt am Main: IKO-Verlag für interkulturelle Kommunikation, 1995.

Stauffer, Robert H. *Kahana: How the Land Was Lost.* Honolulu: University of Hawai'i Press, 2003.

Steel, Frances. *Oceania under Steam: Sea Transport and the Cultures of Colonialism, c. 1870–1914.* Manchester: Manchester University Press, 2011.

Steen, Andreas. "Germany and the Chinese Coolie: Labor, Resistance, and the Struggle for Equality, 1884–1914." In *German Colonialism Revisited: African, Asian, and Oceanic Experiences,* edited by Nina Berman, Klaus Mühlhahn, and Patrice Nganang, 147–160. Ann Arbor: University of Michigan Press, 2014.

Steffen-Schrade, Jutta. "Samoaner im Frankfurter Zoo." In *Talofa! Samoa, Südsee: Ansichten und Einsichten,* edited by Gerda Kroeber-Wolf and Peter Mesenhöller, 368–389. Frankfurt am Main: Museum für Völkerkunde, 1998.

Steinmetz, George. *The Devil's Handwriting: Precoloniality and the German Colonial State in Qingdao, Samoa, and Southwest Africa.* Chicago: University of Chicago Press, 2007.

Stoler, Ann Laura. *Along the Archival Grain: Epistemic Anxieties and Colonial Common Sense.* Princeton, NJ: Princeton University Press, 2009.

———, ed. *Imperial Debris: On Ruins and Ruination.* Durham, NC: Duke University Press, 2013.

Stover, Mary L. "The Individualization of Land in American Samoa." PhD thesis, University of Hawai'i, 1990.

Sunia, Fofo I. F., ed. *The Women of American Samoa, 1900–2000: A Hundred Years of Development and Achievements.* Pago-Pago: Amerika Samoa Humanities Council, 2005.

Takaki, Ronald T. *Pau Hana: Plantation Life and Labor in Hawaiʻi, 1835–1920.* Honolulu: University of Hawaiʻi Press, 1983.

Tavale, Tanuvasa Tofaeono. *Tautua ʻeseʻese NCEA Samoan: Vāega Lua.* Auckland: Fuelavelave Press, 2013.

Teaiwa, Katerina M. *Consuming Ocean Island: Stories of People and Phosphate from Banaba.* Bloomington: Indiana University Press, 2015.

Teaiwa, Teresia K. "bikinis and other s / pacific n / oceans." *Contemporary Pacific* 6, no. 1 (1994): 87–109.

Theroux, Joseph. "H.J.M.: Showman, Author, Farmer, and Crusading Politician." *Pacific Islands Monthly* 52, no. 9 (1981): 59–64.

———. "Rediscovering 'H.J.M.,' Samoa's 'Unconquerable' Harry Moors." *Pacific Islands Monthly* 52, no. 8 (1981): 51–57.

Thode-Arora, Hilke, ed. *From Samoa with Love? Samoan Travelers in Germany, 1895–1911: Retracing the Footsteps.* Munich: Hirmer, 2014.

———. *Für fünfzig Pfennig um die Welt: Die Hagenbeckschen Völkerschauen.* Frankfurt am Main: Campus, 1989.

Thomas, Nicholas. *Islanders: The Pacific in the Age of Empire.* New Haven, CT: Yale University Press, 2010.

Tom, Nancy. *The Chinese in Western Samoa, 1875–1985: The Dragon Came from Afar.* Apia: Western Samoa Historical and Cultural Trust, 1986.

Tomkins, Sandra M. "The Influenza Epidemic of 1918–19 in Western Samoa." *Journal of Pacific History* 27, no. 2 (1992): 181–197.

Trask, Haunani-Kay. *From a Native Daughter: Colonialism and Sovereignty in Hawaiʻi.* Monroe, ME: Common Courage Press, 1993.

Treagus, Mandy. "The South Seas Exhibit at the Chicago World's Fair, 1893." In *Oceania and the Victorian Imagination: Where All Things Are Possible,* edited by Richard D. Fulton and Peter H. Hoffenberg, 45–57. Burlington, VT: Ashgate, 2013.

Trotha, Trutz von. "'One for Kaiser': Beobachtungen zur politischen Soziologie der Prügelstrafe am Beispiel des 'Schutzgebietes Togo.'" In *Studien zur Geschichte des deutschen Kolonialismus in Afrika: Festschrift zum 60. Geburtstag von Peter Sebald,* edited by Peter Heine and Ulrich van der Heyden, 521–551. Pfaffenweiler: Centaurus, 1995.

Tryon, Darrell T., and Jean-Michel Charpentier. *Pacific Pidgins and Creoles: Origins, Growth and Development.* Berlin: Mouton de Gruyter, 2004.

Turner, Victor, and Edith Turner. "Performing Ethnography." *Drama Review* 26, no. 2 (1982): 33–50.

Tworek, Heidi J. S. *News from Germany: The Competition to Control World Communications, 1900–1945.* Cambridge, MA: Harvard University Press, 2019.

Uperesa, Lisa. "Fabled Futures: Migration and Mobility for Samoans in American Football." *Contemporary Pacific* 26, no. 2 (2014): 281–301.

Vaai, Saleimoa. *Samoa Faamatai and the Rule of Law.* Apia: National University of Samoa, 1999.

Vaughan, Christopher A. "Ogling Igorots: The Politics and Commerce of Exhibiting Cultural Otherness, 1898–1913." In *Freakery: Cultural Spectacles of the Extraordinary Body,* edited by Rosemarie G. Thomson, 219–233. New York: New York University Press, 1996.

Wang, Hua. *The Samoan Tangle and Diplomacy of Great Powers, 1871–1900.* Beijing: China Social Sciences Press, 2008.

Wareham, Evelyn. *Race and Realpolitik: The Politics of Colonisation in German Samoa.* Frankfurt am Main: Peter Lang, 2002.

Watters, R. F. "Cultivation in Old Samoa." *Economic Geography* 34, no. 4 (1958): 338–351.

Wehler, Hans-Ulrich. *Das Deutsche Kaiserreich, 1871–1918.* Göttingen: Vandenhoeck & Ruprecht, 1973.

Wenzlhuemer, Roland. *Connecting the Nineteenth-Century World: The Telegraph and Globalization.* Cambridge: Cambridge University Press, 2013.

White, Richard. *Railroaded: The Transcontinentals and the Making of Modern America.* New York: Norton, 2011.

Williams, Eric. *Capitalism and Slavery.* Chapel Hill: University of North Carolina Press, 1944.

Winkler, Jonathan R. *Nexus: Strategic Communications and American Security in World War I.* Cambridge, MA: Harvard University Press, 2008.

Yen, Ching-Hwang. *Coolies and Mandarins: China's Protection of Overseas Chinese during the Late Ch'ing Period, 1851–1911.* Singapore: Singapore University Press, 1985.

Zimmerman, Andrew. *Alabama in Africa: Booker T. Washington, the German Empire, and the Globalization of the New South.* Princeton, NJ: Princeton University Press, 2010.

———. *Anthropology and Antihumanism in Imperial Germany.* Chicago: University of Chicago Press, 2001.

INTERNET SOURCES

Jacobs, Frank. "The Border That Stole 500 Birthdays." *New York Times Opinionator,* July 31, 2012. Accessed May 20, 2021. http://opinionator.blogs.nytimes.com/2012/07/31/the-border-that-stole-500-birthdays/.

Siapo.com. Accessed May 20, 2021. http://siapo.com/kolone-leoso.html; http://siapo.com/mary-pritchard.html.

ACKNOWLEDGMENTS

This book about workers in Samoa is the product of collective labor—both around the world and across communities who care for the past. It would not have been possible without the tireless commitment by generations of Samoan scholars, archivists, and guardians of community knowledge to preserve the memory of their ancestors. As an outlander, I hope that my small contribution inspires more research on working people in Samoa and their links to the wider world.

My research began many years ago in a lecture on U.S. foreign relations by Michael Hochgeschwender, my advisor at the Ludwig-Maximilians-Universität in Munich. His offhand comment that a major war over the Samoan islands was narrowly averted by a tropical cyclone planted the seeds of my interest in Euro-American imperialism in the Pacific. After coming to the United States for graduate school, I somehow remembered this episode and decided to write a research paper on American Samoa for a seminar at Harvard's Charles Warren Center. I would like to thank Walter Johnson and Vince Brown for their early encouragement. My first foray into Samoan history benefited immensely from conversations with fellows Joshua Guild, Paul Kramer, Gunther Peck, Suzanna Reiss, Patrick Wolfe, and Cynthia Young.

Further on in graduate school, I met Sven Beckert, who quickly became my advisor and mentor. Sven's unbridled enthusiasm for history—especially in its labor and global forms—pushed me to ask big questions without losing sight of the details. As both historian and advisor, he is my model. David Armitage emerged at the right time during my research and has been a superb critic and reliable supporter ever since. His scholarship has been a great source of inspiration for my own interest in the Pacific. Jennifer Roberts not only was chair of the American Studies Program during my formative years but has offered crucial advice on my project from the beginning. Damon Salesa has been a passionate mentor, who intervened at crucial moments of my research. His insistence on approaching Samoan and Pacific history beyond the categories introduced by colonialism has deeply reshaped my understanding of workers in Samoa.

My time at Harvard was immeasurably enriched by a community of scholars across the disciplines. For crucial feedback and stimulating conversations, I am thankful to fellows at Harvard's Weatherhead Initiative on Global History, headed by Sven Beckert and Charlie Maier: Claudia Bernardi, Amitava Chowdhury, Sebastian Conrad, Julio Decker, Marcelo Ferraro, Norberto Ferreras, Omar Gueye, Maral Jefroudi, Andrea Komlosy, Marcel van der Linden, Amit Mishra, Steven Serels, Eric Vanhaute, Florian Weber, and Jie Yang. Special thanks to Jessica Barnard for being such a good team player. At Harvard, I have received further guidance from Homi Bhabha, David Blackbourn, Allan Lumba, Werner Sollors, and John Stauffer. Shout-outs to my Harvard American Studies crew Marissa Egerstrom, Brian Goodman, Aaron Hatley, Theresa McCulla, Zach Novak, Sandy Plácido, Scott Poulson-Bryant, Summer Shafer, and Christa Wirth. Arthur Patton-Hock was a rock in the ebbs and tides of graduate school, and I am deeply thankful for his timely advice and general good cheer.

Over the dozen years of research for this book, I have benefited from conversations with colleagues who encouraged me to present papers at conferences and helped me refine my thinking. I would like to thank James Bade for inviting me to give a lecture on telegraphic imperialism in German Samoa at the Goethe Society in Auckland in 2012. Special thanks to Damon Salesa and the late Hugh Laracy for their helpful comments. For their probing questions, I would like to thank participants at the Northeastern University Graduate Conference in 2012; the American Studies Association Conference in San Juan, Puerto Rico, in 2012; the Association for Asian Studies Conference in San Diego in 2013; the European Congress on World and Global History in Paris in 2014; the Labor and Empire Conference at UC Santa Barbara in 2014; and the Circulation of (Post)Colonial Knowledge workshop at the University of Zurich in 2015. At the University of Otago, I would like to thank Judy Bennett for inviting me to join a research workshop on coconuts in the Pacific in 2017, which resulted in a special issue for the *Journal of Pacific History* (2018). My conversations with Judy, April Henderson, Adrian Muckle, Lachy Paterson, and other attendees helped me rethink Samoan copra cooperatives.

Several generous colleagues have read earlier versions of my manuscript, in whole or in parts, as I tried to reenvision it for a broader audience. These include David Armitage, Sven Beckert, David Blackbourn, Chris Capozzola, Charlie Maier, Jennifer Roberts, and Damon Salesa. In Samoa, I am indebted to Malama Meleisea for chatting with me about my research and offering kind words on earlier chapter drafts. *Fa'afetai tele lava!* Over the years, JoAnna Poblete provided intellectual support and shared notes from her own research on U.S. colonials and American Samoa. For additional comments on chapter drafts, I am grateful to Christopher Balme, Michael Hochgeschwender, Bob Rydell, and Hilke Thode-Arora.

After finishing my PhD, I enjoyed the intellectual company of gifted scholars at several institutions of higher learning in the northeastern United States. My heartfelt thanks to my colleagues at Tufts University (Dave Ekbladh and Kris Manjapra), Bard College (Myra Armstead, Christian Crouch, Kevin Duong, Cecile

Kuznitz, Greg Moynahan, Miles Rodriguez, Alice Stroup, and Dominique Townsend), and Smith College (Diana Sierra Beccera, Darcy Buerkle, Jennifer Guglielmo, Liz Pryor, and Neal Salisbury). Writing group members at Bard and Smith allowed me to workshop rough chapter drafts and provided much-needed intellectual and mental support. Since joining Worcester Polytechnic Institute, I have benefited tremendously from the interdisciplinary community and generous spirit of my colleagues in the Humanities and Arts Department. For their support, I would like to thank Kris Boudreau, Steve Bullock, Jim Cocola, Lindsay Davis, Dan DiMassa, Jim Hanlan, Peter Hansen, Kate Moncrief, Rebecca Moody, Geoff Pfeifer, Ángel Rivera, Jennifer Rudolph, John Sanbonmatsu, William San Martín, Dave Spanagel, and Yunus Telliel. Thanks also to colleagues at other institutions: Julio Decker, Julian Go, Justin F. Jackson, Ted Melillo, G. Samantha Rosenthal, Heidi Tworek, and Jessica Wang. Special thanks to colleagues who helped with identifying source material: Ulrike Hertel, Abby Markwyn, Bob Rydell, and Hilke Thode-Arora. Finally, I would like to express my deep gratitude to my students at Harvard, Tufts, Bard, Smith, and WPI, who often asked the most difficult questions.

Over the years, this project has received crucial financial and material support, which has allowed it to blossom and thrive. At Harvard, I would like to acknowledge support from the American Studies Program, the Minda de Gunzburg Center for European Studies, the Charles Warren Center for Studies in American History, the Committee on Australian Studies, the Graduate School of Arts and Sciences, the History Department, the Weatherhead Center for International Affairs, and the Weatherhead Initiative on Global History. At the German Historical Institute in Washington, DC, I would like to thank Britta Waldschmidt-Nelson and Bryan Hart for making my stay both productive and pleasant. As a recipient of this institutional largesse, I am aware of the enormous privilege that allowed me to conduct research and set aside time to write.

My research was made possible with the often-hidden labor of dedicated staff at archives and universities around the world. In Samoa, the staff at the Nelson Memorial Public Library in Apia; the National Archives and Records Authority in Malifa (So'ona'alofa Sina Malietoa, Simi Tanielu); the Archives of the Diocese of Samoa and Tokelau, Shrine of the Three Hearts, in Vauala (Amela Silipa); and the University of the South Pacific, Samoa Campus. In American Samoa, the staff at the American Samoa Historic Preservation Office (Florence Aetonu-Teo, David Herdrich, Joel Klenck, and Epi Suafo'a-Taua'i), the Office of Archives and Record Management (Tua Loken), the American Samoa Community College, and the Feleti Barstow Public Library. In New Zealand, the staff at Archives New Zealand (Jared Davidson and Uili Fecteau) in Wellington and Auckland, and the Alexander Turnbull Library in Wellington. In Australia, the staff at the National Archives of Australia, the National Library of Australia, and the Pacific Manuscripts Bureau at Australian National University, all in Canberra, and at the State Library of New South Wales in Sydney. In Germany, the staff at the Bundesarchiv in Berlin-

Lichterfelde, who responded to my request to look at every available shred of paper (and microfilm) on Samoa with expertise and kindness. Thanks also to the staff at the Bundesarchiv Koblenz and Freiburg i.B. and at the state and city archives in Hamburg, Berlin, and Munich. In the United States, the staff at the National Archives and Records Administration in Washington, DC; College Park, Maryland; and San Bruno, California. Special thanks to the staff at major institutions in the Washington, DC, area: the Smithsonian Institution Archives (Ellen Alers and Mary Markey), the Naval History and Heritage Command, and the Library of Congress (Judith Gray). In addition, I am grateful to staff at the Bancroft Library, the University of California at Berkeley (David Kessler and Susan Snyder), the Mechanics' Institute Library in San Francisco, the Field Museum in Chicago, the Chicago History Museum, the Delaware Historical Society in Wilmington, and the University of Delaware in Newark. At the Tozzer Library at Harvard, I would like to thank Gregory A. Finnegan for his help in identifying ethnographic material. For assistance with images, I am grateful to Amalaratna (ATL), Tony Brunt, Stella Gallahar, Caroline Wolfgramm Irwin, Aïsha Othman (Goethe-Universität Frankfurt am Main), Hamish Rundle (Te Papa), James Taylor, Hilke Thode-Arora (Museum Fünf Kontinente Munich), Reinhard Wendt, Lewis Wyman (LOC), and Robert Zinck (Harvard Imaging Services). And thanks to Isabelle Lewis for the beautiful maps.

My manuscript has improved greatly in the able hands of the editorial staff at Harvard University Press. In particular, I would like to thank my editor, Andrew Kinney, for believing in my project early on and helping me reframe it for a wider audience. Thanks also to the anonymous reviewers for HUP for their incisive and constructive suggestions for revision. And I am grateful to Kim Giambattisto and Jamie Thaman for their work in improving the clarity of the manuscript. All remaining shortcomings are mine.

Over the years, my research (and soul) was sustained by a group of dear friends in the United States and Europe. I shared many citations, drinks, and laughs with them, which helped me put my research in the proper perspective. Among these friends are John F. Bell, Lowell Brower, Collier S. Brown, Raul Hernandez, Raj Hooli, Luvena Kopp, Stephan Kuhl, Pablo Lastra, Mo Lotman, Giovanna Micconi, Wanda H. Moore, Erin Mosely, Stefanie Müller, Edmund Ratka, Stephanie Bosch Santana, Anna Su, Simon Sun, Gernot Waldner, and Philippe Wimmer.

Above all, I would like to thank my family in Germany and the United States. My parents in Germany have supported my passion for history as far back as I can remember. They gave me books, compact discs, flight tickets, and so much more. My sister and my niece have an unmatched talent for reminding me of the truly important things in life. I hope my father, a teacher himself, will learn a bit about Samoan history and what I have been up to over the past decade. My mother asked some of the most pressing questions about my research (most prominently, When will you be done?) and was always there for me when I needed her. It is impossible to thank my parents for all they have done for me. I dedicate this book to them.

Finally, my book would not have come about as it did without my wife, Joy. She danced into my life just as I embarked on my journey into Samoan history. Cheerfully, she dissected my arguments with a lawyer's eye and turned many an unfortunate phrase into something much more elegant. And words cannot describe how our son, Noah, has changed my life. Among many other things, he has never failed to find the right moment to throw a soccer ball at me when I was staring too long at footnotes. On to new adventures.

INDEX